ICTs for Advancing Rural Communities and Human Development:

Addressing the Digital Divide

Susheel Chhabra
Lal Bahadur Shastri Institute of Management, India

Managing Director:	Lindsay Johnston
Senior Editorial Director:	Heather Probst
Book Production Manager:	Sean Woznicki
Development Manager:	Joel Gamon
Development Editor:	Hannah Abelbeck
Acquisitions Editor:	Erika Gallagher
Typesetters:	Lisandro Gonzalez
Print Coordinator:	Jamie Snavely
Cover Design:	Nick Newcomer

Published in the United States of America by
Information Science Reference (an imprint of IGI Global)
701 E. Chocolate Avenue
Hershey PA 17033
Tel: 717-533-8845
Fax: 717-533-8661
E-mail: cust@igi-global.com
Web site: http://www.igi-global.com

Library of Congress Cataloging-in-Publication Data

ICTs for advancing rural communities and human development: addressing the digital divide / Susheel Chhabra, editor.
    p. cm.
  Includes bibliographical references and index.
    ISBN 978-1-4666-0047-8 (hardcover) -- ISBN 978-1-4666-0048-5 (ebook) -- ISBN 978-1-4666-0049-2 (print & perpetual access) 1. Rural development--Effect of technological innovations on. 2. Information technology. 3. Digital divide. I. Chhabra, Susheel.
  HN49.C6I26 2012
  307.1'412--dc23
                                2011043135

British Cataloguing in Publication Data
A Cataloguing in Publication record for this book is available from the British Library.

Associate Editors

List of Reviewers

Table of Contents

Preface..xv

Chapter 1
The Impact of Personal Electronic Communications on Work-Life Balance
and Cognitive Absorption 1
Pruthikrai Mahatanankoon, Illinois State University, USA

Chapter 2
Assessment and Contrast of the Effects of Information and Communication
Technology...15
John Wang, Montclair State University, USA
Bin Zhou, Kean University, USA
Jeffrey Hsu, Fairleigh Dickinson University, USA

Chapter 3
Automatic Language Translation for Mobile SMS...33
S. K. Samanta, University of Essex, UK
A. Achilleos, University of Cyprus, Cyprus
S. Moiron, University of Essex, UK
J. Woods, University of Essex, UK
M. Ghanbari, University of Essex, UK

Chapter 4
Botswana's Novel Approaches for Knowledge-Based Economy Facilitation:
Issues, Policies and Contextual Framework 45
Bwalya Kelvin Joseph, University of Botswana, Botswana

Chapter 5
Children's Maps in GIS: A Tool for Communicating Outdoor Experiences in Urban Planning..........57
Kerstin Nordin, Swedish University of Agricultural Sciences, Sweden
Ulla Berglund, Swedish University of Agricultural Sciences, Sweden

Chapter 6
Participation in Child Welfare Services Through Information and Communication Technologies......73
  Susan Tregeagle, University of Western Sydney, Australia

Chapter 7
Deploying Information and Communication Technologies (ICT)
to Enhance Participation in Local Governance for Citizens with Disabilities....................................91
  John C. Bricout, University of Central Florida, USA
  Paul M. A. Baker, Georgia Institute of Technology, USA

Chapter 8
E-Accessibility and Municipal Wi-Fi: Exploring a Model for Inclusivity and Implementation........109
  Paul M. A. Baker, Georgia Institute of Technology, USA
  Alea M. Fairchild, Vrije Universiteit Brussel, Belgium
  Jessica Pater, Georgia Tech Research Institute, USA

Chapter 9
Adoption and Use of ICTs Among Rural Youth: Evidence from Greece 125
  George Alexopoulos, Agricultural University of Athens, Greece
  Alex Koutsouris, Agricultural University of Athens, Greece
  Irene Tzouramani, National Agricultural Research Foundation, Greece

Chapter 10
Pathways to Participatory Landscape Governance in Northern Laos:
The Role of Information and Communication Technologies...143
  John Daniel Watts, Center for International Forestry Research (CIFOR), Laos
  Vilaphong Kanyasone, Northern Agriculture and Forestry Research Centre, Laos
  Vongvilay Vongkhamsao, National Agriculture and Forestry Research Institute, Laos

Chapter 11
Tlowitsis Re-Imagined: The Use of Digital Media to Build Nation
and Overcome Disconnection in a Displaced Aboriginal Community..158
  Jon Corbett, University of British Columbia Okanagan, Canada
  Raquel Mann, University of British Columbia Okanagan, Canada

Chapter 12
ICTs in Chinese Distance Higher Education: Increased Opportunities
and Continuous Challenges..180
  Xiaobin Li, Brock University, Canada

Chapter 13

The Concerns of Elementary Educators with the Diffusion of Information
and Communication Technology 193

    Armin Samiei, Simon Fraser University, Canada

    Daniel A. Laitsch, Simon Fraser University, Canada

Chapter 14

Examining the "Digital Divide": A Study of Six Pre-Service Teachers'
Experiences with ICTs and Second Language Education... 208

    Francis Bangou, University of Ottawa, Canada

Chapter 15

Leveraging Technology to Promote Assessment for Learning in Higher Education 224

    Christopher DeLuca, University of South Florida, USA

    Laura April McEwen, Queen's University, Canada

Chapter 16

Impact of Podcasts as Professional Learning: Teacher Created,
Student Created, and Professional Development Podcasts.. 237

    Kathleen P. King, University of South Florida, USA

Chapter 17

New Trends and Futuristic Information Communication Technologies
for Engineering Education 251

    Manjit Singh Sidhu, University Tenaga Nasional, Malaysia

    Lee Chen Kang, University Tunku Abdul Rahman, Malaysia

Compilation of References 263

About the Contributors 297

Index 303

Detailed Table of Contents

Preface... xv

Chapter 1

The Impact of Personal Electronic Communications on Work-Life Balance
and Cognitive Absorption 1
    Pruthikrai Mahatanankoon, Illinois State University, USA

E-mail and instant messaging (IM) are essential ingredients of workplace communication. The study examines how the hedonic use of electronic communications influences work-life balance and cognitive absorption. Data collected from white-collar employees in the United States show that work-life balance mediates the relationship between personal e-mail and cognitive absorption, and that personal instant messaging has no impact on work-life balance but has a direct influence on employees' cognitive absorption. The findings suggest that work-life balance may eventually increase cognitive absorption and reduce employees' productivity. The findings provide insight into how different types of personal communication can influence work-life balance as well as into how to manage non-work-related electronic communications in the workplace.

Chapter 2

Assessment and Contrast of the Effects of Information and Communication
Technology.. 15
    John Wang, Montclair State University, USA
    Bin Zhou, Kean University, USA
    Jeffrey Hsu, Fairleigh Dickinson University, USA

This article compares the effects of information and communication technology (ICT) on labor productivity growth and human quality of life in industrialized countries. A mathematical evaluation method based on the concept of Pareto-optimal organization is proposed for this study. This method is easy to apply and uses a linear programming model. The weights for various measurements are determined by objective method and are standard. The method is illustrated with real data from 23 developed countries worldwide.

Chapter 3
Automatic Language Translation for Mobile SMS... 33
    S. K. Samanta, University of Essex, UK
    A. Achilleos, University of Cyprus, Cyprus
    S. Moiron, University of Essex, UK
    J. Woods, University of Essex, UK
    M. Ghanbari, University of Essex, UK

In any form of communication it is vital that both parties can understand the same language, if they cannot a translator is required. Currently mobile users engage the service of a third party provider to translate an SMS text into a different language. The existing services have a number of drawbacks e.g. high cost to the user, not user friendly, they reduce the message space, and are inefficient. To communicate with a foreign person the sender must know the recipients preferred language and device display capability. What is needed is a service where a sender can send message in their native language without regard for the target tongue. We show that a mobile operator can provide a transparent service where the text message is automatically converted to the recipients preferred language. In comparison to the existing system, our implementation is efficient and cost effective and has large implications for commerce, language learning and person-to-person communication. A large number of services such as health care management, education, emergency notification, news, weather, and traffic reports and commerce applications can be delivered to vast mobile populations who are not able to enjoy the benefit of these services due to language barriers.

Chapter 4
Botswana's Novel Approaches for Knowledge-Based Economy Facilitation:
Issues, Policies and Contextual Framework 45
    Bwalya Kelvin Joseph, University of Botswana, Botswana

The Vision 2016, which is a set of strategic plans desired to position Botswana at the completive edge of the socio-economic hierarchy in Africa, is being implemented with concerted efforts from both the private and the public sector, including ordinary citizens. One of the major motivations for drawing this strategy has been the desire to transform Botswana from a resource and industry-based (e.g. agriculture and diamond mining) to knowledge-based economy. This has come from the realisation that in order to compete favourably at a global scale, there is need to put in place efficient knowledge value chains. To this course, several initiatives have been devised and/or implemented by both the government and the public sector. This article surveys the fundamental concepts on which this paradigm shift is hinged and brings out the different issues, initiatives and policies (such as Information and Communications Technology development, nurturing of an appropriate human resource base by way of strategic human resource development plans, investment in intellectual capital, etc.) that have been done so far in Botswana. The article, however, does not claim that it offers a compendium of existing programs towards a knowledge-based economy initiated by Botswana. The article posits that although significant strides have been scored in Botswana's efforts towards a knowledge-based economy, a lot more needs to be done if it were to compete favourably at an international stage.

Chapter 5
Children's Maps in GIS: A Tool for Communicating Outdoor Experiences in Urban Planning 57
    Kerstin Nordin, Swedish University of Agricultural Sciences, Sweden
    Ulla Berglund, Swedish University of Agricultural Sciences, Sweden

Since 2002 the authors have successively developed "Children's Maps in GIS", a method for children's participation in spatial planning. Their studies show that 10-15 year-olds are capable of reading maps and using a GIS-application for communicating their interests in a stable and useful manner. The purpose of this article is to discuss the first stages of implementation in a real world project, in relation to ICT. The authors report experiences from a Swedish municipality using Children's Maps in GIS in a survey with over 600 children as part of a comprehensive planning process and give examples of how data can be visualized. A significant digital divide between different parts of the administration is noted. In the ongoing development into an Internet version of the method the authors aim to increase the access to the GIS-application and develop standard procedures for categorizing and analyzing data.

Chapter 6

Participation in Child Welfare Services Through Information and Communication Technologies...... 73
    Susan Tregeagle, University of Western Sydney, Australia

Case management systems were designed to open the way for increased participation of young people and their families in child welfare interventions, and, their standardised format provides a valuable opportunity to use ICT in social work practice. Existing research is unclear about how effectively case management affects participation, nor, the impact of ICT on social work interventions. This paper describes the findings of qualitative research with service users about their experiences of case management and how ICT could further their involvement in critical decisions for families. Service users are keen to use ICT and this could help overcome the limitations of paper-based case management systems and exploit the communication potential of the internet and mobile phones. However, before ICT could be used, the complex 'digital divide' affecting disadvantaged families would need to be addressed and social workers' understanding and current use of ICT would need to be explored.

Chapter 7

Deploying Information and Communication Technologies (ICT)
to Enhance Participation in Local Governance for Citizens with Disabilities.................................... 91
    John C. Bricout, University of Central Florida, USA
    Paul M. A. Baker, Georgia Institute of Technology, USA

Information and Communication Technologies (ICT) offer a promising technology for citizens with disabilities to participate in local e-governance planning and implementation, provided that underlying issues of social exclusion and technology accessibility are properly addressed. Existing research suggests that for citizens with disabilities gateway issues such as technology access, usability, community- and government-receptivity are barriers to participation in local e-governance. Results from a pilot study indicate that the e-governance landscape for people with disabilities is heterogeneous; likely reflecting both differences within the disability community, as well as among the online governance entities. Systematic changes to the development, implementation, and evaluation of local e-governance for people with disabilities are recommended, informed by an analytical model suitable for empirical testing.

Chapter 8

E-Accessibility and Municipal Wi-Fi: Exploring a Model for Inclusivity and Implementation 109
    Paul M. A. Baker, Georgia Institute of Technology, USA
    Alea M. Fairchild, Vrije Universiteit Brussel, Belgium
    Jessica Pater, Georgia Tech Research Institute, USA

One of the typical design objectives of municipal Wi-Fi systems is the free or low-cost provision of connectivity for citizens, including people with disabilities and others impacted by the digital divide. This paper examines a range of municipal Wi-Fi implementation models for potential impact on e-accessibility. A comparative analysis was undertaken of sample U.S. and European municipal Wi-Fi systems to assess the business model and stakeholders involved in municipal wireless initiatives and to examine the degree of accessibility to or sensitivity of, municipal wireless systems for people with disabilities. As many people with disabilities are currently affected by social disparities in education and income, further marginalization of their communication and information access creates additional access barriers to critical information and full participation in community life.

Chapter 9

Adoption and Use of ICTs Among Rural Youth: Evidence from Greece 125
George Alexopoulos, Agricultural University of Athens, Greece
Alex Koutsouris, Agricultural University of Athens, Greece
Irene Tzouramani, National Agricultural Research Foundation, Greece

In the last few decades, within the rhetoric of the "information age", there is a growing enthusiasm for the (potential) benefits of the dissemination of Information and Communication Technologies (ICTs). This is further enhanced through eGovernment projects undertaken on a worldwide scale. However, a number of issues seem to defy such optimism as far as rural areas are concerned. The critical review of such issues question the thesis that ICTs undoubtedly benefit (human) development. In particular, this paper, drawing on data from a large-scale survey in Greece, identifies the marginal effects of a series of demographic, socioeconomic and spatial characteristics, and information sources on PC and Internet use on the part of young rural inhabitants, especially farmers. The results, pointing toward an emerging intra-rural digital divide, are consequently discussed vis-à-vis eGovernment projects, from the point of view of human development.

Chapter 10

Pathways to Participatory Landscape Governance in Northern Laos:
The Role of Information and Communication Technologies 143
John Daniel Watts, Center for International Forestry Research (CIFOR), Laos
Vilaphong Kanyasone, Northern Agriculture and Forestry Research Centre, Laos
Vongvilay Vongkhamsao, National Agriculture and Forestry Research Institute, Laos

The Landscape Mosaics Project is a global research project coordinated by the Center for International Forestry Research (CIFOR) and the World Agroforestry Centre (ICRAF) and funded by the Swiss Agency for Development Cooperation (SDC). The project examines biodiversity in tropical, forested, multifunctional landscapes in sites adjacent to protected areas. A key thematic component of its research examines the governance of landscapes, and by using a Participatory Action Research approach, the project aspires to facilitate better landscape governance through improved communication between village and landscape level actors. This article examines the initial experiences of the project in its Northern Lao site, located in Vieng Kham District, Luang Prabang Province. The authors describe how the lack of access to information communication technologies have inhibited local actors levels of participation in landscape level governance as well as affected their abilities to effectively and adaptively manage their landscape. Community radio, that provides local actors with the relevant information for more substantially participating in landscape governance as well as information useful for adaptive management, is proposed as one potential solution for improving participatory landscape governance.

Chapter 11

Tlowitsis Re-Imagined: The Use of Digital Media to Build Nation
and Overcome Disconnection in a Displaced Aboriginal Community 158
Jon Corbett, University of British Columbia Okanagan, Canada
Raquel Mann, University of British Columbia Okanagan, Canada

Using the case study of the Tlowitsis, a dispersed indigenous community in British Columbia, Canada, this paper explores the role of ICTs, and in particular participatory video, in nation building. Also, the paper identifies factors that affect both the involvement and exclusion of the membership and addresses the challenges faced and lessons learned. ICTs, in particular new media technologies, offer great potential to overcome the geographic barriers caused by dispersal. However, it remains uncertain how they might contribute to the process of nation building. In this regard, the authors present six fundamental requirements for nation building, and then use these requirements to structure an analysis of the Tlowitsis case study.

Chapter 12

ICTs in Chinese Distance Higher Education: Increased Opportunities
and Continuous Challenges.. 180
Xiaobin Li, Brock University, Canada

The Chinese higher education system is the largest in the world, but distance education, using information communication technologies (ICTs), started later than in developed countries. In this paper, the author examines the benefits of education to human development and provides an overview of the recent development of distance higher education in China. The potential for further developing distance higher education with ICTs is considered. In addition, challenges are discussed and recommendations are made to improve Chinese distance higher education.

Chapter 13

The Concerns of Elementary Educators with the Diffusion of Information
and Communication Technology 193
Armin Samiei, Simon Fraser University, Canada
Daniel A. Laitsch, Simon Fraser University, Canada

In this paper, the authors use a mixed methods study, including a survey and follow up interviews, to investigate the concerns that elementary educators in a school district in British Columbia have regarding the diffusion and integration of Information and Communication Technologies (ICT) in their teaching. The research participants identified four major categories of concerns: the philosophy and pedagogy of ICT integration; accessibility of ICT (including software, hardware and resource personnel); infrastructure technical support; and educational integration of ICT in their teaching. Based on the research findings, the authors propose appropriate intervention methods to address these concerns, including targeted professional development, technical and educational support, and sustained access to proper ICT equipment.

Chapter 14

Examining the "Digital Divide": A Study of Six Pre-Service Teachers'
Experiences with ICTs and Second Language Education.. 208
Francis Bangou, University of Ottawa, Canada

Since the concept of "digital divide" first appeared, many researchers have argued for a more nuanced definition that highlights its complexities and better reveals its impact on the appropriation of ICTs. In this paper, the author analyzes the experiences of six Master of Education (M.Ed.) pre-service teachers learning to integrate ICTs into their practice. These case studies demonstrate how novice teachers' learning processes can be impacted by the unequal distribution of the temporal, material, mental, social, and cultural resources available (van Dijk, 2005). A number of pedagogical and curricular recommendations for the M.Ed. program are then provided.

Chapter 15

Leveraging Technology to Promote Assessment for Learning in Higher Education.......................... 224

Christopher DeLuca, University of South Florida, USA
Laura April McEwen, Queen's University, Canada

Assessment for learning (AFL) is a highly effective strategy for promoting student learning, development and achievement in higher education (Falchikov, 2003; Kirby & Downs, 2007; Nicol & Macfarlane-Dick, 2006; Rust, Price, & O'Donovan, 2003; Vermunt, 2005). However, since AFL relies on continuous monitoring of student progress through instructor feedback, peer collaboration, and student self-assessment, enacting AFL within large-group learning formats is challenging. This paper considers how technology can be leveraged to promote AFL in higher education. Drawing on data from students and instructors and recommendations from an external instructional design consultant, this paper documents the process of pairing technology and AFL within a large-group pre-service teacher education course at one Canadian institution. Recommendations for the improvement of the web-based component of the course are highlighted to provide practical suggestions for instructors to evaluate their own web-based platforms and improve their use of technology in support of AFL. The paper concludes with a discussion of areas for continued research related to the effectiveness of this pairing between assessment theory and technology.

Chapter 16

Impact of Podcasts as Professional Learning: Teacher Created,
Student Created, and Professional Development Podcasts.. 237

Kathleen P. King, University of South Florida, USA

Until now, research on podcasting in education mostly examined teacher created podcasts in K-12 and higher education. This paper explores podcasts in professional learning across several genres of podcasts. Using a popular typology of podcasts, teacher created, student created and professional development podcasts (King & Gura, 2007), this paper compares, contrasts and reveals the potential of multiple educational contexts and instructional strategies, formative instructional design, interdisciplinary strategies, formal and informal learning, and effective uses of data gathering methods. The significance of the study extends from not only the extensive reach of the data gathering and production, but also the robust research model, formative and dynamic instructional design for staff development and recommendations for podcasting research strategies.

Chapter 17

New Trends and Futuristic Information Communication Technologies
for Engineering Education 251

Manjit Singh Sidhu, University Tenaga Nasional, Malaysia
Lee Chen Kang, University Tunku Abdul Rahman, Malaysia

Improving and enhancing education is a goal for higher learning institutions that seek to provide better learning techniques, technologies, and educators and generate knowledgeable students to fulfill the needs of industry. A field in need of significant improvement is engineering. One approach is to review the delivery and pedagogies used in the current educational system. This paper examines the problems faced by staff and students in the field of mechanical engineering. In addition, the authors explore new technologies that enhance and promote the learning process.

Compilation of References 263

About the Contributors 297

Index 303

Preface

The benefits of development paradigms have not reached the people living in remote locations in rural areas in terms of socio-economic development, education and health opportunities which are easily available to people living in urban areas. Community-based development in rural areas provides access to services such as education, health, welfare, and agricultural extensions, facilitating opportunities for the rural population, while still retaining their social, economic, and cultural identities. Information Technology also can provide solutions to reduce problems of rural areas in terms of socio-economic development, education, and empowerment and raise the standard of living conditions. Access to and use of information and communication technologies (ICTs) have become essential for rural communities to attract and retain businesses, enhance educational opportunities and hence remain economically viable in the context of existing and next generation development paradigms.

ICTs have the capability to provide - static and dynamic gainsfrom increase in operating efficiency and from reduced transaction costs. In both cases, the channel for gains is through effective and lower cost information storage, processing and communication. Dynamic gains come from higher growth, potentially raising the entire future streams of consumption.

While technology has had a considerable impact on humanity's progress, it can also fuel inequality and tension. Considerable opportunities exist for investigating the link between ICT design and individual and social development. The digital divide is not only a matter of concern between developing and developed countries, but it is present within developing countries as well. This divide exists between rural and urban dwellers, or within areas of rural dwellers. Various research outcomes show that many rural regions still lag in comparison with urban areas in development and application of ICTs. The opportunities offered by information and communication technologies—telephone, radio, video, Internet—are unevenly distributed. The worldwide surveys indicate that barely six percent of the world's population is linked to the Internet, and many people on the earth have never made a mobile call. There is a growing disparity between information access haves and have nots, and most of them live in rural areas. This has created inequality in terms of employment and other socio-economic opportunities related to new information-based economy.

ICTs can play a major role in reducing the digital divide, which is creating a significant impact in terms of human development parameters. The lower-priced ICT devices, the development of low-cost mobiles, cloud computing, and breakthroughs in wireless access can help bridge digital divide. Digital-based educational tools are facilitating promotion of need-based training programs in rural areas as well as other remote locations. There is a huge demand for broadband access in rural and remote areas in all over the world. Rural communities are eager to be connected to emerging broadband networks so that they should not suffer the same economic fate as many communities that were bypassed by the telephone, the railroad, or the interstate highway systems.

WHERE THE BOOK STANDS

ICTs for Advancing Rural Communities and Human Development: Addressing the Digital Divide reviews the important impact ICTs have on economic, social, and political development and provides analyses of ICTs for education, commerce, and governance. This reference develops strategies and promotes awareness of human development initiatives as they relate to technology development and design.

Organization of the book

The book has been divided into seventeen chapters. The brief coverage of each chapter is given below.

Social networks have attracted individual interests to use ICTs for personal communication for social links in work schedules. This has created an imbalance between their personal and professional life. Chapter 1 examines how the hedonic use of electronic communications influences work life balance and cognitive absorption. Data collected through various research instruments from white-collar employees in the United States show that work-life balance mediates the relationship between personal e-mail and cognitive absorption, and that personal instant messaging has no impact on work-life balance but has a direct influence on employees' cognitive absorption. The findings suggest that work-life balance may eventually increase cognitive absorption and reduce employees' productivity. The findings provide insight into how different types of personal communication can influence work-life balance as well as into how to manage non-work-related electronic communications in the workplace. The recommendations given by the author are expected to ease tension between personal and work life balances.

The advancement and use of ICTs has made a significant impact on labor productivity growth and quality of life in developed countries especially in urban areas. Chapter 2 compares the effects of ICT on labor productivity growth and human quality of life in industrialized countries. A mathematical evaluation method based on the concept of Pareto-optimal organization is proposed for this study. This method is easy to apply and uses a linear programming model. The weights for various measurements are determined by objective method and are standard. The method is illustrated with real data from 23 developed countries worldwide.

Use of SMS for mobile communications has been increased worldwide in the recent years, yet language interpretation and translation in SMSs remains a challenge. Chapter 3 emphasizes that in any form of communication it is vital that both parties can understand the same language, if they cannot a translator is required. Currently mobile users engage the service of a third party provider to translate an SMS text into a different language. The existing services have a number of drawbacks (e.g. high cost to the user, not user friendly, they reduce the message space, and are inefficient). To communicate with a foreign person the sender must know the recipients preferred language and device display capability. What is needed is a service where a sender can send message in their native language without regard for the target tongue. The authors demonstrated that a mobile operator can provide a transparent service where the text message is automatically converted to the recipients preferred language. In comparison to the existing system, the implementation process suggested is efficient and cost effective and has large implications for commerce, language learning and person-to-person communication. A large number of services such as health care management, education, emergency notification, news, weather, and traffic reports and commerce applications can be delivered to vast mobile populations who are not able to enjoy the benefit of these services due to language barriers.

Kknowledge-based development initiatives have become important facets for the economic and social development. Chapter 4 illustrates Botswana's vision 2016, which is a set of strategic plans desired to position this country at the completive edge of the socio-economic hierarchy in Africa, which is being implemented with concerted efforts from both the private and the public sector, including ordinary citizens. One of the major motivations for drawing this strategy has been the desire to transform Botswana from a resource and industry-based (e.g. agriculture and diamond mining) to knowledge-based economy. This has come from the realization that in order to compete favorably at a global scale, there is need to put in place efficient knowledge value chains. To this course, several initiatives have been devised and/or implemented by both the government and the public sector. The author has made survey of the fundamental concepts on which this paradigm shift is hinged and brings out the different issues, initiatives and policies (such as Information and Communications Technology development, nurturing of an appropriate human resource base by way of strategic human resource development plans, investment in intellectual capital, etc.) that have been done so far in Botswana. The chapter, however, does not claim that it offers a compendium of existing programs towards a knowledge based economy initiated by Botswana

GIS has been given emphasis all over the world to help facilitate children in their educational and training interventions. The authors of Chapter 5 have developed "Children's Maps in GIS", a method for children's participation in spatial planning. Their studies show that 10-15 year-olds are capable of reading maps and using a GIS-application for communicating their interests in a stable and useful manner. The chapter examines the characteristics and discusses the first stages of implementation in a real world project, in relation to ICT. The authors report experiences from a Swedish municipality using Children's Maps in GIS in a survey with over 600 children as part of a comprehensive planning process and give examples of how data can be visualized. A significant digital divide between different parts of the administration is noted. In the ongoing development into an Internet version of the method the authors aim to increase the access to the GIS-application and develop standard procedures for categorizing and analyzing data.

Case management systems were designed to open the way for increased participation of young people and their families in child welfare interventions, and, their standardized format provides a valuable opportunity to use ICTs in social work practice. Existing research is unclear about how effectively case management affects participation, nor, the impact of ICT on social work interventions. Chapter 6 explores the findings of a qualitative research project that asked service users about their experiences of case management and how ICT could further their involvement in critical decisions for families. Service providers are keen to use ICT and this could help overcome the limitations of paper-based case management systems and exploit the communication potential of the internet and mobile phones. However, before ICT could be used, the complex 'digital divide' affecting disadvantaged families would need to be addressed and social workers' understanding and current use of ICT would need to be explored.

Information and Communication Technologies (ICT) offer a promising technology for citizens with disabilities to participate in local e-governance planning and implementation. Chapter 7 conducted a thorough literature review on existing research that suggests that for citizens with disabilities gateway issues such as technology access, usability, community- and government-receptivity are barriers to participation in local e-governance. A pilot study conducted by the authors indicates that the e-governance landscape for people with disabilities is heterogeneous, likely reflecting both differences within the disability community as well as among the online governance entities. Systematic changes to the development, implementation, and evaluation of local e-governance for people with disabilities are recommended, informed by an analytical model suitable for empirical testing.

Some of the municipalities of developed and developing countries have installed Wi-Fi systems to enhance Internet penetration for their local development initiatives. Chapter 8 illustrates that one of the typical design objectives of municipal Wi-Fi systems is the free or low-cost provision of connectivity for citizens, including people with disabilities and others impacted by the digital divide. The authors examine a range of municipal Wi-Fi implementation models for potential impact on e-accessibility. A comparative analysis was undertaken of sample U.S. and European municipal Wi-Fi systems to assess the business model and stakeholders involved in municipal wireless initiatives and to examine the degree of accessibility to or sensitivity of, municipal wireless systems for people with disabilities. As many people with disabilities are currently affected by social disparities in education and income, further marginalization of their communication and information access creates additional access barriers to critical information and full participation in community life.

Rural youth are the best target for ICTs penetration for rural development initiatives. In the last few decades, within the rhetoric of the "information age", there is a growing enthusiasm for the (potential) benefits of the dissemination of ICTs. This is further enhanced through eGovernment projects undertaken on a worldwide scale. However, a number of issues seem to defy such optimism as far as rural areas are concerned. Chapter 9 critically reviews such issues indicates ICTs undoubtedly benefit (human) development. In particular, drawing on data from a large-scale survey in Greece, identifies the marginal effects of a series of demographic, socioeconomic and spatial characteristics, and information sources on PC and Internet use on the part of young rural inhabitants, especially farmers. The results, pointing toward an emerging intra-rural digital divide, are consequently discussed vis-à-vis eGovernment projects, from the point of view of human development.

The multiagency development cooperation has become essential for coordination activities among various stakeholders. Chapter 10 draws upon the study of the Landscape Mosaics Project which is a global research project coordinated by the Center for International Forestry Research (CIFOR) and the World Agroforestry Centre (ICRAF) and funded by the Swiss Agency for Development Cooperation (SDC). The project examines biodiversity in tropical, forested, multifunctional landscapes in sites adjacent to protected areas. A key thematic component of its research examines the governance of landscapes, and by using a Participatory Action Research approach, the project aspires to facilitate better landscape governance through improved communication between village and landscape level actors. This chapter examines the initial experiences of the project in its Northern Lao site, located in Vieng Kham District, Luang Prabang Province. It describes as how the lack of access to information communication technologies have inhibited local actors' levels of participation in landscape level governance as well as affected their abilities to effectively and adaptively manage their landscape. Community radio, which provides local actors with the relevant information for more substantially participating in landscape governance as well as information useful for adaptive management, is proposed as one potential solution for improving participatory landscape governance.

Participatory radio, video and other ICT initiatives have helped to bridge digital divide and enhance nation building efforts. Using the case study of the Tlowitsis, a dispersed indigenous community in British Columbia, Canada, Chapter 11 explores the role of ICTs, and in particular participatory video, in nation building. It identifies factors that affect both the involvement and exclusion of the membership and addresses the challenges faced and lessons learned. ICTs, in particular new media technologies, offer great potential to overcome the geographic barriers caused by dispersal. However, it remains uncertain how they might contribute to the process of nation building. In this regard, the authors present six fundamental requirements for nation building, and then use these requirements to structure an analysis of the Tlowitsis case study.

ICTs have made a significant contribution to bridge the educational opportunities available to urban and rural areas using distance education modes. Chapter 12 explores the Chinese higher education system which is the largest in the world, but distance education, using ICTs, started later than in developed countries. It examines the benefits of education to human development and provides an overview of the recent development of distance higher education in China. The potential for further developing distance higher education with ICTs is considered. In addition, challenges are discussed and recommendations are made to improve Chinese distance higher education.

In developing countries the advancement and penetration of elementary education for human development has become important policy initiatives. Advanced ICTs tools can facilitate penetration of education in remote locations where infrastructure support is the limiting factor. Chapter 13 uses a mixed methods study, including a survey and follow up interviews, to investigate the concerns that elementary educators of concerns: the philosophy and pedagogy of ICT integration; accessibility of ICT (including software, hardware and resource personnel); infrastructure technical support; and educational integration of ICT in their teaching. Based on the research findings, the authors propose in a school district in British Columbia have regarding the diffusion and integration of Information and Communication Technologies (ICT) in their teaching. The research participants identified four major categories appropriate intervention methods to address these concerns, including targeted professional development, technical and educational support, and sustained access to proper ICT equipment.

The concern of digital divide in education and professional development has emerged over a period of time with the proliferation of information technologies. It has become essential to examine the impact of digital divide in education. Chapter 14 analyzes the experiences of six Master of Education (M.Ed.) pre-service teachers learning to integrate ICTs into their practice. These case studies demonstrate how novice teachers' learning processes can be impacted by the unequal distribution of the temporal, material, mental, social, and cultural resources available. A number of pedagogical and curricular recommendations for the M.Ed. program are then provided.

Assessment for learning (AFL) is a highly effective strategy for promoting student learning, development and achievement in higher education. However, since AFL relies on continuous monitoring of student progress through instructor feedback, peer collaboration, and student self-assessment, enacting AFL within large-group learning formats is challenging. Chapter 15 considers how technology can be leveraged to promote AFL in higher education. Drawing on data from students and instructors and recommendations from an external instructional design consultant, this chapter documents the process of pairing technology and AFL within a large-group pre-service teacher education course at one Canadian institution. Recommendations for the improvement of the web-based component of the course are highlighted to provide practical suggestions for instructors to evaluate their own web-based platforms and improve their use of technology in support of AFL. The chapter concludes with a discussion of areas for continued research related to the effectiveness of this pairing between assessment theory and technology.

Until now, research on podcasting in education mostly examined teacher created podcasts in K-12 and higher education. Chapter 16 explores podcasts in professional learning across several genres of podcasts. Using a popular typology of podcasts, teacher created, student created and professional development podcasts, this chapter compares contrasts and reveals the potential of multiple educational contexts and instructional strategies, formative instructional design, interdisciplinary strategies, formal and informal learning, and effective uses of data gathering methods. The significance of the study extends from not only the extensive reach of the data gathering and production, but also the robust research model, formative and dynamic instructional design for staff development and recommendations for podcasting research strategies.

Improving and enhancing education is a goal for higher learning institutions that seek to provide better learning techniques, technologies, and educators and to generate knowledgeable students to fulfill the needs of industry. A field in need of significant improvement is engineering. One approach is to review the delivery and pedagogies used in the current educational system. Chapter 17 examines the problems faced by staff and students in the field of mechanical engineering. In addition, the authors explore new technologies that enhance and promote the learning process.

CONCLUSION

Information and Communication Technologies (ICTs) are enhancing efficiency and contributing to socio-economic development for people living in rural and remotely accessible areas. By addressing the digital divide and reducing the inequality, significant growth can be achieved for human development. There is a need to make concreted efforts to ensure that everyone has a chance to share in the benefits of ICTs. It is also essential to encourage international agencies to collaborate more on ICT issues for rural development and to increase parity between privileged and less privileged people. The efforts of various research initiatives and outcomes highlighted in this book have suggested some of the useful and relevant strategies which are expected to promote awareness of human development initiatives as they relate to technology development and design.

Susheel Chhabra
Lal Bahadur Shastri Institute of Management, India

Chapter 1
The Impact of Personal Electronic Communications on Work-Life Balance and Cognitive Absorption

Pruthikrai Mahatanankoon
Illinois State University, USA

ABSTRACT

E-mail and instant messaging (IM) are essential ingredients of workplace communication. The study examines how the hedonic use of electronic communications influences work-life balance and cognitive absorption. Data collected from white-collar employees in the United States show that work-life balance mediates the relationship between personal e-mail and cognitive absorption, and that personal instant messaging has no impact on work-life balance but has a direct influence on employees' cognitive absorption. The findings suggest that work-life balance may eventually increase cognitive absorption and reduce employees' productivity. The findings provide insight into how different types of personal communication can influence work-life balance as well as into how to manage non-work-related electronic communications in the workplace.

INTRODUCTION

E-mail and instant messaging (IM) are emerging options for employee communication within and beyond the workplace. While workplace instant messaging (IM) is relatively new when compared to the worldwide adoption of e-mail, it is becoming increasingly popular among employees.

Instant messaging (IM) requires communicating participants to install free downloadable client IM software from Microsoft, Yahoo, AOL, Skype, and so on. With the capabilities of enhancing workplace relationships and complement existing social networks, such information communication technologies (ICTs) offer the convenience, flexibility and efficiency of reaching anyone from anywhere in the world.

DOI: 10.4018/978-1-4666-0047-8.ch001

Employees realize the benefits of these communication technologies. For example, employees can determine the suitability of their existing communication media when a rapid response is required or when a face-to-face meeting is inappropriate. Employees who use IM and other social networking activities with the intention of staying connected with their superiors have higher job performance ratings (Wu, Lin, Aral, & Brynjolfsson, 2009). Employees also find IM more efficient, less disruptive, and shorter than other forms of electronic workplace communications (Garrett & Danziger, 2008). Given employee self-control and adherence to proper usage policy, organizations may also reap the benefits of these electronic communication technologies by staying connected to their suppliers and clients.

However, given the obscurity of employees' workplace communications as to their utilitarian or hedonic use, several negative consequences may render information communication technologies (ICTs) less appealing to organizations, especially when employees utilize them for non-work-related or personal purposes. In 2006, the ePolicy Institute (www.epolicyinstitute.com) and American Management Association (www.amanet.org) surveyed 416 U.S. companies and found that 26% of the companies had terminated employees for e-mail misuse. The survey also revealed that 35% of employees misused IM at work for sending or receiving improper file attachments (26%), confidential information about their employers (12%), offensive remarks (24%), and sexually related content (10%). Another survey recommends IM monitoring in the workplace, given that 57% of the employees use it at work for personal communications (Swartz, 2005). Because it requires users to download client software and due to its text-based message logging features, IM is less secure than e-mail and is susceptible to viruses and confidentiality problems (Primeaux & Flint, 2004). With ever-growing corporate mobility, employees tend to carry on their e-mail and IM conversations on work-related mobile devices.

Several IM client software vendors also offer IM-over-SMS services to mobile users. SMS (or Short Message Service) refers to asynchronous or semi-synchronous text messaging on mobile phones. Given e-mail and the convergence of IM and SMS, employees have various options for conversing across a variety of electronic communication channels.

The integration of e-mail, IM, and SMS will ultimately exacerbate the problem of personal usage of communication technologies in the workplace. Although some employees may achieve psychological gratification through the excessive use or misuse of the communication technologies (Davis, Flett, & Besser, 2004; Neo & Skoric, 2009; Ruth, 2008; Whitty & Carr, 2004), the study assumes that employees do not suffer from any form of Internet addiction or obsessive-compulsive behavior. However, at some point, personal electronic communications can enhance work-life balance as well as produce cognitive absorption, where *work-life balance* (WB) is understood to be a positive condition of well-being and relaxation at work, and *cognitive absorption* (CA) is understood to be a negative state of being highly involved in non-work-related activities.

The study suggests that personal electronic communications are necessary for a healthy work life, but that they must be managed to cultivate employees' productivity. The purpose of this study is to empirically investigate the effects of personal e-mail (PE) and personal instant messaging (PI) on work-life balance (WB) and cognitive absorption (CA) in work-related settings. The research seeks to examine the following questions:

1. Does personal usage of e-mail (PE) and instant messaging (PI) lead to enhanced work-life balance (WB) and/or cognitive absorption (CA)?
2. Can improving employees' work-life balance (WB) also lead to cognitive absorption (CA)?

An examination of these questions may offer management insights as to how to help enhance employees' balance between work responsibilities and their sense of well-being. The following sections describe the theoretical basis of this study.

BACKGROUND

Three foundational concepts of *workplace* information communication technologies (ICTs) need to be addressed prior to discussion of the proposed research model:

1. *Usage Balance:* There is a need to maintain a balance between work-related and non-work-related usage of ICTs in the workplace. Too much or too little control can lead to dissatisfaction among employees or diminished productivity. Strict monitoring and web traffic filtering can reduce employees' morale and productivity, while the absence of a usage policy can increase organizational liability and misuse of ICTs—the use of ICTs for "workplace deviant behaviors" as established by Robinson and Bennett (1995). As it is nearly impossible and impractical to totally eliminate the misuse of ICTs, organizations can hope only to mitigate the negative consequences of personal electronic communications by implementing appropriate usage policies and installing monitoring software as ways to deter misuse (Flynn, 2004; Flynn & Kahn, 2003).

2. *Degree of Autonomy:* With workplace mobility, employees have higher job autonomy and control over the use of ICTs. ICTs can enable job autonomy, which is defined as the "degree of control or discretion a worker is able to exercise with respect to work methods, work scheduling, and work criteria" (Breaugh, 1985, p. 556). The freedom to expand one's capability to communicate promotes a perceived sense of being autonomous on the job. In other words, job autonomy gives employees the freedom to choose their work procedures, the flexibility to schedule their activities, and the ability to self-evaluate their performance (Breaugh, 1985). In a similar respect, rapid networked computers and Internet-enabled communication devices liberate employees from their physical work environment and allow them to engage in various online communications with colleagues, friends, or family members. Instead of conversing face-to-face, employees have the autonomy to choose a communication media that best fits their needs, time, desire for media richness, and situational context. Hence, the ability to use workplace e-mail and instant messaging for personal purposes enhances employees' sense of autonomy and freedom.

3. *Work-Life Integration:* Work and personal activities can be performed in the modern workplace via ICTs, and in many cases, work-related communication can lead to non-work-related conversations. The concept of work-life integration holds that "people, whose work and non-work lives (especially family) are well integrated function effectively at work and at home, feel a sense of satisfaction with both domains, and experience minimum levels of conflicts between work and family" (Valcour & Hunter, 2004, p. 62). The mediating factor between technology and work-life integration is the distribution of work, which can expand beyond organizational boundaries (Valcour & Hunter, 2004). For example, employees with smart phones (e.g., Blackberry, iPhone, Windows Mobile, etc.) and mobile computers are not bound by the physical space in which they work or play.

RESEARCH MODEL

Regardless of what types of ICTs are used in the workplace, work-related communication often leads to non-work-related activities. The study defines *personal electronic communications* as "any non-work-related electronic communications to anyone within or beyond the workplace that occur during work hours or during paid time". Given current trends in workplace mobility, personal electronic communications also include the use of company-owned communication devices for non-work-related purposes. Therefore, both *personal e-mail* (PE) and *personal instant messaging* (PI) can be characterized as personal electronic communications. *Work-life balance* (WB) is the state of contentment and relaxation while at work. Work-life balance is negatively affected by daily stress and overwhelming responsibilities, which create productivity loss and burnout. The perceived sense of autonomy over workplace ICTs may lessen those effects and help motivated employees ease their mental tension. But if employees get too "involved" in the non-work activities, cognitive absorption may occur. *Cognitive absorption* (CA) is defined as a total involvement in non-work-related ICTs usage (e.g., Internet, e-mail, IM, SMS, MMS, etc.). This study concentrates only on the use of PE and PI with regard to CA. Cognitive absorption (CA) could put into place the conditions for workplace deviance, such as cyber-production deviance (Mahatanankoon, 2006) or cyber-loafing—the "voluntary act of employees' using their companies' internet access during office hours to surf non-job related Web sites for personal purposes" (Lim, 2002, p. 677).

Hypotheses

Most employees are familiar with work-related as well as non-work-related e-mail usages. E-mail is efficient and easy to use. It allows rapid information sharing that permeates an organization (Lucas, 1998). Remote employees find e-mail to be an information-rich medium that enables distributed workforce productivity (Higa, Sheng, Shin, & Figueredo, 2000). In addition, the emergence of easy-to-use IM applications complements the use of e-mail by conveying emotions and feelings via icons and symbols (Lancaster, Yen, Huang, & Hung, 2007). These icons and symbols augment the richness of text-based IM conversation. Work-related IM often leads to social and recreational experiences within the workplace (Rouibah, 2008). Premkumar, Ramamurthy and Liu (2008) find that utilitarian and hedonic beliefs, social norms, critical mass, and ease of use are the determining factors predicting IM activities.

Studies show that information and communication technologies (ICTs) enhance existing social relationships, create a sense of emotional well-being, help resolve conflicts, and motivate team collaboration (Amichai-Hamburger & Furnham, 2007). Blogging—another aspect of ICTs—stimulates social integration and bonding, which enhances an individual's sense of well-being, relationships, and social support (Baker & Moore, 2008; Ko & Kuo, 2008). Kraut et al. (2002) also find that Internet technology usage at home has positive effects on personal well-being and social relationships. Research finds that those who refuse to engage in e-mails, text messaging or other electronic forms of communications are disintegrating themselves from modern society (Batinic & Goritz, 2009), thereby reducing their sense of psychological well-being and increasing their emotional distress (Caplan & Turner, 2007). IM also promotes an individual's sense of well-being by increasing the amount of duration and quality time spent on existing friendships (Valkenburg & Peter, 2007). Employees may use personal electronic communications to reduce stress or to take breaks from overwhelming responsibilities. Based on previous evidence, engaging in personal e-mail (PE) and personal IM (PI) can help increase employees' work-life balance (WB). Therefore, the study proposes:

H1: *Personal e-mail positively affects work-life balance*

H2: *Personal instant messaging positively affects work-life balance*

Cognitive absorption (CA) is the state of total involvement with ICTs—a state in which users experience a sense of temporal dissociation, intense focus, control, curiosity and enjoyment from information technology usage (Agarwal & Karahanna, 2000). It is one of the factors leading to incessant information systems usage (Roca, Chiu, & Martinez, 2006). Educators can increase the acceptance of an Internet-based learning system by designing a system that heightens CA (Saade & Bahli, 2005). In online retailing, web designers create e-commerce websites to maximize users' CA experience (Shang, Chen, & Shen, 2005).

Nonetheless, the seductive nature of Internet, e-mail and IM usage can immerse employees into unplanned or other non-work engagement, which can lead to CA. Rotunda, Kass, Sutton, & Leon (2003) show that CA also has negative psychological and behavioral impacts on individuals. In some cases, personal communication, information seeking, and well-being enhancement can lead to mental distraction (Gordon, Juang, & Syed, 2007). Increased e-mail usage in the workplace could also mean reduced productivity and procrastination (Phillips & Reddie, 2006). Although the influence of peers generally governs the amount and

acceptability of IM behaviors in the workplace (Block & Kollinger, 2007), the covert use of instant messaging for non-work conversations can be quite appealing and engaging for some employees.

Researchers also find correlations among problematic Internet use, task absorption and online procrastination (Thatcher, Wretschko, & Fridjhon, 2008). Since playfulness also plays a role in cognitive absorption (Leonard & Riemenschneider, 2008), it is likely that personal usage of e-mail and IM alters the state of being "balanced," and that this condition later leads to cognitive absorption. Therefore, the study proposes three additional hypotheses suggesting that personal electronic communications (i.e., PE, PI) and WB increase CA.

H3: *Personal e-mail positively affects cognitive absorption*

H4: *Personal instant messaging positively affects cognitive absorption*

H5: *Work-life balance positively affects cognitive absorption*

Figure 1 presents the proposed research model, which holds that the consequences of personal

Figure 1. Proposed research model

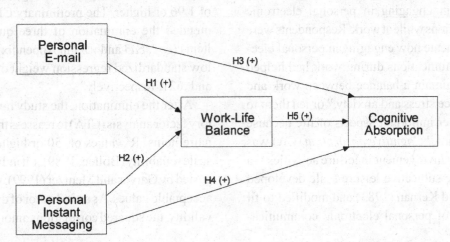

electronic communications can lead to positive work satisfaction as well as to increased involvement of non-work activities.

DATA ANALYSES

Data Collection

A client mailing list of 1,140 white-collar employees (i.e., clerical personnel, technicians, supervisors and managers) from an equipment rental company operating in the United States was used to send out an invitation to take part in the research. Of those who received e-mails pointing to a web-based survey, 115 responded (approximately a 10% response rate). Of the respondents, 60% were female. The majority had at least a bachelor's degree (58.3%) or at least a master's degree (26.1%). Respondents also tended to work full time (83.5%) and held professional (31.3%), clerical (29.6%), or managerial (19.1%) positions. The number of years with current employers was 0-2 years (41.7%), 3-5 years (20.0%), and 6-10 years (25.2%).

Measures

The existing scales were used to measure work-life balance and cognitive absorption. Moorman and Matulich's (1993) scale was modified to capture the essence of *work-life balance* (WB) which resulted from engaging in personal electronic communications while at work. Respondents were asked to indicate how engaging in personal electronic communications during work had helped them to "maintain a balance between work and play," "reduce stress and anxiety," or led them to "neglect other important aspects of life because I work so hard." *Cognitive absorption* (CA) was measured by involvement in leisure activities—a subset of the subjective leisure scale developed by Unger and Kernan (1983) and modified to fit the context of personal electronic communica-

tions. Absorption in leisure or non-work activities means "high involvement or total absorption in an activity" (Unger & Kernan, 1983, p. 383). Respondents were asked to report their feelings when they engaged in personal electronic communications at work. Such items included: "The activities in which I participate totally absorb me," "They help me forget about the day's problems," "Engaging in these activities is like 'getting away from it all', and "I could get so involved that I would forget everything else." To capture information regarding *personal e-mail* (PE) and *personal IM* (PI), respondents were asked to indicate the number of times per week they engaged in personal electronic communications. The scale ranged from the minimum (i.e., "none at all," "1-2 times per week," "3-4 times per week,"…) to the maximum of "11-15 times per week" or "more than 16 times per week."

Validation of Questionnaire Items

To assess the reliability and validity of questionnaire items, Garver and Mentzer (1999) recommend that these items be statistically tested for unidimensionality, scale reliability, and convergent and discriminant validity. Confirmatory factor analysis (CFA) was conducted on all of the questionnaire items (Appendix A). To satisfy the criteria of unidimensionality, item inclusion criteria were based on standardized regression estimates of .70 or higher and a significant t-value of 1.96 or higher. The preliminary CFAs recommended the elimination of three questionnaire items (*ca2, ca3* and *wb3* in Appendix A) due to a low standardized regression weight of .639, .536 and .621, respectively.

After the elimination, the study ran confirmatory factor analysis (CFA) to reassess the questionnaire items. R^2 values of .50 or higher signified scale reliability (Bollen, 1989). Fit indices, as suggested by Garver and Mentzer (1999), were within acceptable values. As an indicator of discriminant validity, the squared correlations among the latent

Table 1. Results of confirmatory factor analysis

QuestionnaireItems	Mean	S.D.	Standardized Regression Weight	R² Values	Variance Extracted	Correlation			
						CA	PE	PI	WB
CA1	2.55	1.19	.991	.983	.809	1.0	.272	.489	.338
CA4	2.48	1.15	.797	.635					
PE1	3.74	2.33	.882	.777	.725		1.0	.468	.267
PE2	4.05	2.39	.818	.669					
PE3	3.88	2.59	.814	.662					
PE4	4.29	2.67	.889	.790					
PI1	3.08	2.63	.955	.912	.873			1.0	.204
PI2	2.90	2.49	.913	.834					
WB1	3.37	1.21	.965	.932	.739				1.0
WB2	3.62	1.19	.740	.548					

Overall Measurement Model Fit: TLI = .930, CFI = .957, RMSEA = .101
Acceptable Threshold: TLI > .90, CFI > .90, RMSEA range = .05-.08

variables were substantially lower than the average variance extracted of a construct (Koufteros, 1999). Table 1 reports standardized factor loadings, scale reliability, and fit indices. The table shows adequate reliability with moderate construct validity (RMSEA=.101) of the questionnaire items used in this study. Appendix A presents the final measurement items used in this study.

Hypothesis Testing

After validating the reliability and validity of the questionnaire items, I tested the proposed hypotheses by examining the structural model's goodness-of-fit and path coefficients of the underlying latent variables. In addition to χ^2/df and Normative Fit Index (NFI)—a comparison between a hypothesized model and the independence model—the same goodness-of-fit indices also were used to assess the proposed research model. Comparative Fit Index (CFI) takes sample size into account, while Tucker-Lewis Index (TLI) is "a measure of parsimony and sample size known to be associated with NFI" (Hair, Anderson, Tatham, & Black, 1998, p. 657). The recommended acceptance values of these indices should be greater than 0.9 (Bentler, 1990). The χ^2/df ratio should be less than 2.0 to indicate accept-

able fit between a hypothetical model and sample data (March & Hocevar, 1985).

PE had a significant impact on WB ($\beta = .11$; $p < .05$), but no effect on CA ($\beta = -.002$; $p = .97$). The impact of PI on WB was non-significant ($\beta = .04$; $p = .43$). PI and WB significantly affected CA ($\beta = .18$; $p < .001$ and $\beta = .24$; $p < .05$, respectively). Both PI and PE accounted for an 8% of the variance in work-life balance—an indication that PE plays only a minimal role in increasing WB. Nevertheless the proposed model explained 32% of the variance in CA. Based on Figure 2, the relationship between PE and CA is mediated by WB whereas PI affects cognitive absorption directly. The goodness-of-fit, path coefficients and square multiple correlations (SMC) of the structural model are illustrated in Figure 2. The goodness-of-fit measures yielded acceptable to moderate fit values (Bentler, 1990). As a result, the study affirms hypotheses 1, 4, and 5 and rejects hypotheses 2 and 3. The implications of the results are discussed in the next section.

DISCUSSION AND IMPLICATIONS

With regard to the first research question, the study shows that not all personal electronic communica-

Figure 2. Results from hypothesis testing

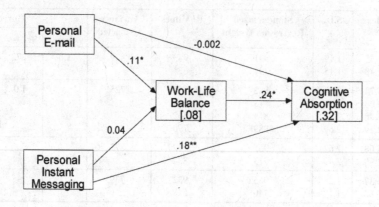

* p < .05; ** p < .001; [ ] = SMC
Chi-square/df = 2.173, CFI=.948; NFI=.909, TLI=.922, RMSEA=.101

tion behaviors lead to enhanced work-life balance and/or cognitive absorption. E-mail is essentially an asynchronous communication tool for which senders and receivers have no expectation of instant responses. Personal e-mail may enhance work-life balance by permitting employees to take time off from work-related tension. Although personal e-mails can be disruptive to continuous workflow, most employees have learned how to avoid e-mail interruptions by reducing the frequency of its use or allotting certain time periods for responding to less sensitive or personal messages. For example, an employee may send an e-mail to schedule a personal lunch meeting and initiate a coffee break, and so on. If used properly, personal use of e-mail may in fact help maintain a sense of balance and cultivate a collegial working environment.

The finding also shows that PE indirectly causes cognitive absorption if it is mediated by work-life balance, but the indirect effect is minimal. Consequently, the management of non-work-related e-mails should emphasize educating and training employees to use appropriate personal message content (e.g., avoiding defamation, harassment, profanity, etc.) and install effective spam filtering software. Employees must understand that all e-mails are not private, as organizations have the right to keep track of and monitor inappropriate content.

Personal IM, on the other hand, has no effect on work-life balance. The finding generates reservations as to IM's benefits in the workplace. Personal IM has a tendency to increase cognitive absorption because the nature of synchronous IM necessitates real-time conversation—an equivalent of online chatting. Employees who engage in IM are alerted via client software when other parties wish to initiate a conversation. Failing to respond within an appropriate time frame often signifies a sense of indifference toward the initiating parties. As IM encroaches into the personal realm, it increases temporal dissociation, focus, and a sense of control over the conversation, as well as of curiosity and enjoyment—the determinant conditions of cognitive absorption. Moreover, the "spillover" effect gives rise to hedonic and non-work-related behaviors. Anyone who has experienced online chatting of any sort will agree that the activity is highly engaging and addictive. Organizations should consider banning personal IM in the workplace or implementing stringent policies for its use, as its liabilities outweigh its benefits. Organizations should put high restrictions on any personal electronic communications

Figure 3. Interrelationships of ICTs, work-life balance and cognitive absorption

Personal E-mail	Leisure-related ICTs
Work-related ICTs	Personal IM

that have minimal impact on employees' sense of well-being and performance.

The second research question is addressed by observing the significant path coefficient between work-life balance and cognitive absorption. Today, workers rely on ICTs for decision-making, communication efficiency and work performance. They also depend on ICTs to build social relationships and to entertain themselves. And since most employees have some perceived sense of control over their ICT usage, it is likely that their personal electronic communications will generally include other non-work-related activities. Whenever possible, organizations should encourage face-to-face activities among employees to enhance the work community's overall sense of well-being. Some organizations support a one-day ban on e-mails and other electronic communications each week as a way to build social relationships.

For workplace settings, the study provides new insights into relationships among different types of personal electronic communications (synchronous versus asynchronous), the state of work-life balance, and the level of cognitive absorption. The findings of this study imply that personal synchronous ICT may increase the level of cognitive absorption, while personal asynchronous ICT does not have the same effect. In other words, asynchronous ICTs do not have the characteristics of subjective leisure activities that effect a sense of temporal dissociation, intense focus, control, curiosity, and enjoyment. As a result, workplace asynchronous ICTs can be less disruptive to workflow and require less cognitive involvement

as compared to synchronous ICTs. For example, employees will probably not turn to e-mails for relaxation or entertainment purposes. While future studies are needed to understand workplace leisure activities, Figure 3 maps different types of ICT usage according to the dimensions of work-life balance and cognitive absorption.

LIMITATIONS AND FUTURE RESEARCH

The study has its limitations due to its small sample size as well as the limited generalizability of its results. Given its response rate of 10%, the study would have benefitted from a larger sample. Non-response bias is also an issue—the respondents who filled out the survey might be employees who engaged in non-work-related activities, while the 90% of non-respondents could be employees who engaged less in non-work related activities in general. These non-respondents could have replied differently to the questions asked by the researchers or might not have found that personal electronic communications increased work-life balance. Future studies can increase the sample size by surveying employees from multiple companies.

The study results also hint at the difficulty of deterring inappropriate usage while maintaining a certain level of employees' workplace satisfaction. Moreover, the nature of the various types of electronic communications could play a significant role in how employees interact with them. Evidence suggests that employees with high levels of focus immersion tend to prefer asynchronous communication—e-mail or SMS; whereas those will low levels of temporal dissociation prefer synchronous communication—IM and online chat (Rutkowski, Saunders, Vogel, & van Genuchten, 2007). Instant messaging—a form of asynchronous or semi-synchronous communication—may require a high degree of cognitive attention and self-efficacy similar to that of short message service (SMS) users (Mahatanankoon & O'Sullivan, 2008). Future studies can reinvestigate the relationships among these variables and investigate these issues for various geographical locations or organizational settings.

CONCLUSION

Although businesses find personal electronic communications convenient and efficient, there are some negative organizational liabilities associated with their use. The study reveals that personal use of e-mail—a form of asynchronous communication—can enhance work-life balance and has no direct impact on non-work involvement. On the contrary, personal IM—a form of synchronous communication—promotes cognitive absorption. Certain types and conditions of personal ICTs require organizational control and monitoring. Employers can encourage physical social activities as a way to reduce excessive usage of non-work-related ICTs.

REFERENCES

Agarwal, R., & Karahanna, E. (2000). Time flies when you're having fun: Cognitive absorption and beliefs about information technology usage. *Management Information Systems Quarterly*, *24*(4), 665–694. doi:10.2307/3250951

Amichai-Hamburger, Y., & Furnham, A. (2007). The positive net. *Computers in Human Behavior*, *23*(2), 1033–1045. doi:10.1016/j.chb.2005.08.008

Baker, J. R., & Moore, S. M. (2008). Blogging as a social tool: A psychosocial examination of the effects of blogging. *Cyberpsychology & Behavior*, *11*(6), 747–749. doi:10.1089/cpb.2008.0053

Batinic, B., & Goritz, A. S. (2009). How does social psychology deal with new media? *Social Psychology*, *40*(1), 3–5. doi:10.1027/1864-9335.40.1.3

Bentler, P. M. (1990). Comparative fit indexes in structural models. *Psychological Bulletin*, *107*(2), 238–246. doi:10.1037/0033-2909.107.2.238

Block, J. H., & Kollinger, P. (2007). Peer influence in network markets: An empirical investigation. *Schmalenbach Business Review*, *59*, 364–385.

Bollen, K. A. (1989). *Structural Equations with Latent Variables*. New York: Wiley.

Breaugh, J. A. (1985). The measurement of work autonomy. *Human Relations*, *38*(6), 551–570. doi:10.1177/001872678503800604

Caplan, S. E., & Turner, J. S. (2007). Bringing theory to research on computer-mediated comforting communication. *Computers in Human Behavior*, *23*(2), 985–998. doi:10.1016/j.chb.2005.08.003

Davis, R. A., Flett, G. L., & Besser, A. (2002). Validation of a new scale for measuring problematic Internet use: Implications for pre-employment screening. *CyberPsychology and Behaviors*, *5*(4), 331–345. doi:10.1089/109493102760275581

Flynn, N. (2004). *Instant Messaging Rules: A Business Guide to Managing Policies, Security, and Legal Issues for Safe IM Communication*. New York: AMACOM/American Management Association.

Flynn, N., & Kahn, R. (2003). *E-Mail Rules: A Business Guide to Managing Policies, Security, and Legal Issues for E-Mail and Digital Communication*. New York: AMACOM/American Management Association.

Garrett, R. K., & Danziger, J. N. (2008). IM=interruption management? instant messaging and disruption in the workplace. *Journal of Computer-Mediated Communication, 13*(1), 23–42. doi:10.1111/j.1083-6101.2007.00384.x

Garver, M. S., & Mentzer, J. T. (1999). Logistics research methods: employing structural equation modeling to test for construct validity. *Journal of Business Logistics, 20*(1), 33–57.

Gordon, C. F., Juang, L. P., & Syed, M. (2007). Internet use and well-being among college students: beyond frequency of use. *Journal of College Student Development, 48*(6), 674–688. doi:10.1353/csd.2007.0065

Hair, J. F., Anderson, R. E., Tatham, R. L., & Black, W. C. (1998). *Multivariate Data Analysis*. Upper Saddle River, NJ: Prentice-Hall.

Higa, K., Sheng, R. L., Shin, B., & Figueredo, A. J. (2000). Understanding relationships among teleworkers' e-mail usage, e-mail richness perceptions, and e-mail productivity perceptions under a software engineering environment. *IEEE Transactions on Engineering Management, 47*(2), 163–173. doi:10.1109/17.846784

Ko, H. C., & Kou, F. Y. (2008). Can blogging enhance subjective well-being through self-disclosure. *Cyberpsychology & Behavior, 12*(1), 75–79. doi:10.1089/cpb.2008.016

Koufteros, X. A. (1999). Testing a model of pull production: a paradigm for manufacturing research using structural equation modeling. *Journal of Operations Management, 17*(4), 467–488. doi:10.1016/S0272-6963(99)00002-9

Kraut, R., Kiesler, S., Boneva, B., Cummings, J., Helgeson, V., & Crawford, A. (2002). Internet paradox revisited. *The Journal of Social Issues, 58*(1), 49–74. doi:10.1111/1540-4560.00248

Lancaster, S., Yen, D. C., Huang, A. H., & Hung, S. Y. (2007). The selection of instant messaging or e-mail: College students' perspective for computer communication. *Information Management & Computer Security, 15*(1), 5–22. doi:10.1108/09685220710738750

Leonard, L. N. K., & Riemenschneider, C. K. (2008). What factors influence the individual impact of the Web? An initial model. *Electronic Markets, 18*(1), 75–90. doi:10.1080/10196780701797698

Lim, K. G. (2002). The IT way of loafing on the job: Cyberloafing, neutralizing, and organizational justice. *Journal of Organizational Behavior, 23*(5), 675–694. doi:10.1002/job.161

Lucas, W. (1998). Effects of e-mail on the organization. *European Management Journal, 16*(1), 18–30. doi:10.1016/S0263-2373(97)00070-4

Mahatanankoon, P. (2006). Predicting cyber-production deviance in the workplace. *International Journal of Internet and Enterprise Management, 4*(4), 314–330. doi:10.1504/IJIEM.2006.011043

Mahatanankoon, P., & O'Sullivan, P. (2008). Attitude toward mobile text messaging: An expectancy-based perspective. *Journal of Computer-Mediated Communication, 13*(4), 973–992. doi:10.1111/j.1083-6101.2008.00427.x

March, H. W., & Hocevar, D. (1985). Application of confirmatory factor analysis to the study of self-concept: First- and higher-order factor models and their invariance across groups. *Psychological Bulletin, 97*, 562–582. doi:10.1037/0033-2909.97.3.562

Moorman, C., & Matulich, E. (1993). A model for consumers' preventive health motivation and health ability. *The Journal of Consumer Research, 20*(2), 208–228. doi:10.1086/209344

Neo, R. L., & Skoric, M. M. (2009). Problematic instant messaging use. *Journal of Computer-Mediated Communication*, *14*(3), 627–657. doi:10.1111/j.1083-6101.2009.01456.x

Phillips, J. G., & Reddie, L. (2007). Decisional style and self-reported email use in the workplace. *Computers in Human Behavior*, *23*(5), 2414–2428. doi:10.1016/j.chb.2006.03.016

Premkumar, G., Ramamurthy, K., & Liu, H. (2008). Internet messaging: an examination of the impact of attitudinal, normative, and control belief systems. *Information & Management*, *45*(7), 451–457. doi:10.1016/j.im.2008.06.008

Primeaux, R. O., & Flint, D. (2004). Instant Messaging: Does it belong in the Workplace? *Intellectual Property & Technology Law Journal*, *16*(11), 5–7.

Robinson, S. L., & Bennett, R. J. (1995). A topology of workplace deviant behaviors: A multidimensional scaling study. *Academy of Management Journal*, *38*(2), 555–572. doi:10.2307/256693

Roca, J. C., Chiu, C. M., & Martinez, F. J. (2006). Understanding e-learning continuance intention: an extension of the Technology Acceptance Model. *International Journal of Human-Computer Studies*, *64*(8), 683–696. doi:10.1016/j.ijhcs.2006.01.003

Rotunda, R. J., Kass, S. J., Sutton, M. A., & Leon, D. T. (2003). Internet use and misuse: preliminary findings from a new assessment. *Behavior Modification*, *27*(4), 484–504. doi:10.1177/0145445503255600

Rouibah, K. (2008). Social usage of instant messaging by individuals outside the workplace in Kuwait: A structural equation model. *Information Technology & People*, *21*(1), 34–68. doi:10.1108/09593840810860324

Ruth, A. (2008). Don't talk to me about e-mail! Technology's potential contribution to bullying. *International Journal of Organisational Behaviour*, *13*(2), 122–131.

Rutkowski, A. F., Saunders, C., Vogel, D., & van Genuchten, M. (2007). "Is it already 4 a.m. in your time zone?": Focus immersion and temporal dissociation in virtual team. *Small Group Research*, *38*(1), 98–129. doi:10.1177/1046496406297042

Saade, R., & Bahli, B. (2005). The impact of cognitive absorption on perceived usefulness and perceived ease of use in on-line learning: An extension of the technology acceptance model. *Information & Management*, *42*(2), 317–327. doi:10.1016/j.im.2003.12.013

Shang, R. A., Chen, Y. C., & Shen, L. (2005). Extrinsic versus intrinsic motivations for consumers to shop on-line. *Information & Management*, *42*(3), 401–413. doi:10.1016/j.im.2004.01.009

Swartz, N. (2005). Workplace e-mail, IM survey reveals risks. *Information Management Journal*, *39*(1), 6.

Thatcher, A., Wretschko, G., & Fridjhon, P. (2008). Online flow experiences, problematic internet use and internet procrastination. *Computers in Human Behavior*, *24*(5), 2236–2254. doi:10.1016/j.chb.2007.10.008

Unger, L. S., & Kernan, J. B. (1983). On meaning of leisure: An investigation of some determinants of the subjective experience. *The Journal of Consumer Research*, *9*(4), 381–392. doi:10.1086/208932

Valcour, P. M., & Hunter, L. W. (2004). Technology, organization, and work-life integration. In E. E. Kossek & S. J. Lamber (Eds.), *Work and Life Integration* (pp. 61-84). Mahwah, NJ: Lawrence Erlbaum.

Valkenburg, P. M., & Peter, J. (2007). Online communication and adolescent well-being: testing the stimulation versus the displacement hypothesis. *Journal of Computer-Mediated Communication*, *12*(4), 1169–1182. doi:10.1111/j.1083-6101.2007.00368.x

Whitty, M. T., & Carr, A. N. (2004). New rules in the workplace: Applying object-relations theory to explain problem Internet and e-mail behavior in the workplace. *Computers in Human Behavior*, *22*(2), 235–250. doi:10.1016/j.chb.2004.06.005

Wu, L., Lin, C. Y., Aral, S., & Brynjolfsson, E. (2009, February). Financial Revenue of Information Technology Consultant. In *Proceedings of the Winter Information Systems Conference*, Salt Lake City, UT. Retrieved August 10, 2009, from http://smallblue.research.ibm.com/

APPENDIX: FINAL MEASUREMENT ITEMS

Cognitive Absorption (CA)

CA1: the activities in which I participate totally absorb me

CA2: they help me forget about the day's problem*

CA3: engaging these activities is like "getting away from it all"*

CA4: I could get so involved that I would forget everything else

Personal E-mail (PE)

PE1: sending or forwarding personal e-mails to your peer or co-workers

PE2: send or forwarding personal e-mails to your family or friends

PE3: reading personal e-mails of your peers or co-workers

PE4: reading personal e-mails of your family and friends

Personal Instant Messaging (PI)

PI1: instant messaging with your peers or co-workers

PI2: instant messaging with family or friends

Work-Life Balance (WB)

WB1: maintain a balance between work and play

WB2: reduce stress and anxiety

WB3: neglect other important aspects of life because I work so hard*

* item dropped from the study

This work was previously published in International Journal of Information Communication Technologies and Human Development, Volume 2, Issue 1, edited by Susheel Chhabra and Hakikur Rahman, pp. 1-17, copyright 2010 by IGI Publishing (an imprint of IGI Global).

Chapter 2
Assessment and Contrast of the Effects of Information and Communication Technology

John Wang
Montclair State University, USA

Bin Zhou
Kean University, USA

Jeffrey Hsu
Fairleigh Dickinson University, USA

ABSTRACT

This article compares the effects of information and communication technology (ICT) on labor productivity growth and human quality of life in industrialized countries. A mathematical evaluation method based on the concept of Pareto-optimal organization is proposed for this study. This method is easy to apply and uses a linear programming model. The weights for various measurements are determined by objective method and are standard. The method is illustrated with real data from 23 developed countries worldwide.

INTRODUCTION

In the announcement of his presidential campaign Barack Obama said, "Let us be the generation that reshapes our economy to compete in the digital age. Let's invest in scientific research, and let's lay down broadband lines through the heart of inner cities and rural towns all across America"

DOI: 10.4018/978-1-4666-0047-8.ch002

(Obama, 2007). In this statement, President Obama acknowledged that investment in science and information technology plays a considerable foundation in the economic success of a country.

There is no doubt that modern information and communication technologies (ICT) are required for innovation, and can be an equalizer for access to education, health and legal services, and to the government. The increasing use of technology in all aspects of society generates confident, creative and productive individuals, furthermore, creates elevated life styles. ICT capability is fundamental to participation and engagement in modern society in today's world and is an essential skill for life.

The last two decades, in particular, have witnessed the widespread adoption of a great number of emerging technologies, notably the personal computer, the cell phone, and the Internet. Together with their multitude of applications, ICT touches on nearly every known economic and societal norm. Today, in many developed countries, the majority of businesses use computers and the Internet as a matter of routine.

The ICT sector, in general, has considerable impacts on economic performance, as it is characterized by very high rates of technological progress, output and productivity growth. These characteristics imply a considerable contribution of the sector to economy-wide performance. The impacts of the sector can be examined in several ways; directly, through its contribution to output, employment or productivity growth, or indirectly, for example as a source of technological change affecting other parts of the economy (Roberts, 2005).

Since the mid-1990s, high rates of economic growth in the U.S. economy and the remarkable acceleration of productivity growth is widely attributed to the ICTs (Hagemann, 2008). During the second half of the 1990s the comparative growth performance of Europe vis-à-vis in the United States has undergone a marked change. Average annual labor productivity growth in the United States accelerated from 1.3% during the period 1980–95 to 1.9% during 1995–2003, EU growth declined from 2.3% to 1.3% (Timmer & van Ark, 2005).

Investment in ICT contributes to capital deepening and can therefore help raise labor productivity (Jalava & Pohjola, 2002; Basu, Fernald, Oulton, & Srinivasan, 2003). The use of ICT throughout the economy may also help firms increase their overall efficiency, thus raising multi-factor productivity (MFP) growth. Moreover, ICT use may contribute to network effects, such as lower transaction costs and more rapid innovation, which should also improve multi-factor productivity (Roberts, 2005).

These impacts can be examined at different levels of analysis, that is, using macro-economic data, industry data or data at the level of individual firms or establishments. Several studies have examined the impact of ICT at the macro-economic level (Colecchia & Schreyer, 2001; Van Ark, Inklaar & McGuckin, 2002; Jorgenson, 2005). These studies show that ICT investment contributed to capital deepening and growth in most OECD countries in the 1990s, though with considerable variation across countries. ICT investment typically accounted for between 0.3 and 0.9 percentage points of growth in GDP per capita over the 1995-2003 period (OECD, 2005b).

The purpose of this article is to evaluate the effects of ICT among 23 various industrialized countries. There are several factors that influence the economic system progress and industrialization of a country. Labor productivity, as mentioned previously, has been examined in various studies as an outcome of ICT investments and measurement of a country development. For the purpose of expansion of the research we'll bring a new aspect to the study and will use quality of life as another category which is also an imperative outcome and a mirror of the industrialized world. This article takes a look at how ICT investment can affect these important outcomes.

LITERATURE REVIEW

The importance of the ICT in the Economy is well documented in the related literature (Stiroh, 2002; Godin, 2004). According to Jeffrey Sachs (2005), director of the Earth Institute at Columbia University, "Information and communication technology has been the single most important new development tool that has come along in our generation". Speaking at ICT sector week, Sachs explained that the singular power of ICT lies in its ability to deliver services at the village level (World Bank, n.d.). Although many scholars agree on the positive impacts of information technologies, there are various opposing views on the issue. We will discuss about these different approaches and ideologies in the literature in a broad-spectrum.

Productivity: Optimistic Perspective

It is logical to assume that higher expenditure on ICT will result in higher levels of productivity. Technology changes the way that we live, changing the way that we do business, communicate and spend money. Technology enables nations to adapt to change, exhibit responsive behavior and be flexible and efficient (Wilkinson, 2006).

The striking acceleration in output and productivity growth in US in the mid-1990s has been much discussed over the years. A consensus has emerged that faster growth can be traced at least in part to the effects of the ICT revolution. According to the various studies, these effects can occur through three transmission channels (Timmer & van Ark, 2005). First, rapid technological progress in the production of ICT goods raises total factor productivity growth in ICT manufacturing industries. Second, falling prices of ICT goods induce an ICT investment boom. This adds to the capital available to workers, making them more productive. The accelerating progress in semiconductor manufacturing technology sustains this substitution of ICT capital for other input types. Third, ICT typically is a general-purpose technology, which is pervasive and will spread with a time lag. It facilitates and encourages firms to introduce more efficient organizational forms. It will eventually boost productivity growth across the economy following significant reorganizations of business processes around ICT capital (Brynjolfsson & Hitt, 2000; Brynjolfsson, Hitt, Yang, Baily & Hall, 2002).

Our researches showed that, there is a great emphasis on the developed countries and their relevant data in the most of the comparison studies. The main reason to this is developing countries "lack the basic infrastructure to build a solid ICT base" (Roberts, 2005, p. 191) and therefore cannot reap its benefits. According to the Economist Intelligence Unit, "technology drives growth, but only after a minimum threshold of ICT development is reached" (Economist Intelligence Unit, 2004, p. 10). It is only after ICT has been developed that it can begin to contribute to a nation's productivity. This threshold is measured by the percent of GNP spent on ICT along with access to telephone mainlines, mobile telephones, internet, personal computers and television. Per capita income plays the biggest role when examining countries that have an existing ICT structure in place versus those who are in the building process. Developed countries have a higher education rate, and thus are more proficient on a computer. When discussing reasons for the digital divide, "computers require education to use, but the Internet requires very little" (Chinn & Fairlie, 2007, p. 18). Investment in human capital is a factor in technology adoption and directly determines the consumer demand as education is positively related to increased income (Chinn & Fairlie, 2007).

While the Economist argues that a threshold must be reached in order to reap the benefits of ICT, Zhang & Lee (2007) say, "ICT is an extremely important factor that contributes to the accelerated rate of productivity of a nation, especially in many newly industrialized economies (NIEs) and developing countries" (p. 65). Their article talks about how the spill over (ICT impacts where the initial investors are not compensated) increases the productivity of the nation. Another study from Brynjolfsson and Hitt (2000) also shows that the use of ICT is only part of a much broader range of changes required to exploit the opportunities offered by the ICT revolution. A rise in ICT use, changes in organizational practices and investment in human capital are highly complementary factors in the productivity performance of firms.

Clearly, the results of our sources conclude that there is a positive relationship between ICT and productivity. With all of the various forms of ICT throughout all sectors of the economy, we can begin to refer to the chosen 23 countries as having an information economy. This includes all of the latest technology and is a fundamental part of the way people conduct their lives (Kudyba & Diwan, 2002). Oliner and Sichel (2000) estimate that ICT "developments account for about two thirds of the acceleration of labor productivity for the nonfarm business sector" (p. 16). This supports the idea that ICT leads to productivity because it "reduces costs by eliminating the redundancies in capital and labor" (Kudyba & Diwan, 2002, p. 10). ICT allows users to streamline their daily tasks and thus improve their quality of life.

The same conclusions were found by Ko, Clark and Ko (2008) through the use of multivariate adaptive regression splines (MARS), a data mining technique. This technique is capable of illustrating relationships in the data, even those that are non-linear, revealing a more complex insight into the topic. The study finds that the most important variable in productivity is the investment in IT stock. This supports our model by quantifying the key variable in our table, percentage of GNP spent on ICT.

Productivity: Pessimistic Perspective

Some scholars argue that the cost for the ICT investment is not worth the potential payoffs. While it has shown a positive correlation with productivity, is it sustainable? Gains for ICT were booming in the 1990s, but slowed in 2000's due to the .com burst. That is the question presented when considering an ICT investment. Economist Kevin Stiroh (2008) says, "The marginal costs depend on the structure of production and the nature of the capital good. The marginal costs depend on the depreciation of the asset (how much value the asset loses as it ages) and the revaluation of the asset (how acquisition price changes over time). For IT investment, the user cost is relatively large and dominated by rapid depreciation and a negative revaluation term as IT rapidly depreciates and loses value over time as better, cheaper models are introduced" (p. 374).

Quality of Life

The Human Development Report, a United Nations publication, has argued that technology "is used to empower people, allowing them to harness technology to expand the choices in their daily lives" (UNDP, 2001, p. 4). They do not claim that ICT is a blanket solution for illiteracy, poor health, or a struggling economy. ICT proves to be beneficial for both developed and developing nations in improving human development. The purpose of the Human Development Report is focus on how ICT can aid global poverty. The technology market is focused on the market pressures, which do not reflect the needs of the poor. The OECD countries account for 19% of the world population and contain 79% of the world's broadband users. To add to how the nations with developed ICT infrastructure can help those without, Kim Dae-Jung, former president of South Korea said, noted that the entire world's prosperity can be elevated by the OECD nations with a strong ICT infrastructure helping those who do not have the same capabilities strengthen/build their own ICT infrastructure. Kim believes that it is the social responsibility of the world to close the technological gap so that all of the world can benefit from ICT.

Technology growth can directly help human development by enhancing capabilities and also impacting the economy through productivity gains. The report outlines four key benefits of ICT as political participation, transparency in planning and transactions, income and health. Rural farmers are being given incentives in using the Internet, helping to connect them to other villages. This creates a more unified country by creating a dialogue between people who without the ICT would never be in contact with on another. This valuable tool helps the farmers stay informed about new farming techniques as well provides opportunities for education. The area of health is being improved by ICT with programs like the Healthnet Project, used primarily in remote areas, allowing the doctors and nurses to do their jobs better by enabling them to procure necessary equipment in addition to providing expert information on how to use this equipment that they otherwise would not have access to. ICT can also aid healthcare professionals with staying informed on the latest pandemics (UNDP, 2001).

Health

Advanced ICTs are important tools in a number of areas of health and include: sophisticated medical equipment enabled by ICT; remote health applications such as telemedicine; and use of large databases of patients to enable better information about, and co-ordination of, treatment. From an individual's point of view, the Internet can be an important source of information about health (OECD, 2008). On the other hand, lack of access to information and communication has been identified as a critical factor in public health crises around the world. The delivery of information on health, as well as various health services, may be facilitated and improved through ICT-based solutions. Providing local points of access to life skills, education, and on-line consultation would be a critical starting point for addressing health care crises in developing countries (OECD, 2005a). Arguably, ICT has had negative effects on health as well, for instance, occupational overuse injuries associated with computer use. Unfortunately, there are very few statistics on ICTs impact on health, positive or negative (OECD, 2008).

Education and Training

Debatably, there are various positive and negative impacts of ICT on learning outcomes. The former could include improvements attributed to the use of ICT in the classroom and the latter the more general influence of intensive ICT use on pupil's cognitive and language skills. Despite the importance of the topic, there appear to be few statistics that show such impacts at a country or international level. In discussing the implications of ICT on learning expectations and educational performance, the OECD/CERI expert meeting of March 2007 report stated that, "it is not surprising that the results, as shown by a number of research reviews, if not contradictory, are at least inconclusive" (OECD, 2008).

ICT and Crime

ICT related crime (.e-crime.) is both a social and an economic problem. The impact of ICT on crime rates could theoretically be examined by looking at statistics on ICT-specific crimes, for instance, identity theft and Internet fraud. It would be of interest to know also whether the advent of ICT-specific crimes substitutes for earlier forms of crime or represents a higher level of criminal activity in terms of number of offences and the damage caused. Of particular interest in an economic sense is the cost of such crime, which accrues to individuals as well as organizations and includes things like goods that are purchased online not being delivered, advance fee fraud, scams and phishing incidents as well as the costs of prevention (Ray, 2008).

Work

ICT changes the way people work and what types of jobs are available. It can also change where people work, with home-based work enabled by ICT having potentially beneficial impacts for individuals and their employers. Clearly, the impact of such changes could be significant for economies and societies (Oliner & Sichel, 2000).

ICT and Data

To conduct any kind of study on the subject, the necessary data should be available to the researches. Earlier comparative studies with a wide coverage of countries have mostly relied on private data sources, such as those provided by the International Data Corporation. These databases contain figures on expenditure on ICT goods, which are used as a proxy for investment using some rough conversion rates such as the share of investment in total expenditure in the US. More recent studies, such as those by Colecchia and Schreyer (2001) and Vijselaar and Albers (2002) make use of genuine investment series but only for a limited number of European countries. Several individual European country studies are also available but due to differences in methodologies, data sources, and definitions, these studies are hard to compare.

In this study, similar to Timmer and Van Ark, we used a harmonized approach to derive an internationally comparable set of investment series for ICT goods for 23 countries. In contrast to most other studies, the definition of ICT investment used here is relatively broad. Three ICT asset types are distinguished, namely 'computers', which comprises the whole category of office, accounting and computer equipment, 'communication equipment' which includes radio, TV and communication equipment, and 'software', including pre-packaged, own account and customized software. Our choice for this broad definition of ICT was partly dictated by the availability of data. But it is also in line with Triplett and Bosworth (2003) who argue in favor of a broad ICT concept. The electronic-driven technological change that is most characteristic of computer and communication equipment is also evident in, for example, photocopiers and related equipment (Timmer & van Ark, 2005).

MODEL DEVELOPMENT

An international comparison of ICT from twenty-three countries is being conducted under five categories: Expenditures on ICT; Institutional efficiency and sustainability; Access to ICT; Productivity; and Quality of life. Each category consists of multiple subcategories and measurements to make up the categories. The data for the comparison were taken from various databases and compiled accordingly. Main resources for the data were Organizations for Economic Co-operation and Development's Directorate for Science, Technology and Industry, the World Bank Group and United Nations Development Program. Table 1 will provide the raw data for each category and subcategory. Based on the items in each category together with the available data from OECD and the International Finance Corporation ICT tables different measurements were selected for each category under evaluation.

The countries we chose for this study are industrialized nations that are the members of Organization for Economic Co-operation and Development. OECD consists of developed nations who are, "committed to democracy and the market economy from around the world". The data availability was the most important reason of deciding on these 23 countries out of 30 OECD members (OECD, 2009a).

Investment in Information and Communication Technology

First, we will explain each category and subcategory as well as discuss the reasons for selecting them for this study. The first category, ICT expenditures, consists of ICT spending as the percentage of GDP, gross domestic expenditure on R&D, researchers on R&D and share of ICT services in value added.

Investment in physical capital is important for growth. It is a way to expand and renew the capital stock and enable new technologies to enter

Table 1. International Comparison of ICT from Twenty-Three Countries

	AU	BE	DE	FI	FR	GE	GR	HU	IC	IR	IT	JA	KO	ME	NE	NO	PO	SP	SN	SD	US
I.	4.44	6.05	6.83	5.89	5.69	4.44	3.88	5.01	6.77	4.1	4.59	3.5	4.18	5.12	4.64	6.66	5.46	4.34	6.69	5.7	5.33
	1.53	0.31	0.28	0.11	0.38	0.89	0.19	0.57	0.6	0.29	0.32	1.2	2.88	1.14	0.45	0.26	0.66	0.54	0.18	0.53	1.89
II.	5,169	5,665	7,727	5,087	5,033	4,537	3,803	3,016	7,171	4,180	7,231	6,117	3,553	1,467	5,558	7,508	2,585	4,592	7,143	7,776	8,049
	7,375	8,272	8,003	7,121	8,472	7,025	4,058	3,184	7,229	5,725	7,568	6,952	5,882	1,768	6,823	10,154	2111*	6,010	7,400	11,900	9,098
	12,416	12,019	15,183	11,768	9,276	10,999	4,731	8,205	8,251	9,809	8,636	11,716	6,047	6,074	13,101	13,739	4,834	8,020	15,715	23,714	20,545
III.	62.5	62.0	80.5	75.9	64.9	83.4	51.1	74.1	59.0	61.6	44.4	83.9	73.2	21.5	66.5	87.4	48.3	42.8	82.2	69.7	87.5
	72*	73*	85.8	84.3	80.9	96.9	95.9	87.4	78.7	90.7	80.8	91.1	85*	36.0	85*	91.7	85.6	66.9	75.9	90.1	73.3
	20.5	13.0	25.0	16.4	14.2	14.1	12.6	15.3	19.9	16.3	10.4	20.9	21.7	13.6	21.9	28.5	14.2	17.9	18.5	17.5	29.4
	49.0	18*	42.2	48.7	26.7	19.5	32.348*	35.2	43.1	36.8	26.7	34.2	35*	41*	27*	39.8	44.1	32.1	35.4	21.6	32.9
IV.	525.4	507.0	492.3	543.5	496.2	491.4	472.3	481.9	491.7	515.5	475.7	498.1	534.1	399.7	513.1	499.7	496.6	480.5	514.3	499.1	495.2
	524.3	529.3	514.3	544.3	510.8	503.0	444.9	490.0	515.1	502.8	465.7	534.1	542.2	385.2	537.8	495.2	490.2	485.1	509.0	526.6	482.9
	525.1	508.8	475.2	548.2	511.2	502.3	481.0	503.3	494.7	505.4	486.5	547.6	538.4	404.9	524.4	484.2	497.8	487.1	506.1	513.0	491.3
V.	151	146	138	188	178	160	166.5*	274	271*	143	162	198*	138	138*	149*	139	217*	157	155	149	198
	158	147	125	171	157	155	155.17*	208	205*	181	147	174*	201	201*	135*	141	201*	136	140	164	184
	2.9	3.6	4.1	3.3	6.7	4.5	3.7	1.3	1.2	2.4	3.6	3.1	2.7	2.8	2.1	2.6	6.6	5.6	4.7	3.7	3.2
	2.2	4.2	4.8	3.8	7.5	5.4	7.6	1.5	1.8	2.3	7.2	3.3	2.6	2.5	2.4	2.3	6.7	9.2	2.6	3.4	2.8

Source: Selected and compiled from Organization for Economic Co-Operation and Development (2007)

Note 1: AU - Australia, BE - Belgium, DE -Denmark, FI - Finland, FR -France, GE -Germany, GR -Greece, HU -Hungry, IC -Iceland, IR -Ireland, IT - Italy, JA - Japan, KO -Korea, ME -Mexico,

NE - Netherlands, NO - Norway, PO - Poland, SP - Spain, SN - Sweden, SD - Switzerland, US - United States

Note 2: I. Expenditures on Educational Institutions: % of GDP (Public, Private); II. Expenditure per student (Primary, Secondary, Tertiary); III. Performance (% Educational attainment of adult population:

(upper secondary or higher); Upper Secondary Graduation Rate, % of Tertiary-type An educational attainment, Tertiary-type An educational attainment Graduation Rate). IV. Student Achievement

(Reading, Math, Science). V. Post graduation performance (Index of Earnings-Men, Index of Earnings-Women, Percentage unemployment ratio-Men, Percentage unemployment ratio-Women).

Note 3*: Information was not available for this cell. Information that was based on comparable counties is noted by an asterisk next to the number.

the production process. ICT has been the most dynamic component of investment in recent years. Investment covers the acquisition of equipment and computer software that is used in production for more than one year. ICT has three components: information technology equipment (computers and related hardware), communications equipment and software. Software includes acquisition of pre-packaged software, customized software and software developed in-house.

Correct measurement of ICT investment is crucial for estimating the contribution of ICT to economic growth and performance. In the national accounts, expenditure on ICT products is considered investment only if the products can be physically isolated (*i.e.* ICT embodied in equipment is considered not as investment but as intermediate consumption). This means that ICT investment may be underestimated and the order of magnitude of the under estimation may differ depending on how intermediate consumption and investment are treated in each country's accounts. In particular, it is only very recently that expenditure on software has started being treated as investment in the national accounts, and methodologies still vary across countries. To tackle the specific problems relating to measurement obstacles and differences, new methods are recently being implemented by OECD member countries (OECD, 2009b). For this particular study, since the collected data was from year 2006, ICT investment and measurement impediments cross countries were in place. Therefore, we believe adding various sub-categories with different measurements would give more reliable results.

As a first measurement, we chose percent of GDP for our analysis. This represents the percentage of gross domestic product for a country which was spent on ICT expenditures. Using percentage values provides an accurate value for comparison purposes among countries of different sizes. It relates the amount spent on ICT as compared to all other contributions to GDP. This is a very useful input from our sample data.

Gross domestic expenditure on R&D percentage is very similar to the Percent of GDP measurement. The percentage that is spent on R&D is an important figure in our model as well. In order for increases in productivity, new technology must be developed and mastered. This is made possible through Research and Development expenditures. Governments such as Korea aim to increase their R&D spending from 3.49% of GDP to 5% by 2012 (The Republic of Korea, 2008). This is a deliberate effort to put an emphasis on building up the country's basic science capabilities.

R&D researchers (per thousand employed, FTE) is another measure on just how far the span of the Research and Development field extends. Researchers are the central element of the research and development system. With more researchers, there is a greater emphasis on developing new technologies. Although, it can be argued that it is actually the quality and skill of the researchers as well as the overall number. Number of R&D researches coupled with Percentage of GDP spent on R&D will provide us with an accurate picture.

The final subcategory shows the value placed on ICT services relative to the investments made by a country in all other business services value added. For this particular subcategory, we chose share of ICT services as a percentage of total business services value added. According to the OECD Factbook 2009, for the 1995-2006 period the share of ICT services has grown most in Finland, Ireland, the Czech Republic and the Netherlands (OECD, 2009b). These are also the countries with high ICT and R&D expenditures. Therefore, we believe this last sub-category will help us to compare the chosen countries in terms of given importance to the sector.

Institutional Efficiency and Sustainability

The second category, institutional efficiency and sustainability consists of three subcategories; telecommunications revenue, telephone subscribers per employee, telecommunications investment. First subcategory, telecommunications revenue, given as a percentage of GDP shows the amount of revenue from the provision of telecommunication services such as fixed line, mobile, and data as a percentage of GDP. It explains us just how much is spent on telecommunication services in each country. The more demand there is for these services, the more revenue that will be generated from them. This also showcases how strong the telecom industry is within each respective country.

Telephone subscribers per employee, our second subcategory in this group, are the number of telephone subscribers (fixed line plus mobile) divided by the total number of telecommunications employees. This measurement helps provide an insight on how sustainable the industry is. With more subscribers per employee, this means companies within a country are successfully leveraging their own technology in order to provide these services to consumers at lower operating costs.

The third subcategory we have for this group is the telecommunications investment. Telecommunications investment as a percentage of revenue is the total telecommunications investment (capital expenditure) that is measured as a percentage of telecommunications revenue. Capital expenditures are necessary to improve upon the current infrastructure and technology used within the industry. A high correlation between telecommunication investment and Gross Domestic Products (GDP) was found (Saunders, 1982; Saunders, Warford & Wellenius, 1983, 1994; Gille, 1986).

ICT Access

The last input we are using for this study is the access to the ICT. We believe, being able to access to the technology conveniently would improve the individuals' everyday life style and can dramatically enhance employee productivity. For this important category, we selected six subcategories to make up the main heading of ICT access.

First subcategory for the ICT access is telephone mainlines. Telephone mainlines is the percentage of telephone lines connecting subscribers to the telephone network. This is an important figure in relation to a country's GDP. A positive relationship between teledensity (number of main telephone lines for every one hundred inhabitants) and GDP per capita was established (Mbarika, Kah, Musa, Meso & Warren, 2003).

The second subcategory is the mobile telephone subscribers. Mobile telephone subscribers are the percentage of subscribers to a public mobile telephone service using cellular technology. This measurement is similar to telephone mainlines and increases telephone connectivity on an individual basis.

Another important subcategory we have is personal computer access. This measures the percentage of personal computers per person. A personal computer is necessary to utilize more advanced features of ICT services such as Internet access. The personal computer has revolutionized how people communicate and do business and in some cases (Skype), cost effectively taken over the traditional telephone line ICT service.

Households with broadband access are the percentage of all households within the country that have broadband access. Broadband access is a high-speed data connection to the Internet. Broadband also allows the consumer to access the Internet while not tying up their traditional phone line as was previously the case with the dial-up access over a modem. The broadband connection can provide a much faster data transmission rate than dial-up modem access.

Households with computer access are the percentage of households that have access to a computer. This may be an at home personal computer or perhaps through that of an easily accessible internet café or at work. Computers have many personal and business software applications as well provide the ability to access the internet.

The final sub-category under ICT Access is access to the Internet. This is the percentage of all households that do have access to the Internet. The Internet provides a deep array of easily accessible information and improves communication ability through the use of email. This is perhaps one of the most important new sub-categories that have the greatest potential to continuously change how we interact and execute business transactions day to day.

Overall, we believe that this category and its subcategories are necessary when comparing information technologies because our research shows that the accessibility can play a big role on the productivity and quality of life. In our opinion, having this category as an input helps add more to the equation as well as helps compare the countries on another level besides economic effects.

Productivity

Productivity is an important factor to having a successful economy. Therefore, it's better if countries try to develop higher productivity rates. Investing in ICT goods and services leads to capital deepening, which in turn leads to increases in labor productivity. Economists believe ICT capital investment has made a sizeable contribution to GDP growth in many developed countries in the past decade, accounting for between 0.3 and 0.8 percentage points of GDP per head growth in the OECD in the 1995-2001 period (The Economist Intelligence Unit, 2004).

For this study, we examine various countries' productivity rates with different measurements as an output of the ICT investments. To get more consistent results, we developed five subcategories under productivity. First of them is GDP per capita measured as constant US dollars, using 2000 constant Purchasing Power Parities (PPPs). Gross Domestic Product (GDP) per capita measures economic activity or income per person and is one of the core indicators of economic performance. GDP per capita is a rough measure of average living standards or economic well-being. Per capita GDP growth can be broken down into a part that

is due to labor productivity growth (measured as GDP per hour worked) and a part that is due to increased labor utilization (measured as hours worked per capita). Growing labor utilization can have considerable impacts on the growth of GDP per capita (OECD, 2009b). Because of these relations, we chose GDP per hour worked/ labor productivity growth rate (%) as our second subcategory.

The next subcategory, unemployment rate, examines the relationship between ICT development and the labor force. The unemployment rate is defined as the number of unemployed persons as a percentage of the labor force, where the latter consists of the unemployed plus those in employment. Again, we felt this was an important statistic to include in our study of the ICT environment. We believe that unemployment rates that are higher than average indicate that the investment in ICT sector is low and the labor productivity is low. Therefore, we ranked the lower unemployment rates better than the higher ones.

To be even more precise, we chose labor productivity per person employed as the next subcategory. Labor productivity per person employed is defined in the dataset as real output (gross value added) divided by total employed persons. We believe this measurement will show us clearly the each individual's output with respect to the all employed persons. This will help us to measure the individual's contribution to overall productivity.

According to the Bureau of Labor Statistics, labor productivity refers to the relationship between output and the labor time used in generating that output. It is the ratio of output per hour. We felt that to get the better result from the study, it was logical to have another subcategory to measure the productivity that shows the labor output. That's the reason we chose labor productivity per unit labor input as our last subcategory in this group.

Quality of Life

For the purpose of generating a greater perspective, we decided to add another output that demonstrates the social impacts of the information technologies. This second important output category, which brings uniqueness to this study, is social benefits, titled as quality of life. It's not easy to measure the humans' quality of life. For this purpose, we tried to find the most relevant data with close attention. The distinctive category has been broken down into three subcategories. These three subcategories are human development index, economic freedom index, and gender-related development index.

Another result of ICT investment in addition to increased productivity is an increase in human development. Traditionally the measure of how developed a country is depends on the economic conditions. The first subcategory we chose is the human development index, which expands the traditional method of measuring how developed a nation is by including other factors that would affect the quality of life such as literacy and life expectancy along with incomes (HRD UNDP, 2009). In 1990 the United Nations Development Program created the Human Development Index (HDI). One way that ICT boosts HDI is by improving the formal education. In line with Sheridan Roberts (2005), "Various studies have shown that ICT plays a major role in improving the quality of formal education in school classrooms and in encouraging further supplemental learning by students at their homes" (p. 201). Other ways that ICT bolsters education is by training students for the future workplace, and thus helping the overall GNP. For less developed countries ICT can help improve adult literacy through broadcast technologies because they "can leverage costs to address the needs of a large number of learners over distance and, with re-broadcast over time, these could potentially offer alternative means of delivering information that would otherwise be inaccessible to illiterate adults" (p. 201). The previous measurements taken in this study are all,

when higher values, components that can positively affect HDI. Consequently, the components that equal a high HDI also equate to a higher GDP and productivity.

Economic freedom index is another measurement taken to access the quality of life. This index was founded by economist Adam Smith in 1776 and is currently annually published by the Heritage Foundation in partnership with the Wall Street Journal. Economic freedom index ranks countries based on ten indicators of how government intervention can restrict the economic relations between individuals. These ten factors are trade policy, taxation, monetary policy, banking system, foreign investment rules, property rights, amount of economic output consumed by the government, regulation policy, size of the black market and extent of wage price controls. A score of 5 means the country has very little freedom while a 1 means the country is very free (The Heritage Foundation, 2009). We believe that there is a direct correlation between economic freedom and ICT/GDP, and therefore thought it would be another good measurement for quality of life. A possible result of an increase in ICT is, "Fifteen years ago 15 countries were rated as free or mostly free. Today, 87 countries are free or mostly free" (Diekmann, 2009, p.6).

The final subcategory is the gender-related development index, which is another facet of HDI. This index is similar to HDI using much of the same data; however this illustrates the disparities in human development between men and women. ICT can help lessen the disparity by providing "an opportunity both to give women wider access to information and services as well as allowing them to develop their own business skills" (Roberts, 2005, p. 202). When women are responsible for working outside the home and caring for the family, typically their physical business mobility is limited and they must overcome any social barriers the country has in place.

As a result, these five categories and their several subcategories will provide a very dependable structure for comparing ICT in different countries. We believe that these three inputs and two outputs we selected will create a formation that takes into account many different factors for the comparisons and will provide impartial results.

MATHEMATICAL EVALUATION

The next step in the creation of the group's comparison of the ICT was to have a method to take the data from Table 1 and alter it into terms that could be compared with one another. To do this, we used a ranking system to scale the data. We took the data from Table 1 and created a ranking system for each subcategory. The scale for each subcategory ranged from 0 to 9.

We, based on the various information discovered during research, consistently created the scale. For example, in the first main category of ICT Expenditures, we created a scale for each of the five subcategories. The raw data from the first subcategory of Percent of GDP spent on ICT was converted to a 0-to-9 scale by ranking the lowest percentage value near 0 and the highest percentage value near 9. The numbers between 0 and 9 were then organized to correlate with the numbers in the middle. We decided that 3.6% will be 0 and that 8.7% will be 9. This was done because the lowest number was near 3.6% and the highest number was near 8.7%. We did a similar analysis for all subcategories. The scales were created based on our opinion of the importance of the values for each subcategory. For some subcategories, higher is better as in the case with Percent of GDP, but in others lower numbers were better, such in the case as Unemployment Rate. In all cases though, the better the country in a subcategory, the higher the ranking, and the closer to ranking of 9 and the worse a countries was the closer the rank would be to 0. Under this method, no matter how poor a country's subcategory number, it could not have a negative rating, only a rating between 0 and 9. The

information about the scales for each subcategory can be seen in the appendix.

After creating the multiple scales for all the subcategories, a new table was created. We converted the raw data obtained and presented in Table 1 into Table 2. Table 2 presents all the data in a comparable format. All the data are now between a score of 0 and 9. The higher the numbers in each subcategory in Table 2 indicate the better performance.

PARETO OPTIMIZATION

The next step in the process was to create Table 3. Table 3 is created through taking the data from Table 2 and using linear programming to create a ranking system. Table 3 takes the data from Table 2 and converts it into scores out of 100 for each main category. The maximum score a country could have in a main category is 100 and the lowest score possible would be close to zero. The higher a score in each main category indicates the better the ICT system is compared to the other ICT systems in the study.

We used this basic equation in the linear programming process to create Table 3. The equation is used for each main heading and subcategories to arrive at a ranking score for each country. It is assumed that the model is linear.

Let

g = the number of categories considered for international comparison,

$Mijr$ = the j-th measurement of the i-th ICT system under category r,

Zkr = the score of the k-th ICT system under category r,

Wjr = the weight to be assigned to measurement j under category r,

Mr = the number of measurements under category r,

n = the number of ICT systems,

Zk = the overall score of the k-th ICT system,

Table 2. International Comparison of ICT Data Scores

	AU	BE	DE	FI	FR	GE	GR	HU	IC	IR	IT	JA	KO	ME	NE	NO	PO	SP	SN	SD	US
I. (A)	6.2	3.0	1.4	3.2	3.6	6.2	7.2	5.0	1.4	6.8	5.8	8	6.6	4.8	5.8	1.6	4	6.4	1.6	3.6	4.4
	7.0	9.4	9.4	9.8	9.2	8.2	9.6	8.8	8.8	9.4	9.4	7.6	4.2	7.8	9	9.4	8.6	9	9.6	9	6.2
II. (B)	5.4	5.8	3.8	5.4	5.0	6.0	6.7	3.5	3.3	6.2	3.2	4.4	7.0	8.0	5.0	3.0	8.0	6.1	3.4	2.8	2.5
	5.8	5.8	5.5	5.9	5.3	6.0	7.5	8.0	5.8	6.7	5.8	6.0	6.6	8.7	6.2	4.4	8.4	6.5	6.2	3.5	5.0
	5.1	5.5	4.3	5.6	6.3	5.9	7.6	6.7	6.7	6.1	6.5	5.7	7.3	7.3	5.0	4.7	7.7	6.8	4.1	1.4	2.8
III. (C)	6.2	6.2	8.1	7.6	6.5	8.3	5.1	7.4	5.9	6.2	4.4	8.4	7.3	2.2	6.7	8.7	4.8	4.3	8.2	7	8.8
	7.2	7.3	8.6	8.4	8.1	9.7	9.6	8.7	7.9	9.1	8.1	9.1	8.5	3.6	8.5	9.2	8.6	6.7	7.6	9	7.3
	4.2	2.6	5.0	3.2	2.8	2.8	2.6	3	4	3.2	2	4.2	4.4	2.8	4.4	5.8	2.8	3.6	3.8	3.6	5.8
	4.9	1.8	4.2	4.9	2.7	2	3.2	3.5	4.3	3.7	2.7	3.4	2.5	4.1	2.7	4	4.4	3.2	3.5	2.2	3.3
IV. (D)	9.0	8.1	7.8	8.7	7.9	7.8	5.9	7.2	7.7	8.5	7.0	8.0	9.5	4.0	8.5	8.0	7.9	7.3	8.7	8.0	7.9
	9.0	9.0	9.0	10	8.0	8	6	8	9	8	7	9	10	4	10	8	8	7	8	10	8
	9.0	8.0	7.0	10	8.0	8	7	8	8	7	8	10	9	4	9	8	8	8	8	9	8
V. (E)	2.0	2.9	2.5	4.5	4.1	3.4	3.2	8	7.9	2.8	3.5	5	2.5	2.5	3	2.6	5.6	3.2	3.2	3	5
	4.8	4.7	2.5	7.1	5.7	5.5	5.2	9.8	9.5	8.1	4.7	7.4	9.1	9.1	3.5	4.1	9.1	3.6	4	6.4	8.4
	6.1	5.4	4.9	6.7	2.3	4.5	4.3	6.7	6.8	6.6	4.4	5.9	6.3	5.2	6.9	5.5	2.4	3.4	4.3	5.3	5.8
	7.8	6.8	6.2	7.2	3.5	5.6	3.4	9.5	9.2	8.7	3.8	7.7	8.4	8.5	8.6	8.7	4.3	1.8	8.4	7.6	8.2

(A) - (E) Values taken from scaling.

Table 3. International Comparison of ICT Ranking System

Country	Expenditures on Educational Institutions	Expenditure per Student	Performance	Student Achievement	Post Graduation Performance	Average
Australia	81.52	67.90	100.00	97.01	88.81	87.05
Belgium	95.92	72.50	76.07	90.00	78.73	82.64
Denmark	95.92	63.22	98.24	90.00	71.20	83.72
Finland	100.00	72.73	100.00	100.00	97.99	94.14
France	94.18	81.82	85.57	85.63	58.16	81.07
Germany	85.87	76.62	100.00	85.03	65.99	82.70
Greece	100.00	98.70	100.00	70.00	63.04	86.35
Hungary	90.86	91.95	93.48	81.44	100.00	91.55
Iceland	89.90	87.01	93.59	90.00	100.00	92.10
Ireland	97.79	79.54	97.77	89.47	96.79	92.27
Italy	97.29	84.41	84.43	80.24	64.36	82.15
Japan	100.00	74.02	97.63	100.00	86.56	91.64
Korea	82.50	94.81	91.55	100.00	93.65	92.50
Mexico	80.72	100.00	83.67	43.11	92.86	80.07
Netherlands	93.27	71.26	90.82	100.00	100.00	91.07
Norway	95.92	61.04	100.00	86.23	91.58	86.95
Poland	88.35	100.00	98.08	85.63	92.86	92.98
Spain	93.57	88.31	74.83	82.04	49.78	77.71
Sweden	97.96	71.26	93.84	91.58	88.42	88.61
Switzerland	92.17	40.23	94.43	100.00	80.00	81.37
US	64.46	57.47	100.00	85.63	86.49	78.81

The score of the k-th education system under category r is calculated via the following linear program:

$$Z_{kr} = Max \sum_{j-1}^{Mr} W_{jr} M_{ijr}$$

Subject to the following constraints,

$$\sum_{j-1}^{Mr} W_{jr} M_{ijr} \leq 100 \ \forall i.$$
$$W_{jr} \geq 0 \ \forall j.$$

Again, after repeating the above linear program r times for r different categories,

$$Z_k = \sum_{r-1}^{g} Z_{kr}$$

Table 2 shows the measurements of the five classes of each country under study. The linear programming model discussed above has some restrictions regarding Wjr. The Wjr must be strictly positive and this way we can avoid assigning zero weight to unfavorable measurements (Kao, 1994). That is, Wjr ≥ € > 0, where € is an infinitesably small quantity. Now, mathematical model is applied to calculate the scores of each grouping, with lower bound Wjr ≥ 0.005. The scores are summarized in Table 3. Subsequently, the total scores Zk are calculated using above equation and are shown in the last column of Table 3. If uniform weights are not acceptable, one can come up with differential weights for each category and the last equation can be changed to

$$Z_k = \sum_{r-1}^{g} W_r Z_{kr}$$

where Wr is the weight for category number r.

The key concept of the linear programming method used is Pareto optimization. Pareto optimization is a concept that helps describe a solution with multiple objectives. In a Pareto-optimal organization any change which makes some people better off makes some others worse off. An organization is Pareto-non-optimal if some people can be made better off without harming anyone else. Each ICT system can be considered as an organization and the measure as indicators of improving people's lives via ICT investment. When several ICT systems are compared with each other, the systems with measurements dominated by other ICT systems are not optimal. The comparison is relative not absolute, hence the score of a system depends on the other ICT system being evaluated. When new education systems are added or old systems deleted, the evaluated score of each system may change accordingly. A linear programming model is formulated using this concept of calculating scores.

In solving the linear program, each ICT system is automatically selecting different weights, which will result in the highest possible score for that ICT system. The important constraint imposed on the weights is that in assigning the selected weights to every ICT system under a given category, the resulted score should not exceed 100.

The important property of this evaluation method is that an ICT system is not required to accomplish a certain level of achievement for every measurement to be optimal. Concentrating on its most suitable groupings might be more advantageous to its evaluated score. The major part of Pareto optimization is the fact that the Pareto optimal solutions can only be improved by making another part of the solution worse. In our example, this means in each category, in order for a country's ICT system to be considered superior, another country's ICT system has to be considered poorer.

The last column of Table 3 creates a final ranking system for the international ICT systems for each country. We felt that some interpretation of the numbers was needed, as described in our concluding remarks, so a simple average did provide a basic frame for comparing the ICT systems.

CONCLUSION

There are numerous countries which have high ICT Expenditures. For example, Finland, Iceland, Ireland, Japan, Sweden, Switzerland, and the US all rank among the top nations in terms of ICT expenditures. The ICT Expenditures for each of these countries, when considered in aggregate, represent the highest overall ICT spending in the world. The underlying data in Table 1 confirms that each of these countries have spent the most on creating better ICT infrastructure services for their people. However, does this high level of ICT spending in fact translate into better Productivity and a higher Quality of Life for the people in these countries?

An examination of the Productivity and Quality of Life Categories from Table 3 reveals that among each of these countries which spent the most on ICT, these also appear to be the ones with the highest levels of Productivity and Quality of Life. At first glance this may lead one to believe that there is a direct relationship between ICT Expenditure and Productivity and Quality of Life. Does this mean all countries should spend more on ICT, and that more ICT spending would result in improvements in both these areas?

Looking further into the scores we also notice that other countries also appear at the top of the results for Productivity and Quality of Life. These countries include Australia, Austria, Canada, Denmark, Luxemburg, Netherlands, Norway, Slovak Republic, and the UK. Norway is one of the top performers in the Productivity and Quality of Life measures, a slim second to only Iceland. Yet, Norway spent roughly only half the amount of Iceland's ICT Expenditures. In addition, Norway spends a smaller percentage of its GDP on ICT than Iceland, yet yields almost the same quality of productivity output.

An explanation for this result may stem from the inefficiencies that exist in the ICT markets of many of the countries who scored the highest in the ICT Expenditures category. For example, one potential cause of inefficiency in the U.S. market stems from government regulation and antitrust intervention in the telecommunications sector. Our study does not try to directly measure this effect; however previous research supports this notion.

Another potential cause of inefficiency is the ICT strategy adopted by each country. For this, we re-examine our Norway and Iceland example, and find that Iceland scores at the top of the scale in the Access ICT category in Table 3. However, the subcategories of the Access category tend to focus primarily on Access at the individual and household levels. Moreover, if we look at Institutional Efficiency and Sustainability, Iceland scores very poorly. In essence, it appears that Iceland manages to provide ICT Access to the vast majority of people and households, but it is done at a somewhat unsustainable cost. In addition, there are inefficiencies built in to their market which has had the effect of driving costs up. Norway, on the other hand, is one of the top scorers in terms of Institutional Efficiency and Sustainability. While Norway doesn't have quite the same levels of Access as Iceland, they do seem to be in a much more stable position economically. Therefore, it can be argued that the expansion of ICT services should be done using a centralized institutional strategy. This would focus on making ICT Access more cost effective and more efficient at a large scale community level, through long range WI-FI and other wireless technologies. This would reduce the high capital investment and maintenance needed to individually reach each household with individual cable lines.

In summary, countries can certainly gain insight from this study, in that increasing the amounts of capital and expenditures being committed to a certain area may not be the only means of improving productivity and quality of life. Governments owe it to their constituents to explore other successful strategies, such as those utilized by Norway. With technology changing so rapidly from day to day, there can be a fine line between overspending and under spending. As a result, key figures such as these should be continually monitored in order to most effectively manage the long term ICT strategy which will result in the greatest benefit to the population.

REFERENCES

Basu, S., Fernald, J. G., Oulton, N., & Srinivasan, S. (2003). The case of the missing productivity growth, or does information technology explain why productivity accelerated in the united states but not in the united kingdom? *NBER Macroeconomics Annual*, *18*, 9–63.

Brynjolfsson, E., & Hitt, L. M. (2000). Beyond computation: Information technology, organizational transformation and business performance. *The Journal of Economic Perspectives*, *14*(4), 23–48.

Brynjolfsson, E., Hitt, L. M., Yang, S., Baily, M. N., & Hall, R. E. (2002). Intangible assets: Computers and organizational capital /comments and discussion. *Brookings Papers on Economic Activity*, *1*, 137–198. doi:10.1353/eca.2002.0003

Chinn, M. D., & Fairlie, R. W. (2007). The determinants of the global digital divide: A cross-country analysis of computer and internet penetration. *Oxford Economic Papers*, *59*, 16–44. doi:10.1093/oep/gpl024

Colecchia, A., & Schreyer, P. (2001). *The impact of information communications technology on output growth* (STI Working Paper 2001/7). Paris: OECD.

Diekmann, F. D. (2009). The new rock stars (economists) & 1 song being sung. *Credit Union Journal, 13*(16), 6.

Economist Intelligence Unit. (2004). *Reaping the benefits of ICT Europe's productivity challenge.* Retrieved July 7, 2009, from http://74.125.47.132/search?q=cache:ZI6UMSLbHXYJ:graphics.eiu.com/files/ad_pdfs/MICROSOFT_FINAL.pdf+ict+relationship+productivity&cd=1&hl=en&ct=clnk&gl= us&client=firefox-a

Gille, L. (1986). Growth and telecommunications. *Information, Telecommunications and Development, 25*-61.

Godin, B. (2004). The New Economy: What the concept owes to the OECD. *Research Policy, 33*(5), 679–690. doi:10.1016/j.respol.2003.10.006

Hagemann, H. (2008). Consequences of the new information and communication technologies for growth, productivity and employment. *Competitiveness Review: An International Business Journal, 18*(1/2), 57–69. doi:10.1108/10595420810874600

Heritage Foundation. (2009). *Index of economic freedom: Link between economic opportunity and prosperity.* Retrieved October 25, 2009, from http://www.heritage.org/ Index/Default.aspx

Jalava, J., & Pohjola, M. (2002). Economic growth in the New Economy: Evidence from advanced economies. *Information Economics and Policy, 14*(2), 189–210. doi:10.1016/S0167-6245(01)00066-X

Jorgensen, D. W. (2005). *Information Technology and the G7 Economies.* Retrieved July 7, 2009, from http://ws1.ad.economics.harvard.edu/faculty/jorgenson/files/IT%20and% 20the%20 G7%20economies_with%20graphx_05-0301.pdf

Ko, M., Guynes Clark, J., & Ko, D. (2008). Revisiting the impact of information technology investments on productivity: An empirical investigation using Multivariate Adaptive Regression Splines (MARS). *Information Resources Management Journal, 21*(3), 1–23.

Kudyba, S., & Diwan, R. K. (2002). *Information technology, corporate productivity, and the new economy.* New York: Quorum Books.

Mbarika, V. W., Kah, M. M., Musa, P. F., Meso, P., & Warren, J. (2003). Predictors of growth of teledensity in developing countries: A focus on low and middle income countries. *The Electronic Journal on Information Systems in Developing Countries, 12,* 1–16.

Obama, B. (2007, February 10). Illinois Sen. Barack Obama's announcement speech. *The Washington Post.* Retrieved July 7, 2009, from http://www.washingtonpost.com/ wp-dyn/content/article/2007/ 02/10/AR2007021000879.html

OECD. (2005a). *Guide to measuring the information society 2005: Directorate for science, technology and industry.* Retrieved July 7, 2009, from http://www.oecd.org/dataoecd/ 41/12/36177203.pdf

OECD. (2005b). *OECD compendium of productivity indicators - 2005.* Retrieved July 7, 2009, from http://www.oecd.org/ dataoecd/6/15/37727582.pdf

OECD. (2008). *Measuring the impacts of ICT using official statistics 2008: Directorate for science, technology and industry.* Retrieved July 7, 2009, from http://www.oecd.org/dataoecd/43/25/39869939.pdf

OECD. (2009a). *OECD member countries.* Retrieved July 7, 2009, from http://www.oecd.org/document/58/0,3343,en_2649_201185_1889402_1_1_1_1,00.html

OECD. (2009b). *Factbook 2009: Economic, environmental and social statistics; science and technology.* Retrieved July 7, 2009, from http://titania.sourceoecd.org/ vl=10066470/cl=24/nw=1/rpsv/factbook/index.htm

Oliner, S. D., & Sichel, D. (2000). The resurgence of growth in the late 1990s: Where are we now and where are we going? *The Journal of Economic Perspectives, 14*(4), 15–44.

Ray, A. K. (2008). Measurement of social development: an international comparison. *Social Indicators Research, 86*(1), 1–46. doi:10.1007/s11205-007-9097-3

Roberts, S. (2005, November 8). Working party on indicators for the information society guide to measuring the information society. In *Directorate for Science Technology and Industry*. Retrieved from http://www.oecd.org/dataoecd/41/12/36177203.pdf

Sachs, J. (2005). *The end of poverty: Economic possibilities for our time*. New York: Penguin Group.

Saunders, R. J. (1982). Telecommunications in developing countries: Constraints on development. *Communication Economics and Development, 1982*(b), 190-210.

Saunders, R. J., Warford, J. J., & Wellenius, B. (1983). *Telecommunications and economic development*. Baltimore: John Hopkins.

Saunders, R. J., Warford, J. J., & Wellenius, B. (1994). *Telecommunications and economic development* (2nd ed.). Baltimore: John Hopkins.

Stiroh, K. (2002). Are ICT spillovers driving the New Economy? Federal Reserve Bank of New York. *Review of Income and Wealth, 48*, 33–57. doi:10.1111/1475-4991.00039

Stiroh, K. (2008). Information technology and productivity: Old answers and new questions. *CESifo Economic Studies, 54*(3), 356–385. doi:10.1093/cesifo/ifn023

The Republic of Korea. (2008, March 28). *R&D spending to reach 5% of GDP: Government*. Retrieved July 7, 2009, from http://www.korea.net/News/News/newsView.asp?serial_no=20080320005&part=107&SearchDay

Timmer, M. P., & Van Ark, B. (2005). Does information & communication technology drive EU-US productivity growth differentials? *Oxford Economic Papers, 57*, 693–716. doi:10.1093/oep/gpi032

Triplett, J. E., & Bosworth, B. P. (2003). Productivity measurement issues in service industries: "Baumol's Disease" has been cured. *Economic Policy Review - Federal Reserve Bank of New York, 9*(3), 23-33.

United Nations Development Programme. (2001). *The human development report: Making new technologies work for human development*. New York: Author.

Van Ark, B., Inklaar, R., & McGuckin, R. (2002). Changing gear? Productivity, ICT and service industries: Europe and the United States. *Economics Program Working Papers, 2*, 1-92.

Wilkinson, M. (2006). Designing an "adaptive" enterprising architecture. *BT Technology Journal, 24*(4), 81–92. doi:10.1007/s10550-006-0099-5

World Bank. (n.d.). *Information & Communications Technologies - 2006 Information & Communications for Development (IC4D) - Global Trends and Policies*. Retrieved April 28, 2009, from http://web.worldbank.org/wbsite/external/topics/extinformationandcommunicationandtechnologieS/0,contentMDK:20831214~pagePK:210058~piPK:210062~theSitePK:282823,00.html

Zhang, J., & Lee, S. (2007). A Time Series analysis of international ICT spillover. *Journal of Global Information Management, 15*(4), 65–78.

This work was previously published in International Journal of Information Communication Technologies and Human Development, Volume 2, Issue 1, edited by Susheel Chhabra and Hakikur Rahman, pp. 18-42, copyright 2010 by IGI Publishing (an imprint of IGI Global).

Chapter 3
Automatic Language Translation for Mobile SMS

S. K. Samanta
University of Essex, UK

A. Achilleos
University of Cyprus, Cyprus

S. Moiron
University of Essex, UK

J. Woods
University of Essex, UK

M. Ghanbari
University of Essex, UK

ABSTRACT

In any form of communication it is vital that both parties can understand the same language, if they cannot a translator is required. Currently mobile users engage the service of a third party provider to translate an SMS text into a different language. The existing services have a number of drawbacks e.g. high cost to the user, not user friendly, they reduce the message space, and are inefficient. To communicate with a foreign person the sender must know the recipients preferred language and device display capability. What is needed is a service where a sender can send message in their native language without regard for the target tongue. We show that a mobile operator can provide a transparent service where the text message is automatically converted to the recipients preferred language. In comparison to the existing system, our implementation is efficient and cost effective and has large implications for commerce, language learning and person-to-person communication. A large number of services such as health care management, education, emergency notification, news, weather, and traffic reports and commerce applications can be delivered to vast mobile populations who are not able to enjoy the benefit of these services due to language barriers.

DOI: 10.4018/978-1-4666-0047-8.ch003

INTRODUCTION

Information and Communication Technology (ICT) is one of the key drivers in global economic growth. In economic terms, ICT facilitates transactions between the seller (i.e. information providers) and the buyer (i.e. information seekers). It appears that economic growth is highly correlated with the growth of ICT services in countries world wide. Current research (Sridhar & Sridhar, 2007) indicates that a 1% increase in telephone penetration (i.e. percentage of population with a telephone) can increase the gross domestic product (GDP) of a country by 0.14%. It can be argued that economic development does not come from telecom service penetration but from the transactions. The efficiency of the transaction can be improved if done by individuals in their preferred (i.e. native) language. This research provides a platform where individuals can transact/communicate in their preferred language irrespective of the language of the other party and hence enhance their quality of life and business.

The need for language translation began when people started travelling from place to place and the first documented cases are between the 3rd and 1st centuries b.c. In modern times, telecommunications have allowed global interaction without the need to travel at all. Currently more than half of world's population has a mobile phone and access to the global facilities (ITU, 2009). Some people use messaging services (e.g. short message and e-mail) more often than conventional voice calls. The mobile short messaging service (SMS) provides a convenient platform where the message can be delivered even if the recipient's phone is engaged in voice communication.

Clearly not all people understand the same language and a textual message in the wrong language may be meaningless. Some messages are generated automatically and generally sent in one language, so many of the recipients may not understand. What is needed is a service that performs language translation according to the preferred language of the recipient, without them even knowing. The literature has focused on SMS language translation; where the service is implemented either in the mobile device (Agrawal & Chandak, 2007) or in the network (Chava et al., 2007; Moka LLC, 2009). For translation in mobile devices an appropriate software interface such as Java Micro Edition (J2ME) is needed. This generally limits the number of languages which can be translated. Therefore devices with larger memory and high processing capability are required (e.g. phones with Symbian or Windows Mobile operating systems) which tend to be costly and can be a barrier to some people. Mobile users can avail the translation service without a costly handset if the translation is performed in the network.

Currently network SMS language translation is done at a centralized server usually belonging to a third party service provider. Mobile users who want to use the SMS translation service indicate the source and target language (e.g. Chinese to English) along with the actual text and then send the message to the service provider as an SMS message. After receiving the message the service provider translates the message and sends it back to the sender. This translation service is used for learning foreign languages and person-to-person communication; where the sender resends the translated message to the recipient.

The current implementation has a number of drawbacks and makes it difficult to deliver the messages which are automatically generated from applications (e.g. mobile commerce). In the current implementation the sender (e.g. mobile user) must have prior knowledge about the recipient's preferred language and or language display capability of the recipient's mobile phone. This increases the complexity if application generated messages are to be delivered in the recipient's preferred language. Using an open source language translation package and a database server we demonstrate that a mobile operator can provide a transparent service where text messages (both from mobile users and application providers) are automatically delivered in the recipient's preferred language.

A large number of services such as health care management, education, emergency notification, news/weather and traffic reports are currently being provided by computer systems. In addition, commerce applications such as insurance, banking, advertisement, auction, sale of goods and services will achieve their objective if delivered in the recipient's preferred language. Service providers can translate the messages at the source but need to maintain a database of language preferences. This not only increases the financial cost, but users are also required to update their preferences for each individual service provider. This research allows message delivery in the recipient's preferred language from all services without the need for language translation at the source.

Telecom operators such as mobile phone companies will be able to connect a large number of services providers to the users. Service providers currently cannot reach everyone due to the barriers created by the diversity of language. SMS usage in December 2008 for six countries shows that the impact of language diversity on the use of SMS is significant. The analysis indicates that SMS usage is greater for those countries where most of the people speak the same language (e.g. the UK, USA and China) compared to those countries where people speak different languages (e.g. Austria, Switzerland and India).

BACKGROUND

SMS subscription (i.e. the percentage of people who use SMS) and usage intensity varies widely across countries but little research has been done in identifying the cause of dissimilar growth among countries of similar economic and social background. One possible reason could be that data related to the SMS subscription and usage is not readily available. A large number of organizations (e.g. International Telecommunication Union)

publish data on land line phones, mobile phones and internet subscriptions for different countries but no such data exists for SMS subscription and its usage. In the past, researchers have investigated the factors affecting the growth of SMS mostly based on a survey conducted face-to-face or by telephone interview. These surveys indicate that the charge and charging mechanisms (He, 2008; Turel et al., 2007), social influence (Lopez-Nicolas et al., 2008), entertainment (Kim et al., 2008; Leung, 2007; Li et al., 2005; Wei, 2008), commerce applications (Kong & Luo, 2006) and discursive use (He, 2008) of the service are the major factors affecting the growth of SMS.

Little research has been done to investigate the impact of language on the growth of SMS. Yan et al. (2006) observed that language is one of the factors behind the dissimilar SMS usage between China's mainland and Hong Kong. Zainudeen, et al., (2006) observed that lower SMS use in India and Sri Lanka compared to Indonesia and the Philippines could be due to fact that most people (in low income groups) in India and Sri Lanka are not familiar with Latin Script (i.e. English) used in SMS communication. We gathered data about SMS usage (as shown in Table 1) as of December 2008 for a few selected countries to investigate whether language is a barrier for the growth of SMS.

From Table 1 it is seen that income and call usage in the UK and Austria are comparable but SMS usage in Austria is much less than that of the UK. If appears that language diversity has a significant impact even if charges for SMS and calls are taken into consideration. A similar impact is observed between India and China. The data in Table 1 indicates that SMS usage is greater for those countries where most of the people speak the same language (e.g. the UK, USA and China) compared to those countries where people speak different languages (e.g. Switzerland, Austria and India). Therefore it can be assumed that SMS usage can be increased if the language diversity is reduced. The use of a messaging service (e.g.

Table 1. SMS usage in six countries

Country	Per Capita Income in $	SMS Charge[1]	Call Volume per user per month	Call Charge[2]	SMS Usage per user per month	Languages Spoken
UK	42,740	0.1	166	0.20	101	Mainly English
Austria	42,700	0.2	168	0.20	43	German and other 7
USA	46040	0.2	345	0.25	200	Mainly English
Switzerland	59,880	0.2	114	0.27	38	German and other 3
China	2,360	0.1	246	0.60	110	Mainly Chinese
India	950	0.6	485	0.60	40	Hindi and other 23

SMS) will enhance the quality of life and business if the user can send the message in their own language and the mobile operator automatically translates and delivers as per the language preference of the recipient.

In a mobile network an SMS is delivered using a store and forward mechanism as shown in Figure 1. Any device capable of sending and receiving a short textual message is designated as a Short Message Entity (SME). A mobile phone or an application server works as an SME. When a mobile user sends a text message, the network first transfers the message to a Short Message Service Centre (SMSC) which stores it for delivery to the recipient. In a similar way, service providers deliver value-added content (e.g. ring tone, news

and weather reports) to the mobile users. The header of the message contains information such as the sender and recipient's phone number. The SMSC stores the message and after collecting the routing information and status of the recipient's handset (e.g. eligible to receive SMS), it forwards the message to the mobile network which delivers to the recipient (Brown et al., 2007).

In the process of delivery from the sender to the recipient the message content (i.e. text) transparently passes through the mobile network and the SMSC. If two people speak the same language (e.g. English) then they can exchange textual messages in their native language. If one speaks English and other German then there are two ways they could communicate: 1) one could have a

Figure 1. SMS delivery in a mobile network

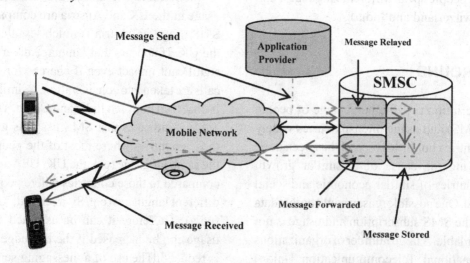

phone which converts from one language to another, and 2) one of them could employ a third party translator. If the conversion is done on the phone then either the sender translates (e.g. English to German) before sending, or the text is sent in the sender's native language and the receiver performs the translation. In either case the device must have the capability to translate many languages if it is to be truly international.

To translate a text message on the mobile, users needs to supply the source and target languages. This is not difficult for a sender if we assume that he/she knows the recipient's language preference. However the receivers face additional difficulty since they need to identify the source language from the received text. The recipient may not be able to identify the language not being a linguistic expert. Therefore the phone needs intelligent software to automatically detect the language and display the text in the user's native tongue. This will increase the cost of the phone which may be prohibitive to some people. In the absence of a high end handset either the sender or the recipient can engage a third party (who makes available a centralized server in the network) to provide the translation service (Chava et al., 2007; Moka LLC, 2009).

NETWORK SMS TRANSLATION

Currently third party providers perform language translation at a centralized server located outside the mobile network. Mobile users connect to the provider through the network and SMSC as shown in Figure 2. The service is used for learning foreign languages and for person-to-person communication. Users, who learn foreign languages, indicate the source and target languages (e.g. English and German) along with the word or the sentence they wish to convert, this is then sent to the translation service provider as an SMS message. The service provider translates the message and sends it back to the sender.

For person-to-person communication (between people who speak different languages) the service can be used either by the sender or the recipient. If the sender wishes to use the service they send the message indicating their language and the recipient's language in a similar way to the language learning. The service provider translates and sends the message back to the sender who resends the translated message to the recipient. If the sent message is in the native language of the sender, then the recipient can use the third party provider to translate to their preferred language.

Figure 2. Current implementation for SMS language translation

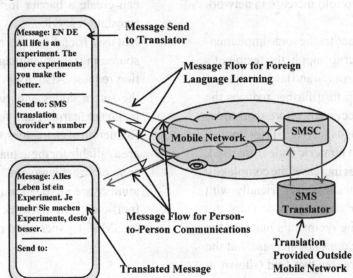

37

Figure 3. SMSC traffic in current SMS language translation

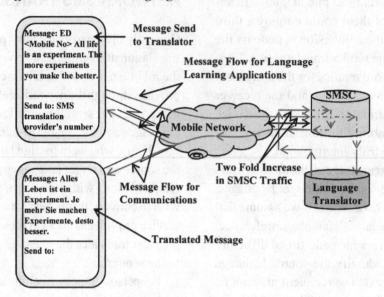

It should be noted that if the sender does not perform the translation the recipient faces the problem of recognising the source language.

Third party translation has a number of drawbacks; it is not user friendly as users need to indicate the source and target language along with the actual text for each translation. The mechanism is not efficient since it reduces the space available for the actual message and increases the traffic in SMSC and mobile network. For person-to-person communication there is a three fold increase in SMSC traffic and a two fold increase in network traffic.

In an attempt to reduce traffic some implementations allow the sender to supply the recipient's number along with the source and target language within the text. This in turn further reduces the available character space and therefore short codes for source and target languages (e.g. ED for English to German or two digit numeric codes) are used. The need for short codes increases the complexity and the system becomes less user friendly with the need to remember language code pairs. As a result of including the recipient's number, the mobile network traffic does not increase, but the SMSC traffic still increases two fold (shown in

Figure 3). Increased SMSC traffic leads to higher cost for the mobile operator and the accompanying higher service charges.

The main drawbacks of the current network based SMS translation services are listed below:

1. High cost to the user; users need to pay a premium fee for each translation request e.g. Lingtastic LLC, one such service provider charges $1.00 per SMS (Watkins, 2008). The cost can be prohibitively high and therefore can create a barrier for the growth of the translation service.
2. Not user friendly; users need to indicate the source and target languages for each translation request. Also, users need to remember the set of codes and rules applicable for language learning and for communication.
3. Reduction of character space; less characters are available for the actual message since the source/ target language, and the recipient's number are included in the text.
4. Inefficient; the network traffic (i.e. traffic on SMSC) is increased two fold.

Under the existing service the sender must have prior knowledge of the recipient's language and/or language display capability of the recipient's mobile phone. As an example a sender may know the recipient's language but may not know whether the phone can display the message. This is a problem for automatically generated messages from application servers such as news, weather reports, security information and notification. Automatic messages are generally sent in a single language (e.g. English). This creates a large barrier since not everyone may understand that language. What is needed is a service that can deliver the messages to the individual recipient in his/her language of preference. If this were the case, the service provider could communicate with any individual regardless of their native tongue. If the provider wished to perform the translation themselves at the source they would need a database containing the language preferences for all users. This would significantly increase the complexity to the sending mechanism. Currently automatically generated messages are sent in batches. The message is composed once and software retrieves the mobile numbers of the recipients from a database. In order to send a message in recipient's language each message has to be sent separately after translation. This increases the cost (i.e. cost for additional software and hardware) for the service provider.

There are other problems in performing translation individually at the service provider's source. Service providers need to collect the language preference of each individual, but people may not be willing to share their information with every provider (e.g. due to privacy). In contrast they will have no hesitation (or choice) in providing the same to their mobile operator who already has other information such as sex, age, spending capabilities etc. Therefore it is appropriate for the mobile operator to perform the message translation and deliver it to the recipient in their preferred language (Rownok et al., 2006).

We show that the operator can perform the SMS language translation automatically by adding a standard language translation software package and a database in the network. By adding an Automatic SMS Language Translator (ASLT) in between the SMSC and the mobile network as shown in Figure 4 mobile operator can allow a sender to send the message in their preferred language without needing to consider the language preferences of the recipient. The ASLT automatically translates the SMS to the recipient's preferred language before delivery. The mobile user needs to only notify the mobile operator once as to the language of preference. The message content will pass through the translation process only if the recipient has subscribed to the service, otherwise it will be transparently forwarded. In the event the translation is required, the content language is identified automatically and translated as per the language preference. Our implementation solves many of the current problems and is laid out in the following.

IMPLEMENTATION

Using the Google Translate Java API (an open source language translation package) and a database server we implement the functionality of ASLT. Our implementation allows message communication in the user's native language and also helps users in language teaching. The implementation is applicable to any messaging service (e.g. SMS, MMS and e-mail) but here we emphasis on SMS.

In Figure 4 we show the architecture of ASLT where a box (containing language translation software, a database server and an ASLT manager) is inserted in the SMS delivery path from SMSC to mobile users. The ASLT manager which is implemented in Java decides whether the translation is required or not. Mobile users who want to receive their communications in their preferred (e.g. native) language indicate their preferences once

Figure 4. Implementation of ASLT in real network

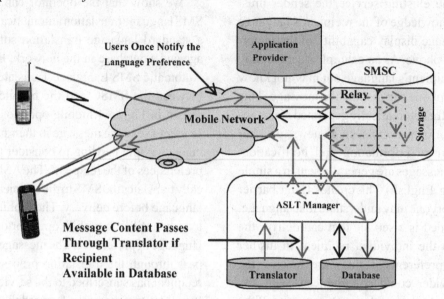

only by sending an SMS which is stored in the database of the ASLT. When an SMS is received (from a mobile user or an application server), the ASLT manager searches the recipient's number in the database. If the entry is not found, the message is transparently delivered. If the number is available in the database, the language preference along with the text content is forwarded to the translator. The translator automatically detects the source language and performs the translation. The translated content is forwarded to the mobile network for ultimate delivery to the recipient. In addition to being user friendly, Figure 4 indicates that in our implementation there is no change in SMSC traffic.

We simulated the functionality of the ASLT on a PC using: The Google-Translate Java API, J2ME (Java Micro Edition) and our own program also in Java. We simulated the origin and reception of the SMS using J2ME as the Short Message Entity (SME). Two SMEs act as sending and receiving mobile devices. In our simulation we allocated numbers 6666666 and 8888888 for the sending and receiving devices. We stored the language preference manually for this simulation. In Figure 5 we show the screenshot of our simula-

tion. A text message: "All life is an experiment. The more experiments you make the better." is sent to the recipient (number "8888888") whose language preference is German. The message is automatically translated to "Alles Leben ist ein Experiment. Je mehr Sie machen Experimente, desto besser." in German and delivered to the recipient's phone. The ASLT implementation in a real world network is relatively straightforward; it works as a relay box and therefore can work independently of other units. It can scale with the network since multiple threads allow translations in parallel.

We acknowledge that there will be a slight delay in searching the recipient's number and to perform the translation. However the delay is reduced if the ASLT is integrated within the SMSC. The ASLT software package can be incorporated easily between the relay and the storage of the SMSC. We are currently engaged in a fully fledged implementation in a network test bed with separate hardware for SMSC and SMEs. A number of mobile operators in India have shown their interest in implementing our ASLT within their real network.

Figure 5. Screenshot of ASLT simulation

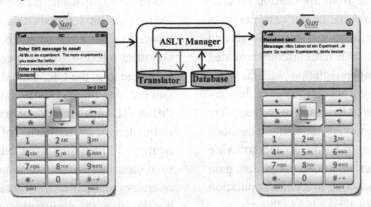

Drawbacks: There are obvious drawbacks of automatic translation since there are difficulties with abbreviations and euphemisms (e.g. u instead of you) frequently used in SMS messages. Research on SMS texting for 11 European Union countries indicates that even though abbreviations such as "lol," "u," "brb," and "gr8," are frequently used they make up only 10% of the total words (Crystal, 2008). Therefore abbreviations may not pose as big limitation to SMS translation as first apparent. Using artificial intelligence, neural network technology (Khalilov et al., 2008) and statistical machine translation it is possible to improve translation accuracy. Some developers (Moka LLC, 2009) currently implement commercial products which translate abbreviations from Chinese to English and vice versa.

BENEFITS

In addition to person-to-person messaging, a large number of applications such as tourism, international business communication, foreign language learning and Business to Consumer (B2C) communications will benefit from our work.

In our implementation, the sender inputs the message in their preferred language (e.g. English) and simply sends the message to the recipient (see Figure 5). There is no need to indicate the source and target language and no requirement to know the preferred language and display capability of the recipient; the recipient automatically receives the message in their preferred language (e.g. German). The communication is seamless, user friendly and unobtrusive. Our implementation is efficient since there is no reduction of character space for the actual message and no increase in the SMSC traffic. Mobile operators themselves can provide the translation service using our relay box without the need for a third party service provider. There will be additional financial cost for the translation software and database server but the cost can be recovered from additional use generated by value added services such as language learning and B2C communications.

Mobile SMS provides potential opportunities for learning foreign languages (Saran et al., 2008). In our implementation language learning is user friendly since learners are freed from the burden of selecting the source and target language for each translation. A mobile user first updates the language preferences such as German if they want to learn the German language. In the same way as a normal SMS messaging, a user inputs a word or a sentence in their native language and sends it to their own mobile number. Message is automatically translated and delivered to the sender.

For B2C communications such as: news, weather reports, and commerce applications, messages often come from application servers. A lot of services such as: health care management, advertisement, auctions, sale of goods and services (CellBazzar, 2009) are currently provided using SMS. Our implementation will facilitate the message delivery from service providers according to the preferred language of the recipient without them even knowing and without the need to change the necessary hardware and software in each individual server. Service providers gain benefit from by connecting to a large population who are currently not accessible to them.

Currently more than half of world's population has a mobile phone and access to the global facilities (ITU, 2009). In developing countries people who do not have easy access to commerce applications (e.g. sale of goods through internet) can now do business using a mobile phone. As an example, similar to eBay people in Bangladesh buy and sell via mobile using CellBazzar (2009). CellBazzar allows people to obtain current market prices in order to buy and sell agricultural products, goods and services through SMS. The service is based on a simple searching mechanism; users only need to read the simple text in English (e.g. buy, sell and name of goods, product and services) and type numeric digits. However, from current (as of April 2009) statistics about the number of goods and services for sale, it is clear that the CellBazzar has failed in enabling people to efficiently sell their agricultural products. One reason may be that most of the people engaged in agriculture cannot read English and need the help of a third party translator. Our implementation will allow the CellBazzar and similar service providers to deliver the information to the peoples in their preferred language (e.g. Bengali) automatically and gain benefit from the additional usage.

CONCLUSION

This research shows that the impact of language diversity on the use of Short Messaging Services (SMS) is significant. Based on SMS usage in December 2008 for six countries our analysis indicates that SMS usage is greater for those countries where most of the people speak the same language (e.g. the UK, United States and China) compared to those countries where people speak different languages (e.g. Austria, Switzerland and India). It appears that the use of SMS will enhance quality of life and improve business if users can send messages in their own language and mobile operators automatically translate and deliver as per the language preferences of the recipient.

We demonstrate a mechanism which allows mobile operators to deliver messages (e.g. SMS) as per the language preferences of the recipient irrespective of the language of the source. Using an open source language translation package and a database server we simulated automatic language translation for SMS text. We show that our mechanism will allow mobile operators to provide textual message delivery in a user's native language without the need for a third party provider (as is currently done). We show that in comparison to the third party provider our mechanism is user friendly and efficient. We demonstrate that using our mechanism a large number of services such as news, weather reports, health care management, vehicular traffic management, and emergency notification can be delivered to those who are currently not able to access these services due to the language barrier.

In a multilingual society governments and public service agencies have a social responsibility to ensure that individuals are not denied access to information. Agencies such as the European Union maintain a veritable army of translators to fulfill these responsibilities. Similar situations exist in the developing worlds such as India and African countries which have language diversity amongst the population. However, developing countries do not have the resources to do the translation, and therefore information access is denied to most of the population. Our work will motivate governments and regulatory authorities to implement policies such that telecom operators provide language translation services by default.

Service providers such as government agencies can deliver messages using SMS. However the cost of communication can be higher due to the barriers created by the diversity of language. A higher cost will in turn reduce the use of SMS for message communication. Using our mechanism telecom operators such as mobile phone companies will be able to connect a large number of service providers to the users and recover the translation cost from additional use of SMS. This in turn will enhance the quality of life and business of vast populations who cannot access these services due to the language barrier.

ACKNOWLEDGMENT

The authors thank officers of BSNL, Indian telecom operator for their feedbacks and comments on the initial draft. The first author thanks both government of India and the British government for providing the financial support for this work under UK-India Education and Research Initiative scheme.

REFERENCES

Agrawal, A. J., & Chandak, M. B. (2007, April 2-4). Mobile Interface for Domain Specific Machine Translation Using Short Messaging Service. In *Proceedings of the 4th International Conference on Information Technology* (pp. 957-958).

Brown, J., Shipman, B., & Vetter, R. (2007). SMS: The Short Message Service. *Computer*, *40*(12), 106–110. doi:10.1109/MC.2007.440

CellBazzar. (2009). *SMS Buy – CellBazaar: Mobile phone market*. Retrieved from http://corp.cellbazaar.com/sms.html

Chava, V., Smith, M. R., & Dudley, W. H. (2007). *System and method for in-transit SMS language translation* (U.S. Patent No. 7272406).

Crystal, D. (2008). *Txtng: the Gr8 Db8. Oxford University Press*.

He, Z. (2008). SMS in China: A Major Carrier of the Nonofficial Discourse Universe. *The Information Society*, *24*(3), 182–190. doi:10.1080/01972240802020101

ITU. (2009). *Measuring the Information Society - The ICT Development Index, 2009 Edition*. Retrieved from http://www.itu.int/ITU-D/ ict/publications/idi/2009/index.html

Khalilov, M., Fonollosa, J. A. R., Zamora-Martinez, F., Castro-Bleda, M. J., & Espaa-Boquera, S. (2008, November 3-5). Neural Network Language Models for Translation with Limited Data. In *Proceedings of the 20th IEEE International Conference on Tools with Artificial Intelligence*, Dayton. OH. Osteopathic Hospitals, *2*, 445–451.

Kim, G. S., Park, S.-B., & Oh, J. (2008). An examination of factors influencing consumer adoption of short message service (SMS). *Psychology and Marketing*, *25*(8), 769–786. doi:10.1002/mar.20238

Kong, J., & Luo, J. (2006, October 25-27). The Innovative Business Model behind the Rapid Growth of SMS in China. In *Proceedings of the International Conference on Service Systems and Service Management* (pp. 1472-1477).

Leung, L. (2007). Unwillingness-to-communicate and college students' motives in SMS mobile messaging. *Telematics and Informatics*, *24*(2), 115–129. doi:10.1016/j.tele.2006.01.002

Li, D., Chau, P. Y. K., & Lou, H. (2005). Understanding Individual Adoption of Instant Messaging: An Empirical Investigation. *Journal of the Association for Information Systems*, *6*(4), 102–129.

Lopez-Nicolas, C., Molina-Castillo, F. J., & Bouwman, H. (2008). An assessment of advanced mobile services acceptance: Contributions from TAM and diffusion theory models. *Information & Management*, *45*(6), 359–364. doi:10.1016/j.im.2008.05.001

Moka, L. L. C. (2009). *Moka Partners with China Mobile for Mobile Chinese to English Language Translation and Language Learning*. Retrieved from http://www.moka.com/ en/news/news-1.htm

Rownok, T., Islam, M. Z., & Khan, M. (2006, December). *Bangla Text Input and Rendering Support for Short Message Service on Mobile Devices*. Paper presented at the 9th International Conference on Computer and Information Technology, Dhaka, Bangladesh.

Saran, M., Cagiltay, K., & Seferoglu, G. (2008, March 23-26). Use of Mobile Phones in Language Learning: Developing Effective Instructional Materials. In *Proceedings of the Fifth IEEE International Conference on Wireless, Mobile, and Ubiquitous Technology in Education*, Beijing, China (pp. 39-43).

Sridhar, K. S., & Sridhar, V. (2007). Telecommunications Infrastructure and Economic Growth: Evidence from Developing Countries. *Applied Econometrics and International Development*, *7*(2), 37–56.

Turel, O., Serenko, A., & Bontis, N. (2007). User acceptance of wireless short messaging services: Deconstructing perceived value. *Information & Management*, *44*(1), 63–73. doi:10.1016/j.im.2006.10.005

Watkins, C. (2008). *SMS text translation and live interpreters arrives on your cell phone with mobile.lingtastic.com*. Retrieved from http://www.lingtastic.com/ LatestNews.htm

Wei, R. (2008). Motivations for using the mobile phone for mass communications and entertainment. *Telematics and Informatics*, *25*(1), 36–46. doi:10.1016/j.tele.2006.03.001

Yan, X., Gong, M., & Thong, J. Y. L. (2006). Two tales of one service: User acceptance of short message service (SMS) in Hong Kong and China. *INFO: The Journal of Policy. Regulation and Strategy*, *8*(1), 16–28.

Zainudeen, A., Samarajiva, R., & Abeysuria, A. (2006). *Telecom Use on a Shoestring: Strategic Use of Telecom Services by the Financially Constrained in South Asia. LIRNEasia*. Retrieved from http://www.regulateonline.org/ content/view/624/71/

This work was previously published in International Journal of Information Communication Technologies and Human Development, Volume 2, Issue 1, edited by Susheel Chhabra and Hakikur Rahman, pp. 43-58, copyright 2010 by IGI Publishing (an imprint of IGI Global).

Chapter 4

Botswana's Novel Approaches for Knowledge–Based Economy Facilitation:
Issues, Policies and Contextual Framework

Bwalya Kelvin Joseph
University of Botswana, Botswana

ABSTRACT

The Vision 2016, which is a set of strategic plans desired to position Botswana at the completive edge of the socio-economic hierarchy in Africa, is being implemented with concerted efforts from both the private and the public sector, including ordinary citizens. One of the major motivations for drawing this strategy has been the desire to transform Botswana from a resource and industry-based (e.g. agriculture and diamond mining) to knowledge-based economy. This has come from the realisation that in order to compete favourably at a global scale, there is need to put in place efficient knowledge value chains. To this course, several initiatives have been devised and/or implemented by both the government and the public sector. This article surveys the fundamental concepts on which this paradigm shift is hinged and brings out the different issues, initiatives and policies (such as Information and Communications Technology development, nurturing of an appropriate human resource base by way of strategic human resource development plans, investment in intellectual capital, etc.) that have been done so far in Botswana. The article, however, does not claim that it offers a compendium of existing programs towards a knowledge-based economy initiated by Botswana. The article posits that although significant strides have been scored in Botswana's efforts towards a knowledge-based economy, a lot more needs to be done if it were to compete favourably at an international stage.

DOI: 10.4018/978-1-4666-0047-8.ch004

1. INTRODUCTION

The recent world economic recession which has largely impacted negatively on the income levels from diamond sells, etc., have forced countries such as Botswana to think twice about their economic mainstay. Botswana has been over-dependent on agriculture and the diamond mining industry for over 3 decades. However, these industries are not sustainable to a more or lesser extent. It is for this reason that Botswana has started shifting towards a Knowledge-Based-Economy (KBE). This strategy is enveloped into the Vision 2016 national vision which aims to improve the socio-economic standing of Botswana. This strategy is hinged on encouraging creativity and innovation and will be spear-headed by the recently established Botswana Innovation Hub (BIH) – which is a localized version of the Malaysian ICT hub model.

Towards a knowledge-based society, there have been several efforts that have been authored at the regional level, such as the Southern African Development Community (SADC) protocol on communications and transport. The logic of this is that initiatives at regional levels have been seen to work e.g. the ESEMK project implemented in the European Union whose main objective was to discuss the possible emergence of a specific European socio-economic model of development in the context of the transition towards a knowledge-based society (Amable & Lung, 2005).

The background to this motivation can also be extended to looking at the value that a KBE brings to the fore in countries such as China, Singapore, Mexico, South Korea, Brazil etc. that have dedicated strategies towards transforming to KBEs. Kuznetsov and Dahlman (2008) have carefully looked at the factors that have affected the transition to KBEs of Mexico and South Korea given their difference in contextual and location aspects. For the Mexican case, the importance of education and institutional reform, encouragement of innovation and entrepreneurship, efficient application of information and communications technologies (ICTs), replication of scientific discoveries in all sectors of the socio-economic sectors, and knowledge revolution contributed a lot to Mexico's transition to a knowledge-based economy. Korea presents a growth model largely based on diversified conglomerates e.g. Daewoo, Samsung Electronics, LG Electronics, KIA motors, Hyundai Motors, etc. (Kuznetsov & Dahlman, 2008). The strategy authored to place Korea at a competitive edge was also partially based on developing their R&D potential. The start point of this development dimension was human development (e.g. massive and effective training) so a strong human resource base is created. This was necessary as one of the major resources that Korea has is its efficient human resource base. Within this framework, human development was extended even to traditional universities through the Brain-21 Korea aimed at encouraging research done by faculty and Masters/PhD students. There was also encouraged a culture that promotes efficient knowledge management at all levels of the socio-economic value chains. The result of these interventions is clearly seen both in Mexico and in Korea as these countries can competent favorably in world economic and knowledge value chains. The aforementioned countries have also seen themselves growing their Gross Domestic Products (GDPs), improving their public service delivery and business processes to fuel the nation's socio-economic mechanisms, etc. These economies have undergone significant structural changes. It is to be noted that propensity to change can be a major factor in determining whether KBE is established or not.

African countries either solely depending on agriculture or mining are slowly transforming into industrial economies where natural resources and labour are the main resources. The current trend is that these countries are now transforming into KBEs where knowledge is the key resource. This is in cahoots with the reasoning brought forward by Leung (2004) that for countries to thrive in this knowledge age, there is need for transformation to knowledge-based economic concepts. However, achieving this may not be feasible if the different other factors that impact on the realization of a KBE are not taken care of. The following gives a list of issues and factors that may impact on establishment of a KBE: culture of innovation, appropriate training programs for the production of appropriate human resource base, putting in place efficient knowledge distribution and dissemination frameworks and channels, encouraging innovation and research, putting in place an enabling environment by having appropriate legal, institutional and regulatory frameworks, etc.

The UNDP (1996) produced a report that outlined Botswana's 2000 human development report that focused on how HIV/AIDS is reducing economic growth and increasing poverty, and provided policy guidance for political action at the highest levels. This report was the gateway for realizing that if a human development strategy were not put in place urgently, Botswana risked developing its economical competence globally. Botswana has the political will as evidenced by its putting in place a logically coherent human resource development strategy and training policy evidenced by the establishment of the Botswana Training Authority (BOTA), inaugurated in October 2000 and mandated under the "Vocational training Act" of 1998. This is in conformance with Gleckman (2009) observation when he made a follow-up to G20 leaders' statements and commitment on humanitarian crisis.

Botswana has now realised that overdependence on diamonds is not doing the country any good and as such the government of the day is pushing for further liberalisation and diversification. In his inaugural address of October 20, 2009, Botswana President Seretse Khama Ian Khama remarked "Closely related to the development of our skills base is the need to move with speed into a knowledge society. Communication, Science and Technology will be key in this. More use of ICT for service delivery, coupled with strength-

ened research and development, should not only give us greater efficiency, but opportunities for diversification beyond diamonds should be enhanced". This is testimony that there is political will to position Botswana as a KBE and that all initiatives towards this are enveloped into government's broad developmental mandate. From the initiatives being put in place, it is evident that Botswana has recognized that the improvement of productivity and enhancement of international competitiveness are some of the critical conditions for national success and competiveness.

To make sure a KBE is established, the strategy should be pursued by employing and encouraging novel frontiers of knowledge with much emphasis being put on research, innovation and creativity; putting in place appropriate policy, legal, institutional, regulatory and monitoring and evaluation frameworks, and effective use of ICT. Moahi (2007) outlined the importance of ICT in today's knowledge value chains when she stated that ICTs have fuelled what is now commonly referred to as the knowledge economy. She further went on to state that the basis of this economy is that we live in a world where the major currency is information and knowledge just as much, if not more than capital and land.

This article is organised as follows: section 2 gives the background of the study detailing the general trends and concepts of KBE. Section 3 presents a case study delving deeper into the status of KBE implementation in Botswana and outlining the issues, challenges and policies that have been put in place in Botswana. Section 4 gives the future trends and recommendations. The article ends with the conclusion which gives a recap of what has been discussed in the article.

2. BACKGROUND

At the center of KBE is innovation and ability to transform existing structures. Innovation is an expression of the productive use of knowledge. A formal definition of innovation is "the application in any organization of ideas new to it, whether they are embodied in products, processes, services, or in the systems of management and marketing through which the organization operates" (Maguire et al., 1994). Alternatively, innovation has also be defined as "innovation if the creative process through which additional economies value is extracted from knowledge; the additional economic value is obtained through the transformation of knowledge into new products, processes and services" (OECD, 1997). To fully understand the workings of the KBE, new economic concepts and measures are required which track phenomena beyond conventional market transactions. As suggested by OECD, improved indicators for the KBE are needed for the following tasks: (i) measuring knowledge inputs; (ii) measuring knowledge stocks and flows; (iii) measuring knowledge outputs; (iv) measuring knowledge networks; and (v) measuring knowledge and learning " (OECD, 1997).

For KBE to be established, there is also an issue of making sure that knowledge distribution channels are in place. This can be achieved through the establishment of formal and informal networks which may be essential to economic performance and knowledge sharing as a public good. Another area that also needs attention is the technological change which entails that countries that do not move with the change are left behind in as far as development may be concerned. Technological change raises the relative marginal productivity of capital through education and training of the labour force, investments in research and development and the creation of new managerial structures and work organization. UNECE Report (2002) states that economic activities associated with the production and utilization of information and knowledge have become an engine of economic growth in the developed market economies, increasingly transforming all the other dimensions of development and the entire societal *modus Vivendi* and *modus operanti* of the humanity.

UNECE Report (2002) further defines KBE as not just being the digital economy, which incorporates the production and use of computers and telecommunication equipment; not quite the networked economy, which incorporates the telecommunication and networking growth during the last decades and its impact on human progress. It defines KBE as a much complex and broader phenomenon and brings out the following dimensions of a KBE: a) The KBE has a very powerful technological driving force – a rapid growth of ICT. b) Telecommunication and networking, stimulated by a rapid growth of ICTs, have penetrated all the spheres of human activity, forcing them to work into an absolutely new mode and creating new spheres. The information society has become a reality. c) Knowledge, based on information and supported by cultural and spiritual values, has become an independent force and the most decisive factor of social, economic, technological and cultural transformation, and d) The knowledge-based economy has allowed a quick integration of the enormous intellectual resources of economies in transition into the European intellectual pool, stimulating the development of the former countries.

Transformation to a KBE starts from the public sector and replicates to all the socio-economic sectors of a nation. Explicitly put, it starts from the doorsteps of the communities when ordinary citizens engulf and adopt ICT usage which is the start-point of appropriate knowledge sharing. This view of ICT adoption is supported by PĂCEŞILĂ (2006) who ascertains that a KBE can't be conceived without technology, especially top technology that allows knowledge transmission and appraisal of functional virtual markets. The knowledge economy in the public sector requires the utilization of the knowledge in order to improve the transparence, the services delivered to the citizens, for a better communication with the citizens/users/clients and in order to improve the knowing degree of their needs (PĂCEŞILĂ, 2006). Kriščiūnas and Daugėlienė (2006) further assert that development of knowledge economy is impossible without the implementation of ICT to the knowledge-based activity. Usually it is stated that a KBE is an economy that makes effective use of knowledge for its economic and social development. This includes tapping foreign knowledge as well as adapting and creating knowledge for its specific needs (Dahlman, 2003). Kalim and Lodhi (2004) looks at the Swedish case of transformation towards a KBE and comes up with the following indicators determining country competitiveness in the realm of KBE: 1) renewal, development and innovation: the "power of innovation"; 2) knowledge capacity: the "power of exchange of knowledge" at a national and international level; 3) human capital and information technologies; and 4) investment in intellectual capital.

Dahlman et al. (2005) asserts that knowledge is fueling economic growth and social development in every region of the world and that ICTs provide the means for developing countries to accelerate their progress or even leapfrog into the current phase of development and to enable their integration into the global economy. For the case of developed countries, the situation is different. KBE allows further specialization, improvements in productivity, and the achievement of sustainable growth: knowledge capital is the only asset that can grow without limits; and new knowledge increases the efficient use of resources that are in finite supply. A practical case or KBE implementation can be that of Finland. Its economic transition has been from the resource-driven to knowledge- and then to innovation-driven development, thanks to the effective use of ICT. Diversification of both technology and exports was a prerequisite for improved performance. Finland's innovation system successfully converted R&D and educational capacity into industrial strengths. Finland's success shows that a strong knowledge economy can be built in a small and comparatively peripheral country. From Finland's case, it can be learnt that specialization in high-tech and R&D intensive production needs to be preceded by

major structural changes in economic and social structures. It is important to note that a knowledge economy is an ensemble of elements that must be in balance. It is not necessarily the lack of technological infrastructure or skilled engineers that restrains economic growth. It might equally well be the lack of entrepreneurs or proper economic incentives and opportunities.

Worldly, especially noteworthy is the shift in the focus and content of industrial policies in the 1990s away from macroeconomic policies and industrial subsidies toward microeconomic "conditions-providing" policies. A specificity of the Finnish "model" has been the early application of a systems view of industrial policy. This systems view could be described as an acknowledgement of the importance of interdependencies among research organizations, universities, firms, and industries due to the increasing importance of knowledge as a competitive asset, especially in the case of small open economies with a well-developed welfare system. Rather, the systems view was concretized through an emphasis on responsive longer-term policies to improve the general framework conditions for firms and industries, especially in knowledge development and diffusion, innovation, and clustering of industrial activities. Dahlman et al. (2005) further notes that education is the key element of a knowledge-based, innovation-driven economy and that it affects both the supply of and demand for innovation. Zeman K. (2005) notes that the results (or outputs) of knowledge-based economy implementation are identified by basic indicators of competitiveness: a) level and growth of labor productivity and GDP; b) employment - environmental sustainability; and c) social cohesion.

In most instances, characteristics of a defined KBE are distinct as outlined above. Besides an overall political, social, cultural and security environment that is conducive to the flourishing of a KBE, there are certain factors that can be identified as critical to the development of a KBE and as indicative of the positioning as well as strengths and weaknesses of a country in that regard. These factors much well to countries in the African context in pursuit of transforming towards a KBE. These factors include the following: 1) Quality of human resources: literacy; secondary enrolment; tertiary enrolment; enrolment in science and technology-related subjects; science graduates; technical graduates; expenditure on education; thinking and innovation skills; a learning culture; lifelong learning facilities; English language skills; receptivity to change; 2) R&D: Public and private sector expenditure on R&D, personnel in R&D, scientists and engineers in R&D, patents filed; 3) Infostructure: newspapers; radios; television; telephone mainlines; mobile telephones; costs of international telephone calls; freedom/availability of information; 4) Infrastructure: investment in ICT infrastructure; electricity; personal computers; Internet hosts; Internet subscribers; Internet usage; 5) Economy: knowledge workers; knowledge-based industries; knowledge-based services; tacit and codified knowledge; knowledge embodied in work processes and products; e-commerce; high-technology exports; venture capital; openness to foreign knowledge workers; entrepreneurship; risk-taking culture.

In the Southern African region, Botswana is seen as the longest surviving democracy (Lekorwe et al., 2001). The bedrock of Botswana's democracy is embedded in the traditional Kgotla system. The Kgotla is a time tested forum where issues of public policy are discussed openly by the community (Lekorwe, 2001; Holm & Molutsi, 1989). The institutional and legal frameworks are somewhat developed supporting almost all socio-economic frameworks. The growth in the diamonds trade has seen Botswana occupy a place as one of the most stable economies of Africa and boasts of having one of the fastest growing economies worldwide. However, all this developmental strands are thwarted by high unemployment rates, escalation of the HIV-AIDS virus, etc. From colonial times to the recent present, Botswana has largely been a resource-based economy. That is to say, its survival has always

been dependent on producing natural resources for further processing by the developed world. One such important resource has been diamonds. Of late, Botswana has started transcending towards a knowledge-based economy. In contemplating to be a full-fledged knowledge-based economy, Botswana needs to tackle several challenges that may impend its becoming a KBE. One such challenge is reducing its overdependence on diamonds as a major contributor to the nation's GDP, and reducing the over escalating spread of HIV-AIDS, developing a solid human resource base baked enough to face the challenges of the knowledge age, etc. The next section gives a detailed analysis of Botswana's vision towards turning into a KBE.

3. BOTSWANA'S CASE: RESOURCE TO KNOWLEDGE-BASED

Botswana has been among the fastest-growing economies in Africa over the past 40 years. Sound macroeconomic policies and good governance have parlayed the country's diamond resources into a remarkable transformation from one of the poorest countries in the world at independence to upper middle-income status. At independence in 1966, Botswana was one of Africa's poorest countries. It had a weak human capacity (22 university graduates), few assets, underdeveloped infrastructure (12 kilometers of paved road), and an abattoir as the only "industry." With such statistics, there was no option but to strongly rely on resources (e.g. diamonds, cattle) as the economic mainstay. However, recently, there has been reduction in the demand for diamonds or even meat which are the major exports from Botswana due to the world recession which had hit bad in 2007/08. Factors such as declining fertility rates, increased women participation in economic activities, access to better health, increased literacy, escalating HIV-AIDS infection rates, etc may have effect on the growth rate of the population. This and many other factors too numerous to mention here have called for a need to diversify the economy and eventually

Figure 1. KAM 2008 report

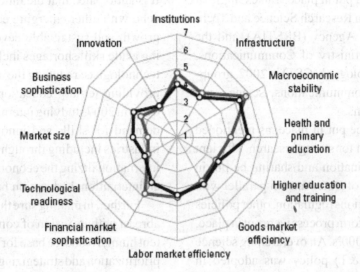

move to knowledge-based. The following chart from KAM 2008 (Figure 1) shows how Botswana features against different benchmarks that used to assess the development of a country.

Botswana is currently ranked as a first-stage transition economy. The above chart has shown that Botswana has to do a lot if it were to be at the competitive edge in this knowledge age. This justifies the government declaration that Botswana has to move towards placing itself as a KBE. Botswana is generally praised for its pursuit of sound economic policies, which have enabled it use its diamonds wisely. Its policy stance has been guided by Vision 2016, which sets a broad

policy agenda for poverty reduction and macro-economic stability. To make sure that the legal, institutional and the regulatory framework, together with an enabling environment for the maturity of KBE, there have been a lot of initiatives that have been put in place to make sure that this vision is realized. On the policy front, some work has already been done, with the development of a Science and Technology (S&T) Policy (Botswana Ministry of Finance, 1998) and the setting up of the National Commission for Science and Technology (NCST), which plays the role of overall policy advisor to government on S&T matters (see Table 1). Other complementary in-

Table 1. Summary of key S&T Agencies and functions

Agency	Date Established	Major Function
National Commission for S&T (NCST)	May 2002	S&T research Policy advisory matters
Botswana Research, S&T Investment Agency (BRSTIA)	2006/07	Co-ordinate and monitor all government R&D funding (S&T research Purchasing matters)
Government owned National Research Centers	See different research institutes	Policy Advocacy matters
Botswana National Association of Scientists and Technologists -BNAST	-	Policy Advocacy matters
Tertiary Education Council (TEC)	March 1999	Higher education policy development, institutional guidelines and support

stitutions have been put in place. Tan example of this is the Botswana Research Science and Technology Investment Agency (BRSTIA), and the set-up of a new Ministry of Communications, Science and Technology (MCST) in 2002, grouping together all communications, science and technology functions.

For a KBE, to be put in place, as mentioned above, there is need for strong research, efficient knowledge dissemination and sharing be put in place. For the case of Botswana, in parallel with the telecommunications regulation, other policies supportive of the reform process were put in place, in 1996 and early 2000's. An overarching science and technology (S&T) policy was adopted in 1998. The policy gives priority to strengthening telecommunications infrastructure and the use of ICTs, and attracting women to professions and careers in the field of science and technology.

Another strategy that has been seen from Botswana is the emphasis that has been on training the potential human resource for the country. Within this framework, Botswana has put in place fiscal policies that specifically look at the advancement of education from the grassroots to the tertiary level (TKS, 2006). This has seen the establishment of the Tertiary Education Council (TEC) by Act of Parliament Cap 57:04 of 1999 to be responsible for "…promotion and coordination of tertiary education and for the determination and maintenance of standards of teaching, examination and research in tertiary institutions (Section 5(1)). The government of Botswana understands that for the country to transform towards a KBE, there is need to have a very well trained human resource base. This effort has been complimented by putting in place other policies in support of training a better human resource base. These include the College of Agriculture Act (1991), Botswana College of Distance and Open Learning Act (1998), Botswana Examinations Council Act (2002), the Vocational Training Act (1998), the Botswana International University of Science and Technology- BIUST Act (2005). Of the much talked about amongst these policies is the BIUST act of 2005.

It is anticipated that the rationale for BIUST will echo with other emerging economies: economic growth and sustainable development; overcoming acute skill shortages including engineers and technologists; reducing the unreasonable costs of providing tertiary education for over 7000 students in 2007 studying internationally; addressing demand for skills and innovation for advanced industries including through technology transfer; internationalizing the economy; and aspiring to be an international education hub (Wilmoth, 2006).

Further, in making sure that Botswana remains abreast with its vision of coming up with competent human resource base for the purposes of KBE prioritization and strategizing, new education policies have been put in place. One of these so called 'vibrant' policies has been the putting in place of Human Resource Development Strategy, approved by Parliament on January 21, 2009. This has been a follow-up on TEC which was established by an act of parliament in 1999 specifically to standardize the quality of education in tertiary education institutions in Botswana. Also, the new tertiary education policy of April 2008 aims to change the landscape for the better of tertiary education in Botswana. This confirms that the institutional and regulatory framework towards production of competent human resource base has somewhat already been established in Botswana.

On another front, Botswana continues to show commitment in encapsulating ICT into its cultural norms. Widespread campaigns are evident in Botswana in encouraging the use of ICTs in almost all socio-economic setups. This encouragement of using ICTs in all socio-economic strata conforms to efficient knowledge sharing and management which is one of the pillars to establishing a KBE as efficient in service delivery, production systems, research knowledge sharing is facilitated. This commitment to putting in place efficient knowledge sharing paradigms and revamping ICT usage is further evidenced by the Botswana Telecommunication Company's (BTC) signatory status to three consortia that are intended to develop undersea optical fibre systems: the East

Africa Submarine System (EASSY), to run along-side the eastern coast of Africa from Port Sudan through East African seaports down to Mtunzini in South Africa; the West Africa Festoon System (WAFS), intended to run alongside the western coast of Africa from Nigeria through Gabon, DRC down to Angola, and possibly Namibia; and the Africa West Coast Cable (AWCC), proposed to run alongside the western coast of Africa from South Africa, Namibia through to the United Kingdom. Plans are also underway to establish an IT hub in Botswana. This is going to make sure that Botswana is seen as the most advanced country in as far as ICT usage is concerned. Once this subscription has transcended into tangible deployment of optical across all corners of the country, the cost to send data from one place to the next will be substantially reduced as through-put, data latency and transmission speed will be improved. As aforementioned, the institutional framework to pioneer the dream of transforming the country into a KBE has been set to some appreciable extent. The following table shows some of the regulatory agencies that have been put up in different socio-economic realms.

These different endeavors outlined here point out the commitment that Botswana has towards transforming itself as a knowledge-based economy. Looking at the different initiatives outlined above, it is evident that the institutional framework is quiet advanced. The only component that seems to be lacking and that no one pays much attention is the legal and regulatory framework. It is anticipated that a defined legal and regulatory framework with the local context flavor be put in place. This will help create trust and protect the weaker members of the society in the ICT environment.

4. FUTURE TRENDS

Looking at different platforms for a sound environment for KBE, the UNECE Report (2002) concludes that the strategy proposed for the improvement of the country's information and communication system should include the following benchmarks: a) the establishment of an independent regulatory body; b) the modification of license issued to incumbent telecom operators; and c) the development and adoption of standards in the quality of telecommunications services. For the case of Botswana, have these aspects been incorporated into the KBE transformation strategy? However, these benchmarks may be too hard to measure especially in the African context. It is thus imperative to understand that, in virtually all sectors, developing countries are still very far from the technological frontier, they still need to put priority on developing effective means of tapping the pre-existing and rapidly growing stock of global knowledge. Developing countries, like Botswana, need to put more weight than they do now on understanding, acquiring, adapting, diffusing, and using existing knowledge, including indigenous knowledge. This includes putting in place basic technological infrastructure such as norms and standards, metrology, testing, and quality control, as well as strong dissemination mechanisms and institutions such as technical information centers, productivity organizations, and agricultural and industrial extension agencies. Botswana has made considerable strides even when looked at using these guidelines and although has some work to do in liberalization of its financial markets, tackling the HIV-AIDS pandemic, addressing unemployment, reducing poverty amongst majority of its citizens, etc. it thus recommendable that a locally-drawn roadmap for transforming to a KBE be done.

To be able to eventually put in place a competent KBE agenda, there is need to consider the following principles:

A. There is need to promote more foreign-direct investment which will be consider of knowledge produced by local research and create more employment.

B. The quality of human resources will be the single most important factor. More and more citizens of Botswana need to be encouraged to go to school as education plays a crucial part in developing human capital and will play a critical role in shifting the economy towards a KBE. Lifelong learning should be ignored as it can provide the organizing principle which integrates economic development, social justice, cultural, political and scientific-technological literacy, national unity and cohesion as well as capacity-building for international competitiveness which is prerequisite to putting in place a KBE.

C.   There is need to establish a National KBE Development Council which will be specifically responsible for coordinating all the efforts towards establishing a KBE.

D.   The Private sector and the ordinary citizens should be involved in drawing the plans towards the establishment of a KBE.

E.   There is need to have good public governance and low levels of corruption as these are essential to the knowledge economy.

F.   There is need to put in place of an enabling environment by putting strong regulatory frameworks so that both the dynamism of the economy and social cohesion and welfare be maintained in the future.

G.   Just as the case for Finland outline above, it is important to encompass two attitudes: an independent spirit of self-reliance and a "can-do" mindset and a strong spirit of cohesiveness, high moral values, an emphasis on equality, and relatively equal distribution of national resources. These two characteristics can be preached to the ordinary citizens so that they buy-in to the idea of establishing a KBE and what should be done, thereof.

H.   There is need to preach the willingness of the ordinary citizens to interact with the outside world in an open but strongly nationalistic way and for Botswana to have a flexible economy that is able to react to changing conditions (like putting in place proper

diversification mechanisms to reduction in diamond demand which is the economic mainstay), and have in place a responsive education system.

I.   Policies should be put in place to make sure that information is readily available to almost all socio-economic sectors and that people can have access to it at a reasonable cost.

J.   There should be deliberate policies in place to make sure that the culture of innovation is encouraged throughout all the socio-economic setups.

If these principles and other attributes not mentioned here are observed and implemented, chances are high that the course for transformation from a resource to a knowledge-based economy by Botswana is likely to be reached.

5. CONCLUSION

This article has surveyed the fundamental concepts on which this paradigm shift from a resource-based to knowledge-based economy is founded. The article has looked at the major characteristics of a KBE and has contrasted it with the industrial and/or resource based economy. It brings out different initiatives that may be embarked on in transition from a resource to a KBE such as ICT development, nurturing of an appropriate human resource base, promoting a culture of innovation, investment in intellectual capital, etc. specifically, the article has looked at the status of endeavors and initiatives done by Botswana towards shaping itself as a KBE, and also has emphasized the role of research and efficient knowledge management paradigms in shaping a country as a KBE. The article also briefly looks at the Finland case of transforming to a KBE as a good example of how a small country can transform from a resource, to an industrial and then to a KBE. The lessons outlined in the Finland case in the course of discussion has helped this article come up with specific recommendations on what Botswana should do if this vision of transforming to a KBE is to be realized.

From the surveys made and the initiatives discussed in this article, it has been seen that Botswana has put in place start-up policies consolidating the transition of its economy from a resource to a knowledge-based one. It is thus suffice to say that the country is in tract to transforming to a KBE. The commitment towards this transformation is however left to the government and a few individuals which makes this vision very difficult to implement. It is thus important that strategic initiatives be put in place to sell this idea to the general population of Botswana so that amalgamated efforts can be devoted towards the same. For a truly KBE to be unleashed in Botswana, there is ultimate need to make sure that cross-sector integration and keeping in mind KBE's multi-dimensionality (e.g. innovation, entrepreneurship, product differentiation, the importance of just-in-time delivery, sound institutional, legal and regulatory mechanisms, etc.) is considered at all times.

The recommendations given in this article may be strategic in realizing this KBE transformation dream for the case of Botswana. However, it is worth mentioning that future research works needs to be done on how certain stringent challenges such as reduction of HIV-AIDS infection rates, massive unemployment levels, overdependence on diamonds, etc. needs to be reduced or incorporated into KBE transformation policies so that this may not rob the country of its dream.

REFERENCES

Amable, B., & Lung, Y. (2005). The European Socio-Economic Models in a Knowledge- based society: The objectives of the ESEMK project. *Actes du GERPISA*.

Dahlman, C. J. (2003). Using knowledge for development: a general framework and preliminary assessment of China. In B. Grewal, L. Xue, P. Sheehan, & F. Sun (Eds.), *China's future in the knowledge economy: Engaging the new world* (pp. 35-66). Melbourne, Australia: Centre for Strategic Economic Studies, Victoria University and Tsinghua University Press.

Dahlman, C. J., Routti, J., & Ylä-Anttila, P. (2005). *Finland as a knowledge economy: Elements of success and lessons learned*. Washington, DC: International Bank for Reconstruction and Development European Forecasting Network. (2004). *The Euro area and the Lisbon strategy*. Milan, Italy: Author.

Gleckman, II. (2009). *Global Governance and Policy Coherence: Before and After the G20 Summit, Global Policy Coherence 2009 Project*. Institute for Environmental Security.

Kalim, R., & Lodhi, S. (2004). *The Knowledge-Based Economy: trends and implications for Pakistan*. Retrieved May 15, 2009, from http://www.pide.org.pk/.../The% 20Knowledge%20Based%20Economy.pdf

Kriščiūnas, K., & Daugėlienė, R. (2006). The assessment models of Knowledge-Based Economy penetration. *Engineering Economics, 5*(50). ISSN 1392-2785.

Kuznetsov, Y., & Dahlman, C. J. (2008). *Mexico's Transition to a Knowledge-Based Economy Challenges and Opportunities*. Washington, DC: International Bank for Reconstruction and Development.

Lekorwe, M., Molomo, M., Molefe, W., & Moseki, K. (2001). *Public attitudes toward democracy, governance and economic development in Botswana* (Afrobarometer Paper No.14). Afrobarometer.

Leung, K. C. (2004). Statistics to measure the knowledge-based economy: The case of Hong Kong, China. In *Proceedings of the 2004 Asia Pacific Technical Meeting of Information and Communication Technology (ICT) Statistic*. Retrieved July 16, 2009, from http://www.unescap.org/.../ 18.Statistics_to_measure_the _Knowledge-Based_Economy- Hong_Kong.pdf

Maguire, C., Kazlauskas, C., & Weir, A. D. (1994). *Information systems for innovative organizations*. London: Academic Press

Moahi, K. G. (2007). Globalization, Knowledge Economy and the implication for Indigenous Knowledge. *International Review of Information Ethics (IRIE), 7*. ISSN 1614-1687

OECD. (1997). *The OECD Report on regulatory reform: Synthesis*. Retrieved July 10, 2009, from http://www.oecd.org/dataoecd/ 17/25/2391768. pdf

PĂCEŞILĂ M. (2006). The impact of moving to Knowledge Based Economy in the public sector. *Management & Marketing Craiova, 1*, 113-118. Retrieved June 12, 2009, from http://www.ceeol. com/aspx/ getdocument.aspx?logid=5&id

TKS- Towards a Knowledge Society. (2006). *A proposal for a tertiary education policy for Botswana. Technical report*. Retrieved July 27, 2009, from http://www.tec.org.bw/ tec_doc/ tec_rep_10_2006.pdf

UNDP. (1996). *Human Development – at the heart of today's policy agenda*. New York: Author.

UNECE. (2002). *Towards a Knowledge-Based Economy: ARMENIA – country readiness assessment report*. Retrieved May 30, 2009, from http://www.unece.org/operact/enterp/ documents/ coverpagarmenia.pdf

Wilmoth, D. (2008). *Innovation in private higher education: the Botswana International University of Science and Technology*. Washington, DC: IFC International Investment Forum on Private Education.

Zeman, K. (2005). *Transformation towards Knowledge-Based Economy. Conference on Medium-Term Economic Assessment*. Retrieved May 10, 2009, from www.aeaf.minfin.bg/.../ Karel_Zeman_paper_CMTEA2005.pdf

This work was previously published in International Journal of Information Communication Technologies and Human Development, Volume 2, Issue 1, edited by Susheel Chhabra and Hakikur Rahman, pp. 59-74, copyright 2010 by IGI Publishing (an imprint of IGI Global).

Chapter 5
Children's Maps in GIS:
A Tool for Communicating Outdoor Experiences in Urban Planning

Kerstin Nordin
Swedish University of Agricultural Sciences, Sweden

Ulla Berglund
Swedish University of Agricultural Sciences, Sweden

ABSTRACT

Since 2002 the authors have successively developed "Children's Maps in GIS", a method for children's participation in spatial planning. Their studies show that 10-15 year-olds are capable of reading maps and using a GIS-application for communicating their interests in a stable and useful manner. The purpose of this article is to discuss the first stages of implementation in a real world project, in relation to ICT. The authors report experiences from a Swedish municipality using Children's Maps in GIS in a survey with over 600 children as part of a comprehensive planning process and give examples of how data can be visualized. A significant digital divide between different parts of the administration is noted. In the ongoing development into an Internet version of the method the authors aim to increase the access to the GIS-application and develop standard procedures for categorizing and analyzing data.

INTRODUCTION

It is considered that children (0-18 years) should be afforded the opportunity to influence those matters that affect or concern them, as outlined in Article 12:1 of the UN Convention of The Rights of the Child (UNICEF, 1990), a convention signed, and

in effect implemented, by most countries around the World. The local environment is such an issue concerning children, this is identified in the UN action plan Agenda 21 (United Nations, 1993) where it is stated that young people's participation is vital to the realization of a sustainable society. Therefore there is an expectation for young people's experiences and wishes to be included in local-authority planning.

DOI: 10.4018/978-1-4666-0047-8.ch005

In the background section of this article we report on our theoretical framework and describe the method Children's Maps that we have developed through our research. In the result section we document how this method was used outside the research-context in a municipal as a part of a comprehensive planning process. In the discussion section we comment on the results and make comparisons with experiences from previous research-pilots. Finally we draw conclusions on further development of the method.

BACKGROUND

This paper reports on research carried out within the discipline of Landscape architecture although the theoretical framework shows an interdisciplinary approach including planning theory, social theory as well as theory of environmental psychology, geography and GIScience.

Children, Planning and Participation

In today's construction of childhood, children are acknowledged as active social and cultural actors (Holloway & Valentine, 2003; Christensen & Prout, 2002). According to Christensen & O'Brian (2003, p. 2) they are also recognized as informants and participants in research, having "emerged as key source for understanding their everyday life". Christensen further stresses the relevance for planning of children's "emplaced knowledge […] full with personal and social meaning, built up through their everyday encounters" with their local environment" (Christensen, 2003, p.16). The overall idea of governance using communicative planning (e.g., Healey, 1997; Healey, 1999) with reference to Habermas' theories on communicative rationality and communicative action (e.g., Habermas, 1984) today is widely practiced in developed countries. However, this practice is criticized for lacking strategies for handling of biased power relations. This means that less powerful stakeholders, and especially those whose perspectives deviate from existing policies, are at risk of being unable to achieve the influence that their arguments call for (Flyvbjerg, 2001; Sager, 1994; Sager, 2006).Children and youth tend to fall into this category, putting their participation at risk of being reduced to pseudo-democratic practices, such as manipulation, decoration or tokenism, the lower steps in the "Ladder of Young People's Participation" (Hart, 1997). Case studies in various European countries highlight tendencies towards superficial participation resulting in little real influence (Rogers, 2006; Tonucci, Prisco, & Horelli, 2004) and unwillingness or inability from decision-makers to take children's interests into account has been noted by many researchers (Chawla, 2002a; Lynch, 1977; Matthews, 1998; Wilhjelm, 1999; Woolley et al., 1999).

Conversely, literature shows a strong support for the idea that planning and design of the physical environment attracts the interest of young people and it is therefore possible to include them in society's democratic processes (Horelli, 1998; Percy-Smith & Malone, 2001; Urban Green Spaces Taskforce, 2002; Norsk form, 2005.) Furthermore, following our personal experiences, there is a desire among many planners to engage children and youth to a larger extent. We, as well as Freeman & Aitken-Rose (2005) have noticed a growing interest toward child-focused and youth-focused methodologies for working with adolescents.

There is an obvious need to find solutions to the dilemma of how to incorporate young peoples' perspectives into local planning processes (e.g., Christensen & O'Brian, 2003; Driskell, 2002). A model for enhancing children's participation in decision-making is the "Pathways to participation", developed by Shiers (2001). Shiers, drawing on Hart (1997), identifies five levels of participation. The model can be used as a tool for planning for participation. Level 3, "Children's views are taken into account" is the minimum you must achieve if you endorse the UN Convention on the Rights of the Child. The higher levels of participation require that children are involved in decision making processes (level 4) and children share power and responsibility for decision-making (level 5). A method aiming to enhance children's participation should be useful at least at level 3.

Several initiatives concerning the empowerment of children within spatial planning and related issues have been influenced by the UN Convention of the Right of the Child. Among these are the "Town of Children Project" started in 1991 which has engaged more than 200 Italian municipalities (Baraldi, 2003), the UNESCO Project "Growing up in Cities" (Chawla, 2002b; Driskell, 2002), and the "Children as Community Researchers", initiated by Roger Hart and launched by UNICEF (UNICEF, 2001). These varied approaches highlight the diversity of methodologies available for children's participation in planning of cities.

The changes brought about by globalization and the diffusion of information and communication technology (ICT) is gradually opening up new opportunities for the involvement of young people in planning and development of cities (Horelli & Kaaja, 2002). One such example is a tool in the form of an Internet-based design game "The Adventure Forest" invented by Finnish researchers (Kyttä, Kaaja, & Horelli, 2004); other example is the sharing of knowledge on the Internet site "The FreeChild Project" (The FreeChild Project, 2008);

There are several reports concerning the institutional constraints of adapting new methods and technologies within the planning practice (Horelli & Kaaja, 2002; Vonk, Geertman, & Shot, 2005). An assumed reason for this is that most current tools are too inflexible and incompatible for most planning tasks, being oriented towards technological problems rather than planning problems (Vonk et al., 2005)

A method for communicating children's outdoor experiences into every-day planning practices should be an easy-to-handle method that can collect, store, analyze and visualize data that is relevant and trustworthy to all participants in a planning process. The first step is then to make data concerning children's use and perceptions of the outdoor environment available in a planning decision system in a way that is true to the child's own views.

Geographic Information

Geographic information, often represented in the form of maps, plays an important role in planning practice; today almost all of this information is digital and part of a geographic information system, GIS. Although the use of GIS has increased in Sweden in the public sector since 2003, there is still a gap between those who can and those who cannot use GIS for more advanced applications. To look at static digital maps is still the most common use of GIS (ULI, 2008).

MacEachren (2004, pp. iii-iv) points out that the map is evolving as an interactive interface to geospatial information, not just a static representation of information. He states that understanding the processes of map-making and the perceptual-cognitive processes through which these representations are understood are of importance in decision making and the enhancement of the role of maps in collaborative activities.

Maps and cartography has been critically discussed since the 1990's with relation to linking geographic knowledge with power (Crampton & Krygier, 2006). They note drawing on Pickles (1995) that "Maps are active: they actively construct knowledge, they exercise power and they can be powerful means of promoting social change" (Crampton & Krygier, 2006, p.15).

Geovisualization of data enhance visual thinking in exploring data and in collaboration processes (Jiang, Huang, & Vasek, 2003). Children tend to develop a visual competence in an early age. Of special interest is specifically children's understanding of a map as a representation of the real world. Plester, Blades, and Spencer (2006), describe how children during the first school years learn to master correspondence and to interpret direction and distance, i.e. skills needed to understand the representation of an environment in an aerial photograph or map.

If we focus on GIS as a data collecting tool, is it useful when collecting information from children? When it comes to drawing on digital maps the competence of children above 10 years of age concerning interpretation of symbols, scale etc can be expected to be as good (or bad) as that of adults (Plester et al., 2006). Positive experiences of the use of digital maps with children are reported by for example Kyttä et al. (2004) and Berglund (2008). Holloway and Valentine (2003) in their study of children and ICT comment that children on the whole tend to be more technically competent in the use of computers than their parents are.

Elwood (2006) points out that GIS has a history of being an expert tool in a rational, expert-driven planning process. Information that can be displayed visually is privileged as are the use of quantitative techniques for spatial analysis. This may implicate that other forms of knowledge may be excluded from processes in which GIS is used. The widespread use of Internet and mobile GIS makes it important to discuss the digital divide with aspect to access to GIS and to spatial data (Elwood, 2006). So why use GIS? "Elwood answers (2006, p. 693) "In spite of its limitations and challenges, GIS is tremendously important because it is such a powerful mediator of spatial knowledge, social and political power …" The use of such an expert tool as GIS, can give the information from the children some legitimacy (Elwood, 2002).

Research with Children in School

There is a significant amount of literature regarding pupils of 11-12 years of age. In our judgment this is due not only to their experience of place but also to their writing and reading abilities and in some cases the fact that technical skills of children from this age group are supposedly developed,

providing the researcher with multiple options concerning methodology.

School is a frequently used environment for research with children. In school you find an organization that can assist with information and the permissions needed for research that concerns children. If the aim and the methods of the research can make it fit into the curriculum at school, a win-win situation could be created. If this is not possible it might be regarded unethical to ask for the time of teachers and pupils.

According to the report "Benchmarking Access and Use of ICT" (Korte & Hüsing, 2006), all Swedish schools have access to computers and Internet, but the access is inconsistent across schools, with students and teachers at independent schools having more access to ICT than students and teachers in municipal schools. This includes hardware as well as connection to broadband and software (Skolverket, 2009). Furthermore, most teachers in Sweden do not feel that that they have sufficient knowledge of ICT, and roughly half of the teachers do not believe that ICT encourages learning. That puts Sweden almost at the bottom of the list for ICT use in schools in Europe (Skolverket, 2009).

The Method Children's Maps

Since 2002 we have in our research successively developed "Children's Maps in GIS", a method for communicating young people's outdoor experiences into urban planning. The method Children's Maps consist of several activities: contact with school and parents, information to children, the use of a GIS-application and feed-back to the children and teachers (Berglund, 2008; Berglund, Nordin, & Eriksson, 2009). In the following we refer to the method as "Children's Maps" and depending on the context, we use young people as well as children and youth, students and children for labeling our target group.

We aimed at developing a method that was easy to manage within the school context, and stimulating and fun for children to participate with. We tested the method with and adapted it for children from 10 to 15 years of age. As we were aware of that GIS technology may empower or disempower actors and institutions as described in Elwood (2002) we wanted to build a GIS-application that should not demand technical skills or expensive software or databases. The result should be trustworthy and relevant to a town district level in the planning practice.

We have in several research pilots (Berglund & Nordin, 2007; Berglund, 2008; Berglund et al., 2009) tried to answer the following questions: Can we attain location bound information that is relevant to planning and suitably reliable, with the help of children? Will this information be accepted by planning authorities? Are children able and willing to document their movements using GIS on digital maps that are used within today's planning? Can the children's school become a mediator between the children and the planners; can it be the place for developing and implementing the method?

During the period 2003-2006, the method was tested with children and teachers in several research-pilots in different locations in Sweden. Several tests were carried out in Stockholm; in a high-status inner-city district as well as in a low-status outer-city district with a high proportion of immigrant families within an interdisciplinary research project "Children and Open spaces in the City – Accessibility, Use and Influence". In 2006 we got an opportunity to test the method in a rural context (a village, Örbyhus) as we got funding from the Road Administration. In that project we adjusted the method to better catch questions concerning traffic safety. In all our studies, we supplied computer, software and supervision for the children participating, and did not ask for any IT-qualifications from the teacher. We have through diverse means, evaluated the function and the trustworthiness of the method. We have found no special complications regarding the use of the method in the different research-contexts.

Our studies show that 10-15 year-olds are capable of using a GIS-application for communicating their experiences and interests into the local urban planning process in a stable and useful manner. We found it easy to fit the project into schools and to get some teachers to run a special teacher's application. The development and tests are described in detail in Berglund (2008) and supplemented in Berglund et al. (2009).

The GIS-application can be described as a computerized questionnaire. Each student answers seven questions individually. The student answers the question by making a sketch map directly on the screen, and when required, the student includes text information as an attribute to the geographical object created in the sketch map. An overview of the procedure is presented in Table 1. The exercise generally takes about 15 minutes and is carried out during class hours. The software is an application built in ESRI ArcView 3. Laptops are used to store the application as well as the data collected.

The teachers participating in a study are using an application that works in the same way as the children's application. They indicate routes and places that are used for teaching by themselves or used by other teachers of their school.

APPLICATION OF THE METHOD IN REAL-WORLD USE IN TÄBY

We have in the text above described the method Children's Maps through our research-pilots. What was still lacking was the evaluation of the implementation into planning practice. In 2008, the municipal of Täby wanted to use the method "Children's Maps" to get information about how children and young people perceive and use the outdoor environment in Täby. The project was called "Place to grow" (our translation) and a part of the comprehensive planning process. This gave us an opportunity to test if the method Children's Maps could be transferred from research to prac-

Table 1. Questions included in the survey and data inputs that are possible to make. The questions are directly translated from Swedish and not adapted to English speaking children

Questions on the screen	Geographic data	Attribute
A call to register a new student by writing a unique number		School, grade, number and sex
1.Where do you live?	Point object(s)	No attributes
2.What routes do you use to school?	Poly-line object(s)	Means of travel: walk, cycle, walk/cycle to public transportation Comments: Free wording
3.What routes do you use in your free-time?	Poly-line object(s)	Movements: walk, run, walk the dog, walk/cycle to public transportation Destination: friends, activity or else Comments: Free wording
4.Where do you go when you are outdoors?	Polygon(s)	Common activities all year around: meet friends, play, play boll, training, sun-bath, barbeque, skate Common activities in winter time: Ice-skating, skiing, play, sliding Comments: Free wording
5.Are there places that are hazardous or make you feel uncomfortable?	Point object (s)	Comments: Free wording
6.Do you have a favorite place?	Point object (s), max 3 objects	Comments: Free wording
7.Do you have any suggestions for improvements?	Point object (s)	Comments: Free wording

tical use. We decided to use the version that we had developed and tested in 2006 with special focus on traffic safety (Berglund et al., 2009). Our conclusions from the research-pilots are that this version works well as an over all tool and that traffic safety has proved to be of high interest in local planning with a child perspective.

By participating in the project we wanted to get some answers on the following questions:

• How can the method work outside the research context?
• How can the information be accessed, handled and valued within a local authority?

Täby has about 62 000 inhabitants and is situated 15 km north of Stockholm city. The residential areas consist partly of block of flats and partly of areas with private homes. In the centre of the municipal are a big shopping mall and some sports arenas. The topography is varied, and green areas with woods and lakes are situated close to the

residential areas. For an overview, please, look at http://maps.google.se/maps, search for Täby.

The initiative for a co-operation came from Technical Office at the municipal administration in Täby. Technical Office is divided into five units: Building Permits Unit, Surveying Division, Street and Park Unit, Water and Sewage Unit and Urban Planning Unit. The project leader and the project members came from the Street and Park Unit. The unit works with developing and maintenance of streets, roads, parks and forests. The aims of the project "Place to Grow" were (Täby kommun, 2009b):

• To make the voices of children and youth heard in urban planning in Täby,
• To gather the results into a planning-friendly tool for all who plan and design the public places and out-door environments in the municipality,

- To get concrete maps concerning places and routes that children and youth use, and in what way they use them,
- To get some general information about what children and youth see as good or bad about the neighborhoods of Täby,
- To draw conclusions from the answers about which places and routes ought to be protected, developed or changed.

During 2008, surveys were carried out in 28 out of 42 schools in Täby that have students in the age between 11-18 years. The schools were chosen to give a good geographical representation of the municipality. In all a total of 635 children from 34 classes participated. 54% of the children were 11-12 years, 37% were 15-16 years and 9% were 17-18 years old (Täby kommun, 2009b). In Table 2 there is an overview of the schools participating in the project. Schools with children with special needs did not participate.

The Surveying Division of Täby provided the digital maps with detailed and updated information. As data were in MapInfo–format (tab) they had to be exported to ESRI ArcView format (shape) and then loaded into the Children's Maps GIS application on laptop-computers.

The Use of the Method Children's Maps in Täby

The method used in Täby is very much like the method described earlier in this article, with some

exceptions. Besides the spatial information the project "Place to grow" wanted to get as much verbal comments from the children as possible about their perceptions of dangerous or unpleasant places (question 5). The supervisor clarified that boring or weary places could be marked as well. The supervisors also reminded the children to think about the winter aspect (part of question 4) (Täby kommun, 2009b).

This project did not prioritize the participation of the teachers. However, 16 teachers from 11 schools were given the opportunity to take part. All schools, teachers and children participated voluntarily.

The data was transferred from the lap-tops into the data server administrated by the IT-department of the local government. Before storing the data, some harmful comments on individuals were taken away by the project team. A copy of the data set was sent to us for research purposes and back-up. The administration of data showed to be a time-consuming activity when using the application developed for small-scale research in a large scale survey.

REPRESENTATION OF DATA

The project team had full access to data through an internal digital support system. The team represented data in several maps and charts presented it in a report (Täby kommun, 2009b). The project also produced additional information as

Table 2. Numbers of schools participating sorted on level and school form

	Total number of schools	municipal	independent	Not participating
Compulsory schools Age: 11-16 years	24 participating of 37 possible	16 participating of 19 possible	8 participating of 18 possible	7 schools with children with special needs, 6 of them are independent schools
Upper secondary schools Age: 16-18 years	4 participating of 7 possible	1 participating of 2 possible	3 participating of 5 possible	1 school for students with special needs, 2 schools with vocational education

field notes, analysis and presentations that have not been published.

A summary of the results is a part of the comprehensive plan (exhibited for consultation until September, 15, 2009), under the heading Public Interests – important out-door places for children and youth. The comprehensive plan highlights the following conclusion:

"[...] many popular places have some qualities in common – space, variation, people and vicinity. [...] The biggest problem for children in the local environment is traffic, followed by lack of illumination and worries about other people's behavior. Bad maintenance is another factor that makes places difficult to use." (Täby kommun, 2009a, p. 39).

The results were also presented on a seminar April 14, 2009. Participants were politicians and employees representing the Technical Office, the Child Care and Elementary School and Culture and Leisure. In the seminar and in the report "Place to Grow" (Täby kommun, 2009b), the following aspects were brought forward.

In general there are no big differences noted between how boys and girls are moving around except in the 9th grade (15-16 years), where there are some notable differences. The boys report more physical activities than the girls. The girls report that they "hang around", looking at activities, talking to each other. When it comes to safety/ security, girls 15 years and older, have made more comments than the boys on places that they perceive as insecure. Such places can be where people are gathering at nights, empty places or badly illuminated places like woods and parks. Places to meet friends are a favorite in all ages. Many children have marked places indoors as the shopping mall, training grounds or at a friend's home as a favorite place. Most comments in all ages about insecure places concerns traffic, lack of illumination and suspicious and unsavory people. Places that are often used also have most marks

as dangerous or insecure places. The explanation given is that these are places the children know well, and therefore have a lot of information about. An example is the central shopping mall that has most marks for favorite place and as a place that can be perceived as insecure. A closer look at the comments shows that the indoor environment, with a lot of people and activities is perceived as secure, and the parking lot outside is perceived as empty no mans land and insecure. Also, the children have made some comments on rebuilding of parks that in one case has been successful according to the comments, in another case the comment from the children are "it was better before". Some new places for skating and biking are asked for in the survey, and that information is also highlighted in the report.

The participants of the seminar expressed their appreciation of the information of children's use and perceptions on the local environment and saw connections to prioritized issues like on school-road safety and security issues in the outdoor environment, as well as a basis for prioritizing maintenance of streets and parks.

A follow-up meeting was held on May 18, 2009 with one researcher and people in the local administration that were most likely to use the information from the children (the GIS-expert from Surveying Division and employees from the Street and Park Unit and from the Urban Planning Unit together with Child Care and Elementary School and Culture and Leisure departments). The question was: what part of the dataset is the most interesting, and how do you want to access it? The following alternatives were discussed: a) plain thematic maps (Figure 1), b) map visualizing some attributes e.g. places for meeting friends (Figure 2), c) summarized maps (Figure 3), and d) text information connected to geographical object (Figure 4).

The participants from the administration anticipated to use the information in urban planning and in the detailed planning of projects concerning traffic safety, green-structure planning and

Figure 1. A thematic map showing all the places marked in a part of Täby without editing afterwards. The attributes are not visualized. Symbolization of the basic map is different from what the children saw on the screen when drawing the sketch map.

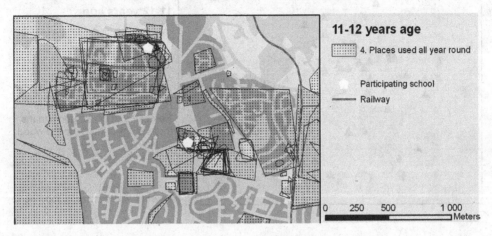

Figure 2. A map showing places for meeting friends. It is one of the multiple-choice options that are given in question number 4. Each bar represents one annotation from one child.

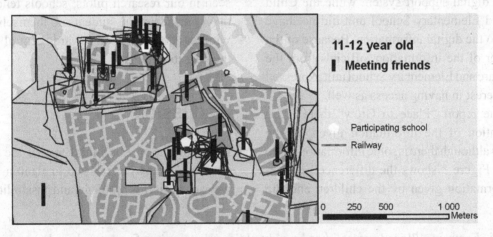

Figure 3. A representation using the centroids of each polygon to construct a density map. When there are many centroids of the polygons close to each other, the color gets darker.

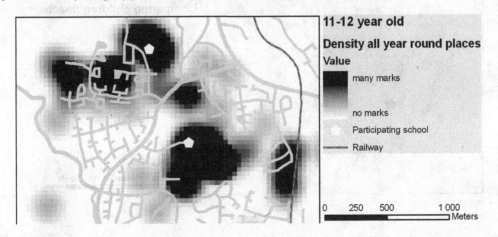

Figure 4. A map showing places that are perceived as hazardous or dangerous. Connected to the symbol are text annotations made by the children. The examples on the right are directly translated from Swedish.

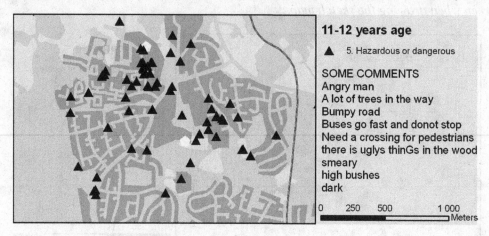

maintenance of open spaces. The Technical Office had access to data from the survey, through the internal digital support system while the Child Care and Elementary School unit did not have access to the digital information. Because of the character of the information, officials from the Child Care and Elementary School unit expressed their interest in having access as well.

In the report "Place to Grow" there is no presentation of the information given by the teachers although there is some information in the dataset. Figure 5 shows the difference between the information given by the children and the

information given by the teachers of one of the schools. It shows the same pattern that we have seen in our research pilots; schools tend to use other areas than the students do themselves, and with less concentration towards central parts of the neighborhoods.

DISCUSSION

By reporting on this initial test of the method Children's Maps in a real-world planning project we want to discuss problems and possibilities with

Figure 5. Focus in "Place to grow" has been on children's mapping. Some teachers have contributed with information as in this example.

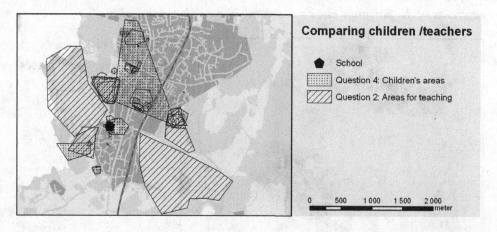

implementation into a local government context. We also reflect on empowerment of children and school and on the digital divide within the local authority administration.

On a general level we could ask if the project "Place to Grow" shows that Children's Maps can function as a vehicle to facilitate young peoples influence on the local environment. One conclusion is that the project allows the opportunity for children to participate to a degree that corresponds with level 3 "Children's views are taken into account, and given due weight in decision making" (Shier, 2001, p. 111). A weakness of the method is that young people are delivering data, yet have neither ownership nor control over it. The maps produced are adapted to the conventional planning process, which we judge crucial for the information to be taken into account in real-world planning. The power of the children is embedded in the fact that their knowledge and perceptions are visualized, and have the same technical significance as other forms of planning information. At this point, the deliberation between different aspects becomes political issue.

Lessons Learned by Stepping Out of the Research Context

The method has shown to function outside the research context as a tool for collecting and storing information. Information from over 600 children concerning their use and perceptions of the local environment has been collected within the local administration. On the whole the results are consistent with the results from the research–pilots. The seven questions (see Table 1) in our research studies are tested in different social contexts and in different age-groups. The development and tests are described in detail in Berglund (2008) and supplemented in Berglund et al. (2009). By using the same pre-formulated questions in every survey we assert that the questions are not biased by any ongoing planning debate or by personal agendas.

The "Place to Grow" project had no procedures to communicate back to the children (and teachers) on the impact of their participation. Even if their information is taken into account, they may not be aware of it and the project did not provide for further communication within the planning process. This must be regarded as a weakness when considering the empowerment of children, making it less likely to positively influence their attitude to future contributions to society. Feed-back is, however, prescribed by us in the steps for the use of Children's Maps. This is based on numerous studies of participation projects with children stating that being listened to and getting feed-back are cornerstones needed for a fair involvement of children in a participation process (Chawla, 2002b). In this sense the "Place to Grow" project is incomplete, as well as our own research-pilots.

As reported, some of the results from the project "Place to grow" have been integrated in the consultation for the comprehensive plan yet it is too early to assess the real impact on the local environment or on the empowerment of the children. If the administration can not assimilate the information in its different activities, it may be another case of tokenism (Hart, 1997).

The supervisors came from the Street and Park Unit of Täby Municipality. The result indicates that the supervisors have encouraged the children to make comments on favorite places (question 6) and suggestions for improvements (question 7), besides the expressed aim of gathering as much verbal information as possible about unpleasant and dangerous places. The extent of the comments from Täby is larger than from the research-pilots. The influence from the supervisors can imply that the children are used as a transmitter for the supervisors own views, which could lead others to assess the information as less trustworthy. On the other hand, the Children's Maps can be seen as a tool for getting on speaking terms with children and youth, and thus gaining information that is otherwise difficult to attain. This is important to consider when choosing persons to instruct the children.

One bias that the Täby case highlights is the choice of schools participating in mapping. If the case is just a small project, concerning one small village this might not be an issue. When the method is used for gaining information about a whole municipality, there needs to be some consideration on how the schools and classes are chosen. In Täby, schools and classes with students with special needs were excluded. We have not reflected or tested how the method can or cannot be used by children with different kind of disabilities. But to exclude these students from the use of Children's Maps is certainly not our intention.

In the report "Place to grow", it is noted that most of the children were able to orientate on the map quite well, except from one district with a very hilly topography, were the slopes are not shown in the basic orientation map (Täby kommun, 2009b, p. 16). This is an aspect that we have not encountered earlier and, of course, it is important that the basic map used for orientation represents features in the landscape that are important for children.

Another point to observe is the low number of teachers participating in the mapping. The project leader was reluctant to include teachers' mapping in the project as the focus was on how children used and perceived the outdoor environment. However, we know from our own pilots that teachers might be reluctant to use the computer themselves to input information. Some have willingly done so while others have preferred to be helped by the supervisor. This observation is in line with the reporting from the Swedish National Agency for Education (Skolverket, 2009). We have not engaged ourselves in developing the teacher's graphical interface to the same degree as the children's version. The interface that we have used has still to prove that it functions. As the teacher does not report a personal use but functions as a representative for the school's use of the outdoor environment, it is not considered

to be a significant problem that not all teachers are involved. The school's use and need for good environments and safe routes for transportation can be reported by those teachers who are willing and able to do so.

The project "Place to grow" shows that there is a great demand for information from children and from various administrations. In Täby there were demands of information from different units within the Technical Office as well as from the Child Care and Elementary School and from Culture and Leisure. The most obvious demands came from the park unit, from the traffic department and from people involved in "Safe in Täby" (our translation), a project within the local government.

As we have stated earlier in this article, maps (and GIS) represent power and this means that parts of the administration that cannot express their interests in maps (or GIS) have a weaker position when it comes to maintaining their interests in urban planning. Child Care and Elementary School Unit have until now had little interest in geographic information. This may be a result of different approaches toward different sources of information and technologies within an administration.

The seminars showed that the written comments were of high interest. As our focus is on the spatial information, we have not considered how to analyze or categorize the written information. The participants wanted the information to be categorized for easy access. Qualitative analyzes of the text information calls for time and competence to carry it out in a qualified way. One solution is to have standard categories in the questionnaire, yet if we restrict the children to placing information into predefined categories, we are afraid that this will produce biased and incomplete results. By this we mean that it is better to let children express themselves in their own words in relation to personal feelings such as favorite places, dangerous places and wishes for change. It is then possible to make different interpretations while the source material is kept intact. This ambition may lead to a somewhat less administration-friendly representation, yet the strength of the written text is that it provides an easier medium to hear the voice of the child, than by simple markings on the map.

Digital Divide

The geographical databases produced by local government in Täby are of high quality regarding scope, scale of details and actuality. It is mainly used as a background map for the internal digital system, containing a large amount of different information used in administration. Geographic information was not accessible for Child Care and Elementary School units within the internal digital support system. The preliminary finding from Täby tells us that the use of GIS is still inconsistent across the administration, and that it is still a technique that demands training to master. In Täby, as in many municipalities in Sweden, there are just a couple of people engaged in the technical support of the data system that have the mandate to set up and decide the functionalities that can be obtained by users in administration. The GIS-expert plays a crucial role in deciding what is possible to do or not.

The full potential of the internal digital system with interactive maps seems not to have been used or even requested. The same situation is reported from research on bottlenecks with implementation of planning support system (Vonk et al., 2005). If the information stored in digital information system is not relevant for you, why use the systems? Interactive maps and multimedia representation of data helps the user to construct knowledge. If important information is stored in files, charts and archives or unreadable static maps they have very little influence. If relevant information, such as children's experiences of the outdoor environment, is accessed through an interactive information system, this will enhance the use of the information, and maybe even transform it into knowledge.

Need for Improvements on Children's Maps

Problems with the GIS-application in its current stage are; access to the GIS application, the adaptation of the maps in the GIS-application to each case and the administration of data. From the very beginning we aimed at an Internet solution, we now have funding for transferring the GIS-application into Internet so we will address issues of unequal access to hardware between different schools as mentioned by the Swedish National Agency for Education (Skolverket, 2009). We will also develop standard procedures for categorizing and analyzing data, making the threshold as small as possible for the user to interactively explore the data.

Parallel to this, we will write a manual describing, among other things, how the supervisors should conduct themselves when using the method and how we consider it could be combined with other means for gaining deeper information and higher levels of participation. We will also develop guidelines concerning feed-back to children and teachers and further explain the role of the teacher's map.

CONCLUSION

The information that young people and teachers can provide is asked for in many contexts, not only in urban planning. The use of GIS as an interactive tool for analyses and presentations is not well established in Swedish local authorities. In Täby it is still an expert tool, and especially the social administration has not integrated the technique in the daily work. Here the representation on static maps still plays an important role in communication processes between the municipal administrations as well as with the public.

We look forward to transferring Children's Maps to Internet. We do not aim for the application to be open for use by everyone, only accessible within projects, to secure that the information given by children and youth is not misused. Besides, local authorities, a school, or an organization with children's wellbeing on the agenda could get access to the tool. As the use of Google maps and Web 2.0 is spreading, we think it is more important than ever that the knowledge and the interests of children and youth are made visible and accessible. We believe that the presence of Children's Maps on Internet will contribute to this and in the end hopefully be helpful in giving young people the influence on local planning and maintenance of their neighborhoods that they have the right to.

REFERENCES

Baraldi, C. (2003). Children's social participation in the town of adults. In Christensen, P., & O'Brian, M. (Eds.), *Children in the city: Home neighbourhood and community* (pp. 184–205). London: RoutledgeFalmer.

Berglund, U. (2008). Using children's GIS maps to influence town Planning. *Children. Youth and Environments, 18*(2), 110–132.

Berglund, U., & Nordin, K. (2007). Using GIS to make young people's voices heard in urban planning. *Built Environment, 33*(4), 469–481. doi:10.2148/benv.33.4.469

Berglund, U., Nordin, K., & Eriksson, M. (2009). *Barnkartor i GIS och trafiksäkerhet* (Children's maps in GIS and traffic safety) (Tech. Rep.). Uppsala, Sweden: Rapporter Institutionen för stad och land.

Chawla, L. (2002a). Toward better cities for children and youth. In Chawla, L. (Ed.), *Growing up in an Urbanizing World* (pp. 15–34). London: Earthscan.

Chawla, L. (Ed.). (2002b). *Growing up in an urbanising world*. London: Earthscan.

Christensen, P. (2003). Place, space and knowledge: Children in the village and the city. In Christensen, P., & O'Brian, M. (Eds.), *Children in the City: Home neighbourhood and community* (pp. 13–28). London: RoutledgeFalmer. doi:10.4324/9780203167236

Christensen, P., & O'Brian, M. (2003). Children in the city: Introducing new perspectives. In Christensen, P., & O'Brian, M. (Eds.), *Children in the city: Home neighbourhood and community* (pp. 1–12). London: RoutledgeFalmer. doi:10.4324/9780203167236

Christensen, P., & Prout, A. (2002). Working with ethical symmetry in social research with children. *Childhood, 9*(4), 447–497. doi:10.1177/0907568202009004007

Crampton, J. W., & Krygier, J. (2006). An introduction to critical cartography. *ACME An International E-Journal for Critical Geographies, 4(*1), 11-33. Retrieved Mach 29, 2009 from http://www.acme-journal.org

Driskell, D. (2002). *Creating better cities with children and youth*. London: Earthscan.

Elwood, S. (2002). GIS use in community planning: A multidimensional analysis of empowerment. *Environment & Planning A, 34*, 905–922. doi:10.1068/a34117

Elwood, S. (2006). Critical issues in participatory GIS: Deconstructions, reconstructions, and new research directions. *Transactions in GIS, 10*(5), 693–708. doi:10.1111/j.1467-9671.2006.01023.x

Flyvbjerg, B. (2001). *Making social science matter: Why social inquiry fails and how it can succeed again*. Cambridge, UK: Cambridge University Press.

Freeman, C., & Aitken-Rose, E. (2005). Future shapers: Children, young people, and planning in New Zealand local government. *Environment and Planning. C, Government & Policy, 23*, 227–256. doi:10.1068/c0433

Habermas, J. (1984). *The theory of communicative action* (*Vol. 1*). Boston, MA: Beacon Press.

Hart, R. A. (1997). *Children's participation: The theory and practice of involving young citizens in community development and environmental care.* London: Earthscan.

Healey, P. (1997). *Collaborative planning: Shaping places in fragmented societies.* Basingstoke, UK: Palgrave Macmillan.

Healey, P. (1999). Institutionalist analysis, communicative planning, and shaping places. *Journal of Planning Education and Research, 19*(2), 111–121. doi:10.1177/0739456X9901900201

Holloway, S., & Valentine, G. (2003). *Cyberkids: Children in the information age.* London: RoutledgeFalmer.

Horelli, L. (1998). Creating child-friendly environments: Case studies on children's participation in three European countries. *Childhood, 5*(2), 225–239. doi:10.1177/0907568298005002008

Horelli, L., & Kaaja, M. (2002). Opportunities and constraints of internet-assisted urban planning with young people. *Journal of Environmental Psychology, 22*, 191–200. doi:10.1006/jevp.2001.0246

Jiang, B., Huang, B., & Vasek, V. (2003). Geovisualisation for planning support systems. In Geertman, S., & Stillwell, J. (Eds.), *Planning support system in practice* (pp. 177–191). Berlin: Springer.

Korte, W. B., & Hüsing, T. (2006). *Benchmarking Access and Use of ICT in European Schools 2006.* Retrieved from http://empirica.com/publikationen/ documents/No08-2006_learnInd.pdf

Kyttä, M., Kaaja, M., & Horelli, L. (2004). An internet-based design game as a mediator of children's environmental visions. *Environment and Behavior, 36*(1), 127–151. doi:10.1177/0013916503254839

Lynch, K. (Ed.). (1977). *Growing up in cities: Studies of the spatial environment of adolescence in Cracow, Melbourne, Mexico City, Salta, Toluca, and Warszawa.* Cambridge, MA: MIT Press.

MacEachren, A. (2004). *1995). How maps work: Representation, visualization, and design* (pp. iii–iv). New York: Guilford.

Matthews, H., Limb, M., & Taylor, M. (1999). Young people's participation and representation in society. *Geoforum, 30*, 135–144. doi:10.1016/S0016-7185(98)00025-6

Norsk Form. (2005). *Barnetråkk: Barns tilgjengelige uteareal* (Children's tracks: Children's accessible outdoor environments). Retrieved June 20, 2009 from http://www.norskform. no/?V_ITEM_ID=1282

Percy-Smith, B., & Malone, K. (2001). Making children's participation in neighbourhood settings relevant to the everyday lives of young People. *PLA Notes, 42*, 18–22.

Pickles, J. (Ed.). (1995). *Ground truth: The social implications of geographic information systems.* New York: Guilford.

Plester, B., Blades, M., & Spencer, C. (2006). Children's understanding of environmental representations: Aerial photographs and model towns. In Spencer, C., & Blades, M. (Eds.), *Children and their environments: Learning, using and designing spaces* (pp. 42–56). New York: Cambridge University Press. doi:10.1017/CBO9780511521232.004

Rogers, P. (2006). Young people's participation in the renaissance of public space: A case study of Newcastle upon Tyne, UK. *Children. Youth and Environments, 16*(2), 105–130.

Sager, T. (1994). *Communicative Planning Theory. Avebury.* UK: Avebury Press.

Sager, T. (2006). The logic of critical communicative planning: Transaction cost alteration. *Planning Theory, 5*(3), 223–254. doi:10.1177/1473095206068629

Shiers, H. (2001). Pathways to participation: Openings, opportunities and obligations. *Children & Society*, *15*, 107–117. doi:10.1002/chi.617

Skolverket. (2009). *IT-användning och IT-kompetens i förskola, skola och vuxenutbildning* (IT usage and IT skills in preschool, school and adult education) (Dnr 75-2007:3775). Retrieved from http://www.skolverket.se/ publikationer?id=2192

Täby kommun. (2009a). *Det nya Täby: Översiktsplan 2010-2030, utställningshandling maj 2009, allmänna intressen* (The new Täby: Comprehensive plan 2010-2030, consultation May 2009, public interests). Retrieved June 20, 2009 from http://www.taby.se

Täby kommun. (2009b). *Plats att växa* (Place to grow). Retrieved June 13, 2009 from http://www.taby.se/Miljo-natur-halsa/ Planeringsdokument/ Plats-att-vaxa/

The FreeChild Project. (2008). Retrieved November 15, 2009 from http://www.freechild.org

Tonucci, F., Prisco, A., & Horelli, L. (2004). A comparison of the models for children's participation in decision-making, in Rome and Helsinki. In L. Horelli & M. Prezza (Eds.), *Child-Friendly Environments: Approaches and lessons* (pp. 83-93). Espoo, Finland: Helsinki University of Technology.

ULI. (2008). *Lägesbild GI Sverige: en lägesbild av användandet av geografiska informationssytem i Sverige, resultat från delundersökningen offentliga sektorn* (Situational awareness GI Sweden: Study on use of geographic information and geographic information technology in Sweden, public sector). Retrieved from http://www.geoforum.se/page/158/332

UNICEF. (1990). Convention on the rights of the child. In *First Call for Children* (pp. 43–79). New York: UNICEF.

UNICEF. (2001, March). *The children as community researchers*. Retrieved November 15, 2009 from http://www.unicef.org/ teachers/researchers/

United Nations. (1993). [*Earth summit - the United Nations programme of action from Rio*. New York: United Nations Dept. of Public Information.]. *Agenda (Durban, South Africa)*, 21.

Urban Green Spaces Taskforce. (2002). *Green spaces, better place: Final report*. London: Department for transport, local government, and the regions.

Vonk, G., Geertman, S., & Shot, P. (2005). Bottlenecks blocking widespread usage of planning support systems. *Environment & Planning A*, *37*, 909–924. doi:10.1068/a3712

Wilhjelm, H. (1999). *Hvor har du vært? - ingen steder: Miljøtilknyttende infrastruktur og barns hverdagsliv - en kunnskapsoversikt* (Where have you been? nowhere: Environmental infrastructure and children's everyday life- a review). Trondheim, Norway: Norsk senter for barneforskning.

Woolley, H., Spencer, C., Dunn, J., & Rowley, G. (1999). The child as citizen. *Journal of Urban Design*, *4*(3), 255–282. doi:10.1080/13574809908724451

This work was previously published in International Journal of Information Communication Technologies and Human Development, Volume 2, Issue 2, edited by Susheel Chhabra and Hakikur Rahman, pp. 1-16, copyright 2010 by IGI Publishing (an imprint of IGI Global).

Chapter 6
Participation in Child Welfare Services Through Information and Communication Technologies

Susan Tregeagle
University of Western Sydney, Australia

ABSTRACT

Case management systems were designed to open the way for increased participation of young people and their families in child welfare interventions, and, their standardised format provides a valuable opportunity to use ICT in social work practice. Existing research is unclear about how effectively case management affects participation, nor, the impact of ICT on social work interventions. This paper describes the findings of qualitative research with service users about their experiences of case management and how ICT could further their involvement in critical decisions for families. Service users are keen to use ICT and this could help overcome the limitations of paper-based case management systems and exploit the communication potential of the internet and mobile phones. However, before ICT could be used, the complex 'digital divide' affecting disadvantaged families would need to be addressed and social workers' understanding and current use of ICT would need to be explored.

INTRODUCTION

Young people and families involved with child welfare services have few opportunities to communicate about, or exercise power over, their lives. In typical western child welfare service systems, service users have limited opportunities to con-

DOI: 10.4018/978-1-4666-0047-8.ch006

tribute to planning their future (2004). They do not feel listened to or able to influence authorities (Create Foundation, 2001). Some young people experience multiple workers and foster homes, leading to loss of important information and poor understanding of how contribute to decisions (Cashmore & Paxman, 2006). Parents whose children live in the care system can be painfully excluded (Klease, 2008) becoming alienated from opportunities to reclaim their children (Victorian Government, 2003). This paper poses the questions of whether Information & Communication Technology (ICT) could have a role in addressing these issues and what would need to happen to open such an opportunity.

One way in which ICT could be employed in child welfare is in conjunction with standardised case management systems. Case management systems have been developed over the past twenty years as part of an attempt to reform child welfare services and have spread rapidly, internationally (Cheers, Kufeldt, Klein, & Rideout, 2007). Part of their aim is to provide opportunities for families to be heard, be involved in decision-making venues and limit the autonomy of social workers (Jackson & Kilroe, 1996). However, the existing research is unhelpfully divided as to the impact of these systems on child welfare power relations and on how use of extensive written material affects participation. Social workers have also been generally reluctant to consider the impact of ICT on their work (Sapey, 1997; Tregeagle & Darcy, 2007) and to look at the potential of ICT for communication.

This article explores these issues by describing research on service users' experiences of their participation in case managed interactions. It examines existing literature on ICT from a range of disciplines which could have implications for service users' ability to communicate in child welfare settings. This research shows that ICT could enhance participation and limit social workers' exercise of power if used in conjunction with case management systems, however, considerable barriers still need to be overcome.

The theoretical position underpinning this paper is one of social constructionism and the ideas of 'social shaping'. In this view, technology is seen to be shaped by social processes; however, aspects of the technology also 'afford' particular possibilities and introduce limitations upon the way that a technology is used (Hutchby, 2001, 2003). These 'affordances', in turn, shape social

processes. Hence, the way a technology is used requires an understanding of the social processes affecting the development of the technology *and* the varied ways that the technology can be employed. The 'affordances' of a technology may be different for different people; the use of the technology may be the result of the context in which the technology is employed. A particular technology may have a range of possibilities and limitations and these may not always have been foreseen in the original design. In this view, the applications of ICT are not necessarily inevitable or beneficial when used with highly disadvantaged individuals and must be understood as complex and not easy to predict.

Applying this theoretical framework to ICT in child welfare services shows that the take-up and impact of technology has significant implications for the ability of service users to participate. For example, the use of computers can be seen as shaped by social factors such as poverty, age and power relationships, which restrict access. ICT may alter capacity to communicate between particular groups of people, for example social workers (frequently tertiary educated), or by service users (predominantly have low literacy levels and are young). The technology may be used in a variety of contexts (such as offices or home) and may have multiple applications (such as data collection or social networking). The use of ICT in child welfare may also be very different from its intended design (such as using the internet for pedophile grooming of children). The 'lived' experience of highly disadvantaged families therefore needs to be explored carefully before we can consider its role in child welfare practice.

DEFINING CASE MANAGEMENT SYSTEMS IN CHILD WELFARE

Two case management systems are explored in this study. These are Looking After Children (LAC), a system originally developed in United

Kingdom and adapted to Australian legislation for children living in foster or residential care. The second 'sister-program' is Supporting Children and Responding to Families (SCARF) based on the UK Framework for Assessment of Children in Need and their Families, developed for children still living with their own families. Both systems are organised in age-related stages, and assess seven 'domains' of a child's life (health, education, identity, social presentation, self-care skills, emotional and social development and relationships). SCARF contains two additional areas of assessment- that of the parental capacity and also the family's ability to function in the community. These, or similar case management systems, are widely used in the United Kingdom, Sweden, Hungary, Canada and Australia (Cheers et al., 2007).

These systems consist of interrelated forms which attempt to shape the assessment of a child's life and develop plans to bring about change in the young person's welfare. They are extensive questionnaires for assessment and planning and include highly prescriptive instructions to social workers. The case management systems specify when information is to be collected, when decisions are to be made and how the various professionals in a child's life are to inter-relate. Answers in some areas are provided in tick-box form, but, other questions require short narrative accounts. The forms require a significant level of literacy and organisation and appear highly bureaucratic; they are inter-connected through a series of instructions, and each form must be checked against previously completed forms. They are most often used in paper form however; electronic systems have also been developed predominantly to be used by social workers and not directly with families. The electronic systems' functions are, thus far, largely confined to collecting and analysing data (Cheers & Morwitzer, 2006; Jones, 2006).

One important social work process attempted through LAC-based case management is that of a change in 'power relations' between social workers and service users. The authors of case management aimed to give service users greater control over decisions than in more traditional social work practice. Young people and parents supposedly were extended greater opportunities to participate in decision-making and workers' power were significantly restricted. Despite initial controversy, there is now research showing that opportunities for participation in decision making by service users have increased (Kufeldt, Simard, Vachon, Baker, & Andrews, 2000), although to a more limited extent than envisaged by their authors (Tregeagle & Mason, 2008).

Strategies employed in the case management systems aim to increase the opportunities for service users to be 'listened to' and express views. The authors of these systems described their motivation as improving decision-making by having service users better inform their social worker (Jackson & Kilroe, 1996, p. 9) and encouraging service users to be more committed to decisions that have been made (Tolley, 2005). Their strategies include:

- Questions to elicit service users' understandings of service users' circumstances
- Consultation 'booklets' to allow both young people and adults to contribute to planning
- Questions which identify impediments to service users communicating their views, such as learning disability.

Other elements of the text provide direct strategies for service users to be involved in decision-making meetings:

- There are requirements for service users to formally approve case decisions, and for workers to record dissent (This applies to young people defined in LAC as those over the age of ten and is reinforced by the need for the service user to sign forms.)
- There is a focus on an individual 'named' child (to ensure that individual children are

de-segregated and not treated simply as part of a family or sibling group)

- There are requirements for ongoing detailed discussion between workers and service users .

Text-based strategies also attempted to restrict worker autonomy and to place obligations on social workers to facilitate participation. Workers needed to:

- Record and account for actions taken following decision making
- Record the reason that service users did not attend meetings - thereby placing a stronger onus on workers
- Confirm circulation of documents to service users.

Case management systems were developed to create a 'partnership' between workers and service users in which power is shared (Jackson & Kilroe, 1996 p. 10), however, not necessarily to the extent of power being equally shared between workers and service users.

BACKGROUND: CASE MANAGEMENT, PARTICIPATION AND ICT

Case management systems have been highly controversial in child welfare practice and their impact on participation has been central to debate. Whilst the role of ICT has increased in the general community and amongst social workers since the implementation of these systems, there has been division over the role of ICT in affecting social work practice and significant criticism has been expressed. These debates are explored below to identify how this research may contribute.

Case Management and Participation Debate

The case management approach and its impact on participation has been controversial. The uses of written texts and extensive forms have been described as alienating for young people (Bell, 1998, 1999; Munro, 2001). There have been criticisms of the approach, which is seen to impinge on relationships with the professional and to 'empty' the relationship between workers and service users (Garrett, 2003). The systems have also been criticised as restricting social workers' professional autonomy by imposing managerial accountability on them, and encroaching on workers' time for engaging with family members (Searing, 2003). In Canada, social workers have reported concern that LAC restricted time available for practitioners and service users to interact. Furthermore, these social workers identified the repetitive, stigmatising and intimidating nature of case management as contributing to situations in which service users lied or remained silent in response to intrusive questions (Drolet & Sauve-Kobylecki, 2006). Early commentators claimed that case management actively stopped children from expressing their views:

...[LAC] reduces the space for children to contribute to determining what is in their best interest and what outcomes they themselves want to achieve (Munro, 2001, p. 134).

In Australia, Wise (1999) reported poor involvement of family members in interventions, with many young people not understanding the way they were meant to participate or the purpose of gathering information:

...some adolescents ...were mistrustful of the process, and were not especially frank about sensitive issues (Wise, 2003a, p. 15).

Other research has contradicted these findings, claiming that participation for young people had improved when compared with previous practices. Specifically, two Scottish evaluation reports described greater involvement in decision making (Francis, 2002; Wheelaghan & Hill, 2000). Young people were described as feeling 'that they were more involved than formerly in developing their plans' (Wheelaghan & Hill, 2000, p. 161). In an English study, Thomas (2005) reported that child welfare managers believed young people were more involved in decision-making than in previous practice. In Canada, researchers claimed that young people using case management had significantly improved their participation compared to more traditional methods of compiling case information (Kufeldt et al., 2000, p. 189). Young people considered that they had greater control over documentation and more regular communication with, and accountability from, workers (Kufeldt, McGilligan, Klein, & Rideout, 2006). There has been little attention given to parents' experiences, although an English evaluation reported that parental participation had increased compared to previous practice (Cleaver & Walker, 2004). In Australia, Fernandez (2007) showed a positive working relationship in programs for young people at home, and noted that families engaged more with workers who used a collaborative approach.

This polarized debate is underpinned by a variety of research claims about service users' views, however, much of this research is not adequate. Previous studies were undertaken in the early stages of implementation of the systems, when service users were still dependent on welfare agencies and where workers and service users may have been unused to the systems. Draft forms had sometimes been used and these were not necessarily relevant to the circumstances. Previous studies have also not addressed whether a change in technology could better achieve more effective participation. This study aimed to conduct research in established practice of LAC and

SCARF with service users who had completed their contact with welfare agencies and thus may have felt freer to speak.

The Debate Over the use of ICT in Social Work

The impact of computers in social work has been seen as problematic –in striking contrast to other areas of human services (Christensen, Griffiths, & Jorm, 2004). Since the 1990s, in parallel with implementation of case management systems, the general community and social workers have increasingly used ICT. However, it has been used in a limited way in child welfare, with little interest shown in the communication potential with service users.

ICT has so far been applied to case management primarily to allow the collection of data and analysis by social workers. Collecting data was a clear motivation for the development of the original paper-based case management system: *Another advantage of adopting standard measures of outcome is that they create consistency in the collection of information* (Parker, Ward, Jackson, Aldgate, & Wedge, 1991, p. 13). Social workers saw that data collection had both professional and managerial implications:

... the chief beneficiaries of such an exercise should not be the organisation or its employees, but the children and young people for whom the service is provided (Jackson & Kilroe, 1996, p. 14).

Data collection was also increasingly important for supervision of staff, maintaining information on young people and for reform of the system because data could be used as a basis for research (Wise, 2003b). ICT made the collection and use of this data easier. The use of ICT has been actively pursued both in Australia (Cheers & Morwitzer, 2006) and in England, where case management systems have been redeveloped and designed in electronic format specifically to allow computerised reporting to central government and analyse the costing of services (Jones, 2006).

This use of computers and the role of electronic data bases, generally in social work, has been strongly contested. ICT debate has been linked with managerial, rather than service users' focus (Henman & Adler, 2003; Hough, 1996). Munro (2005) has argued that frontline workers' needs for information and decision-making are not adequately addressed. Garrett (2004) draws attention to the increasing use of ICT for surveillance in juvenile justice and child welfare- he identifies data in the UK integrated system as part of governments 'joined up thinking, the e-government agenda and marketisation' (Garrett, 2005, p. 5). Parton (2008, 2009) identified computerisation as moving social work practice from narrative 'to an endeavour increasingly framed by the logic of the database' (Parton, 2008, p. 261). This impact was associated with: greatly increased accountability; loss of knowledge through the restricted way that data is collected; distortion of identity, individuals being 'constructed according to the fields that constitute the database' (Parton, 2008, p. 263) and information becoming increasingly more important than people (Parton, 2009). Australian researchers have also noted the impact of indicators on practice (Tilbury, 2004) and the increased ability to collate data may exacerbate these problems. Case management systems have been criticised as part of this wider concern, however, the communication potential of ICT has not been extensively explored in child welfare (Tregeagle & Darcy, 2007).

There are indications that ICT could be useful to social work communications. As I have argued elsewhere (Tregeagle & Darcy, 2007), ICT fundamentally changes the initiation, distribution and consumption of texts in ways that may affect how social work is experienced (Fairclough, 1992). ICT may encourage service users to initiate and maintain communication and may have a significant impact on service users' ability to exercise power in the relationship. The very nature of ICT, with its associations of interactivity, egalitarianism, young people's proficiency and fun (Ben-Ze'ev, 2004) may encourage service users to start communicating. Research into the way the internet is used in spontaneous on-line communication (Ben-Ze'ev, 2004), shows that physical and social barriers may be altered by ICT, as the internet can reduce social embarrassment. The greater anonymity of the internet could assist in making approaches for help less stigmatising. ICT may offer opportunities to initiate communication for people who may otherwise be discouraged by their low level of education and poor literacy. The internet can be a source of company and entertainment (Ben-Ze'ev, 2004). ICT has been shown to be more useable with the socially anxious and it offers advantages to those dealing with taboo subjects (Tyler, 2002)—an issue extremely relevant to child welfare. The internet has also been shown to reduce status differences in communication (Joinson, 2001). Websites can tailor words to the audience, supplemented by graphics or photos, and bring other qualities to communication. ICT could allow service users greater ability to initiate communication by letting service users control the timing and by reducing physical, social and educational barriers to communication. Many human service websites attribute their success to the opening up of access, removing barriers to initiation of communication and allowing control over sequencing of communication (Christensen et al., 2004).

There is a range of hypotheses about how ICT could encourage initial and ongoing communication, such as:

- The capacity to present the self in a better light (Joinson, 2005);
- The absence of socially restricting features which stop communication in face-to-face relationships, for example shyness (Ben-Ze'ev, 2004) or where personal appearance is an issue (Walther, 1996);

- The advantages of asynchronous relationship (Joinson, 2005);
- Allowing people time to consider the responses that they give;
- Greater anonymity (Ben-Ze'ev, 2004; Joinson, 2005), although even situations where privacy is not guaranteed do not dispel the impression of anonymity (Joinson, 2005);
- Greater focus on individual feelings and relationships;
- Feeling more akin to other people who communicate electronically (Joinson, 2005);
- The provision of greater personal detail in on-line communication as a means of reducing uncertainty (Walther, 1996);
- The development of a 'feedback loop' which means that self-disclosure is reinforced (Walther, 1996).

THE STUDY

This research aims to examine service users' experiences of case management, participation and ICT in order to contribute to the debates explored above. The wide-spread use of technology for meaningful relationships, engagement of other human services in ICT based communication and increasing evidence of the important impact of ICT on altering communication mean that further exploration of ICT in social work is needed. As will be observed in the research findings below, most service users want greater efficiency in communication with workers and young people increasingly expect this to be electronic.

The Study Method

This study was undertaken in Australia, a country which has pioneered the use of ICT with case management (Cheers & Morwitzer, 2006) and which has strong community take-up of computers and

the internet (OECD, 2006). The study was undertaken as part of a University-industry partnership between the University of Western Sydney and Barnardos Australia, a non-government service provider which holds licenses for using case management systems in eastern Australia.

Qualitative methods were used to understand the complex factors involved in service users' experiences. This approach was adopted to explore the depth of people's experiences and minimise the impact of the researcher on establishing the parameters of the study (Alvesson, 2002; Gubrium & Holstein, 2003). Thirty-two individuals (in twenty-five families) participated in semi-structured interviews. Participants had between two and eight years' experience of using a case management system, and had completed their involvement with the welfare agency. Participants included fourteen young people, two fathers and sixteen mothers. The youngest participant was eight years old and the oldest two parents were in their forties. Six of these participants were Aboriginal.

The research aimed at trustworthy findings of a range of participants which allows general applicability (Alvesson, 2002). The research was submitted to the University of Western Sydney Human Research Ethics Committee and was conducted in eight different welfare programs: in agencies in New South Wales and the Australian Capital Territory in 2006/7. Potential participants were approached through welfare agency managers and asked to contact the researcher. All referrals were followed up with written information describing promise of confidentiality, access to support and opportunities to withdraw at any time. Participants could choose to be involved through face to face electronic interviews or group discussions. However, all choose individual interviews with the researcher. It is significant that the offer of computer-mediated interviews was not taken up by service users as it may indicate a reluctance to discuss sensitive matters with strangers on line. An illustrated booklet of the interview questions was developed to assist individuals who preferred a visual format. An Aboriginal participant was recruited as a co-researcher for interviews with Aboriginal participants. Participants were reimbursed for the time they spent attending interviews. The research project was successful in reaching young people, very poor adults and those under welfare scrutiny; each of these groups is known to be difficult to engage in research (Curtis, Robert, Copperman, & Liabo, 2004; Gilbertson & Barber, 2002; Heptinstall, 2000; Leonard, 2005; Valentine, Butler, & Skelton, 2001).

The interviews explored the experience of the everyday use of participation in the welfare intervention, how the paper LAC and SCARF forms had been used in interactions with social workers and current use of technology and future aspirations for ICT. Service users were asked whether they felt listened to and involved in decision-making, their views of the accountability of workers and the impact of the written forms on their experiences. Interviews also covered service users' current access to computers, the ways in which they used the internet and their interest in using ICT to negotiate with social workers.

Analysis of the data began in the semi-structured interviews and continued through extensive reiterative coding. Transcripts of interviews were sent back to participants to check the accuracy of representation. The researcher transcribed all interviews with specific emphasis on accuracy. The NVIVO computer-based analysis package was used to assist in analysis of the records of interview and academics were involved in the checking coding categories used by the researcher. A number of reiterations of coding were undertaken. Concepts and categories were examined and actively reviewed (for example initial analysis was coded according to hierarchical theories of power sharing, however as data showed different findings, other theoretical positions were explored (Tregeagle, 2008)). Whilst majority views were noted, particular attention was paid to diverse experiences and atypical responses. Analysis of the research continually focused on the importance of power relationships within the research setting (Alvesson, 2002; Gubrium & Holstein, 2003). Attempts to open opportunities for service users to exercise power were actively pursued, for example, children may have been intimidated by the adult researcher and this issue was addressed through discussion about the importance of children's unique experiences to the study and use of child-friendly venues and prompts.

The Study Findings

The study found many examples of positive participation amongst families who had used case management with social workers. The majority of service users described being satisfied with the way that they contributed to decision-making when using case management systems. However, their experience of power relations was different from that 'expected' by the authors of the systems and there were significant problems with the use of written text and the impact of external power on the intervention. Some relationships took time to develop and, in a small minority of situations, negotiations between service users and social workers completely failed. Service users were interested in using ICT with their social workers to increase their participation. However, they described significant barriers to being able to get access to computers and the internet; and some had no experience with the technology and were disinterested.

Service Users' Satisfaction with Participation in Case Managed Interventions

Most service users felt listened to and described actions being taken in response to their requests. Service users frequently described getting the practical assistance that they expected and stated that they felt emotionally and socially supported. For example one young person was clear:

I never felt that I had a problem that was dismissed

Some children reported being moved from their foster families when they had made significant complaints. Service users generally described establishing a 'positive relationship' with their worker when using case management systems.

Despite the majority of service users describing positive participation, some took time to develop a relationship with their workers and a small number never achieved this and refused to engage in active communication. There were times that service users were clear that they were in conflict with their workers or restricted what they told them:

Everyone knows the boundaries to go to speak to the worker.

When I came down to it, if I didn't like something on the forms, if I felt something was a bit too personal or something I'd just lie

It seemed that service users were restricted by power external to the intervention and sometimes would not answer questions posed in the case management systems because they feared legal or social repercussions. Service users frequently approached the intervention as a negotiation with their workers, by controlling information. At other times, they chose not to take the opportunity to exercise power and instead deferred to their worker's judgement. Furthermore, disagreement over the aims of assistance had led a small minority of service users to significantly limit their engagement with social workers. In one example, older adolescents, who lived in stable placements, did not like using the case management system as it detracted from their feeling 'normal'. In another example, a young mother wanted more help than she received and resented the fact that workers focused on her children. These participants withdrew from active engagement with their workers.

An additional area of some disappointment for young people was the way in which childhood was understood, and the limitations this placed on participation. Young people identified three areas of concern. Firstly, they spoke of wanting social and emotional support after eighteen years of age because, although legally being adults, they did not yet feel able to manage independently (case management systems were not used after the legal age of independence). Secondly, some young people wanted their views considered separately from their parents and objected when this was not implemented by their social workers. (It appeared that workers did not actually consult independently with the young people who were living in their own families, despite instructions to do so.). Thirdly, a number of young people were concerned by stereotyped views of their behaviour based on age categories.

While case managed interventions *did* appear to offer opportunities for service users to exercise power, there were significant discrepancies between the ways the systems attempted to alter power relations and the experiences of different service users exposed to the same system. Both service users and social workers exercised power in ways that operated outside the written text-based attempts to affect power relations. Furthermore, service users' participation was affected by power relations external to the intervention, including social attitudes towards children. Case management appears an important way of increasing participation, but also one where changes could be made to improve participation.

A major impediment to participation, described by service users, was the limitation imposed by the use of ' paper form' 'technology'. Service users were either critical or ambivalent about the case management forms. When service users actively used the forms they said they had difficulties with the written text. Young people and parents clearly identified case management systems as highly bureaucratic and 'belonging' to the welfare agency. For this reason it often came as a surprise to service users that the forms helped them to develop insight into their circumstances by looking at the forms and being able to review progress. Nonetheless, literacy requirements did create problems and service users felt intimidated and resented the imposition of the forms' repetition and structure. They had problems keeping track of the forms (for example when they moved house) and in trying to maintain privacy within families. The forms were also reminders of emotionally disturbing events and sometimes service users wanted to get rid of reminders about difficult times.

Service Users' Attitudes to Using ICT with Case Management Systems

Given the limitations of pen and paper technology in case managed intervention and the increasing importance of exploring ICT outlined above, this study explored the issue of service users' interest in using ICT with their social workers. The study examined the use of e-mail, instant messaging and social networking sites- the most common internet applications at the time of the study. The participants in this study were largely reliant on Government income maintenance or in very low-paid work; they were all living below the poverty line. The findings indicate significant limitations in service users being able to access ICT.

Many, but not all, service users were open to using the internet with their social workers. Some owned computers or were keen to use them with the internet. The majority of young people and parents found communication over the internet attractive and convenient and felt it addressed problems such as their ability to keep copies of forms. There were some individual differences in willingness to use the internet with the oldest and youngest in the research not so interested. Some of the young men were also less interested in using the internet, except for school work.

Overall, approximately two-thirds of the service users in this study were not likely to communicate with their workers using ICT, de-

spite most wanting to do so. There was a range of reasons. Firstly, most service users could not afford the expense of computers, software and internet connections. Only eight participants had working computers in their homes—four of these had been supplied by foster families and two of the participants living with their own families were in one household. Many service users had had computers in the past, but had lost access because of the need to pawn them or because of social disruption. Eleven participants had lost their home computers for varied reasons: some families broke up, one family experienced a house-fire, others had unaffordable leasing arrangements and some computers had been pawned due to financial need. Four families actually had computers in the home but were unable to afford the technical assistance required to get them working. In one household there were three donated computers, none of which worked! One young person had lost access to a computer when she left foster care. All the participants with working computers had internet access. Those participants who did not have home internet access were able to access the internet from other locations if they wished to.

While there were other locations apart from the home that service users could access the internet, these had significant privacy problems when interacting with social workers. All school children had access to the internet at school, and many participants aged between 18 and mid-30s used friends' computers or internet cafes, although for some this was not convenient and their use was infrequent.

A second limitation to communication between service users and social workers was the result of different ways that social workers and service users used the internet. In contrast to social workers, service users did not like to use e-mail, and were unlikely to check for mail or to respond to messages; a number felt that e-mail took time and effort, as well as skills they were not comfortable with. Many stated that there was no point in

Table 1. Access to home computers and the internet amongst categories of the research participants

	Currently have a functioning computer at home	Formerly had access to a home computer	Never had a home computer
Young people who used LAC (7)	4 (computer supplied by foster or adoptive family)	1	2
Young people whose family used SCARF (7)	1	5	1
Adult interviewees who used LAC or SCARF (18)	3	5	10
Total: 32	8	11	13

checking as they rarely received e-mails. Typical is this response by an eighteen-year-old:

I don't read e-mails. I look at them but, I dunno, it's just something about reading and writing back—it just takes too much effort for me. I dunno—if the worker had e-mailed me, I probably would have looked at it but not really have taken it in.

Service users also did not seem comfortable with the time delays between sending and receiving an e-mail message. Both adults and young people expressed the view that e-mails were not an appropriate form of communication with welfare agencies:

... I think e-mail ... puts up more of a barrier sort of thing, I'd rather talk to someone on the phone, and it's a lot more personal.

Two young people, who were both in care many hours away from their statutory workers, said that they had initiated e-mail contact with workers but that this had been restricted to practical issues, such as arrangements for meetings.

Young people, including the younger mothers interviewed, preferred IM (Instant Messaging) as their primary use of the internet, a facility not used with their social workers with families. Service users' preference for IM was consistent with research that indicates that IM has emerged as a significant form of communication amongst

young people in the general community (Pakula, 2006). Participants in this study frequently used IM for long periods of time during a day, where they had internet access, or had previously had access to the internet, or were among the small number who used internet in libraries and cafes. They said that it was very important to their social relationships. Some much disrupted families had adapted their use of IM to address their families' communication problems. A mother of five, who refused to allow contact between the children and her violent ex-partner, had effectively used the internet to maintain contact between the children and their father, and she had also used it to overcome her own social isolation:

Q: Did you use the internet a lot?
A: Yeah MSN, talking to my mum and friends ... Every day, I would do all my housework, put the kids to bed and like sit there, late at night, and get friends on-line.

In another family, the boy's siblings lived with different step-families in three different states. Following a further relationship breakdown, in which access to the internet was lost, IM contact between the children had stopped. The use of particular types of IM has been shown to differ among particular social groups, for example Indigenous young people seem to use a particular system (Blanchard, 2008). These findings indicate that IM, rather than e-mail communication proved to be particularly relevant to, and highly valued by, families who lived in poverty and had disrupted relationships.

The third factor limiting use of the internet in child welfare interventions was service users' reluctance to use computer-mediated communication in the early stages of the intervention. It appeared that a level of trust was needed before service users would use ICT with social workers. Nevertheless, service users were very conscious of their increasing disadvantage in not having access to the internet and they frequently said that they wished to use computer-mediated communication more.

Descriptions by service users of how social workers used ICT with them indicated that social workers were currently reluctant to do so, and did not attempt to communicate this way even when the internet was available to service users. The reasons for this are not yet clear. It may be that social workers' duty of care' to ensure the wellbeing of young people is a barrier, for example, social workers may be reluctant to use ICT because of the potential dangers of the internet, or because of their limited understanding of the effect of computer-mediated communication (Blanchard et al., 2008). However, this paper has also suggested that social workers and managers have dominated the use of ICT for management purposes and they may be reluctant to give up their dominance.

COULD ICT INCREASE SERVICE USER PARTICIPATION?

This section explores some of the ways that ICT may increase participation of families in child welfare interventions, particularly in contrast to the current use of paper-based technologies. The study has noted significant difficulties in the 'paper-based' technology currently used in case management.

ICT may increase participation by altering the ways written texts are distributed. ICT may

reduce social workers' control over distribution while simultaneously allowing service users greater control over when and how they can access records kept (Tregeagle & Darcy, 2007). Currently, social work written records must be kept in specific physical locations and can be mislaid or mistakenly fall into unauthorised hands. The internet may allow for more efficient and reliable distribution of files and thus offer service users more control over the child welfare intervention. ICT can also offer the potential for information to be easily distributed to service users because this can be done automatically, for example automatic reminders of meetings or deadlines for decisions could be generated automatically.

ICT may also increase the possibilities for service users to use the LAC and SCARF forms over time, increasing the opportunity for self reflection. The internet may make it easier for service users to maintain forms over the long term; forms may not be so easily lost or accidentally found by other people not authorised to see them.

Despite these potentially positive attributes it is also important to recognise that ICT may bring significant disadvantages to communication in child welfare interventions. In the past, loss of face-to-face contact was seen as a potential loss in the development of relationships (Tidwell & Walther, 2002). This is now rejected by researchers and on-line relationships are now viewed as potentially highly meaningful (Tidwell & Walther, 2002). Nevertheless, there is new understanding that communication could be different on-line. Computers may bring rigidity to the social work relationship through controlling the questions asked and the range of answers which may be given through pre-determined tick-boxes. Negotiating on-line relationships has been shown to have quite different dynamics to interacting face-to-face. An example is on-line flaring behaviour in which it is easier to lose one's temper; and this may significantly affect child welfare interventions (Thompson & Nadler, 2002). There may be loss of assessment capacity because of on-line image-management, deceit, or the capacity to physically 'distance' in communication. ICT may also lead to the potential exclusion of individuals who are not interested in computer-mediated communication (Facer & Furlong, 2001). There may also be individual differences in communication skills on the internet which may make it harder for some service users to participate as effectively as in face-to-face relationships (Orgad, 2005).

In addition to these limitations, there is also growing awareness that the internet can open opportunities for exploitation of young people and that socially disadvantaged young people may not be well equipped to deal with these issues. Websites for young people may attract paedophiles. They may also lead to a substantial amount of time spent away from face-to-face socialising, and create opportunities for bullying (Maher, 2008). There are also more subtle effects such as a loss of privacy (through disclosing 'too much' information about themselves), an overload of information (with users not being able to discriminate between different forms of information) and problems of identity theft through deception and fraud (Palfrey & Gasser, 2008). These problems need to be carefully considered.

All of the research outlined above has been undertaken in areas outside child welfare and the particular conditions of this research may not apply in this specialised area. In child welfare, service users may be particularly fearful of or resistant to workers, alternately they may be overly trusting because they have poor social skills. There is also a wide age and educational range among service users. Specific research must therefore be undertaken with child welfare service users before ICT can be used confidently for communication in child welfare.

DISCUSSION

This discussion explores the areas in which ICT could be used in conjunction with case manage-

ment systems to increase service user participation in child welfare interventions. ICT, used in particular ways, could enable service users to better initiate, distribute and use text. Assistance and control could both be changed and alterations in genre make communication more attractive.

Assistance to families could be enhanced. ICT allows more opportunity for emotional support through ease of contact between social workers and family members. The internet has been shown to increase emotional support in the general community (Ben-Ze'ev, 2004; Blanchard, Metcalf, Degney, Herman, & Burns, 2008) and ICT could enhance social support of service users. The internet, as with mobile phones (Hoyles & Tregeagle, 2007), could be used to reduce social isolation and allow social workers to reach out to service users. The internet may allow quicker initiation of communication to better identify where assistance is needed (although still shaped by the case management system). It may be easier for service users to use mobile phones and the internet (probably IM) to contact their social workers, rather than having to rely on the existing face-to-face contact initiated by social workers. ICT may increase the opportunities for the development of insight as it could allow family members to examine their 'forms' easily, at times that suit them. (As noted earlier the development of insight was a feature of the paper-based systems for a limited number of service users.). It could be used more actively than pen and paper because of the user-friendly genre of internet websites, easier distribution of forms through e-mail or a shared website and the ability of service users to decide when to use the case management forms, rather than completing them at the social worker's convenience; service users could consume texts over the longer term and return over time to examine issues on websites at times that suited them in more private ways. Finally, ICT could be seen as a way of making access to information easier if computers were made available to service users — the internet could assist in addressing the problem of insufficient information identified in this study (although the choice of websites could be a way of social workers attempting to shape service users' behaviour).

Attempts by social workers to control service users' behaviour could be altered in three ways. Firstly, through reducing intrusion of workers' values as service users could access forms independently by using them on-line. Secondly, by offering increased opportunities for service users to control the sequence of communication. Thirdly, by challenging social workers' concepts of childhood—young people's competency with technology is likely to confront social workers who feel that young people, as a group, are less competent than adults. ICT has a potentially creative and constructive role in contributing to the assessment, the provision of assistance and the way control may be exercised in case managed interventions.

Websites used in conjunction with case management could introduce changes in genre which help overcome problems of written texts: The capacity to personalise web-sites (perhaps with a picture of the young person such as in Face Book) could offer opportunities for service users to identify *with* case management records. Use of passwords could reduce the likelihood of untimely reminders of past events compared to paper-forms. Use of the internet for storage of documents may enable families to retain information into the future more effectively than in the current paper forms.

However, before these advantages can be explored, there are three barriers which must be considered. Firstly the current difficulty that service users experience in getting access to technology. Secondly, the predominant use of ICT by social workers for data gathering and intra-professional communication and limited experience and perhaps interest in using ICT to communicate. Thirdly, and related to the last point, the poorly resolved debate of how ICT may affect social work communication. Altering these factors will be a challenge for resources and for

social workers themselves who may be reluctant to share the potential of ICT.

CONCLUSION

This paper has explored the potential for standardised case management systems to be teamed with ICT to increase family members' involvement in child welfare decision making. Whilst the case management systems have been shown to have a more limited impact on participation than may have originally been envisaged, they do allow greater opportunities for family members to be heard, than is currently the situation. There are important reasons to consider using ICT with these systems to increase participation in child welfare interventions. This paper has drawn attention to the wide-spread expectations that ICT will be used, including the aspirations of service users to take advantage of the efficiencies allowed by the internet. Understandings of communication over the internet show that earlier social work fears about impact on relationships and debate restricted to the impact of data bases are inadequate responses. Problems with written-text in case management interventions are significant and ICT could assist in addressing current barriers to communication.

This paper urges social workers to reconsider ICT in their work – there is the danger that service users are becoming increasingly disadvantaged because of their exclusion from the now mainstream new communication technologies. Young people and their parents are open to the use of ICT and some service users have found there are innovative ways to solve social problems through access to the internet.

REFERENCES

Alvesson, M. (2002). *Postmodernism and Social Research*. Buckingham, UK: Open University Press.

Bell, M. (1998). 1999). The Looking After Children materials. A critical analysis of their use in practice. *Adoption & Fostering, 22*(4), 15–22.

Ben-Ze'ev, A. (2004). *Love Online: Emotions on the Internet*. Cambridge, UK: Cambridge University Press. doi:10.1017/CBO9780511489785

Blanchard, M., Metcalf, A., Degney, J., Herman, H., & Burns, J. (2008). Rethinking the digital divide: Findings from a study of marginalised young people's information communication technology (ICT) use. *Youth Studies Australia, 27*(4), 35–41.

Cashmore, J., & Paxman, M. (2006). Wards Leaving Care: Follow up five years on. *Children Australia, 31*(3), 18–25.

Cheers, D., Kufeldt, K., Klein, R., & Rideout, S. (2007). Comparing Care: The Looking After Children system in Australia and Canada. *Children Australia, 32*(2), 21–28.

Cheers, D., & Morwitzer, J. (2006). Promoting resilient outcomes in Australia with the Looking After Children Electronic System (LACES). In Flynn, R. J., Dudding, P. M., & Barber, J. G. (Eds.), *Promoting Resilience in Child Welfare*. Ottawa, Canada: University of Ottawa Press.

Christensen, H., Griffiths, K., & Jorm, A. F. (2004). Delivering interventions for depression by using the Internet: Randomised controlled trials. *British Medical Journal, 328*(7434), 265–268. doi:10.1136/bmj.37945.566632.EE

Cleaver, H., & Walker, S. (2004). From Policy to Practice: The implementation of a new framework for social work assessments of children and families. *Child & Family Social Work, 9*, 81–90. doi:10.1111/j.1365-2206.2004.00314.x

Create Foundation. (2001). *Participation in Case Planning Processes. A Consultation with Children and Young People in Care about their Experiences of Decision Making*. Sydney, Australia: Create Foundation.

Curtis, K., Robert, H., Copperman, J., & Liabo, K. (2004). "How come I don't get asked no questions?" Researching "hard to reach" children and teenagers. *Child & Family Social Work, 9*, 167–175. doi:10.1111/j.1365-2206.2004.00304.x

Drolet, M., & Sauve-Kobylecki, M. (2006). The needs of children in care and the Looking After Children approach: Steps towards promoting children's best interests. In Flynn, R. J., Dudding, P. M., & Barber, J. G. (Eds.), *Promoting Resilience in Child Welfare*. Ottawa, Canada: University of Ottawa Press.

Fairclough, N. (1992). *Discourse and Social Change*. Cambridge, UK: Polity Press.

Fernandez, E. (2007). Supporting children and responding to families: Capturing the evidence on family support. *Children and Youth Services Review*. doi:10.1016/j.childyouth.2007.05.012

Francis, J. (2002). Implementing the Looking After Children in Scotland materials: Panacea or stepping-stone? *Social Work Education, 21*(4), 457–463. doi:10.1080/02615470220150401

Garrett, P. M. (2003). *Remaking Social Work with Children and Families. A Critical Discussion of the "Modernisation" of Social Care*. London: Routledge. doi:10.4324/9780203380765

Garrett, P. M. (2004). The electronic eye: Emerging surveillant practices in social work with children and families. *European Journal of Social Work, 7*(1), 57–71. doi:10.1080/136919145042000217401

Garrett, P. M. (2005). Social work's 'electronic turn': Notes on the deployment of information and communication technologies in social work with children and families. *Critical Social Policy, 25*(4), 529–553. doi:10.1177/0261018305057044

Gilbertson, R., & Barber, J. C. (2004). The systemic abrogation of standards in foster care. *Australian Journal of Social Work, 57*(1), 31–45. doi:10.1111/j.0312-407X.2003.00112.x

Gilbertson, R., & Barber, J. G. (2002). Obstacles to involving children and young people in foster care research. *Child & Family Social Work, 7*(4), 253–258. doi:10.1046/j.1365-2206.2002.00251.x

Gubrium, J. F., & Holstein, J. A. (Eds.). (2003). *Postmodern Interviewing*. Thousand Oaks, CA: Sage.

Henman, P., & Adler, M. (2003). Information technology and the governance of social security. *Critical Social Policy, 23*(2), 139–163. doi:10.1177/0261018303023002002

Heptinstall, E. (2000). Gaining access to looked after children for research purposes: Lessons learned. *British Journal of Social Work, 30,* 867–872. doi:10.1093/bjsw/30.6.867

Hough, G. (1996). *Information Technology in the Human Services: Whose Dreams, Whose Realities?* Paper presented at the HUSITA 4 Dreams and Realities: Information Technology and the Human Services, Finland.

Hoyles, B., & Tregeagle, S. (2007, 1-3 May). *Harnessing Information and Communication Technology in work with young people.* Paper presented at the Are we there yet? Conference, Melbourne, Australia.

Hutchby, I. (2001). Technologies, texts and affordances. *Sociology, 35*(2), 441–456.

Hutchby, I. (2003). Affordances and the analysis of technologically mediated interaction. *Sociology, 37*(3), 581–589. doi:10.1177/00380385030373011

Jackson, S., & Kilroe, S. (1996). *Looking After Children: Good Parenting, Good Outcomes Reader*. London: The Stationery Office.

Joinson, A. N. (2001). Self-disclosure in computer-mediated communication: the role of and visual anonymity. *European Journal of Social Psychology, 31,* 177–192. doi:10.1002/ejsp.36

Joinson, A. N. (2005). Internet Behaviour and the Design of Virtual Methods. In Hine, C. (Ed.), *Virtual Methods: Issues in Social Research on the Internet*. New York: Berg.

Jones, H. (2006). The Integrated Children's System: A resilient system to promote the development in children in care. In Flynn, R. J., Dudding, P. M., & Barber, J. G. (Eds.), *Promoting Resilience in Child Welfare*. Ottowa, Canada: University of Ottowa Press.

Klease, C. (2008). Silenced stakeholders: Responding to mothers' experiences of the child protection system. *Children Australia, 33*(3), 21–28.

Kufeldt, K., McGilligan, L., Klein, R., & Rideout, S. (2006). The Looking After Children assessment process: Promoting resilient children and resilient workers. *Families in Society, 87*(4), 565–574.

Kufeldt, K., Simard, M., Vachon, J., Baker, J., & Andrews, T. L. (2000). *Looking After Children in Canada: Final Report*. Report to Social Development Partnerships of Human Resources Development Canada: University of New Brunswick University Laval.

Leonard, M. (2005). *With a capital "G": Gatekeepers and gate-keeping in research with children*. Unpublished manuscript, Queens University Belfast, Ireland.

Maher, D. (2008). Cyberbullying: An ethnographic case study of one Australian upper primary school class. *Youth Studies Australia, 27*(4), 50–57.

Munro, E. (2001). Empowering looked after children. *Child & Family Social Work, 6,* 129–137. doi:10.1046/j.1365-2206.2001.00192.x

Munro, E. (2005). What tools do we need to improve identification of child abuse. *Child Abuse Review, 14*, 374–388. doi:10.1002/car.921

OECD. (2006). *Are students ready for a technology rich world?* Retrieved July 20, 2006 from www.pisa.oecd.org

Orgad, S. (2005). From online to offline and back: Moving from online to offline relationships with research informants. In Hine, C. (Ed.), *Virtual Methods: Issues in Social Research on the Internet.* New York: Berg.

Pakula, K. (2006, July 1-2). OMG! Your such a chatterbox. *Sydney Morning Herald,* p. 21.

Palfrey, J., & Gasser, U. (2008). *Born digital: Understanding the first generation of digital natives.* New York: Basic Books.

Parker, R., Ward, H., Jackson, S., Aldgate, J., & Wedge, P. (1991). *Looking After Children: Assessing outcomes in child care.* London: HMSO.

Parton, N. (2008). Changes in the form of knowledge in social work: From the "social" to the "informational". *British Journal of Social Work, 38*, 253–269. doi:10.1093/bjsw/bcl337

Parton, N. (2009). Challenge to practice and knowledge in child welfare social work: From the "social" to the "informational"? *Children and Youth Servcies Review,* (doi:10.1016/j.childyouth.2009.01.008).

Sapey, B. (1997). Social work tomorrow: Towards a critical understanding of technology in social work. *British Journal of Social Work, 27*(6), 803–814.

Searing, H. (2003). The continuing relevance of casework ideas to longterm child protection work. *Child & Family Social Work, 8*, 311–320. doi:10.1046/j.1365-2206.2003.00279.x

Thomas, N. (2005). Has anything really changed? Managers' views of looked after children's participation in 1997 and 2004. *Adoption & Fostering, 29*(1), 67–77.

Tidwell, L. C., & Walther, J. B. (2002). Computer-mediated communication effects on disclosure, impressions and interpersonal evaluations. Getting to know one another a bit at a time. *Human Communication Research, 28*(3), 317–348. doi:10.1111/j.1468-2958.2002.tb00811.x

Tilbury, C. (2004). The influence of performance measurement in child welfare policy and practice. *British Journal of Social Work, 34*, 225–241. doi:10.1093/bjsw/bch023

Tolley, S. (2005). SCARF: Supporting Children and Responding to Families. *National Child Protection Council Newsletter, 13*(2), 16–19.

Tregeagle, S. (2008). *Service Users' Experiences of Case Managed Interventions.* Paper presented at the Australian National Foster Care Conference.

Tregeagle, S., & Darcy, M. (2007). Child Welfare and Information and Communication Technology: Today's challenge. *British Journal of Social Work.* doi:10.1093/bjsw/bcm048

Tregeagle, S., & Mason, J. (2008). Service user experience of participation in child welfare case management. *Child & Family Social Work.* doi:10.1111/j.1365-2206.2008.00564.x

Tyler, T. R. (2002). Is the Internet changing social life? It seems the more things change, the more they stay the same. *The Journal of Social Issues, 58*(1), 195–205. doi:10.1111/1540-4560.00256

Valentine, G., Butler, R., & Skelton, T. (2001). The ethical and methodological complexities of doing research with "vulnerable" young people. *Ethics Place and Environment, 4*(2), 119–124. doi:10.1080/13668790120061497

Victorian Government. (2003). *Public parenting: A review of home-based care in Victoria.* Melbourne, Australia: Victorian Government.

Walther, J. B. (1996). Computer-mediated communication: Impersonal, interpersonal and hyperpersonal interaction. *Human Communication Research, 23,* 3–43.

Wheelaghan, S., & Hill, M. (2000). The Looking After Children records system: An evaluation of the Scottish pilot. In Iwaniec, D., & Hill, M. (Eds.), *Child Welfare Policy and Practice* (pp. 143–164). London: Jessica Kingsley Publishers Ltd.

Wise, S. (1999). *The UK Looking After Children Approach in Australia.* Paper presented at the 11th Biennial Foster Care Organisation Conference, Melbourne, Australia.

Wise, S. (2003a). An evaluation of a trial of Looking After Children in the State of Victoria, Australia. *Children Australia, 17,* 3–17.

Wise, S. (2003b). Using Looking After Children to create an Australian out-of-home care database. *Children Australia, 28*(2), 38–44.

This work was previously published in International Journal of Information Communication Technologies and Human Development, Volume 2, Issue 2, edited by Susheel Chhabra and Hakikur Rahman, pp. 17-33, copyright 2010 by IGI Publishing (an imprint of IGI Global).

Chapter 7
Deploying Information and Communication Technologies (ICT) to Enhance Participation in Local Governance for Citizens with Disabilities

John C. Bricout
University of Central Florida, USA

Paul M. A. Baker
Georgia Institute of Technology, USA

ABSTRACT

Information and Communication Technologies (ICT) offer a promising technology for citizens with disabilities to participate in local e-governance planning and implementation, provided that underlying issues of social exclusion and technology accessibility are properly addressed. Existing research suggests that for citizens with disabilities gateway issues such as technology access, usability, community- and government-receptivity are barriers to participation in local e-governance. Results from a pilot study indicate that the e-governance landscape for people with disabilities is heterogeneous; likely reflecting both differences within the disability community, as well as among the online governance entities. Systematic changes to the development, implementation, and evaluation of local e-governance for people with disabilities are recommended, informed by an analytical model suitable for empirical testing.

INTRODUCTION

Technology is tasked with enhancing the 'reach' of humanity, and so-called 'technologies of citizenship' are meant to help vulnerable populations increase their capacity for participation

DOI: 10.4018/978-1-4666-0047-8.ch007

(Dowse, 2009). Information and Communication Technologies (ICT), such as the Internet, and wireless devices such as mobile phones and other Web-accessing technology, have been proposed as tools for enhancing the participation of people with disabilities in the public domain. People with disabilities use ICT both as consumers of, and contributors to public goods, services and

Copyright © 2012, IGI Global. Copying or distributing in print or electronic forms without written permission of IGI Global is prohibited.

policies (Jaeger, 2006). More especially, ICT hold the promise of enhancing the participation of people with disabilities in 'governance' or the web of coordinated governmental and non-governmental exchanges aimed at addressing social issues and public policy goals (Polat, 2005). The online dimension of governance, electronic or 'e-governance' is enabled by ICT. Individual participation has the greatest potential for impact at the local level of e-governance, as compared to larger regional, national or transnational aggregations, making local e-governance a good unit of analysis for examining the participation-enhancing qualities of ICT. Social and communication networks that link people to information, resources and each other lie at the core of e-governance participation. The principle challenge to participation in e-governance for people with disabilities stems from the fact that people with disabilities face social exclusion and accessibility barriers to communication technologies (Stienstra & Troschuk, 2005).

The relative value of ICT in the context of participation in local e-governance by people with disabilities is contingent upon inclusion and access; noting that rapid technological change, disablist attitudes and strong normalization pressures in a global society constitute barriers to both social inclusion and access (i.e., Roulstone, 2003). By enabling decentralized, distributed environments of exchange, ICT have occasioned the collapse of distance as a barrier in e-governance, but they have not occasioned a parallel collapse of social distance, which manifests itself in technical interface, social and interpersonal barriers. These barriers are embedded in both the ICT architecture and the transactions it carries. The question of how to make e-governance effective as an approach to enhancing the local government participation of people with disabilities arises naturally from this discussion.

A significant first step in addressing this question of effectiveness is to explore the role of the e-governance ICT 'environments'; social and technological, in influencing local government participation. This paper critically examines the extant research literature and reports Web-based pilot study findings to propose an analytical model, suitable for empirical testing that links aspects of the users and ICT environment to e-government participation. The analytical model describes how the ICT environment mediates key transactions between person-level traits of citizens with disabilities and system-level e-governance participation. Recommendations for future research, policy and practice are generated from the model.

Local government has a critical role to play as the front-line resource for local services, information and social goods, as well as being the most accessible point for participative democracy in the lives of disadvantaged, marginalized populations (Odendaal, 2003). However, the experience of people with disabilities engaged in partnerships with local government authorities point to enduring barriers to participation attributable to unequal power relations, negative perceptions of ability, lack of knowledge, and inadequate consultation (i.e., Barnes, 2002; Piggot, Sapey, & Wilenius, 2005; Riddington, Mansell, & Beadle-Brown, 2008). These challenges to local government participation do not stem from ICT, nor is ICT their solution. However, the social networks and social capital that ICT can facilitate are relevant to a solution. Both the social inclusion challenges and the role of ICT in providing a solution will be discussed later.

As governments around the globe have sought to increase ease of access to public information, services and feedback they have used the Web as a platform for communication and outreach (Martinez-Moyano & Gil-Garcia, 2004). This Web-based platform has become known as electronic government, or digital government; commonly shortened to 'e-government.' E-government is typically one of several nodes in e-governance, albeit an important one. There exists a great deal of variation in the sophistication in e-government services, varying along lines of

Web page accessibility, clarity, recentness of information, integration with services, capacity for public exchange, and linkages to reliable pages off-site (Asgarkhani, 2005; Martinez-Moyano, & Gil-Garcia, 2004). In the United States alone, the sheer number of local governments in the United States, estimated at 87,525 (U.S. Census, 2002) virtually assures a great deal of variation in e-government. The complexity of the system is increased when governance, a critical mechanism for extending the reach of local government is factored in.

Governance refers to both a process and a network, inherently political in nature that links statutes, resources, services, information and goods (Torres, Pina, & Acerete, 2006). Governance takes place through the delivery of public services, information and tools (Polat, 2005). People with disabilities constitute a marginalized population whose needs are poorly understood in local governance affairs (Kazemikaitiene & Bileviciene, 2008). What is called for is 'good governance;' an approach that alters the relationship between government and the various communities that compose 'the public' opening channels for citizen discourse and participation (Polat, 2005). Good governance is grounded in accessible and responsive mechanisms of government, as well as in non-governmental nexuses of exchange and coordinated action, to achieve public policy goals and address social issues (Polat, 2005).

Involving citizens in governance, alternately framed as 'citizen governance' or 'democratic governance', shifts the emphasis from service delivery and organization to knowledgeable community, as well as individual involvement in decision making, through neighborhood or community meetings and consultations, engaging local government directly (John, 2009; Polat, 2005). The social exclusion, marginalization and socioeconomic disparities experienced by people with disabilities makes citizen involvement the core emphasis in discussions of local governance, which calls attention to the need for strategies and resources that address inequality-related barriers to participation in local governance. E-governance uses ICT to link electronic, or e-government resources with the civil, administrative and political spheres in service of more responsive public planning, activity and outreach (Odendall, 2003; Torres et al., 2006).

The aim of e-governance is to enhance the interactions between citizens and government, but is contingent upon the social and political frameworks in which it is embedded (Torres et al., 2006). This same thesis obtains for the ICT that form the connective tissues of e-governance networks. ICT can provide bridges to representative democracy, especially at the local level where some observers have decried a diminishment of interest in local government. For such bridges to representative democracy to be effective the interfaces and online media must be accessible to all users and local government entities must make policy choices, adopt management strategies and embrace a culture of institutional inclusiveness (Polat, 2006).

Whilst ICT can provide a suitable medium for citizens with disabilities to participate in local government through the medium of e-governance, several preconditions must be met: that the ICT is not only accessible, or available and functional for users in general, but also 'usable, that is to say, adaptable to the needs and preferences of specific end users. In addition, the e-governance network must be designed for public discourse, consultation and debate, giving the citizens' inputs and discourse equal weight with that of officials (Asgarkhani, 2005; Jaeger, 2006).

There is a dearth of studies on the effectiveness of e-governance resources for persons with disabilities – of major consequence to both the citizenry and government (Kazemikaitiene & Bileviciene, 2008). However, the extant literature indicates that for a variety of reasons, citizens with disabilities constitute a group that can be difficult to consult with on governance issues, due to lack of Internet connectivity and accessibility, as well as content barriers (Sienstra & Troschuk, 2005). Content barriers are complex to address, due to assumed levels of knowledge, or more broadly, ICT literacy, on the part of users (Anderson et al., 2004). Computer literacy and knowledge of the Web may be less prevalent among people with disabilities than in the general population. Certainly, people with disabilities have lower rates of computer ownership and Internet access, and continue to face accessibility issues, due to low usage of existing usability guideline, guideline limitations, and a diverse user population (Leuthold, Bargas-Avila, & Opwis, 2008).

People with disabilities are a heterogeneous group with vastly different needs for ICT adaptations, as well as different resources reflecting attributes of their impairments and the compensatory or assistive technologies available to them (Anderson, Bohman, Burmeister, & Sampson-Wild, 2004). Although they are subject to common trends, such as social exclusion and barriers to participation, they cannot be considered in a monolithic fashion, so the local e-governance system must have built in flexibility and responsiveness to a diverse group of citizens. The environment in which ICT influences participation of people with disabilities in local e-governance must, therefore, be reckoned to have social as well as technological dimensions, and to involve individual or personal level variables as well as institutional and systemic factors.

THEORETICAL CONTEXT

The civic engagement of persons with disabilities must be placed in a theoretical context that links the major factors influencing local e-governance participation: citizenship, the digital divide, social networks, social capital, and the ecological perspective. Each of these factors will be discussed in turn.

Citizenship

'Citizenship' is a basic characteristic of democratic access, of which voting and the electoral process play major roles (Redley, 2008). Citizenship is more broadly conceptualized in terms of social, political and civic or civil participation, and includes both rights and corresponding responsibilities (e.g., Barton, 1993; Rummery, 2006). At the centre of the concept of citizenship is the balance between rights and responsibilities; a balance that is poised in a larger context of power politics, despite the fact that democracy is presumed to involve equality among citizens (John, 2009; Roulstone, 2007). For people with disabilities, who experience a lower power position than the general population, and for whom the interests of the general population in a representative democracy too often prevail, the emphasis must be upon rights because responsibilities require the means to discharge them. In the absence of necessary resources or capacities, 'responsibilities' become a yolk in the guise of equal accountability among an unequal citizenry. The 'active citizen', an individual who is employed and contributing to the 'enterprise culture,' is tendered as the model against which individual behavior is benchmarked. Those persons who are insufficiently 'active' are deemed less substantial citizens (Barton, 1993; Ebersold, 2007). Other authors have decried the role of disabling barriers, including an emphasis on productivity and forced dependence on goodwill in the lack of recognition and diminishment of citizenship status for persons with disabilities (Ebersold, 2007; Rummery, 2006).

Citizenship is clearly linked to issues of identity, and for people with disabilities 'identity' is often linked to a particular explanatory model of disability. This model, in turn guides their efforts at obtaining equal citizenship (Hughes, 2009). Several models of disability are relevant to this discussion: the social model, the medical model, the multi-causal or integrated model, and the biosocial model. Many individuals either explicitly or implicitly identify their disability, and thus their peer group in terms of one of these models (Hughes, 2009). The social model of disability posits that disability is a social construction and sets aside considerations of bodily changes, whereas the medical model focuses on bodily impairments, focused on the normalization of impaired bodies (Freund, 2001). The World Health Organization's International Classification of Functioning Disability and Health (ICF) presents a model of disablement that maps the interactions between personal, health condition, social and environmental factors into a single framework, thereby integrating social and medical models (Stucki, Reinhardt, Grimby, & Melvin, 2008).

The social model has spurred a social movement focused on rights-based accommodations, whereas the medical model has inspired a health movement focused on illness-based accommodations. An integrated health and rights model has prompted an emergent group of 'biological citizens' to focus on overcoming illness with due consideration to social and political reform (Hughes, 2009). Citizens who are stalwarts of the social model of disability will focus on reconstituting society, whereas citizens who are stalwarts of a biosocial model will seek change in dialogue with the medical community (Hughes, 2009). These distinctions have direct relevance to local e-governance inasmuch as the individual with a disability whose identity gravitates towards the biological or biosocial citizen will likely want local e-governance to engage him or her in health consultations, information and exchange far more than the individual who leans towards a social citizen identity and thus emphasizes social and political change. These are, of course, broad characterizations.

Political efficacy, which refers to one's sense of mastery of the political process, is also very important to fostering responsive e-governance. For people with disabilities, political efficacy, together with political participation, are lower for people with disabilities than the general population (Schur, Shields, & Schriner, 2003). People with disabilities seem to believe that government is less receptive to their needs (Schur et al., 2003). This appears to be particularly true for individuals who are unemployed, with education and income as major issues (Schur et al., 2003), again suggesting social and structural barriers related to exclusion. Connection to social networks, community or interpersonal 'connectedness' has been positively linked to citizenship, suggesting an alternative model for full citizenship to the productivity-centric model (Ebersold, 2007; Redley, 2008). Righting this imbalance to favor the citizenship of persons with disabilities requires both access to productive roles held by 'active' citizens, and a deepening of community and strategies to redress power inequalities. In principle, local government ought to afford persons with disabilities with more opportunities to create and deepen community through online connections that extend offline to local venues. Given that in principle, local government is more readily influenced by its citizens than larger polities, persons with disabilities ought to be able to take on more active roles.

Digital Divide

Worldwide differences in ICT accessibility and ICT literacy, corresponding to differences in wealth at the national level, as well as within country differences has been identified as a threat to the effectiveness of e-government (Asgarkhani, 2005). People with disabilities continue to face a digital divide characterized by ICT accessibility and usability gaps (Ritchie & Blanck, 2003). Moreover, the 'digital' in the divide is confounded by the socioeconomic divide, which is both cause and effect, reminding us that closing the gaps entails offline as well as online barriers to participation (Bricout, Baker, Ward, & Moon, 2010; Kazemikaitiene & Bileviciene, 2008). The participation of people with disabilities in governance is rendered problematic in part by economic and social disparities, inequities and negative public perceptions, amounting to a non-responsive system (Edwards, 2008). Similarly, in the e-governance context, people with disabilities have encountered systematic barriers to participation due to lack of Internet connectivity and accessibility, Web literacy, as well as content barriers (Stienstra & Troschuk, 2005).

As has been noted previously, people with disabilities are a heterogeneous group, or what might be termed 'multiple accessibility audiences,' when it comes to online materials (Anderson et al., 2004). Barriers to ICT access vary with education level and employment status as well as type and severity of impairment, financial resources and adaptive technology costs. For some groups, such as people who are blind, delays in adaptive technology may be most problematic. For other groups, such as individuals with neurological disabilities, adaptations may be prohibitively costly, while for still others, such as individuals with intellectual disabilities, appropriate content may not have been developed (Dobransky & Hargittai, 2006). To the extent that the data exist, the track record of tools and legislation to help promote accessibility in making E-government sites accessible around the globe has been uneven (Hong, Katterattanakul, & Joo, 2008; Wong & Welch, 2004). Federal legislation in the United States, namely, the 1998 Amendments to Section 508 of the Rehabilitation Act, mandates accessible electronic and information technologies for all Federal Agencies. Internationally, the World Wide Web Consortium's (W3C), Web Content Accessibility Guidelines (WCAG) 2.0 launched in December, 2008 provide principles and guidelines for online accessibility (WC3, 2008).

Online accessibility remains challenging for some groups. For instance, the WCAG guidelines are not comprehensive enough for blind Internet users (Leuthold et al., 2007) or people with cognitive disabilities (Anderson et al., 2004). Moreover, our current state of knowledge may be lacking in terms of generating optimal guidelines, or more broadly, accessibility tools and training.

People with intellectual disabilities constitute a case in point. Only very recently have the online habits of people with intellectual disabilities been studied: in terms of online or e-learning (Fitchen et al., 2009), computer competence (Wong, Cha, Li-Tsang, & Lam, 2009) and use of blogs (McClimens & Gordon, 2009). The findings of the Wong et al. study in particular confirm the need for additional training in the use of ICT by people with intellectual disabilities based on a careful assessment of their readiness in terms of key cognitive and spatial skills, thus moving far beyond the considerations of current guidelines.

Online Social Networks and Social Capital

By employing Web 2.0 media, such as blogs and social networking sites, it is possible to traverse, or at least influence the offline sphere from the virtual sphere. Online social networks have the capacity to influence the offline sphere in terms of social networks and social capital (Soderstrom, 2009; Williams, 2006). Social networks describe the nature of linkages between individuals, whereas social capital captures the reciprocal bonds of relational trust. Online social networks facilitate extended relational ties, termed 'weak (network) ties' conducive to collective action and community building, and 'bridging' social capital, or reciprocal trusting relationships that link individuals to groups outside their habitual circle, offline as well as online (Williams, 2006). There is evidence to suggest that online social interactions enhance social capital formation (Best & Krueger, 2006). For persons with disabilities the social network is typically not as large as people without disabilities, most notably, their ties tend to be exclusive, rather than inclusive, to the detriment of participation (Clement & Bigby, 2009). Borrowing from research in the general population, it is anticipated that the presence of community related social networks and social capital will influence the political participation of persons with disabilities (i.e., Ikeda & Richey, 2005). Thus, a reasonable argument can be made that online social networks can provide persons with disabilities a mechanism for enhancing social capital and social networks both online and offline to augmenting both their participation in society, citizenship status and role.

Social networking ICT can be deployed strategically to span the online-offline boundary, specifically aimed at closing the participation gap in local governance by people with disabilities. More specifically, online social networks can be used to redress the power asymmetry between persons with disabilities and the general population by means of the medium's social networking and social capital building capabilities. The ensuing symmetrical balance of power would increase both the investment in, and receptivity of local government towards persons with disabilities. E-governance is intriguing because it can either serve as an instrument to enhance civic participation, or as a mechanism for socially progressive technological policy and design. From a policy standpoint, E-governance can be deployed strategically to span the online-offline boundary, specifically aimed at closing the participation gap in local governance by people with disabilities. An analytical framework, using an ecological perspective is proposed to illustrate the role of ICT in facilitating local governance participation for people with disabilities.

Ecological Perspective

An ecological approach to understanding the context of disabled citizen engagement is grounded in Bronfenbrenner's social ecology model (Bronfenbrenner, 1992), which requires that the transactions between the individual with a disability and his or her environment be taken into account. The environment is conceived as a series of concentric rings around the individual, with which she or he transacts in the course of activities, beginning with the most immediate environment, or micro

system, for example, the family, to the most distal environment, or macro system, for example culture in the guise of norms (Bricout & Gray, 2006). Such transactions result from 'negotiations' between person and environment that are not strictly attributable to either the person or the environment, but are nonetheless grounded in context: for example, civic engagement activities, such as seeking polling station information with local government online, may combine aspects of personal preferences in terms of proximate locations, together with considerations of the limited availability of accessible polling environments (Ward, Baker, & Moon, 2009). The ecological perspective also assumes that people are adaptive and that the particular adaptation will reflect the opportunities, resources and impediments arising from their transactions with the relevant environment (Trickett, 2009). For citizens with disabilities their transactions with local e-governance take place at several levels: at the institutional level as they engage in exchanges with e-government or non-governmental organizations online, at the personal level as they participate in social media, such as blogs, Facebook or Twitter, and across levels as they use social media, such as Facebook or Twitter to interact with government or government officials.

RESEARCH DESIGN

Web Study

A Web-based study was conducted as part of a larger study on Web 2.0 accessibility for people with disabilities. The purpose of the study was to explore the factors surrounding engagement by people with disabilities in local e-governance, including e-government sites and social networking sites. The study aims were to: (a) analyze the use of online social media for local e-governance communication and, (b) to analyze the acces-

Table 1. Top ten small digital cities

City	Population
Lynchburg, VA	72,596
Flower Mound, TX	69,307
Jupiter, FL	48,879
Blacksburg, VA	41,796
Charlottesville, VA	46,302
Annapolis, MD	36,524
Medford, OR	73.212
Delray Beach, FL	64,717
Manchester, CT[1]	56, 385
Boynton Beach, FL	68,291

NB: [1] Manchester was omitted from the search due to the number of non-related results that emerged during the search process.

sibility, readability, content, and interactivity of governance-related Websites on disability issues.

First, social media communication by local e-government was examined. The local government sample was drawn from the ten best 'digital' small cities' as rated by the 2008 Digital Cities Survey. The presence and use of local e-government information in selected social media was explored. Second, a cross-platform examination of Web site accessibility, readability and grade level scoring indexes was conducted on nine high-traffic Websites.

Survey of Local E-Government-Social Media Use

The first phase of the research examined the interactive links between best digital small cities local government Websites, Web pages in social media sites, and use of local e-government information. This investigation was in response to two research questions: (1) how is local e-government content integrated into key social media spaces, and (2) how do people make use of that content? Facebook and Twitter were selected as the social media for study because of their dominance and continued user growth. In the absence of a direct indicator of e-government content use by the public the number

of government content 'fans' and 'followers,' for Facebook and Twitter respectively, were used.

Survey of E-Governance Website Accessibility

The second phase of the research explored several dimensions of the accessibility of selected high-traffic Websites to users with disabilities. This investigation was guided by two research questions: (1) how accessible are key local government and e-governance Websites, and (2) how do different types of Websites: e-government, non-profit and Web 2.0 (disability blogs) compare in terms of accessibility?

Methods

The ten digital cities 2008 'small city' category (30,000 - 74,999) winners were selected for study because of the advanced use of Web technologies (e-government and non-governmental) in those municipalities. Complete data were available online for nine of the ten cities, the exception being Manchester, Connecticut. Data were gathered on the following variables: (1) number of government Web pages, (2) number of Facebook fans of government pages, (3) number of government Twitter

Table 2. Government presence on Facebook

	Jul 2008 Pop (US Census)	# govt pages	# of fans of govt pages	Total # of pages	% of fans of govt pages vs. total fans	govt pages %total pages
Annapolis, MD	36,524	5	810	89	2.6%	5.6%
Blacksburg, VA	41,796	2	3059	17	45.3%	11.8%
Boynton Beach, FL	68,291	2	410	15	21.0%	13.3%
Charlottesville, VA	46,302	4	1585	66	7.2%	6.1%
Delray, FL	64,757	6	511	14	28.2%	42.9%
Flower Mound, TX	69,307	6	1384	31	40.3%	19.4%
Jupiter, FL	48,879	0	0	2	0.0%	0.0%
Lynchburg, VA	72,596	4	533	29	5.8%	13.8%
Medford, OR	73,212	3	103	14	14.1%	21.4%
Average						**14.9%**

profiles, and (4) number of followers of Twitter profiles. These data permit a preliminary picture of government-social media linkages. In order to establish a rough measure of government-social media permeability the percentage of Facebook fans of government and the percentage of Twitter followers of government profiles were calculated.

Web site accessibility on nine high-traffic Websites was assessed using WCAG 2.0 standards, while readability was evaluated using the Flesch-Kinkaid reading ease, and grade level measured using Flesch-Kinkaid scoring indexes. Those nine Websites were: (1) the 1st, 5th and 10th-ranked best small 'digital' cities rated by the 2008 Digital Cities Survey, (2) three non-profit sites; the Municipal Research and Services Center of Washington (state), the National Organization on Disability, and the International Commission on Technology & Accessibility, and (3), three prominent disability blogs: the U.S. Social Security Disability Blog, the Disability Blogger and the Disability Blog Carnival. The accessibility data provide a preliminary exploration into the readiness of those Websites to engage users with disabilities on issues pertaining to local e-governance.

RESULTS

The results from the local e-government social media use survey data (Table 2 and Table 3) show a great deal of variability between cities, and within cities depending on the social medium. The percentage of Facebook fans of government pages, compared to total fans ranged from 0% to 45.3% with a mean score of 18.3%. The number of Facebook fans varied from zero for Jupiter, Florida, to 3,059 for Blacksburg, Virginia. However, Jupiter had no Facebook pages, so perhaps a better comparison would be between Flower Mound, Texas with 1,384 fans and Delray, Florida with 511 fans, both of which had six government pages. Interestingly, Flower Mound had the most groups (2) in the top five Facebook pages which suggests more significant 'uptake' of the e-government content.

Followers of government profiles on Twitter, as a percentage of all followers also showed a considerable variability, from 16.8% to 81.2% with a mean score of 54.5%. Flower Mound, which was a stand-out in Facebook along several dimensions, was also a 'use-intensity' leader in Twitter, with the largest percentage of government profile followers (81.2%), despite a modest

Table 3. Government presence on Twitter

	Jul 2008 Pop (US Census)	# of govt twitter profiles	# of govt profile followers	Total # of twitter profiles	% followers of govt pages vs. total fans	govt pages % total pages
Annapolis, MD	36,524	4	1087	12	36.6%	5.6%
Blacksburg, VA	41,796	2	401	6	81.2%	11.8%
Boynton Beach, FL	68,291	1	164	4	71.9%	13.3%
Charlottesville, VA	46,302	6	1288	14	68.2%	6.1%
Delray, FL	64,757	3	1193	12	63.0%	42.9%
Flower Mound, TX	69,307	5	967	19	16.8%	19.4%
Jupiter, FL	48,879	2	278	14	31.3%	0.0%
Lynchburg, VA	72,596	4	1009	10	69.7%	13.8%
Medford, OR	73,212	5	1355	19	43.7%	21.4%
Average						29.6%

number (2) of government profiles. Indeed, the intensity of use appears to be a better measure of uptake than number of pages or profiles alone. Thus, Jupiter, without any government Facebook pages, nonetheless is a relative 'hot spot' for followers of its one Twitter profile at 71.9%. Similarly, Charlottesville, which appears to draw tepid responses on Facebook, eliciting only 7.2% of total fans for its four government pages drew a very robust 63% of total fans for its three Twitter profile followers, suggesting that its Twitter profiles have more impact than its Facebook pages. At the same time, the different nature of the Facebook medium and Twitter must be taken into account. Facebook offers far more diversions and competing content than Twitter, which may systematically depress the uptake of Facebook e-government content vis-à-vis Twitter. Overall, it is clear that e-government content finds an audience in the 'digital' cities, so a local e-governance must incorporate these media explicitly. The single most profound limitation of this survey is that it was not possible to specify users with disabilities, so the sample is drawn from the general population. Clearly, the results are only suggestive and exploratory at best. It is not possible to ascertain the disability status of users of e-government social media for a variety of practical and ethical reasons.

The results from the e-governance website accessibility survey (see Table 4 and Table 5) show that the municipal, non-profit and blog sites were fairly consistent, and positive, in their accessibility ratings. The National Organization on Disability (NOD) site rating is noticeably lower than the others, whereas the Charlottesville site is higher, but all sites rated 'A' or better (A, AA, or AAA). Those ratings were arrived at using the WCAG guidelines across the operability, understandability and robustness categories for which data were available. Grade level equivalence for written content, measured by the Flesch-Kincaid method, varied independently of the WCAG categories. Similarly, ease of reading, measured by the same method was independent of grade level, speaking to the complexity of the broader 'accessibility' issue.

However, a trend is still visible between grade level and reading ease, with higher grade level tending towards an inverse relationship with ease. Moreover, the high mean grade level of the non-profit Association Websites (18.8) and low level of ease (9.1) is markedly different from both the cities' averages (14.2 reading; 35.1 ease) and the

Table 4 High traffic websites: WCAG guideline content accessibility scores

		Perceivable *	Operable	Understandable	Robust
City Websites	Lynchburg, VA	A	AA	AA	A
	Charlottesville, VA	A	AAA	AAA	A
	Boynton Beach, FL	A	AA	AA	A
Association Websites	Municipal Research and Services Center of Washington (State)	A	AA	AA	A
	National Organization on Disability	A	A	A	A
	International Commission of Technology & Assessment	A	AA	AA	A
Blogs	Disability Blog Carnival	A	AA	AAA	A
	The Disability Blogger	A	AA	AA	A
	The Social Security Disability Blog	AA	AA	AA	A

NB: *No media on Webpage
Perceivable: "Information and user interface components must be presentable to users in ways they can perceive." (W3C, 2008 p. 6)
Operable: "User interface components and navigation must be operable: (W3C, 2008 p.11)
Understandable: "Information and the operation of user interface must be understandable." (W3C, 2008 p. 14)
Robust: "Content must be robust enough that it can be interpreted reliably by a variety of user agents, including assistive technology." (W3C, 2008 p. 17)

Table 5. High traffic websites: Flesch-Kinkaid content accessibility

		Flesch-Kincaid Reading Ease	Flesch-Kincaid Grade Level
City Websites	Lynchburg, VA	25.5	15.7
	Charlottesville, VA	35.9	14.0
	Boynton Beach, FL	43.9	12.9
	CATEGORY MEAN	**35.1**	**15.1**
Association Websites	Municipal Research and Services Center of Washington (State)	32.9	14.4
	National Organization on Disability	-9.1	21.9
	International Commission of Technology & Assessment	3.5	19.1
	CATEGORY MEAN	**9.1**	**18.5**
Blogs	Disability Blog Carnival	22.7	13.8
	The Disability Blogger	26.2	15.9
	The Social Security Disability Blog	55.9	11.14.2009
	CATEGORY MEAN	**34.9**	**13.6**

NB: Higher Reading Ease test scores indicate easier to read; Grade Level scores correspond to U.S. grade level.

blogs' (13.6 reading; 34.9 ease). Much of the analyzed blog content comes from people with disabilities, the targeted end-users and citizen group. The finding that such end-user content is on average significantly easier to read and more modest in grade level than the non-profits' content strongly suggests that a more inclusive e-gover-nance will require that all network collaborators calibrate their content to the user's preferences and literacy level. Thus, readiness to engage citizen users with disabilities appears to be vari-able and there is clearly need for improvement. Although the blogs examined were disability-focused, as were two of the non-profit associations, the remainder of the Websites (4:9) were general in their focus. This, in addition to the purposive nature of the small sample, forbids generalizability of the results to either disability-focused e-governance sites, or to general e-governance sites. As in the case of the social media survey, the data are suggestive and exploratory.

ANALYTICAL MODEL OF LOCAL E-GOVERNANCE ENVIRONMENT

The findings from the pilot study, considered in tandem with the research literature suggest that the environment in which local e-governance takes place has several dimensions. The model of ICT local e-governance environment captures those dimensions and the complex interactions between them. The complete model can be found in Figure 1. Consistent with a social ecological approach, the model posits that people with disabilities interact as unique individuals with idiosyncratic competencies, framed here in terms of 'individual capacity for local e-governance participation'. That individual capacity is understood to consist of a literacy

component and a political efficacy component. The individual or person-level factors are important to the model because of the heterogeneity of the population and its consequences to the adoption of ICT for participation in local e-governance. As the research literature indicates, the capacity of ICT to mediate the individual's participation in local e-governance has two dimensions: a social dimension and a technical dimension. The social dimension is rooted chiefly in the social capital and social networks that the individual can bring to bear, using online networks. The technical dimension is rooted principally in the interactive potential of the online medium, related to the accessibility of the interface ('Web accessibility') and the readability of the content ('Web content'). The pilot study findings provide additional evidence for the elusiveness and inconsistency on the technical dimension across e-governance elements (local government, non-profits and blogs). In fact, participation in the local e-governance system is clearly contingent upon the receptivity of that system towards collaboration and resource coordination. More generally, the e-governance network must collectively demonstrate a willing-

Figure 1. Model of ICT local e-governance environment

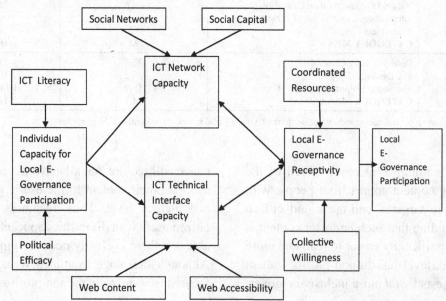

ness to engage people with disabilities, both as an intermediary step to local e-governance participation and as a feedback mechanism into building ICT network capacity.

Testing the Model

For some components of the model, standardized measures or established assessment protocols exist; for example, political efficacy measures, measures of computer literacy and knowledge of the Web, as aspects of ICT literacy. The social and Web components of ICT capacity are similarly amenable to assessment using tools already developed in the research literature. However, additional empirical research is clearly needed, given the nebulous nature of local e-governance in terms of system components and boundaries, the indefinite nature of resource coordination, and more especially the unknown parameters of 'collective willingness'. A sensible plan of research would begin with a descriptive study, using a purposive sample of local e-governance 'agents', preferably, local e-government, non-profit organizations and social media platforms that host e-governance content/interaction, to explore the nature and parameters of e-governance 'receptivity'. This study could be followed by a more sophisticated longitudinal study of the key model relationships over time. One of the strengths of the model is that it identifies 'leverage points' or factors that could be targeted for change that would yield a 'multiplier effect' in the system. Unfortunately, the most critical such point identified by the model, e-governance receptivity, is also the least clearly articulated. We propose that a reasonable indicator of e-government receptivity could be developed, by generating a composite index based on number of bi-direction channels, weighted by activity and diversity of activity. Given the relatively new state of multi-channel municipal initiatives this index is still in a conceptual phase. The proposed model thus remains tentative and preliminary in nature.

Policy and Practice Barriers and Opportunities

The model suggests that as potentially advantageous as ICT-based governmental services could be, it might yet fail to enhance e-governance participation. The history of technological deployment is replete with examples of poorly implemented public sector projects. One of the least anticipated risks is a peripheral one that relates to the *ramifications* of implementation rather than the implementation, as such. The failure of many otherwise well-intentioned systems has frequently been linked to the application of top-down design components that may overlook or misunderstand the needs and interests of impacted constituencies. We believe that without robust community use analysis (i.e., discernment of constituent needs and system design parameters), e-governance systems run the risk of failing to meet the needs of various constituencies within the population of persons with disabilities (Baker & Ward, 2002). In terms of an applied policy implementation, the model suggests that initial context survey and user needs assessment should be undertaken as part of the specification process. This could serve as a preliminary step in a comprehensive system design process, as the individual capacity for local e-governance participation, ICT literacy and political efficacy components are put to empirical test.

More formally, following the model, the first design consideration would be to undertake a community audit or assessment, to obtain a robust understanding of the characteristics, needs and objectives of the varied constituencies. This includes user characteristics, namely, the ICT and e-governance participation capacities and limitations of citizens with disabilities. Normatively, this would require an effort by local government to make participation a system design objective; in other words, a high-priority value. Additionally, the design process might include a critical evaluation ascertaining system accessibility, both programmatically and conceptually, in terms of the model's capacity building components. In this latter category, technology interface adaptations, such as making Web-based screen presentations readable by text-reading technology may be supplemented by additional design features, for instance, alternative presentations that would provide accessibility to users with communication or cognitive disabilities. Another consideration would be to build a menu of applications and services that, through delivery in an online format, increases the general ease and ability of persons with disabilities to engage public sector services. A final consideration would entail iterative input from those most likely to benefit for accessible services, in the design, testing and planning for system sustainability. There are additional, more complex barriers operating at different levels that might be measured, indirectly, by the local e-governance receptivity component of the model.

In the proposed model there is an iterative flow. Hence, when governments, constrained by laws and regulations within a physical world, extend their presence, reach and responsibilities into the virtual dimension, new legal issues will inevitably arise. Given the variability of user readiness, local resources, and competing public priorities, questions surrounding the adequacy of local governance ICT accessibility will admit no definitive answer. Nonetheless, as governments continue down the current path of virtualization, questions about the adequacy of local e-governance to the task of citizen engagement and participation for people with disabilities will have to be addressed. Moving beyond baseline e-governance network assessment, ongoing monitoring of the channels and subsequent fine-tuning of the system implementation, while not fully developed in our model, could address these issues.

CONCLUSION

Local e-governance encompassing virtual spaces requires that we re-conceptualize the way in which government operates. Specifically, it is critical to expand our notion of governance in terms of enhanced accessibility to community services and information, engagement with citizens, outreach and community development that is truly bi-directional or even multi-directional and founded in dialogue. This can be achieved, in part, with the deployment of the rich ecosystem of ICT-based communications and participation modes. These modes range from Web-based systems, social networking portals, twittering, e-mail, and voice over IP (VOIP), to immersive virtual environments. We have proposed a model for assessing and determining resources that could be brought to bear. We have also considered the possibilities for systemic coordination of those resources, decentralized in nature and arising from the disparate efforts of 'partners' responding to an emerging market of Web-involved citizens with disabilities. The multiplicity of virtual municipal channels would also take advantage of the motivated and willing providers in each domain of e-governance.

There are many practical realities to keep in mind as well. First, the user audience of virtual environments is about 73% of the population in the United States (Pew, 2008). By definition, these individuals have access to computers and the Internet. The model highlights the need for accessible e-governance to include resources for connectivity to be made available to citizens with disabilities, the majority of whom do not have Internet at home. In addition, citizens with disabilities must acquire a sufficient level of ICT literacy once 'connected' to make optimal use of local e-governance resources. Thus, the local community assessment component of the model must ensure not only that services and information are accessible, but also that they can be fully engaged, by ensuring that the user community knows *how* to engage them. The issue of ICT literacy, like the issue of access is intimately related to the larger socioeconomic context. People with disabilities are a marginalized population and must have access to more social, human and economic capital to acquire the necessary resources for both online participation and active citizenship. At the present time, accessible e-government entails a steep learning curve for local government; especially in the case of more advanced, immanent virtual environments.

Government receptivity hinges, in part, on creating user tools that help a first-time visitor engage. Developing such tools will be of paramount importance to the success of the online community. It will also signal a serious concern for the user/citizen. Considered from the perspective of system sustainability, the model's coordinated resources component points to the need for managers, administrators and policy makers to be present and active in the virtual environment on a regular basis. Without this presence, the e-governance platform runs the risk of generating mere "empty halls"; a situation in which the lights will be on but no one is at home, so to speak. Furthermore, in the absence of not only the instruments of participation, but also the resources to exercise persuasion, persons with disabilities will be unable to influence policy makers. More broadly, they will be excluded from the emerging discourse around deciding normative and legal conflicts between the real and virtual spheres of governance. Social media online (networking) outlets such as Facebook, Second Life, and Twitter could provide leverage towards greater local government engagement and inclusion. These social media allow the local community to engage the broader world as the obverse; for the world to embrace the community. In addition, online social media actually build community, locally as well as in a distributive fashion across communities. For people with disabilities this means building capacity to become more active in the public sphere collectively, as well as individually. This incipient democratic movement in no way negates the vital role of local government as a partner, nor does it obviate the need for public policy and public resources to create conditions favorable to increased civic engagement by people with disabilities. In fact, as our local governments begin the transition into a more 'digital persona' embedded in e-governance networks, it is imperative that the issues of participation and citizenship for people with disabilities raised in this paper are addressed.

ACKNOWLEDGMENT

The authors wish to acknowledge the research assistance of Jessica Paterson (GTRI) and partial research support of the Rehabilitation Engineering Research Center for Wireless Technologies, sponsored by the National Institute on Disability and Rehabilitation Research (NIDRR) of the U.S. Department of Education under grant number H133E060061. The opinions contained in this paper are those of the authors and do not necessarily reflect those of the U.S. Department of Education or NIDRR.

REFERENCES

W3C. (2008). Web content accessibility guidelines (WCAG) 2.0. *W3C Recommendation 11 December 2008*. Retrieved November 7, 2009 from www.w3.org/TR/ WCAG/#guidelines

Anderson, S., Bohman, P., Burmeister, O., & Sampson-Wild, G. (2004). User needs and e-Government accessibility: The future impact of WCAG 2.0. In Stary, C., & Stephanidis, C. (Eds.), *User Interface for All* (pp. 289–304). Berlin: Springer Verlag.

Asgarkhani, M. (2005). Digital government and its effectiveness in public management reform: A local government perspective. *Public Management Review*, 7(3), 465–487. doi:10.1080/14719030500181227

Baker, P. M. A., Bell, A., & Moon, N. W. (2009). Accessibility in municipal wireless networks: System implementation and policy considerations. In Reddick, C. (Ed.), *Strategies for local e-government adoption and implementation: Comparative studies, advances in e-government research book Series*. Hershey, PA: IGI Global.

Baker, P. M. A., & Ward, A. C. (2002). Bridging temporal and spatial "gaps": The role of information and communication technologies in defining communities. *Information Communication and Society*, 5(2), 207–224. doi:10.1080/13691180210130789

Barnes, M. (2002). Bringing difference into deliberation? Disabled people, survivors and local governance. *Policy and Politics*, 3(3), 319–331. doi:10.1332/030557302760094694

Barton, L. (1993). The struggle for citizenship: The case of disabled people. *Disability, Handicap & Society*, 8(3), 235–248. doi:10.1080/02674649366780251

Best, S. J., & Kreuger, B. S. (2006). Online interactions and social capital: Distinguishing between new and existing ties. *Social Science Computer Review*, 24(4), 395–410. doi:10.1177/0894439306286855

Bricout, J. C., Baker, P. M. A., Ward, A., & Moon, N. (2010). Teleworking and the digital divide. In Ferro, E., Dwivedi, Y., Gil-Garcia, R., & Williams, M. (Eds.), *Overcoming digital divides: constructing an equitable and competitive information society* (pp. 155–178). Hershey, PA: IGI Global.

Bricout, J. C., & Gray, D. B. (2006). Community receptivity: The ecology of disabled persons' participation in the physical, political and social environments. *Scandinavian Journal of Disability Research*, 8(1), 1–21. doi:10.1080/15017410500335229

Census, U. S. (2002). *Federal, State, and Local Governments: 2002 Census of Governments*. Retrieved July 1, 2009 from http://www.census.gov/ govs/www/cog2002.html

Chadwick, A. (2003). Bringing e-democracy back in: Why it matters for future research on e-governance. *Social Science Computer Review*, 21(4), 443–455. doi:10.1177/0894439303256372

Clement, T., & Bigby, C. (2009). Breaking out a distinct social space: Reflections on supporting community participation for persons with severe and profound intellectual disability. *Journal of Applied Research in Intellectual Disabilities*, 22, 264–275. doi:10.1111/j.1468-3148.2008.00458.x

Dowse, L. (2009). Some people are never going to be able to do that. Challenges for people with intellectual disability in the 21st Century. *Disability & Society*, 24(5), 571–584. doi:10.1080/09687590903010933

Ebersold, S. (2007). Affiliating participation for active citizenship. *Scandinavian Journal of Disability Research*, 9(3-4), 237–253. doi:10.1080/15017410701685893

Edwards, C. (2008). Participative urban renewal? Disability, community and partnership in New Labour's urban policy. *Environment and Planning*, 40(7), 1664–1680. doi:10.1068/a39199

Fitchen, C., Ferraro, V., Asuncion, J., Chowjka, C., Barile, M., Nguyen, M., Klomp, R., & Wolforth, J. (2009). Disabilities and e-learning problems and solutions: An exploratory study. *Educational technology & Society*, 12(4), 241-256.

Fruend, P. (2001). Bodies, disability and spaces: The social model and disabling spatial organizations. *Disability & Society*, 16(5), 689–706. doi:10.1080/09687590120070079

Hong, S., Katterattanakul, P., & Joo, S. (2008). Evaluating government accessibility: A comparative study. *International Journal of Information Technology & Decision Making, 7*(3), 419–515. doi:10.1142/S0219622008003058

Hughes, B. (2009). Disability activisms: social model stalwarts and biological citizens. *Disability & Society, 24*(6), 677–688. doi:10.1080/09687590903160118

Ikeda, K., & Richey, S. E. (2005). Japanese network capital: The impact of social networks on Japanese political participation. *Political Behavior, 27*(3), 239–252. doi:10.1007/s11109-005-5512-0

Jaeger, P. (2006). Telecommunications policy and individuals with disabilities: Issues of accessibility and social inclusion in the policy and research agenda. *Telecommunications Policy, 30*, 112–124. doi:10.1016/j.telpol.2005.10.001

John, P. (2009). Can citizen governance redress the representative bias of political participation? *Public Administration Review, 69*(3-4), 494–502. doi:10.1111/j.1540-6210.2009.01995.x

Kazemikaitiene, E., & Bileviciene, T. (2008). Problems of involvement of disabled persons in eGovernment. *Technology and Economic Development, 14*(2), 184–196. doi:10.3846/1392-8619.2008.14.184-196

Leuthold, S., Bargas-Avila, A., & Opwis, K. (2008). Beyond Web content accessibility guidelines: Design of enhanced text user interfaces for blind Internet users. *International Journal of Human-Computer Studies, 66*, 257–270. doi:10.1016/j.ijhcs.2007.10.006

Martinez-Moyano, I., & Gil-Garcia, J. R. (2004). Rules, norms, and individual preferences for action: An institutional framework to understand the dynamics of e-government evolution. In Traunmueller, R. (Ed.), *E-Government 2004* (pp. 194–199). Berlin: Springer-Verlag.

McClimens, A., & Gordon, F. (2009). Presentation of self in E-veryday life: How people labeled with intellectual disability manage identity as they engage the blogosphere. *Sociological Research Online, 13*(4).

Odendaal, N. (2003). Information and communication technology and local governance: Understanding the difference between cities in developed and emerging economies. *Computers, Environment and Urban Systems, 27*, 585–607. doi:10.1016/S0198-9715(03)00016-4

Pew Internet & American Life Project. (2008). *Degrees of Access* (May 2008 data). Washington, DC: Pew Research Center's Internet & American Life Project. Retrieved July 1, 2009 from http://www.pewinternet.org/Presentations/2008/Degrees-of-Access-%28May-2008-data%29.aspx

Piggot, L., Sapey, B., & Wilenius, F. (2005). Out of touch: Local government and disabled people's employment needs. *Disability & Society, 20*(6), 599–611. doi:10.1080/09687590500248365

Polat, R. K. (2005). The Internet and democratic local governance: The context of Britain. *The International Information & Library Review, 37*, 87–97. doi:10.1016/j.iilr.2005.04.001

Redley, M. (2008). Citizens with learning disabilities and the right to vote. *Disability & Society, 23*(4), 375–384. doi:10.1080/09687590802038894

Riddington, C., Mansell, J., & Beadle-Brown, J. (2008). Are partnership boards really valuing people? *Disability & Society, 23*(6), 649–665. doi:10.1080/09687590802328550

Ritchie, H., & Blanck, P. (2003). The promise of the internet for disability: A study of on-line services and website accessibility at Centers for Independent Living. *Behavioral Sciences & the Law, 21*, 5–26. doi:10.1002/bsl.520

Roulstone, A. (2003). Disability, new technology and the redefinition of space-opportunities and challenges. *Cognitive Processing, 4*, 1–12.

Roulstone, A. (2007). Citizenship and vulnerability: Disability and issues of social and political engagement. *Disability & Society, 22*(3), 329–337. doi:10.1080/09687590601141741

Rummery, K. (2006). Disabled citizens and social exclusion: The role of direct payments. *Policy and Politics, 34*(4), 633–650. doi:10.1332/030557306778553132

Schur, L., Shields, T., & Schriner, K. (2003). Can I make a difference? Efficacy, employment, and disability. *Political Psychology, 21*(1), 119–149. doi:10.1111/0162-895X.00319

Soderstrom, S. (2009). Offline social ties and online use of computers: A study of disabled youth and their use of ICT advances. *New Media & Society, 11*(5), 709–727. doi:10.1177/1461444809105347

Stienstra, D., & Troschuk, L. (2005). Emerging citizens with disabilities in eDemocracy. *Disability Studies Quarterly, 25*(2), e13.

Stucki, G., Reinharrdt, J. D., Grimby, G., & Melvin, J. (2008). Developing research capacity in human functioning and rehabilitation research from the comprehensive perspective based in the ICF-model. *European Journal of Physical Rehabilitation Medicine, 44*, 343–351.

Torres, L., Pina, V., & Basilio, A. (2006). E-governance developments in European Union cities: Reshaping government's relationship with citizens. *Governance: An International Journal of Policy. Administration and Institutions, 19*(2), 277–302.

Trickett, E. J. (2009). Community psychology: Individuals and interventions in community context. *Annual Review of Psychology, 60*, 395–419. doi:10.1146/annurev.psych.60.110707.163517

Ward, A., Baker, P. M. A., & Moon, N. (2009). Ensuring the enfranchisement of people with disabilities. *Journal of Disability Policy Studies, 20*, 79–92. doi:10.1177/1044207308325996

Williams, D. (2006). On and off the 'Net: Scales for social capital in an online era. *Journal of Computer-Mediated Communication, 11*, 593–628. doi:10.1111/j.1083-6101.2006.00029.x

Wong, A., Chan, C., Li-Tsang, C., & Lam, C. (2009). Competence of people with intellectual disabilities on using human-computer interface. *Research in Developmental Disabilities, 30*, 107–123. doi:10.1016/j.ridd.2008.01.002

Wong, W., & Welch, E. (2004). Does e-government promote accountability? A comparative analysis of Website openness and government accountability. *Governance: An International Journal of Policy, Administration, and Institutions, 17*(2), 275–297.

This work was previously published in International Journal of Information Communication Technologies and Human Development, Volume 2, Issue 2, edited by Susheel Chhabra and Hakikur Rahman, pp. 34-51, copyright 2010 by IGI Publishing (an imprint of IGI Global).

Chapter 8
E–Accessibility and Municipal Wi–Fi:
Exploring a Model for Inclusivity and Implementation

Paul M. A. Baker
Georgia Institute of Technology, USA

Alea M. Fairchild
Vrije Universiteit Brussel, Belgium

Jessica Pater
Georgia Tech Research Institute, USA

ABSTRACT

One of the typical design objectives of municipal Wi-Fi systems is the free or low-cost provision of connectivity for citizens, including people with disabilities and others impacted by the digital divide. This paper examines a range of municipal Wi-Fi implementation models for potential impact on e-accessibility. A comparative analysis was undertaken of sample U.S. and European municipal Wi-Fi systems to assess the business model and stakeholders involved in municipal wireless initiatives and to examine the degree of accessibility to or sensitivity of, municipal wireless systems for people with disabilities. As many people with disabilities are currently affected by social disparities in education and income, further marginalization of their communication and information access creates additional access barriers to critical information and full participation in community life.

WI-FI, ACCESSIBILITY, AND INCLUSIVITY

The progressively more common connectivity provided by wireless devices offers local governments 1) an opportunity to provide new and innovative services to citizens, and 2) the possibility

to expand access to those who might otherwise be excluded, yet would benefit from enhanced connectivity (U.S. NTIA, 2000, 2002). Municipal wireless systems[1] (municipal Wi-Fi/muni Wi-Fi) have been promoted as a tool for the provision of widespread wireless connectivity with associated benefits. Municipal officials, telecom providers, and concerned citizens in cities and regions have

DOI: 10.4018/978-1-4666-0047-8.ch008

rushed to develop plans to deliver Wi-Fi systems. A key rationale cited by municipalities for deploying these networks is their potential to bridge the digital divide by facilitating wider accessibility to broadband connectivity (Bar & Park, 2006; Chesley, 2009). According to a recent *Ars Technica* article (Fleishman, 2008), more than 300 systems in the United States have been implemented or are planned. However, a good number of initial start-up projects had been downsized or abandoned, even before the beginning of the recent economic recession (Fleishman, 2008). Similar estimates for the EU are difficult to come by, in part because actual system implementation is more problematic under EU regulation.[2]

To some extent, there is a "chicken and egg" relationship between the diffusion and adoption of these systems, and the perceived need for these systems. Broadband technology, and in this case, wireless implementations, has been seen as key to enhancing Internet diffusion (Papacharissi & Zaks, 2006; Sirbu, Lehr, & Gillett, 2006; Dingwall, 2007; Wallsten, 2005). Industry stakeholders and researchers have identified broadband access as necessary for the evolution of advanced communications services, as well as for associated economic growth (Gillett, Lehr and Osorio, 2003). The United States Congress also directed states and the FCC to encourage broadband deployment in a timely manner.[3] Despite these stated goals for faster broadband deployment, the U.S. has not adopted an official policy or regulation aimed at promoting or developing broadband deployment (FCC, 2005; FTC Report, 2006). The Broadband Technologies Opportunities Program, part of the American Recovery and Reinvestment Act of 2009, was recently funded $4.7 billion to support the deployment of broadband infrastructure in unserved and underserved areas. The program also encourages sustainable adoption of broadband services, making the need for implementing regulations and policy more timely than ever before.[4] Rationales for the development of municipal Wi-Fi systems include bridging the digital divide, enhancing economic development, reducing the cost of government, improving the level of services provided to the public, increased opportunities for education, and offering an alternative to the expensive process of physically cabling or laying fiber optics (Shein, 2005). Wi-Fi systems could ideally deliver Internet access to individuals at much lower cost than traditional broadband technology, and provide coverage via a ubiquitous "cloud" model or the creation of a network of "hot-spots".

Similarly, in the EU, the widespread introduction of broadband at affordable prices has been one of the chief objectives of the EU's i2010 action plan. The European Commission aims to achieve 100% high-speed internet coverage for all citizens by 2010 as part of the European Economic Recovery Plan. The EU is committed to ensuring that the continent's more remote and economically disadvantaged regions get the support they need to share in the benefits of economic growth. Digital technologies such as broadband Internet access can play a part in narrowing disparities between regions and helping to promote social and economic cohesion. The European Commission's Broadband Gap Policy has supported actions to develop an inclusive Information Society that embraces those who live in geographically less accessible areas (Dimireva, 2009).

While municipal Wi-Fi systems can potentially bridge aspects of the digital divide, significant policy, economic, and technological barriers to access still exist for people with disabilities, who constitute a sizable population. There are some 51.2 million Americans (about 18 percent of the population) and more than 84 million persons with different types of disabilities in all EU/EEA countries, all part of an estimated 650 million globally (UN, 2008) who have some kind of long-term or conditional disability, including sensory, physical, mental, or self-care needs (Baker & Bellordre, 2003). Accessible, universally designed Wi-Fi systems offer increased opportunity to access information and services, either in the home or public places. However, a review of the literature suggests that few Wi-Fi systems (Baker, Hanson, & Myhill, 2009) specifically address the disability community, even though, theoretically, the Americans with Disabilities Act of 1990 (ADA) mandates equal opportunity and access to U.S. municipal programs and services for people with disabilities (Blanck, Hill, Siegel, Waterstone, & Myhill 2006).

A lack of attention to the needs of the disability community, either individually or as an underserved group, and whether due to uncertainty about municipal obligations under the ADA or simple lack of awareness about access barriers faced by people with disabilities, may inadvertently further this "disability" digital divide. A consequence of this oversight exacerbates, rather than remedies, the problem of access for individuals with disabilities and undermines the fundamental objective of social inclusion in planning and executing municipal wireless systems. In fact, some implementations of municipal Wi-Fi in the U.S. may run afoul of the ADA, taking into account the outcome of a recent legal settlement impacting websites[5].

Wireless devices can deliver specialized information services in multiple formats for people with disabilities, offering enhanced employment opportunities, access to health care information and on-line services, emergency preparedness, and greater participation in a community. Access may be limited, however, by a general lack of awareness of technologies or access options, as well as economic, technological, and regulatory restrictions. For individuals with disabilities, equal access to accessible content, services information, and telecommunications technologies remains a major concern (Baker & Moon, 2008; Baker, Hanson, & Myhill, 2009; Klein, Myhill, Hansen, Asby, Michaelson, & Blanck, 2003; Myhill, Cogburn, Samant, Addom, & Blanck, 2008).

In the U.S., a variety of barriers exist to the full participation of people with disabilities, and it has been only relatively recently (2007) for instance, that websites were explicitly recognized as issues of concern. The U.S. Department of Justice's Project Civic Access provides guidance to state and local governments on the accessibility of websites (DOJ, 2008), and while not specifically addressing access to wireless systems, access to them might become a regulatory issue downstream.[6]

In the EU, the core group of disabled persons for whom e-accessibility is relevant comprises some 84 million persons in Europe, of whom 50 million are in the age range 15-64 and 34 million are in the age range 65 and above.[7] As there is a wide variety of impairments, needs are very diverse and, likewise, a great variety of solutions are needed. Up to 15% of the population across the European Union has a disability, such as a visual, hearing, speech, cognitive, or motor impairment[8]. The elderly population is also very concerned with access issues, as disability (that is, functional limitations) correlates strongly with age. In the EU about 16% of the population is over 65, a number forecasted to rise rapidly in the coming years.

Joining these two streams, then, we believe that given the presence of an underserved population, people with disabilities, and the public sector's interest in crafting approaches to increase participation in the information society, that municipal Wi-Fi systems represent a potential means to bridge this access gap. But several factors arise in the deployment of these public systems. First, considering system usability and accessibility, what are the considerations that go into the design of these systems? Information systems are composed of a variety of elements, including network design and constraints, management and sustainability of the systems, information (content), and interface design issues. We are especially concerned with interface related issues of access and intended use or programmatic accessibility of the information content of the systems. The latter, dealing with implementation of policy, program directives and regulations and general governance is a manifestation of a more subtle issue of access for people with disabilities. These might be considered the dependent variables in a more traditional research design.

Second, we explore the influence of the stakeholders on the design of Municipal Wi-Fi systems. We posit that the ultimate Wi-Fi system is, to some extent, a function of the influence of the different stakeholders in the design and implementation process. The mix of participants involved in a given system implementation is a function of the political and business climate of the locality, as well as social and cultural norms, though the manifestation can be affected by geography. In the U.S., there is some evidence (Tapia, Maitland, & Stone, 2006) that ideological debate on municipal wireless initiatives has propagated the idea that only two business model options exist for broadband networks: privately owned or publicly owned and operated systems. However, a review of the literature, as well as our exploratory study, suggests that a number of other models have emerged and countless hybrid possibilities exist. Many municipalities are of the mindset that broadband is a new type of utility, and they are deploying their own networks. This is exemplified by Finland's recent move to guarantee to each citizen the right to 1 MB/sec broadband access as a civil right (Straus, 2009), This is also evident in the support of innovation and R&D in this domain by companies such as JoikuSpoft and FON, the world's largest Wi-Fi community.

While the public private dichotomy is a not uncommon approach to the issue we feel that it is more useful to categorize deployment models according to the following typology:

- *Public models*: Under this approach, municipalities have the greatest control over services and content; however, with costs borne by local government, these systems are most likely to experience financial constraints, exacerbated by political factors.
- *Private models*: These systems offer businesses the greatest direct control over

process, design and capacities, and have the widest array of possibilities for financial sustainability; but because they favor profit-based models they are least likely to make design decisions that optimize such social concerns as the accessibility of these systems for people with disabilities.
- *Private/Public Partnership (PPP) models*: This approach may provide the most effective balance between profit and public objectives, and hence serve the public interest in a sustainable manner. The downside is that public/private initiatives run the risk of drifting to a business model when costs become prohibitive, and consequently lose public accountability features. This model is also highly sensitive to the mix of stakeholders involved in system design and implementation.

Municipal Wi-Fi systems, however implemented, represent a valuable approach to helping people with disabilities overcome some of the barriers to information and participation access that they face (GCATT, 2004). As noted above, a key design objective of many municipal wireless networks has been the digital inclusion of "disadvantaged" communities. However, this usually is achieved at some cost; hence, the issue of sustainability becomes a critical concern.

IMPLEMENTATION MODELS IN MUNICIPAL WI-FI

A deployed information system, such as the Wi-Fi systems under discussion in this article, represents the final outcome of an array of cost, functional, technological, and other "soft" (political, cultural, etc.) design factors. For instance, accessibility is an issue when considering the users of a system. Accessibility of wireless networks can occur in several ways. Accessibility can be "bolted on," that is, features can be retrofitted onto established systems, which is not atypical of an assistive technology approach. Alternatively, a universal design approach considers the characteristics of the users and attempts to design systems so that they, *a priori*, can accommodate the various needs, and characteristics of the users. More broadly, Gunasekaran and Harmantizis (2008) observe that there are many public policy issues centered on municipal Wi-Fi, as evidenced by the political and legal conflicts with regard to the local government's right to build communication networks. The key arguments are centered on cost, competition, and failure to achieve the social fairness expected from the municipal Wi-Fi deployment (Tapia & Stone, 2005). On the other hand, Wi-Fi proponents cite benefits for municipalities entering into the broadband market. For example, Wi-Fi access technology can be used as a low-cost solution to provide broadband access to low-income households and small businesses, thus bridging the digital divide (Bar & Park, 2006).

As a rule, the literature regarding Municipal Wi-Fi does not have much discussion on approaches for long-term system sustainability or alterative implementation strategies and business models (Baker & Moon, 2008; Baker, Hanson, & Myhill, 2009; Powell & Shade, 2006; Powell, 2008). Though any such strategy will generally rely on one of the three aforementioned models that are in usage at this time: the public, private and community models, resulting in at least six combinations and variations of these (FTC, 2006; Van Audenhove et al., 2007; Merienrath et al., 2006). Research on value networks in municipal Wi-Fi suggests that it is not unusual for a municipal Wi-Fi network to have two, or even three, stakeholder groups working together for a network to be realized. Stakeholder roles can be divided in the form of public-private cooperation, filled in through different domains, or they can become integrated.

Components

Based on the work of literature from Van Audenhove et al (2007), Tapia, Maitland, and Stone (2006) and others noted previously, we propose a system model composed of several elements:

- *Infrastructure/Site Provision*: In many cities, a part of the PPP-structure already exists and a network builder/operator will use existing infrastructure and public resources to build and/or to run the network. Typically, municipal optical fiber networks provide an information backbone, and public buildings and infrastructure such as poles, traffic lights, communication towers, etc. are used for the installation of base-stations, as well as to provide for power for the components. This leveraging of existing infrastructure makes the roll-out of networks considerably less expensive. Frequently, municipalities will offer use of this infrastructure in exchange for free or subsidized use of the network for city services and free access for selected groups.

- *Infrastructure Manufacturing Vending*: Vendors provide such critical IT infrastructure as WLAN-stations and routers, and they might be separate from systems designers or operators. In most cases, component suppliers play an important role in the structure of the network building, at least indirectly, if not directly involved.

- *Network Building*: Another key element involves the builder/systems integrator of network architecture and builder of the physical aspects of the Wi-Fi network. This role is sometimes undertaken by different parties, either as a collaboration or coordination of separate efforts.

- *Network Operation*: The ongoing operation of the physical network is another important aspect. In the telecom sector, this is the "home ground" of telecom- and cable operators. In the WLAN-world, we see both new private parties arising that specialize in the management of these networks, as well as public sector involvement.

- *Service Provision*: This is an important role within the value network. The entity providing the service "contact" is the agent that develops a relationship with the citizen. In a public model, the municipality typically takes on this role. In a vertical setup, the network operator takes this role. In a horizontal setup, operators can grant a private ISP entry to the network. In a wholesale model, this party will often also provide the billing, advertising, security, and, possibly, the application development.
- *Applications Provision*: The development and offer of specific applications is also important. If done via an Internet service provider (ISP), parties can offer specific services on the platform. This service can be private or publicly organized and be offered independently via Internet in the form of so-called "walled gardens" with access limited to citizens/users from a given municipality.

Van Audenhove et al. (2007) examines a cross-section of municipalities in the U.S. and the EU selected to represent cases of existing business models and stakeholders in the municipal Wi-Fi market, which are combined (per Van Audenhove

et al., 2007) to develop Table 1. We combine these into two categories, Network Management and Service Provision.

For network management, they make the following classifications:

- **Private Player:** Network managed by private operator on basis of a PPP-agreement (license, concession, etc.). Municipal authority is concerned with the availability of sites, backbones, etc.
- **Public Player:** The municipal authority is owner of the network and manages this itself.
- **Open site:** Municipal authority oversees its site, other parties involved in building of a network.
- **Community Player:** The network is managed by the community.

For service provision, they make the following classifications:

- **Private Player:** The service provisioning is managed by a private operator.
- **Public Player:** One or more public players manage service provisioning.
- **Wholesale:** Several private players are involved in service provisioning.
- **No specific ISP:** Services are not specifically assigned to one ISP.

Table 1. Business model types and examples

Model type:	Examples in action:
Private – private	Bristol (UK), Cardiff (UK), Westminster (UK), Minneapolis (U.S.)
Private – wholesale	Philadelphia (U.S.), Portland, OR (U.S.)
Public-public	St. Cloud, FL (U.S.)
Public - wholesale	Stockholm (SE)
Open site	Bologna (IT), Decatur, GA (U.S.)
Community	Leiden (NL), Turku (FI), New York City (U.S.)

Accessibility Business Model: Beyond Just Service and Application Provisioning

In terms of mobile business frameworks, Lehner and Watson (2001) concentrate on a stakeholder perspective, a service and applications perspective, and a market player's institutional perspective. In the latter, they propose relevant research problems such as the business models, useful alliances, and the interaction between market players, among other considerations.

In principle, municipal Wi-Fi systems are deployed to strengthen two types of service delivery: access to the Internet generally, as well as access to new (municipal) services and applications. In examining the services and applications area, the primary stakeholders are application providers, content providers and content aggregators. Portals are also important players in this category. The other actors are application developers, middleware developers, content owners, and system integrators. E-business players implementing a mobile strategy and professional service providers, such as the consultancies, are also active in this sector (Camponovo & Pigneur, 2003). However, one must remember that the underpinnings of a business allow the business to function profitably at a particular price point. Although some would argue that the choices of infrastructure and network actors do not matter in municipal Wi-Fi systems for accessibility discussions, we point out here that these actors do matter in terms of economically viable implementations that allow accessibility to be addressed.

EXPLORATORY STUDY

Methodology: E-accessibility in a Mobile Context

E-accessibility (that is, simple connectivity to a wireless network) in a strict sense is not neces-

sarily a problem, *per se*, but *accessibility*, more broadly constructed, may be problematic. By analogy, consider that while a building such as a library may have a ramp allowing physical access (analogous to connectivity) to its internal space, but if there are no elevators to other floors, or if books and other materials are placed out of reach, then the *accessibility* of the facility as a construct is compromised. Therefore, while it might be argued that connectivity to a network constitutes access in the simplest sense, a municipal wireless network, as a public construct, must go beyond that as accessibility must be programmatic as well to ensure inclusive participation and engagement.

As a way of teasing out this aspect of accessibility, an exploratory effort was made at discerning the total accessibility of Municipal Wi-Fi networks beyond the connectivity criteria. Project staff evaluated system websites and online documentation (including secondary sources) of the selected representative municipal Wi-Fi projects for accessibility and/or awareness of disability related issues as pertinent. In the cases where there was no website, *per se*, information was gathered from secondary sources such as online articles from newspapers, magazines, and sites that keep track of municipal wireless projects. Systems were evaluated for the level of consideration/awareness of the needs of disadvantaged populations in general as well as specific discussion of people with disabilities (PWD) based on the following indicators. An Accessibility Level (AL) scale was developed to catalog the type or level of awareness (i.e., consideration of disability issues) that went into each network design and deployment policy.

- AL(1) Little/no consideration - no specific mention of PWDs or disadvantaged populations
- AL(2) Moderate consideration - peripheral mention of underprivileged groups; no detailed goals or discussion of intended impacts

Table 2. Awareness of people with disabilities in assessed EU municipal Wi-Fi implementations

	Category 1	Category 2	Category 3	Category 4
Municipality	AL(1)	AL(2)	AL(3)	AL(4)
Bristol (UK)	X			
Cardiff (UK)	X			
Turku (Finland)		x		
Stockholm (Sweden)		x		
Bologna (IT)		x		
Leiden (NL)		x		

- AL(3) substantial consideration - detailed discussion of disadvantaged communities with specific goals and ideals, but nothing specific to PWDs
- AL(4) = Specific discussion of PWDs and the benefits of municipal wireless for this community

In addition to basic design parameters, a number of external factors could impact the level of accessibility of these projects. One key characteristic was the phase of deployment of the project, as systems tend to evolve as technology and the policy environment in which they operate change. In the target systems under study here, the extent to which system accessibility is addressed was determined by analyzing awareness level (the level of consideration given to disadvantaged members of the community) evidenced in the stated objectives/goals of the project. Source material, either from the project websites, proposal and bid materials or other public documents, as noted above, was coded and ranked using a five point Likert scale ranging from "no consideration" to "high consideration" in regard to mention of, or recognition of the specific needs of the disabled population. A summary of the Awareness Level (AL) of information from the web survey was generated to accompany each case assessment.

Results

European Municipal Wi-Fi – Accessibility Sensitivity Analysis

Again, applying the approach of Van Audenhove et al. (2007), it appears that the municipalities of Leiden and Turku have the widest scope of applications for their networks, and this would also fit with the type of inclusive social characteristic of Dutch and Finnish cultural values. However, in our analysis for disabilities of these and other municipal Wi-Fi implementations shown in Table 2, we did not find detailed descriptions of the benefit or use for PWD's and no network received more than a Category 2 rating based on available materials.

Observations from our analysis:

- **Bristol (UK):** No mention of disadvantaged or persons with disabilities.
- **Cardiff (UK):** No mention of the disabled community, the material represented more of a British Telecom (BT) focus on business in the community, and tourist information, etc.
- **Turku (Finland):** Coded as having a higher community sensitivity/awareness component in that the system allows other members of the community to use access points (which suggests a heightened acces-

Table 3. Awareness of people with disabilities in assessed U.S. municipal Wi-Fi implementations

	Category 1	**Category 2**	**Category 3**	**Category 4**
Municipality	AL(1)	AL(2)	AL(3)	AL(4)
Minneapolis, MN		x		
Philadelphia, PA				x
Portland, OR		x		
St. Cloud, FL	x			
New York City, NY		x		
Decatur, GA	x			

sibility) however there are no references specifically to people with disabilities

- **Stockholm (Sweden):** Again, while there was little specifically that evidenced heightened e-accessibility, the site received a higher rating as there was more awareness of the social implications of municipal Wi-Fi based on reference to a tool using Wi-Fi and cell phones to guide blind people by voice
- **Bologna (IT):** Bologna Wi-Fi is targeted towards people who do not have other means of Wi-Fi as well as municipal workers, students, and teachers so it discusses certain communities which may be disadvantaged but it does not mention people with disabilities, *per se*.

U.S. Municipal Wi-Fi - E-accessibility Analysis

The analysis of the U.S. municipal Wi-Fi projects suggests that most municipal Wi-Fi projects are closely associated with the levels of economic development within the communities. While other considerations, like emergency response and education were also heavily prevalent, analysis of only one community indicated high awareness to people with disabilities (PWDs). Wireless Philadelphia is very explicit with the levels of inclusion that they support. 25% of all Wireless Philadelphia's *Digital Inclusion Partners* focus on severe PWD

(Digital Impact Group, n.d.). Philadelphia was the only municipality that had public record of such diverse stakeholders

Observations from our analysis:

Minneapolis, MN
- Mentions different underserved user sectors, including underprivileged groups, but no mention of disadvantaged or people with disabilities

Philadelphia, PA
- Large direct partnership with multiple disability communities
- Frequently mentions *digital inclusion* within mission and goals
- Direct linkage to the following disability focused groups: Community Council for Mental Health, COMHAR, Home Care Associates, JEVS Human Services, Ready Willing & Able, PATH, Elwyn Institute, PMHCC, and Horizon House

Portland, OR
- Large focus on community involvement and education
- Sharing of public and private based nodes with the whole community.

St. Cloud, FL
- Just mentions that they want to help their community but no mention

of disadvantaged or people with disabilities

New York City, NY
- ○ Still in development – only accessible in certain parks around the city
- ○ No direct mention of people with disabilities or disadvantaged groups.

Decatur, GA
- ○ Recently fully built-out
- ○ No direct mention of people with disabilities or disadvantaged groups

Comparative Analysis of Municipal Wi-Fi Models and Accessibility Awareness

Examining the combination of business model, stakeholders, and awareness level (AL) of PWD, we show, in Table 4, some initial connection between AL for PWD and type of business model.

FINDINGS AND CONCLUSIONS

The design and implementation of wireless technologies in general and, more specifically, the deployment of municipal Wi-Fi systems creates additional opportunities for increased access to ubiquitous, low-cost Internet connectivity. This possibility has consequently raised questions of *who* will fund, own, design, deploy, and manage these networks, and under what terms and conditions (Tapia, Maitland, & Stone, 2006; Van Audenhove et al., 2007). This research study is an extension of two lines of research, one generally related to issues of increased universal access to information resources, and the other related to issues of e-accessibility, or access for a specific group of individuals with functional limitations, that is, people with disabilities. Our concern in this research is for those who are often excluded in terms of e-accessibility. While much has been

Table 4. Summary of Business model, stakeholder and AL category classification

City	Type of Business Model	AL (1-4)	Stakeholder(s) involved
Bristol	Private – Private	1	City of Bristol, CitySpace, BelAir, Clear Channel AdShell
Cardiff	Private – Private	1	Council of Cardiff, British Telecom, IBM, Mitel, Apropos, Nortel
Minneapolis, MN[910]	Private – Private	2	U.S. Internet of Minnetonka, USI Wireless
Philadelphia, PA[11121314]	Private – Wholesale	4	City of Philadelphia, Wireless Philadelphia, Vision for Equality, College of Physicians of Philadelphia, Partners in Digital Inclusion,
Portland, OR[1516]	Private – Wholesale	2	City of Portland, MetroFi, Intel, DuVinci Inc.,
St. Cloud, FL[171819]	Public – Public	1	City of St. Cloud, HP, Intel, MRI, national ISPs such as Sprint and Warner, Cyberspot
Stockholm	Public – Wholesale	2	Stockholm city, Svenska Bostader, Ementor, Stoklab, private ISPs
Bologna	Open Site	2	City of Bologna, University of Bologna, RoamAD/ HI-TEL Italia, Acantho
Decatur, GA[2021]	Open Site	2	City of Decatur, Agnes Scott College, City Schools of Decatur, Columbia Theological Seminary, Downtown Development Authority, Cisco, Get the Speed, Civitium
Leiden	Community	2	Wireless Leiden, Leiden University, HCCInet, Sun Microsystems, CeTIM, AA24, city of Leiden,
Turku	Community	2	OpenSpark, City of Turku, 4 universities in Turku, Amica Biocity, Buffalo Tech
New York City[2223]	Community	1	Nycwireless, Bryant Park Restoration Corp., Alliance for Downtown New York,

written on issues of socio-economic digital divides, very little research has been conducted on accessibility components of Wi-Fi systems or issues of access by people with disabilities.

The first finding evident from the stakeholder list suggests a linkage between type of stakeholder group and awareness of the needs for inclusivity/e-accessibility. That is, the greater the involvement from institutions that enable wider public participation (universities, health care institutions, specific communities), the higher the AL rating the municipal wireless system exhibited. While on the face of this, one interpretation of these phenomena suggests that private business models do not actively seek applications for people with disabilities, on further inspection this is not necessarily the case. The private model implies a different driver set for initial implementation and perhaps different business goals. Public models with either government or third party funding for initiation of the municipal Wi-Fi project may be a factor in consideration. This is one area for further exploration.

A second finding suggests that the more diverse the stakeholder group, the wider the range of consideration of Wi-Fi user requirements. This is logical as the more stakeholders participate, the wider the range of views become available. The trade-off here is one of efficiency. As the number and range of stakeholder interests increases, articulation of the objectives as well as agreement on system objectives becomes more complex. On the other hand, the broader the base of user/constituents the greater the political "capital" deployable by the interested parties, and thus an easier case is made for expenditures on resources for this type of municipal initiatives. A similar effect could be expected in private systems, in which case support for the system would be manifested though market mechanisms evidenced by such indicators as subscriptions or users paying for system access.

Third, we can conclude that key differences exist even within broad model categories. For instance, in the Philadelphia implementation, service provision was initially done on a wholesale basis with tiered fees. In the face of changing business climate, this was ultimately revised, with the withdrawal of Earthlink as network operator in June 2008, and the transfer of network ownership to Network Acquisition Co. LLC, a Philadelphia company formed by some local telecom and Internet veterans. EarthLink has subsequently terminated operating agreements and pulled out of all markets in 2008, including Philadelphia, New Orleans, and San Francisco, because it was unable to develop a sustainable revenue stream from Wi-Fi networks it was building. The municipal Wi-Fi division has since been shut down. This model has proven to be problematic in the U.S., as well for the international companies (MetroFi's 9 systems and the smaller Kite, SkyPilot; and Strix) that also have ceased operation.

Network Acquisition made the network available for free to anyone who could access it, which eliminated the need for Wireless Philadelphia's special rate[24]. We believe this was related to 1) a changing cost structure, and 2) a different structure for the network operator. Wireless Philadelphia has renamed itself the Digital Impact Group as of May 2009, and it now focuses on helping the underprivileged get the tools to gain access to Wi-Fi.

While we have identified a range of variables that are associated with the accessibility of Municipal Wi-Fi systems (among others, the nature, type and cooperation of stakeholder, the pricing of service provisioning due to the infrastructure investment, the access to digital tools), the exploratory design of the research and our small sample doesn't allow us to conclude definitely that any one of the factors is the driver of accessibility in the U.S. or EU contexts. With the assumption that people with disabilities have the basic digital technologies and do not necessarily need special equipment beyond their current adapted technologies for internet access, the issue is not so much a matter of insurmountable access issues, but system design and implementation. This does not have to be the case. However, ancillary research in the adoption of information technologies shows that a heightened awareness and certain regulatory and policy initiatives can encourage the use of universally designed systems. These are systems that are designed *a priori* for e-accessibility, or ones in which they are easily adaptable for the needs of a wide range of users and capabilities. Finally, in addition to a more inclusive design philosophy, we are curious as the specific role of participatory stakeholder engagement in facilitating system accessibility.

A potential drawback of our approach is that our surrogate variable (programmatic accessibility as well as system connectivity) for general information on system accessibility came from the public information provided by the Wi-Fi project websites or public literature. Thus, if there are additional capabilities available, we would not have factored them into our analysis. On the other hand, our approach can be considered to be more accurately representative of the status quo, and hence be what individual with disabilities would encounter in their attempts to access systems, or find more information about them. We have also focused on the provision of wireless *access,* as the other side of the equation. Barriers to the accessibility of *wireless devices* is an equally important issue, but beyond the range of this study. A more robust effort at assessing the design process including the inclusion of marginalized populations would include a larger sample as well as interviews with key stakeholders. We would also desire that the study had gone beyond the generally well-connected developed states to other countries with lower levels of connectivity.

In conclusion, the results of this pilot study suggest that the value of further exploration of the design, implementation and operation of Municipal Wi-Fi systems is merited with respect to the accessibility of systems, and the considerations that impact them. More specifically, from both a design standpoint, as well as from a sustainability impact, further research is merited on the role of stakeholder participation in the operation of Wi-Fi system business models, and the cooperative arrangements assembled to deploy these systems. Finally, from a policy perspective, we believe that such research needs to consider the role of the other contextual factors in the understanding of the sustainability of Municipal Wi-Fi networks and the design and mission of these systems, especially as it pertains to varying degrees of e-accessibility.

ACKNOWLEDGMENT

We wish to acknowledge the support of the European Union Center of Excellence at the Georgia Institute of Technology, the Center for Advanced Communications Policy (CACP), Georgia Tech Research Institute (GTRI), and the Rehabilitation Engineering Research Center (RERC) for Wireless Technologies, sponsored by the National Institute on Disability and Rehabilitation Research (NIDRR) of the U.S. Department of Education under grant number H133E060061. The opinions contained in this paper are those of the authors and do not necessarily reflect those of the U.S. Department of Education or NIDRR.

Special thanks to colleague Leo van Audenhove, SMIT, VUB, for access to the 2006 working paper that preceded the 2007 South African publication. We also acknowledge the research assistance of Matias Medina, recent graduate of Vesalius College / VUB, and CACP research associate Avonne Bell, who assisted on background research for this project, and research scientist Nathan Moon, who provided editorial assistance.

REFERENCES

About WifiPDX - Free wireless internet in Portland on WifiPDX. (n.d.). *In Free Portland WiFi - Free wireless internet in Portland on WifiPDX*. Retrieved June 05, 2009 from http://www.WiFipdx.com/about/

Baker, P. M. A., & Bellordre, C. (2003). Factors Influencing Adoption of Wireless Technologies – Key Policy Issues, Barriers, and Opportunities for People with Disabilities. *Information Technology and Disabilities, 9*(2).

Baker, P. M. A., Hanson, J., & Myhill, W. (2009). The Promise of Municipal WiFi and Failed Policies of Inclusion: the Disability Divide. *Information Polity, 14*(1-2).

Baker, P. M. A., & Moon, N. W. (2008). Access Barriers to Wireless Technologies for People with Disabilities: Issues, Opportunities and Policy Options. In Langdon, P., Clarkson, J., & Robinson, P. (Eds.), *Designing inclusive futures*. London: Springer Verlag. doi:10.1007/978-1-84800-211-1_14

Ballon, P. (2007). Changing business models for Europe's mobile telecommunications industry: The impact of alternative wireless technologies. *Telematics and Informatics, 24*, 192–205. doi:10.1016/j.tele.2007.01.007

Ballon, P., Audenhove, L., Poel, M., & Staelens, T. (2007). Business models for wireless city networks in the EU and the US: public inputs, and returns. In *Proceedings of the 18th European Regional ITS Conference*, Istanbul, Turkey.

Baltuch, J. (2005). *Free Municipal Wireless, Pays Big Dividends*. St. Cloud, FL: MRI.

Baltuch, J. (2006). St Cloud, Florida citywide Wi-Fi update: Launch plus 30 days. *MuniWireless*. Retrieved June 6, 2009 from http://www.muniwireless.com/municipal/

Bar, F., & Park, N. (2006). Municipal Wi-Fi Networks: The Goals, Practices, and Policy Implications of the U.S. Case. *Communications and Strategies, 61*(1), 107–126.

Blanck, P., Hill, E., Siegal, C., Waterstone, M., & Myhill, W. (2006). *Disability civil rights law and policy: Cases and materials* (1st ed.). St. Paul, MN: Thomson/West Publishers.

Campanovo, G., & Pigneur, Y. (2003, April 23-26). *Business model analysis applied to mobile business*. Paper presented at the 5th International Conference on Enterprise Information Systems, Angers, France.

Chesley, K. A. (2009). The Future of Municipal Wireless in the United States and Europe. Retrieved May 22, 2009 from http://ssrn.com/abstract=1408808

City of Decatur. Administrative Services. (2009, January). *Wireless Network Complete* (Press release). Retrieved June 7, 2009 from http://www.decaturga.com/ cgs_citysvcs_atr_technology_wireless.aspx

City of Minneapolis. Communications. (2008, December 18). *Wireless Minneapolis results in new funding to help bridge the digital divide* (Press release). Retrieved June 5, 2009 from http://www.ci.minneapolis.mn.us/ news/20081218DigitalInclusionAwards.asp

Digital Impact Group - Make a Digital Difference. (n.d.). Retrieved June 07, 2009 from http://www.wirelessphiladelphia.org/ digital_partners.cfm

Dimireva, I. (2009, September). Geographical eInclusion. *EU Business News - EUbusiness.com*. Retrieved November 13, 2009 from http://www.eubusiness.com/ Internet/Internet/eInclusion/

Dingwall, C. (2007). Municipal Broadband: Challenges and Perspectives. *Federal Communications Law Journal, 59*(2), 69–106. Retrieved from http://www.law.indiana.edu/ fclj/pubs/v59no2.html.

Fleishman, G. (2008, November 17). Second wind for muni WiFi? Mesh-networking startup hopes so. *Ars Technica*. Retrieved May, 2009 from http://arstechnica.com

Georgia Centers for Advanced Telecommunications Technology (GCATT). (2004). U.S. Wireless Policy and People with Disabilities: A Status Report. In H. Mitchell, P. M. A. Baker, & A. Bakowsi (Eds.). Atlanta, GA: GCATT and Wireless RERC. Retrieved April 24, 2007 from Gillett, L., & Osorio. (2003, September). *Local Government Broadband Initiatives*. Paper presented at the MIT Program on Internet and Telecoms Convergence.

Gunasekaran, V., & Harmantzis, F. C. (2008). Towards a Wi-Fi ecosystem: Technology integration and emerging service models. *Telecommunications Policy, 32*, 163–181. http://www.cacp.gatech.edu/Policy/ Briefings/EU_Policy_Report_9-21_(B).pdf. doi:10.1016/j.telpol.2008.01.002

Jussi, L. (2006). *Municipal WLAN: Case Examples in Finland (Tech. Rep.)*. Helsinki, Finland: Helsinki University of Technology.

Klein, D., Myhill, W., Hansen, L., Asby, G., Michaelson, S., & Blanck, P. (2003). Electronic Doors to Education: Study of High School Website Accessibility in Iowa. *Behavioral Sciences & the Law, 21*(1), 27–49. doi:10.1002/bsl.521

Kramer, R., Lopez, A., & Koonen, A. (2006). Municipal broadband access networks in the Netherlands - three successful cases, and how New Europe may benefit. In *Proceedings of the ACM International Conference on Access networks* (p. 267).

Lehner, F., & Watson, R. (2001) *From e-commerce to m-commerce: research directions* (working paper). Regensburg, Germany: University of Regensburg, Chair of Business Informatics.

Merinrath, S., Richard, M., & Middleton, C. (2006, October 19). *Public Forum: Municipal broadband networks: an idea whose time has come*? Lecture presented at the Alternative Telecommunications Policy Forum, Ottawa, Canada. Retrieved June 7, 2009 from www.cwirp.ca

National Federation of the Blind et al v. Target Corporation. (2007, March 8). *United States District Court, Northern District of California - San Francisco Division* (Justia, 4,154,104, Dist. file).

Papacharissi, Z., & Zaks, A. (2006). Is broadband the future? An analysis of broadband technology potential and diffusion. *Telecommunications Policy, 30*, 64–75. doi:10.1016/j.telpol.2005.08.001

Personal Telco Project. (n.d.). Retrieved June 4, 2009 from http://www.personaltelco.net/

Philadelphia, W. Communications. (2009, February 27). *Expanded Horizons and Empowerment for Families with Sons and Daughters with Disabilities* (Press release). Retrieved June 4, 2009 from http://www.wirelessphiladelphia.org/wp_release_vfe_event_022709.pd

Philadelphia Family TIES. (n.d.). Retrieved June 4, 2009 from http://www.phillyhealthinfo.org/vision_for_equality/index.php/

Powell, A. (2008). WiFi Publics: Producing Community and Technology. *Information Communication and Society, 11*(8), 1068–1088. doi:10.1080/13691180802258746

Powell, A., & Shade, L. R. (2006). Going Wi-Fi in Canada: Municipal and community initiatives. *Government Information Quarterly, 23*(3-4), 381–403. doi:10.1016/j.giq.2006.09.001

Ross, H. (Director) (2006, September 26). The Philadelphia Municipal Wireless Project (Podcast series episode). In *NTEN: Nonprofit Technology News. Portland, Oregon: ODEO*. Retrieved June 5, 2009 from http://odeo.com/episodes/1988269-Part-1- The-Philadelphia-Municipal-Wireless-Project

Shein, D. M. (2005). *Municipal Wireless: A Primer for Public Discussion (Tech. Rep.)*. Rochester, New York: Rochester Institute of Technology, Center for Advancing the Study of Cyber Infrastructure.

Sirbu, M., Lehr, W., & Gillett, S. (2006). Evolving Wireless Access Technologies for Municipal Broadband. *Government Information Quarterly, 23*, 480–502. doi:10.1016/j.giq.2006.09.003

St. Cloud Florida. *CyberSpot General Information*. (n.d.). Retrieved June 5, 2009 from http://www.stcloud.org/ index.aspx?NID=402

Tapia, A., Maitland, C., & Stone, M. (2006). Making It Work for Municipalities: Building Municipal Wireless Networks. *Government Information Quarterly, 23*(3-4), 359–380. doi:10.1016/j.giq.2006.08.004

Tapia, A., & Stone, M. (2005, September 23-25). *Public–private partnership and the role of state and federal legislation in wireless municipal networks*. Paper presented at telecommunications policy research conference (TPRC), Arlington, VA.

Television series episode. (2009, May 18). In *Wireless in the City*. New York: Fox News. Retrieved June 5, 2009 from http://www.myfoxny.com

United Nations Economic and Social Council (UN). (2008). *Mainstreaming Disability in the Development Agenda, Note by the Secretariat*. Retrieved November 30, 2009 from http://www.un.org/disabilities/

United States of America, Department of Justice. (n.d.). *Project Civic Access*. Retrieved May, 2009 from http://www.ada.gov/civicac.htm

United States of America, Federal Trade Commission (FTC). (2006). *Municipal Provision of Wireless Internet*. Washington, DC: Federal Trade Commission.

U.S. NTIA. (2000). *Falling Through the Net: Toward Digital Inclusion*. Washington, DC: Department of Commerce, Economics and Statistics Administration.

U.S. NTIA. (2002). *A Nation Online: Entering the Broadband Age*. Washington, DC: Department of Commerce, Economics and Statistics Administration.

USI Wireless - Wireless Minneapolis History. (n.d.). In *USI Wireless high-speed broadband wireless internet services*. Retrieved June 05, 2009 from http://www.usiwireless.com/ service/minneapolis/history.htm

Using the public airwaves to connect and strengthen communities in New York City. (n.d.). *NYCwireless*. Retrieved June 05, 2009 from http://www.nycwireless.net/about/

Van Audenhove, L. V., Ballon, P., Poel, M., & Staelens, T. (2007). Government Policy and Wireless City Networks: A Comparative Analysis of Motivations, Goals, Services and Their Relation to Network Structure. *The Southern African Journal of Information and Communication, 8*, 108–135.

Wallsten, S. (2005). Broadband Penetration: An Empirical Analysis of State and Federal Policies. *AEI-Brookings Joint Center for Regulatory Studies*. Retrieved April 25, 2007 from http://downloads.heartland.org/17468.pdf

Wireless Communities Georgia. (2007, June 29). *Civitium. Wireless Philadelphia - Digital Impact Partners*. (n.d.). Retrieved June 4, 2009 from http://wirelessphiladelphia.org/ digital_partners.cfm

ENDNOTES

[1] A competing model of area connectivity, is WiMax ("World Interoperability for Microwave Access"). WiMAX/IEEE 802.16 is a global standard-based technology for Broadband Wireless Access Equivalent to Wi-Fi Alliance for IEEE 802.11 (see "Wimax An Efficient Tool To Bridge The Digital Divide (November, 2005) Prepared by Guy

Cayla, Stephane Cohen and Didier Guigon, on behalf of WiMAX Forum.

[2] Muni WiFi is difficult in Europe because EU rules limit the amount of government aid that can go into these networks, until relatively recently there was a bias against the perception that local governments would be competing with private enterprises.

[3] Telecommunications Act of 1996, Pub. L. No. 104-104 § 706, 110 Stat. 153 (codified as amended at 47 U.S.C. § 157 (2000)).

[4] Broadband Technology Opportunities Program – National Telecommunications and Information Administration. BTOP Funding awarded under the American Recovery and Reinvestment Act of 2009

[5] National Federation of the Blind (NFIB) v. Target Corp. (Case No. 06-01802 MHP), settled in August 2008, in which the retailer Target agreed to ensure website accessibility. [www.nfbtargetlawsuit.com]

[6] The technical assistance document issued in 2003 entitled, "Accessibility of State and Local Government Websites to People with Disabilities" cites the accessibility requirements for those entities receiving federal funds notes that alternative equivalent access is currently acceptable, this might change in the future. [http://www.ada.gov/websites2.htm]

[7] Based on Eurostat data.

[8] Report of the Inclusive Communications (INCOM) subgroup of the Communications Committee (COCOM) COCOM04-08.

[9] City of Minneapolis press release, Dec 2008

[10] USI Wireless - Wireless Minneapolis History

[11] Philadelphia Family TIES Program partnership with Wireless Philadelphia. Empowers families caring for people with developmental disabilities.

[12] Wireless Philadelphia Press Release ""Expanded Horizons and Empowerment" For Families with Sons and Daughters with Disabilities"

[13] Wireless Philadelphia Partners in Digital Inclusion that serve the disability community

[14] Interview with Holly Ross director of NTEN programming. Review of the Philadelphia Municipal Wireless Project. Podcast NTEN Podcast

[15] WiFiPDX – Wireless Portland

[16] PersonalTelco

[17] Baltuch 2005

[18] Baltuch 2006

[19] CyberSpot General Information

[20] City of Decatur website "Wireless Decatur"

[21] Civituim's discussion of the Wireless Communities of Georgia Initiative

[22] NYCwireless about page.

[23] MyFox news "Wireless in the City"

[24] Philadelphia Business Journal, "Wireless Philadelphia reboots to bring Wi-Fi to the masses", http://philadelphia.bizjournals.com/philadelphia/stories/2009/01/05/story8.html

This work was previously published in International Journal of Information Communication Technologies and Human Development, Volume 2, Issue 2, edited by Susheel Chhabra and Hakikur Rahman, pp. 52-66, copyright 2010 by IGI Publishing (an imprint of IGI Global).

Chapter 9
Adoption and Use of ICTs Among Rural Youth:
Evidence from Greece

George Alexopoulos
Agricultural University of Athens, Greece

Alex Koutsouris
Agricultural University of Athens, Greece

Irene Tzouramani
National Agricultural Research Foundation, Greece

ABSTRACT

In the last few decades, within the rhetoric of the "information age", there is a growing enthusiasm for the (potential) benefits of the dissemination of Information and Communication Technologies (ICTs). This is further enhanced through eGovernment projects undertaken on a worldwide scale. However, a number of issues seem to defy such optimism as far as rural areas are concerned. The critical review of such issues question the thesis that ICTs undoubtedly benefit (human) development. In particular, this paper, drawing on data from a large-scale survey in Greece, identifies the marginal effects of a series of demographic, socioeconomic and spatial characteristics, and information sources on PC and Internet use on the part of young rural inhabitants, especially farmers. The results, pointing toward an emerging intra-rural digital divide, are consequently discussed vis-à-vis eGovernment projects, from the point of view of human development.

INTRODUCTION

Over the last decades, within the discourse of 'information/knowledge society/economy', the (potential) impact of Information and Communication Technologies (ICTs) on (sustainable) devel-

opment, enabling low-cost creation, access and distribution of information, and re-structuring and re-organising the spheres of production, distribution and circulation, has become a much contested issue. Debates have also emerged concerning the 'dream' of the pioneers of the 'information age', who envisaged ICTs (particularly the Internet) as the mechanism towards self-government (Maki-

DOI: 10.4018/978-1-4666-0047-8.ch009

nen & Naarmala, 2008; Norris, 2001; Quintelier & Vissers, 2008; Raman, 2008; Small, 2006).

In particular, the use of ICTs in government (eGovernment) has been anticipated to have noteworthy potential benefits such as the improvement of the delivery of services to citizens, business and industry; the augmentation of transparency, efficiency and effectiveness; and, the reinforcement of democracy (i.e., through the spread of relevant and accurate information and democratic and participatory political ideas, and stimulating participation). Nowadays, there is indeed a growing, worldwide development of eGovernment initiatives, defined as "A government that applies ICT to transform its internal and external relationships" (UN, 2003a). According to the United Nations World Public Sector Report (UN, 2003b) over 173 countries had, by 2003, developed government web sites thus indicating a clear move towards (some form of) eGovernment.

However, the term eGovernment, in spite of capturing the attention and efforts of politicians, businesses and citizens at various levels, is not unanimously defined. In the first place, debates exist as to whether concepts such as E-Government, e-democracy, digital government and E-Governance "are the same, different or complementary or whether they should be subsumed under the umbrella of E-Government research" (Helbig et al., 2009, p. 90). Secondly, some definitions are rather narrow, focusing on service delivery, reflecting thus the efforts of governments to advance the development of on-line public services, while others are broader and view eGovernment as an effort to transform government, that is to affect the level and style of political participation and transform the nature of politics (Beynon-Davis, 2007; Dada, 2006; Polat, 2005). Thus, eGovernment can be used as a broad concept, encompassing the transformation of both the business of governance (eServices and eAdministration) and governance itself (eDemocracy).

The latter dimension denotes the use of ICTs to facilitate greater citizen participation, i.e., to support informed deliberation and enhance participation in decision making (Beynon-Davis, 2007; Helbig et al., 2009). ICT-supported participation in processes involved in government and governance has also been termed as eParticipation (Macintosh, 2006). In this respect, Mahrer's model presents eGovernment as a continuous cycle of political communication between various actors from society-media-politics (Mahrer & Krimmer, 2005); for Muhlberger (2004) the Internet can reinforce the 'virtuous cycle' between political interest, political knowledge and participation.

Finally, some authors argue for the need of a holistic conception for eGovernment that would escape solely technical considerations and would thus take full account of the socio-technical nature and thus of the complexity (human, technological, economic, managerial, organizational, social/cultural, and legal issues) of the phenomena (Beynon-Davis, 2007; Fuchs, 2009; Madon, 2005).

The impressive development of ICTs and especially their appeal to youth (re: mobilisation thesis; Norris, 2001) has led many to support the optimistic scenario claiming that new media can fill the existing 'communicative void', i.e., stimulate political participation as well as revitalize and strengthen civil society (Dutta-Bergman, 2005; Helbig et al., 2009; Quintelier & Vissers, 2008; Van Dijk, 2005). However, many remain sceptical if not pessimistic vis-à-vis the effectiveness of ICTs, particularly the Internet, in stimulating higher levels of political participation. On the one hand, researchers raise doubts about the success of eGovernment projects (Helbig et al., 2009) and/or the establishment of new vs. the reinforcement of traditional functions by political institutions (Needham, 2004 in Small, 2006). On the other hand, others take a critical stance on the potential such government initiatives have. For example, Bimber (1998) argues that the effectiveness of the projects aiming at increasing the information provided to citizens does not ensure an increase on the political participation, while Foster (2000) argues that information is a qualitative rather than a quantitative matter. Furthermore, the capacity of governments, commercial interests and media corporations to manipulate/misuse new media further supports the dystopic scenario (Makinen & Naarmala, 2008).

THE DIGITAL DIVIDE

Scholars argue that various social groups cannot benefit from eGovernment due to problems of access and use of ICTs, especially the Internet. Thus, for example, the UN, while appreciating media's importance to social justice and acknowledging that access to information is a basic human right, also note the persistence of the so-called 'digital divide' (UN, 2006, p. 25).

The term owes to concerns expressed in the United States where, since the mid-1990s, NTIA (National Technical Information Administration) undertook a series of studies focusing on access to technological resources and documented persistent differences in the rates at which members of different groups use the new media. Thus, attention was given to the dichotomous distinction between people who have access to the Internet or not resulting from varying socioeconomic, cognitive, and cultural resources (Buente & Robbin, 2008; DiMaggio & Hargittai, 2001; Warschauer, 2003; Zheng & Walsham, 2008).

Since then, the issue has become the source of lively debates. Furthermore, concerns about the dichotomous approach to the digital divide emerged. The approach was found to be oversimplified if not confusing - since other phenomena such as differences in use were either ignored or confused with physical access (DiMaggio & Hargittai, 2001; Gunkel, 2003; Selwyn, 2004; Van Dijk & Hacker, 2003). Consequently, by 2000, a conceptual shift emerged, signalling the move towards the study of the digital divide as a) not only a technological, but a social problem, i.e., a phenomenon reflecting broader social, economic, cultural, and learning inequalities, and b) concerning not only physi-

cal access but the required skills for using it and what users do with computers/the Internet as well (Buente & Robbin, 2008; Cho et al., 2003; Dewan & Riggins, 2005; DiMaggio & Hargittai, 2001; Fuchs, 2009). The focus has further expanded to issues of social exclusion and inclusion, also addressing broad socioeconomic inequalities as well as political and institutional arrangements and equity (Norris, 2001; Selwyn, 2002; Van Dijk & Hacker, 2003; Zheng & Walsham, 2008). Hence, the digital divide proves a multifaceted, "complex and dynamic phenomenon" (Van Dijk & Hacker, 2003, p. 315). Accordingly, different forms of access can be considered as layered, material access being at the bottom (Clement & Shade, 2000; Van Djik, 2006; Fuchs, 2009).

Consequently, various frameworks have been proposed to address the digital divide. For example, Van Dijk and Hacker (2003), distinguish four kinds of barriers to access and the type of access: material access; mental access; skills access; and usage access. Chen and Wellman (2003) divide the digital divide in four different categories: technological access; technological literacy; social access; and, social use. Fink and Kenny (2003) based on their literature review on the topic, propose at least four possible interpretations of the digital divide: a gap in access to ICTs; a gap in the ability to use ICTs; a gap in actual use; and, a gap in the impact of use. Conceiving of the digital divide as a multidimensional phenomenon implies that, despite their importance, no single factor (such as gender, age, race, education, income or geographic location; see, for example: Dada, 2006; Dewan & Riggins, 2005; Korupp & Szydlick, 2005; Yu, 2006) can alone fully explain the first order (physical access) gap. As far as the second level (ability to use) digital gap (and the resulting 'knowledge gap') is concerned, there is no consensus among scholars on the factors predicting Internet use. In this respect, education, gender, autonomy of use, motivation, family structure, information technology literacy and IT skill (and experience), social support, type of employment, language, kinds of information (content), involvement in social/civic pursuits, satisfaction have been found to have an effect on use (e.g., Chen & Wellman, 2004; Cho et al., 2003; Dewan & Riggins, 2005; Gil-Garcia et al., 2006; Hargittai & Hinnant, 2008).

The Urban-Rural Divide

Therefore, contrary to the proponents of ICTs, who take an optimistic view and highlight the positive (potential) effects of ICTs to create new economic, social and political opportunities, another strand takes a pessimistic view stressing that the existing socioeconomic inequalities do not allow for such prospects. Thus, for example, Forestier et al. (2002), argue that telecommunications have historically been a significant factor on increasing inequality, which is exacerbated by new ICTs, particularly the Internet.

In the framework of (agricultural and rural) development and poverty alleviation, ICTs' potential impact has drawn the attention of both scholars and practitioners and has resulted in lively debates as well. For the FAO, for example, the challenge in assisting farmers and, generally, rural populations to develop implies the need for new technologies, new skills, changed attitudes and practices, and new ways to collaborate. This, in turn, requires that rural populations have access to relevant information and knowledge and ICTs are envisaged to play a decisive role in or drive (rural) development (see: Koutsouris, 2006).

However, despite the fact that much of the literature on the use of ICTs concerns the potential that relevant investments may offer for rural areas, such a 'techno-optimist' account ignores the fact that on a worldwide scale rural areas are lagging behind in terms of access and taking advantage of the benefits of the ICTs (Koutsouris, 2006). Indeed, for many years, rural communities have been, in both developing and developed countries, referred to as the 'last mile of connectivity' (Paisley & Richardson, 1999). The digital divide(s) between urban and rural areas is well established

by research in the US, Canada, Australia and the European Union (Demoussis & Giannakopoulos, 2006; Fucks, 2009; Gil-Garcia et al., 2006; Ramirez, 2001; Willis & Tranter, 2006). Furthermore, Donnermeyer and Hollifield (2003) have found that there is also a digital divide between rural communities as well as between rural people at the same place.

Farmers and ICTs

Especially as far as farmers are concerned, research findings, in both developed and developing countries, point to the need to approach ICTs with caution. In this respect, the case of developed countries is revealing. Research in the USA has pointed out that, not only farmers had opposed the use of personal computers in the past (Lasley & Bultena, 1986), but that nowadays the Internet and email are less used than other sources (Brashear et al., 2000; Howell & Harbon, 2004; Lasley et al., 2001; Vergot et al., 2005). Furthermore, research in the US shows that the adoption and use of ICTs differs among different sections of the farming community due to factors such as farm size and type of production, gross annual income level, age and education (Bardon et al., 2007; Burke & Sewake, 2008; Hall et al., 2003; Howell & Harbon, 2004). Similar is the evidence from England and Ireland (Warren, 2002; Wims, 2007). Therefore, concern is expressed for a widened digital divide thus leaving many with little understanding of the technology (ICTs) and its potential applications.

THE GREEK SETTING

In Greece, according to the Observatory for the Greek Information Society's latest report (OGIS, 2009) the adoption of PCs and the use of Internet at home has, between 2005 and 2008, risen from 43% to 54% (vs. EU27: 68% and EU15: 72%, in 2008) and from 24.21% to 39.4% (vs. EU27: 60% and EU15: 64%, in 2008). In parallel, there has been a substantial increase in households' broadband connections from 1% to 23% (vs. EU27: 49% and EU 15: 52%, in 2008). Large differences are observed according to gender, age and education. Furthermore, Greek rural areas are lagging behind in the use of both PCs (20.5% vs. 37.5% in urban areas; 2006) and the Internet (15.9% vs. 30.1% respectively) (VPRC, 2007). Major factors impending the use of Internet, especially in rural areas, are poor infrastructure, the high cost of services and equipment and the lack of training and thus of IT skills (OGIS, 2009). Overall, according to the UN (2008), Greece rates, among 192 countries, 44th in terms of the eGovernment Readiness Index (and last among the Southern Europe EU member-states), and 104th in terms of the eParticipation Index.

Aims and Methodology

In the light of the above discussion this article aims at identifying the existence (or not) of (some form of) a 'digital divide' within rural areas in Greece. More specifically, it aims at exploring which characteristics (socio-demographic, economic, etc.) of (young) rural inhabitants relate to the use of PCs, the ownership of PCs and the use of Internet. Therefore, analysis addresses differences occurring within, first, the totality of (young) rural inhabitants (whether farmers or not) and, second, the farming community, utilising a Probit analysis framework. The findings, in turn, are critically discussed vis-à-vis eGovernment and human development prospects in rural areas.

The current piece of work utilises data drawn from a large-scale survey concerning young rural inhabitants in the framework of the 'Agrogenesis' project[1]. The target group comprised rural inhabitants 18-45 years old, in 7 out of the 52 Greek Prefectures. In order to take into account the heterogeneity of rural Greece, a multi-stage proportional stratified random sampling procedure was employed in cooperation with the National Statistics Service of Greece (NSSG)[2]. Data were collected (2005) through personal interviews on the basis of a structured questionnaire[3]; 853 completed questionnaires (91.4% of the target being 916 questionnaires) were used in the analysis that follows. A series of data concerning demographic, socioeconomic and spatial characteristics and information sources are examined in order to decompose their marginal effects upon use of PCs, ownership of PCs (PC at home) and use of Internet. A number of relevant explanatory variables is thus processed utilising a Probit analysis framework.

The Probit Model

A Probit model deals with a choice between two alternatives (Greene, 2000). It quantifies the relationship of the probability (a number between zero and one) to various characteristics. The Probit model uses the functional form: $\Pr ob[y_t = 0] = 1 - \Phi(x_t\beta)$, where $\Phi(\bullet)$ is the cumulative normal distribution; that is, $\Phi(z)$ is the probability that a random variable with a normal distribution, zero mean, and unit variance does not exceed z. The dependent variable is not a continuous but a dichotomous, binary variable. The probability depends on a vector of independent variables (x_t) and a vector of unknown parameters β. The task of estimation is to find the best values for these parameters. Since $x_t\beta$ has a normal distribution, interpreting Probit coefficients requires thinking in the Z metric. The interpretation of a Probit coefficient, β, is that a one-unit increase in a predictor leads to increasing the Probit score by β standard deviations. Estimation of Probit model is attained by maximizing the likelihood function. Goodness of fit and inferential statistics are based on the log likelihood and chi-square test statistics.

The dependent variables in the following Probit models are: PC use, PC ownership (PC at home) and use of Internet. These are binary dependent variables, taking on a value of 1 if the respondent has 'access/use or ownership' and 0 if not. The tentative explanatory variables comprise both continuous and binary variables, as shown in Table 1.

Table 1. Definition of variables used in the probit models

Variable	Description	Total Sample	Farmers
Dependent			
Computer use PC ownership Internet use	1 = Yes, 0 = No 1 = Yes, 0 = No 1 = Yes, 0 = No		
Independent			
Gender	Male = 1, Female = 0	+	+
Educ 1	Education > 9 years	+	+
Age X1	Age < 31 years old	+	+
Age X2	Age 31-35 years old	+	+
Age X3	Age 36-40 years old	+	+
Age X4	Age > 40 years old	+	+
Age Y1	Age of spouse < 31 years old	+	+
Age Y2	Age of spouse 31-35 years old	+	+
Age Y3	Age of spouse 36-40 years old	+	+
Age Y4	Age of spouse >40 years old	+	+
Educ 2	Education of spouse > than 9 years	+	+
Languag1	Knowledge of foreign language 1 = Yes, 0 = No	+	+
Q10new	Children at home 1 = Yes, 0 = No	+	+
Mount	Dummy; equals 1 if the area is mountainous	+	+
Lessfav	Dummy; equals 1 if the area is less favoured	+	+
Plain	Dummy; equals 1 if the area is plain	+	+
Income1	Income less than 6000€ equal to 1, else=0	+	+
Income2	Income 6000-12000€ equal to 1, else=0	+	+
Income3	Income more than 12000 € equal to 1, else=0	+	+
Plant	Dummy; equals 1 if the main orientation of the farm is plant production		+
Animal	Dummy; equals 1 if the main orientation of the farm is animal production		+
Q21.1	Mobility for education 1 = Yes, 0 = No	+	+
Q21.2	Mobility for job 1 = Yes, 0 = No	+	+
Q21.3	Mobility due to family affairs 1 = Yes, 0 = No	+	+
Q36AGR	Dummy; equals 1 if main job is farmer, else = 0	+	+
Q36YP	Dummy; equals 1 if main job is not farming, else = 0	+	
Q17.3yp	Dummy; equals 1 if there is spouse works outside agriculture, else=0		+
Q45.1yp	Dummy; equals 1 if farmer holds a second job, else=0		+
Q25new	Participation in collective action 1 = Yes, 0 = No	+	+
Q97new	Vocational education 1 = Yes, 0 = No	+	+
Q122new	Modern agriculture requires specialised knowledge & skills 1 = Yes, 0 = No	+	+
Q126new	Willingness to pay for advice 1 = Yes, 0 = No	+	+

continued on following page

Table 1. Continued

Variable	Description	Total Sample	Farmers
Q127new	Willingness to access advice through the Internet 1 = Yes, 0 = No	+	+
Q64Info	Knowledge of 'young farmers' programme 1 = Yes, 0 = No	+	+
Q74Info	Knowledge of 'modernization schemes' in farming 1 = Yes, 0 = No	+	+
Print	Main source of information: printed materials 1 = Yes, 0 = No	+	+
RTV	Main source of information: Radio & TV 1 = Yes, 0 = No	+	+
Internet	Main source of information: Internet 1 = Yes, 0 = No	+	+
Personal	Main source of information: personal conducts 1 = Yes, 0 = No	+	+
Q84new	Future plans for expanding farm 1=Yes, 0=No		+
Q60new	Satisfaction with farm income 1=Yes, 0=No		+
YearPC1	Use of computer = 1 year or less	+	+
YearPC2	Use of computer = 2-3 years	+	+
YearPC3	Use of computer > 3 years	+	+

Key Characteristics of Young Rural Inhabitants

The sample comprises of 65.5% men and 34.5% women; 63.9% have farming as their main occupation while the categories of self employed and private sector employees are represented with 12.2% each; the remaining 11.7% is distributed in one-figure percentages among civil servants, other professions or housewives. Nevertheless more than ¾ of the non professional farmers (non-farmers) are also engaged in agriculture - as a secondary activity.

The average age in the sample is 39.1 years with the most populated age-group being the 41-45 years one (46%) followed by those of 36-40 (29%), 31-35 (15.6%) and equal or less than 30 (9.4%). This distribution does not change significantly between farmers and non-farmers as far as the two first cohorts are concerned; however differences occur as far as the last two groups are concerned (17.8% and 7.7% respectively for farmers and 12% and 12.3% respectively for non-farmers).

46.2% of the sample reside at plain – dynamic areas and 53.8% in Less Favoured Areas (LFAs)[4] and mountainous ones; the majority of famers is found in the latter ones (61.3%) while the majority of the non-farmers in the former ones (58.9%). Furthermore, 43.1% of the sample has higher secondary education and 22.9% lower secondary education, with another 6.5% holding higher education degrees, thus leaving 27.9% of the total with only elementary education[5]. Among farmers, 33.1% have elementary education and only 2.4% have obtained a higher education degree. On the other hand, 48% of the non-farmers have higher secondary education and 13.7% higher education degrees.

Young rural inhabitants are familiar with technology (the use of cell phones, and radio-TV exceeds 90% of the total); additionally, 26.2% (19.5% of the farmers; 38% of the non-farmers) use PCs; among them, 81% have a PC at home (90.4% of the farmers; 72.6% of the non-farmers) and 74.7% have Internet access (65.7% of the farmers; 82.2% of non-farmers). Nevertheless, personal contacts are the major source of information as far as agricultural issues are concerned (95%) while RTV are the main sources of information for general information (70%). The Internet accounts for 1% and 3.7% respectively. Furthermore, PC and Internet use mainly cover occupational (62.3%, i.e., 59.6% for farmers and 64.7% for non-farmers; 57.8%, i.e., 60% and 56.3% respectively), information (58.6%, i.e., 53.6% and 62.9% respectively; 75.9%, i.e., 80% and 72.9% respectively) and entertainment needs (47.3%, i.e., 53.8% and 41.4% respectively; 41.6%, i.e., 40% and 42.7% respectively). Finally, everyday Internet use was reported by 25% of the sample (18.8% for farmers and 29.5% for non-farmers), some days of the week by 45.7% (46.4% and 45.3% respectively), once a week by 22.6% (26.1% and 20%) and rare by 6.7% (8.7% and 5.3%).

More than 55% of the farmers (and more than 70% of the non-farmers) ignore the main programmes employed in Greece ('young farmers' programme and 'farming modernisation' schemes) since the mid 80s. Given an increasing understanding (71% of the total; 76.5% of farmers; 61.5% of the non-farmers) that nowadays farming requires specialised knowledge and skills rural youth, almost unanimously (>90%), stated that they would certainly like to have access to advisory services, but only 41.5% of the total (47.4% of the farmers; 31.1% of the non-farmers) showed a will to pay for such services. Furthermore, 41.8% of the total sample (40.2% of farmers; 44.3% of non-farmers) expressed their propensity to access advice through the Internet - but farmers are highly uncertain (43.3%) as compared to non-farmers (26.3%).

Results of the Probit Model for Young Rural Inhabitants

For the analysis of the total sample the Probit models are estimated using a standard maximum likelihood approach. The maximum likelihood estimates of the Probit model are presented in Table 2. Results indicate that at least 84% of the observations were correctly predicted (84% for computer use, 86% for computer at home and 93% for internet use). The overall models are significant at the 0.0000 level according to the Model chi-Square Statistic (366.19, 302.54 and 599.55 respectively). The McFadden R^2 for the three models are 0.3736, 0.3436 and 0.7156. Both goodness-of-fit measures indicate that the Probit models perform reasonably well, considering the cross-sectional nature of the data. Marginal effects indicate the effect of one unit change in an exogenous variable on the probability of PC or Internet use.

Results of the first models show that there is a common set of variables influencing all three models. These are: knowledge of a foreign language (Languag1, marginal effects= 0.243, 0.206 and 0.523 respectively); education of spouse (Educ2= 0.119, 0.085 and 0.039); mobility (moved away from residence area) for education (Q21.1= 0.171, 0.102 and 0.042) as well as belief that success in modern agriculture requires specialised knowledge and skills (Q122new= 0.091, 0.090, 0.030) and, as expected, propensity to use the Internet for advice (Q127new= 0.231; negligible in the other two cases).

Furthermore, young rural inhabitants with higher than lower secondary education are 10% more likely to use PCs (Educ1, marginal effect= 0.100). The probability to use PCs is also higher by 18.4% for those holding an off-farm job (Q36YP), by 8.4% for those with vocational education (Q97new), by 9.8% for those willing to pay for advisory services (Q126new), by 10.7% for those who are knowledgeable of the 'young farmers' programme (Q64Info) and, finally, by 36.7% for those who use the Internet as their main source for information (Internet). On the contrary, those who left the area for work are 7.8% less likely to use PCs (Q21.2).

In the case of ownership of PC (PC at home), besides education (Educ1= 0.086), holding an off-farm job (Q36YP= 0.116), having vocational education (Q97new= 0.088), willingness to pay for advisory services (Q126new= 0.052) and

Table 2. Probit models for young rural inhabitants

	Computer use				Computer at Home				Internet use			
	Estimate		Marginal Effects		Estimate		Marginal Effects		Estimate		Marginal Effects	
Variable	Coef.	St. Err.	Coef.	St. Err.	Coef.	St. Err.	Coef.	St. Err.	Coef.	St. Err.	Coef.	St. Err.
Gender	0.2075	0.1660	0.5251	0.0420	0.0688	0.1693	0.0135	0.0333	-0.3009	0.2770	-0.0183	0.0172
Educ 1	0.3974*	0.1425	0.1005	.0.0356	0.4402*	0.1524	0.0866	0.0292	-0.0049	0.2556	-0.0003	0.0155
Age X1	-0.3328	0.3592	-0.0841	0.0909	-0.4108	0.3594	-0.0808	0.0706	0.2085	0.5855	0.0126	0.0359
Age X2	-0.1848	0.3193	-0.0467	0.0808	-0.5569**	0.3259	-0.1095	0.0641	-0.3927	0.5233	-0.0239	0.3226
Age X3	-0.4829	0.2962	-0.1221	0.0749	-0.8647*	0.2995	-0.1701	0.0587	-0.6134	0.4872	-0.0373	0.0305
Age X4	-0.2872	0.2787	-0.0726	0.0705	-0.5421**	0.2780	-0.1066	0.0546	-0.4948	0.4662	-0.0301	0.0288
Age Y1	-0.3521	0.3022	-0.8907	0.0763	-0.5727**	0.3293	-0.1126	0.0646	-0.7319	0.5052	-0.0445	0.0319
Age Y2	0.0558	0.2859	0.0141	0.0723	-0.1124	0.3037	-0.0221	0.0597	-0.5216	0.4913	-0.0317	0.0305
Age Y3	-0.0338	0.2888	-0.0085	0.0730	0.0032	0.3020	0.0006	0.0594	-0.3184	0.4660	-0.0193	0.0285
Age Y4	-0.1408	0.2899	-0.0356	0.0733	-0.1579	0.3081	-0.0318	0.0605	-0.5138	0.4577	-0.3129	0.0287
Educ 2	0.4722*	0.1555	0.1194	0.0393	0.4354*	0.1620	0.0856	0.0319	0.6519**	0.2756	0.0397	0.0186
Languag1	0.9621*	0.1431	0.2433	0.0360	1.0478*	0.1539	0.2061	0.0303	0.8602*	0.2490	0.5239	0.0187
Q10new	-0.0806	0.2218	-0.0204	0.0561	0.1690	0.2380	0.0332	0.0467	-0.1702	0.3610	-0.0103	0.0221
Mount	-0.0496	0.2929	-0.0125	0.0741	-0.1434	0.2848	-0.0282	0.0560	-0.4901	0.4900	-0.0298	0.0304
Lessfav	-0.1073	0.2847	-0.0271	0.0720	-0.2218	0.2777	-0.0436	0.0546	-0.2668	0.4748	-0.0162	0.0291
Plain	0.1866	0.2748	-0.0472	0.0695	-0.4626**	0.2668	-0.0910	0.0526	-0.5675	0.4416	-0.0345	0.0284
Income1	-0.6467	0.4716	-0.1636	0.1188	-0.4716	0.5222	-0.0928	0.1024	-0.0660	0.7806	-0.0040	0.0475
Income2	-0.3872	0.4701	-0.0979	0.1187	-0.1689	0.5205	-0.0332	0.1023	-0.2221	0.7817	-0.0135	0.0477
Income3	-0.4132	0.4697	-0.1045	0.1186	-0.2935	0.5204	-0.0577	0.1022	-0.0583	0.7706	-0.0035	0.0469
Q21.1	0.6791*	0.1836	0.1718	0.0482	0.5224*	0.1821	0.1028	0.0369	0.6978*	0.2596	0.0425	0.0192
Q21.2	-0.3089**	0.1871	-0.0781	0.0478	-0.2755	0.1958	-0.0542	0.0389	-0.1114	0.2947	-0.0067	0.1810
Q21.3	-0.3697	0.2441	-0.0935	0.0620	-0.2467	0.2602	-0.0485	0.0513	-0.5865	0.3637	-0.0357	0.2368
Q36AGR	0.2999	0.3141	0.0758	0.0793	0.4417	0.3466	0.0869	0.0679	-0.7801**	0.4610	-0.0475	0.0295
Q36YP	0.7277**	0.3127	0.1840	0.0788	0.5939**	0.3450	0.1168	0.0675	-0.7703	0.4794	-0.0469	0.0307
Q25new	0.00007	0.0005	0.00001	0.0001	-0.0003	0.0005	-0.00006	0.0001	0.00001	0.0010	-0.000001	0.00006
Q97new	0.3328*	0.1634	0.0841	0.0413	0.4475*	0.1666	0.0880	0.0328	-0.6079	0.2600	-0.0037	0.0159
Q122new	0.3612*	0.1399	0.0914	0.0355	0.4600*	0.1478	0.0905	0.0295	0.4940**	0.2349	0.0300	0.0158
Q126new	0.3893*	0.1307	0.0985	0.0329	0.2672**	0.1351	0.0525	0.0266	0.2647	0.2219	0.0161	0.0136
Q127new	0.0009*	0.0001	0.2310	0.00004	0.0008*	0.0001	0.0001	0.00003	0.0006**	0.0003	0.00003	0.00001
Q64Info	0.4231	0.1618	0.1070	0.0408	0.4216*	0.1662	0.0829	0.0325	0.0572	0.2710	-0.0348	0.01659
Q74Info	-0.0846	0.1673	-0.0214	0.0423	-0.0653	0.1699	-0.1285	0.0334	-0.2360	0.2684	-0.0143	0.1638
Print	0.4977	0.3867	0.1259	0.0978	0.5760	0.3888	0.1133	0.0766	0.6937	0.5421	0.0422	0.3440
RTV	0.1121	0.4155	0.0283	0.1051	0.0054	0.4073	0.0010	0.0801	-0.4578	0.6703	-0.0278	0.0411
Internet	1.4532**	0.7099	0.3676	0.1819	0.7652	0.5487	0.1505	0.1088	0.3632	0.8164	0.0221	0.0501
Personal	-0.1613	0.1503	-0.4080	0.0379	-0.1826	0.1567	-0.0364	0.0307	-0.0883	0.2486	-0.0538	0.1519
YearPC1									2.4239*	0.4149	0.1476	0.0459
YearPC2									2.5253*	0.2837	0.1538	0.0439
Year PC3									3.1613*	0.2821	0.1925	0.0560

continued on following page

Table 2. Continued

	Computer use		Computer at Home		Internet use	
	Estimate	Marginal Effects	Estimate	Marginal Effects	Estimate	Marginal Effects
Model chi-square	366.19		302.54		599.55	
McFadden's R	0.3736		0.3436		0.7156	
% correct predictions	84		86		93	

* significant at the 0.01 level, ** significant at the 0.05 level

knowledge of the 'young farmers' programme (Q64Info= 0.082), all age categories but the lowest (i.e. AgeX2, AgeX3, AgeX4) as well as the lowest age category of the spouse (AgeY1) are negatively related to adoption. Similarly, those living in plain areas are 9.1% less likely to own a PC at home (Plain= -0.091).

Finally, in addition to the aforementioned common set of variables, Internet use relates positively to the years one uses PCs (YearPC1, YearPC2, YearPC3; marginal effects=0.147, 0.153 and 0.192 respectively) and negatively with main occupation been farming (Q36AGR= -0.047).

Results of the Probit Models for Farmers

For the analysis of the farmers (sub)sample the Probit models are also estimated using a standard maximum likelihood approach. The maximum likelihood estimates of the Probit model are presented in Table 3. Results indicate that at least 88% of the observations were correctly predicted (88% for computer use and for computer at home and 96% for internet use). The overall models are significant at the 0.0000 level according to the Model chi-Square Statistic (218.65, 202.87 and 315.92 respectively). The McFadden R^2 for the three models are 0.4076, 0.4052 and 0.7635. Both goodness-of-fit measures indicate that the Probit models perform reasonably well, considering the cross-sectional nature of the data. Marginal effects indicate the effect of one unit change in

an exogenous variable on the probability of PC or Internet use.

Results of the models for farmers show that there is, again, a common set of variables influencing all three models. These are: age of spouse less than 31years old (AgeY1= negative), spouse education higher than lower secondary schooling (Educ2= positive), knowledge of foreign language (Languag1= positive), mobility for studies (Q21.1= positive), and propensity to access advice through the Internet (Q127new= positive).

In the case of PC use, additional variables refer to mobility for work (Q21.2= negative), involvement in public affairs (Q25new= positive), willingness to pay for advise (Q126new= positive) and Internet as the main source of information (Internet= positive). In the case of having a PC at home additional, to the common variables are: involvement in public affairs (Q25new= positive), vocational education/training (Q97new) and Internet as main source of information (Internet= positive). Finally, in the case of Internet use, additional variables refer to gender (Gender= negative), mobility for work (Q21.2= negative), and years of PC use (YearPC1, YearPC2, YearPC3= positive).

DISCUSSION

The present piece of work aims at identifying the existence (or not) of (some form of) a 'digital divide' within rural areas in Greece, utilising data

Table 3. Probit results for farmers

Variable	Computer use		Computer at Home		Internet use	
	Sign	Sig.	Sign	Sig.	Sign	Sig.
Gender	-		-		-	**
Educ 1	+		+		-	
Age X1	-		-		-	
Age X2	+		+		-	
Age X3	+		-			
Age X4	-		-			
Age Y1	-	*	-	*	-	**
Age Y2	-		-		-	
Age Y3	-		-			
Age Y4	-		-			
Educ 2	+	*	+	*	+	**
Languag1	+	*	+	*	+	*
Q10new	+		+		+	
Mount	-					
Lessfav	-					
Plain	-		-			
Income1	-		-		+	
Income2	-		-		+	
Income3	-		-		+	
Plant	-		-		-	
Animal	-		-		-	
Q21.1	+	*	+	**	+	*
Q21.2	-	**	-		-	**
Q21.3	-		-		-	
Q17.3yp	+		+		+	
Q45.1yp	-					
Q25new	+	*	+	*	+	
Q97new	+		+	**	+	
Q122new	+		+			
Q126new	+	**	+		+	
Q127new	+	*	+		+	**
Q64Info	+		+			
Q74Info	-					
Print	-					
RTV	-		+		+	
Internet	+	**	+	*	+	
Personal	-					
Year PC1					+	*

continued on following page

135

Table 3. Continued

Variable	Computer use		Computer at Home		Internet use	
	Sign	Sig.	Sign	Sig.	Sign	Sig.
Year PC2					+	*
Year PC3					+	*
Q84new	+		+		+	
Q60new	-		-		-	
Model chi-square	218.65		202.87		315.92	
McFadden's R	0.4076		0.4052		0.7635	
% correct predictions	88		88		96	

* significant at the 0.01 level, ** significant at the 0.05 level

drawn from a large-scale survey concerning young rural inhabitants (18-45 years old).

The use of PCs and the Internet on the part of young rural inhabitants is found to be affected by a number of characteristics mainly relating to educational attainment (moved away from residence area for education; knowledge of foreign language; spouse's education; as well as own vocational education – re: PC use) and thus attitudes towards knowledge (modern agriculture requires specialised knowledge and skills; willingness to pay for advice; and, as expected, propensity to search for advice in the Internet) as well as occupation (i.e., non-farmers). Ownership of PC is also affected by age, with older inhabitants and younger spouses been less likely to own a PC. The latter probably owes to the fact that young women who stay at home and get married relatively young are 'left behind' i.e., do not move away from rural areas (a common phenomenon in the Greek countryside) and generally have low educational level. Further, the finding that inhabitants of plain areas are less likely to have PC at home may owe to the fact that multiple information sources are available in such areas (compared to mountainous and LFAs) as well as that since the majority of young non-farmers live in such areas they may use PC at work or in Internet cafes[6]. Finally, Internet use relates to experience with PCs (measured as years of PC use)[7].

The same characteristics determine, in general lines, farmers' behaviour as well. Nevertheless,

it is interesting to note that a) spouse's age appears to play a role in all three cases examined; b) farmers' engagement in public affairs appears to determine PC use and ownership; and, c) gender appears to influence Internet use (i.e., women are less likely to use the Internet).

A further finding is that, contrary to - based on the literature review - expectations, income appears to influence none of the dependent variables (PC use, Internet use or PC ownership). Yet, it can be argued that this is due to the influence of education and occupation which, in turn, 'obscures' the influence of income[8].

Therefore, the preceding analyses are in line with previous studies addressing the (general) phenomenon 'digital divide'. Moreover, it seems that, besides the well established urban-rural divide, further 'sub-divides' emerge within rural areas: on the one hand, between non-farmers and farmers and, on the other hand, among farmers. Cultural resources (educational attainment within the household and attitudes towards knowledge) appear to determine a great part of this phenomenon (also due to relationships to occupation and income). This may obscure the influence of the presence of children at home and deserves further exploration. Occupation emerges as the second important factor determining PC and Internet use with farmers being left in the 'wrong side' of the divide.

Two points are worth mentioning here. First, the present piece of work reaffirms the finding that 'who you are' is strongly related to whether or not you use the internet, and what you use it for (Selwyn et al., 2005). Second, education has been found to be a major factor determining differential Internet use (Gil-Garcia et al., 2006; Hargittai & Hinnant, 2008). Tentatively, given the prominence of education in determining PC and Internet use in the preceded analysis, a 'second level' divide is also in place. The fact that this paper only begins to analyse the topic of an emerging intra-rural digital divide, and that findings are limited by the availability of data (the survey, data were drawn from, was not designed to specifically address the topic under consideration) implies the need for further investigation. In order to acquire a more nuanced account of the 'sub-divides' within rural areas, research concerning the 'second level divide' and 'unfavourable inclusion' (Zheng & Walsham, 2008), as well as the relationship between different groups of non-users (Reddick, 2000) and media use selection, is deemed necessary.

CONCLUSION: ON HUMAN DEVELOPMENT

Further to such considerations, it is highly probable that the 'digital divide' has major repercussions as far as the advent of eGovernment in terms of (human) development is concerned. Following Sen, development concerns the enlargement of people's opportunities for choice; therefore, citizens have an entitlement to acquire capabilities including those of being well-informed and able to participate in society (Alkire, 2005; Hargittai & Hinnant, 2008; Madon, 2005; Mansel, 2002; Zheg & Walsham, 2008). Therefore, the questions of a) which ICT options are available, and b) whether people have the ability to use them to participate in democratic processes, arise.

From the preceding analysis it is shown that considerable, identifiable segments within the Greek rural society (notably a large part of farmers) are being deprived of access to PCs and the Internet. This, in turn, means that they are excluded from certain information concerning, for example, political and public affairs and, thus, from participation in political, social and cultural practices etc. Moreover, as long as electronic information is increasingly embedded in and mediating people's lives, it seems highly probable that those who do not have (or are not able to acquire) the ability to use new media, particularly the Internet, will not have the capabilities to participate in democratic processes and improve their lives.

In order to avoid a self-reinforcing cycle that will deepen the gap while also widening the 'democratic deficit', policies concerning new media must take on board issues of democracy, social development and equity together. This, in turn, means that policies should concentrate on citizens' rights and entitlements to the opportunity to acquire both physical access and new media literacies. The latter implies the facilitation of people to acquire both technical and cognitive capacities (i.e., to acquire, interpret and use information as part of a civil society and in the context of their everyday lives), which, in turn, will increase their abilities to effectively use electronic spaces to enhance their opportunities to make choices between alternatives and participate in public deliberation/ democratic processes.

However, it seems that currently governments heavily focus on the 'access to technology' problem, with eGovernment services' development being based on a 'customer-centric' model (Cibbora, 2005), i.e., an inflexible model that provides people with information and services, rather than on tools to enable capabilities. Therefore, it remains uncertain as to what contribution current eGovernment projects make to overall development.

Nevertheless, experience from the fields of rural development and rural extension (Koutsouris, 2006, 2008) points towards an alternative: that is, participatory processes. In such a case the 'supply-driven' approach is reversed as follows: first, people's and communities' interests are identified; then, the type of information necessary to satisfy such needs is determined; finally, the way technology can support those interests is decided. In this respect, the development of eGovernment projects should be planned and evaluated in common with the people concerned and thus with respect to their context. This for rural areas and especially farmers implies an understanding of the local knowledge systems which is mainly based on experience and the support of local organizations, and concerns both farm and non-farm decisions.

In the light of our research findings and discussion, the effort put on eGovernment projects, mainly concerning the offer of more information and services online, is questionable. Such a techno-centric (technological deterministic) approach in creating a developmental process fosters material access and technology adoption per se and thus fails, on the one hand, to appreciate the complexity of the factors stalling eGovernment, and in general ICT projects in rural areas (i.e., the digital divide phenomenon) and, on the other hand, to address those people and groups who have least access to new media and seem to be socially and politically marginalised. This, in turn, tentatively has major repercussions as far as (human) development is concerned.

Therefore, although "the idea that ICTs are intrinsically desirable and beneficial to the society is still prevalent", the present study confirms that "ICTs can contribute to the exacerbation of social exclusion, or can be tools to bridge gaps" (Trauth & Howcroft, 2006; in Zheng & Walsham, 2008, p. 222). And, while this study draws on the experience of Greece, the lesson may be universal.

REFERENCES

Alexopoulos, G., Koutsouris, A., & Tzouramani, I. (2008, November). *Characteristics of the demand for advisory and educational services in rural areas: Results of field research among young rural inhabitants*. Paper presented at the 10th Panhellenic Conference of Rural Economy, Thessaloniki, Greece.

Alkire, S. (2005). Why the capability approach? *Journal of Human Development and Capabilities, 6*(1), 115–135. doi:10.1080/146498805200034275

Bardon, R., Hazel, D., & Miller, K. (2007). Preferred information delivery methods of North Carolina forest landowners. *Journal of Extension, 45*(5). Retrieved January 20, 2009, from http://www.joe.org/joe/ 2007october/a3.shtml

Beynon-Davies, P. (2007). Models for e-government. *Transforming Government: People. Process and Policy, 1*(1), 7–28.

Bimber, B. (1998). The Internet and Political Transformation: Populism, Community, and Accelerated Pluralism. *Polity, 31*(1), 133–160. doi:10.2307/3235370

Brashear, G., Hollis, G., & Wheeler, M. (2000). Information transfer in the Illinois swine industry: How producers are informed of new technologies. *Journal of Extension, 38*(1). Retrieved January 20, 2009, from http://joe.org/joe/ 2000february/rb4.html

Buente, W., & Robbin, A. (2008). Trends in Internet Information Behavior, 2000-2004. *Journal of the American Society for Information Science and Technology, 59*(11), 1743–1760. doi:10.1002/asi.20883

Burke, K., & Sewake, K. (2008). Adoption of computer and internet technologies in small firm agriculture: A study of flower growers in Hawaii. *Journal of Extension, 46*(3). Retrieved January 20, 2009, from http://www.joe.org/joe/ 2008june/rb5.shtml

Chen, W., & Wellman, B. (2003). Charting and Bridging Digital Divides. *I-Ways, Digest of electronic commerce policy and regulation, 26*, 155-161.

Chen, W., & Wellman, B. (2004). The global digital divide – within and between countries. *IT & Society, 1*(7), 39–45.

Cho, J., de Zuniga, H., Rojas, H., & Shah, D. (2003). Beyond access: The digital divide and Internet uses and gratifications. *IT & Society, 1*(4), 46–72.

Cibbora, C. (2005). Interpreting e-government and development. *Information Technology & People, 18*(3), 260–279. doi:10.1108/09593840510615879

Clement, A., & Shade, L. R. (2000). The Access Rainbow: Conceptualising universal Access to the Information/Communication Infrastructure. In Gurstein, M. (Ed.), *Informatics: enabling communities with information and communications technologies* (pp. 32–51). Hershey, PA: IGI Global.

Dada, D. (2006). The failure of E-Government in developing countries: A literature review. *The Electronic Journal of Information Systems in Developing Countries, 26*. Retrieved May 11, 2009, from http://www.ejisdc.org/ojs2/ index.php/ejisdc/article/ viewFile/277/176

Demoussis, M., & Giannakopoulos, N. (2006). Facets of the digital divide in Europe: Determination and extend of Internet use. *Economics of Innovation and New Technology, 15*(3), 235–246. doi:10.1080/10438590500216016

Dewan, S., & Riggins, F. (2005). The digital divide: Current and future research directions. *Journal of the Association for Information Systems, 6*(12), 298–337.

DiMaggio, P., & Hargittai, E. (2001) *From the 'Digital Divide' to 'Digital Inequality': Studying Internet Use as Penetration Increases* (Working Paper 15). Princeton, NJ: Princeton University, Center for Arts and Cultural Policy Studies.

Donnermeyer, J., & Hollifield, A. (2003). Digital divide evidence in four rural towns. *IT & Society, 1*(4), 107–117.

Dutta-Bergman, M. (2005). Access to the internet in the context of community participation and community satisfaction. *New Media & Society, 7*(1), 89–109. doi:10.1177/1461444805049146

Fink, C., & Kenny, C. (2003). W(h)ither the digital divide? *Info, 5*(6), 15–24. doi:10.1108/14636690310507180

Forestier, E., Grace, J., & Kenny, C. (2002). Can information and communication technologies be pro-poor? *Telecommunications Policy, 26*, 623–646. doi:10.1016/S0308-5961(02)00061-7

Foster, S. P. (2000). The Digital Divide: Some Reflections. *The International Information & Library Review, 32*(3/4), 437–451. doi:10.1006/iilr.2000.0136

Fuchs, C. (2009). The Role of Income Inequality in a Multivariate Cross-National Analysis of the Digital Divide. *Social Science Computer Review, 27*(1), 41–58. doi:10.1177/0894439308321628

Gil-Garcia, R., Helbig, N., & Ferro, E. (2006). Is It Only About Internet Access? An Empirical Test of a Multi-dimensional Digital Divide. In *Proceedings of EGOV 2006* (pp. 139-149). New York: Springer. DOI: 10.1007/11823100

Greene, W. H. (2000). *Econometric Analysis* (4th ed.). Upper Saddle River, NJ: Prentice Hall.

Gunkel, D. J. (2003). Second thoughts: toward a critique of the digital divide. *New Media & Society, 5*(4), 499–522. doi:10.1177/146144480354003

Hall, L., Dunkelberger, J., Ferreira, W., Prevatt, J. W., & Martin, N. (2003). Diffusion-adoption of personal computers and the internet in farm business decisions: Southeastern beef and peanut farmers. *Journal of Extension, 41*(3). Retrieved January 20, 2009, from http://www.joe.org/joe/2003june/a6.shtml

Hargittai, E., & Hinnant, A. (2008). Digital inequality: Differences in young adults' use of the Internet. *Communication Research, 35*(5), 602–621. doi:10.1177/0093650208321782

Helbig, N., Gil-Garcia, R., & Ferro, E. (2009). Understanding the complexity of electronic government: Implications from the digital divide literature. *Government Information Quarterly, 26*(1), 89–97. doi:10.1016/j.giq.2008.05.004

Howell, J., & Harbon, J. (2004). Agricultural landowners' lack of preference for internet extension. *Journal of Extension, 42*(6). Retrieved January 20, 2009, from http://www.joe.org/joe/2004december/a7.shtml

Korupp, S., & Szydlick, M. (2005). Causes and trends of the digital divide. *European Sociological Review, 21*(4), 409–422. doi:10.1093/esr/jci030

Koutsouris, A. (2006). ICTs and rural development: Beyond the hype. *Journal of Extension Systems, 22*(1), 46–62.

Koutsouris, A. (2008). The battlefield of (sustainable) rural development: The case of the Lake Plastiras, Central Greece. *Sociologia Ruralis, 48*(3), 240–256. doi:10.1111/j.1467-9523.2008.00465.x

Lasley, P., & Bultena, G. (1986). Farmers' opinions about third-wave technologies. *American Journal of Alternative Technology, 1*, 99–110.

Lasley, P., Padgitt, S., & Hanson, M. (2001). Telecommunication technology and its implications for farmers and Extension Services. *Technology in Society, 23*, 109–120. doi:10.1016/S0160-791X(00)00039-7

Macintosh, A. (2006). eParticipation in Policymaking: the research and the challenges. In P. Cunningham & M. Cunningham (Eds.), *Exploiting the Knowledge Economy: Issues, Applications and Case Studies* (pp. 364-369). Amsterdam: IOS press.

Madon, S. (2005) Evaluating the developmental impact of E-Governance initiatives: An exploratory framework. *The Electronic Journal of Information Systems in Developing Countries, 20*. Retrieved May 11, 2009, from http://www.ejisdc.org/ojs2/index.php/ejisdc/article/view/123

Mahrer, H., & Krimmer, R. (2005). Towards the Enhancement of E-democracy: Identifying the Notion of the 'Middleman Paradox'. *Information Systems Journal, 15*(1), 27–42. doi:10.1111/j.1365-2575.2005.00184.x

Makinen, O., & Naarmala, J. (2008). The changing concept of the digital divide. In M. Iskander (Ed.), *Innovative Techniques in Instruction Technology, E-learning, E-assessment, and Education* (pp. 406-409). New York: Springer. DOI: 10.1007/978-1-4020-8739-4_71

Mansel, R. (2002). From Digital Divides to Digital Entitlements in Knowledge Societies. *Current Sociology, 50*(3), 407–426. doi:10.1177/0011392102050003007

Muhlberger, P. (2004). Access, skill and motivation in online political discussion: Testing cyberrealism. In Shane, P. M. (Ed.), *Democracy online: The prospects for political renewal through the Internet* (pp. 225–238). New York: Routledge.

Norris, P. (2001). *Digital divide: Civic engagement, information poverty, and the Internet worldwide*. Cambridge, UK: Cambridge University Press.

OGIS - The Observatory for the Greek Information Society. (2009). *The digital Greece indicators: 4th annual report*. Athens, Greece: OGIS.

Paisley, L., & Richardson, D. (1999). *The first mile of connectivity: Why the first mile and not the last?* Rome, Italy: FAO.

Polat, R. K. (2005). The Internet and political participation. *European Journal of Communication, 20*(4), 435–459. doi:10.1177/0267323105058251

Quintelier, E., & Vissers, S. (2008). The Effect of Internet Use on Political Participation: An Analysis of Survey Results for 16-Year-Olds in Belgium. *Social Science Computer Review, 26*(4), 411–427. doi:10.1177/0894439307312631

Raman, V. (2008). Examining the 'e' in government and governance: A case study in alternatives from Bangalore City, India. *The Journal of Community Informatics, 4*(2). Retrieved May 24, 2009, from http://www.ci-journal.net/index.php/ciej/article/view/437/405

Ramirez, R. (2001). A model for rural and remote information and communication technologies: a Canadian exploration. *Telecommunications Policy, 25*, 315–330. doi:10.1016/S0308-5961(01)00007-6

Reddick, A. (2000). *The dual digital divide: The information highway in Canada*. Ottawa, Canada: The Public Interest Advocacy Centre.

Selwyn, N. (2002). *Defining the 'Digital Divide': Developing a Theoretical Understanding of Inequalities in the Information Age* (Occasional Paper 36). Cardiff, UK: Cardiff University, School of Social Sciences.

Selwyn, N. (2004). Reconsidering political and popular understandings of the digital divide. *New Media & Society, 6*(3), 341–362. doi:10.1177/1461444804042519

Selwyn, N., Gorard, S., & Furlong, J. (2005). Whose internet is it anyway? Exploring adults' (non)use of the internet in everyday life. *European Journal of Communication, 20*(1), 5–26. doi:10.1177/0267323105049631

Small, T. (2006). Review: Electronic Democracy: Mobilisation, Organisation, and Participation via New ICTs. *Canadian Journal of Communication, 31*(2), 475–476.

UN. (2003a). *World Public Sector Report 2003: E-Government at the Crossroads*. New York: UN.

UN. (2003b). *UN Global E-government Survey 2003*. Retrieved June 1, 2009, from http://unpan1.un.org/intradoc/ groups/public/documents/ UN/ UNPAN016066.pdf

UN. (2006). *UN Millenium Development Goals Report 2006*. New York: UN.

UN. (2008). *UN E-Government Survey 2008. From E-Government to Connected Governance*. New York: UN.

Van Dijk, J. (2005). *The deepening divide*. Thousand Oaks, CA: Sage.

Van Dijk, J. (2006). Digital divide research, achievements and shortcomings. *Poetics, 34*, 221–235. doi:10.1016/j.poetic.2006.05.004

Van Dijk, J., & Hacker, K. (2003). The digital divide as a complex and dynamic phenomenon. *The Information Society, 19*, 315–326. doi:10.1080/01972240309487

Vergot, P., Israel, G., & Mayo, D. (2005). Sources and channels of information used by beef cattle producers in 12 Counties of the Northwest Florida extension eistrict. *Journal of Extension, 43*(2). Retrieved January 20, 2009, from http://www.joe.org/joe/ 2005april/rb6.shtml

VPRC. (2007). *Comparative report on the 'National research on new technologies and the information society*. Athens, Greece: VPRC & National Network for Research and Technology.

Warren, M. F. (2002). Digital divides and the adoption of information and communication technologies in the UK farm sector. *International Journal of Information Technology and Management, 1*(4), 385–405. doi:10.1504/IJITM.2002.001207

Warschauer, M. (2003). *Technology and Social Inclusion: Rethinking the Digital Divide*. Cambridge, MA: MIT Press.

Willis, S., & Tranter, B. (2006). Beyond the 'digital divide': Internet diffusion and inequality in Australia. *Journal of Sociology (Melbourne, Vic.), 42*(1), 43–59. doi:10.1177/1440783306061352

Wims, P. (2007). Analysis of adoption and the use of ICTs among Irish farm families. *Journal of Extension Systems, 23*(1), 14–28.

Yu, L. (2006). Understanding information inequality: Making sense of the literature of the information and digital divides. *Journal of Librarianship and Information Science, 38*(4), 229–252. doi:10.1177/0961000606070600

Zheng, Y., & Walsham, G. (2008). Inequality of what? Social exclusion in the e-society as capability deprivation. *Information Technology & People, 21*(3), 222–243. doi:10.1108/09593840810896000

ENDNOTES

[1] The 'Agro-genesis' project (www.agrogenesis.gr), run within the EQUAL II framework under the coordination of the Greek Confederation of Agricultural Co-operative Unions (PASEGES), aimed at exploring young (18-45 years old) rural inhabitants' attitudes towards various forms of provision of extension and educational services as well as their relevant needs (see: Alexopoulos et al., 2008).

[2] Such a procedure was deemed necessary in order to account for spatial differences (i.e., plain, semi-mountainous and mountainous areas), urbanisation (urban, semi-urban and rural municipalities) as well as to obtain a sample fairly representative of the actual population age categories, based on the latest available Census (NSSG, 2001). Following such a stratification, NSSG selected municipalities/communities within the 7 Prefectures as well as the sample and the supplementary sample, both on a random numbers basis.

[3] The questionnaire comprised of 86 questions organised in 9 sections. Besides the socioeconomic profile of the interviewees, issues such as their participation in various programmes and training schemes, their experience from existing services, the challenges they face as farmers and/or rural inhabitants, etc., were explored. Among such issues, aspects relating to the use of PCs and of the Internet were also addressed.

[4] In the European Union, since 1975 (EC Directive No 75/268/EEC of 28.April 1975 on mountain and hill farming and farming in certain less-favoured areas; Brussels, Official Journal L 128, 19/5/1975), less-favoured area (LFA) is a term used to describe an area with natural handicaps, or that is mountainous or hilly, as defined by its altitude and slope. The LFAs schemes provide 'compensatory allowances' to farmers in mountainous areas or in other areas where the physical landscape results in higher production costs. According to the last amendment (Council Regulation (EC) No 1257/1999 of 17 May 1999 on support for rural development from the European Agricultural Guidance and Guarantee Fund (EAGGF) and amending and repealing certain Regulations; Brussels, Official Journal L 160, 26/06/1999) compensatory allowances are granted to farmers in mountain areas (Article 18), other less-favoured areas (Article 19), and areas affected by specific handicaps (Article 20).

[5] According to the Greek schooling system, elementary (primary) education lasts 6 years, lower secondary education (Gymnasium) 3 years and higher secondary education (Lyceum) 3 years. Compulsory education concerns the first 9 years (Gymnasium degree), while to proceed to higher education (technological or university) one needs a Lyceum degree (i.e., 12 years of schooling).

[6] Confirmed by bivariate analysis (crosstabulations).

[7] Furthermore, bivariate analysis (crosstabulations) shows that density of use is affected by occupation.

[8] Bivariate analyses (crosstabulations) show statistically significant relationships between, on the one hand, income and, on the other hand, education, occupation, PC use and Internet use.

This work was previously published in International Journal of Information Communication Technologies and Human Development, Volume 2, Issue 3, edited by Susheel Chhabra and Hakikur Rahman, pp. 1-18, copyright 2010 by IGI Publishing (an imprint of IGI Global).

Chapter 10
Pathways to Participatory Landscape Governance in Northern Laos:
The Role of Information and Communication Technologies

John Daniel Watts
Center for International Forestry Research (CIFOR), Laos

Vilaphong Kanyasone
Northern Agriculture and Forestry Research Centre, Laos

Vongvilay Vongkhamsao
National Agriculture and Forestry Research Institute, Laos

ABSTRACT

The Landscape Mosaics Project is a global research project coordinated by the Center for International Forestry Research (CIFOR) and the World Agroforestry Centre (ICRAF) and funded by the Swiss Agency for Development Cooperation (SDC). The project examines biodiversity in tropical, forested, multifunctional landscapes in sites adjacent to protected areas. A key thematic component of its research examines the governance of landscapes, and by using a Participatory Action Research approach, the project aspires to facilitate better landscape governance through improved communication between village and landscape level actors. This article examines the initial experiences of the project in its Northern Lao site, located in Vieng Kham District, Luang Prabang Province. The authors describe how the lack of access to information communication technologies have inhibited local actors levels of participation in landscape level governance as well as affected their abilities to effectively and adaptively manage their landscape. Community radio, that provides local actors with the relevant information for more substantially participating in landscape governance as well as information useful for adaptive management, is proposed as one potential solution for improving participatory landscape governance.

DOI: 10.4018/978-1-4666-0047-8.ch010

INTRODUCTION

The Landscape Mosaics Project is a global research project coordinated by the Center for International Forestry Research (CIFOR) and the World Agroforestry Centre (ICRAF) and funded by the Swiss Agency for Development Cooperation (SDC). The project examines biodiversity in tropical, forested, multifunctional landscapes including protected areas. In particular, the project asks the following questions about biodiversity in these forest patches:

- How are forest products used and by whom?
- What are the socioeconomic values of the services provided by these forests – ranging from non-timber forest products to watershed protection and biodiversity conservation - and where relevant, are there potential incentives to conserve them?
- What role do these forest patches have in biodiversity conservation?
- How are these resources governed from the national to the village level? and,
- Who are the people in the landscape and what is their vision for the future management of the landscape?

The two final questions form the basis of the intervention component of the project. The overarching intention of the project is to facilitate the emergence of a multi-level communication system linked to a platform that brings village and landscape level actors together. The ideal platform would be where the visions of actors can be negotiated and incorporated into the planning and management of the landscape.

The project aimed to work with district and village groups using a Participatory Action Research (PAR) approach. The objectives of this approach were to improve the capacity of different actors at the village and district level, especially women, to formulate their visions, negotiate plans and

adaptively manage their landscape. Initial results from ICRAF and CIFOR tend to support the idea that improved communication can lead to better conservation and improved livelihoods because government plans and strategies better reflect the wishes of local people (Komarudin et al., 2008; van Noordwijk et al., 2001). These activities would all take place in landscapes often characterized by the lack of infrastructure for supporting suitable alternative communication strategies that rely on information communication technologies.

This article will focus on the initial experiences of facilitating the emergence of a multi-level communication platform in the context of one of the sites of the Landscape Mosaics Project, Vieng Kham District, in the northern part of Laos. The project in Laos works in conjunction with the National Agriculture and Forestry Research Institute (NAFRI), the Northern Agriculture and Forestry Research Centre (NAFReC), and the District Agriculture and Forestry Office (DAFO) in Vieng Kham. The project identified the nascent official government structure known as the "*kumban*" or village cluster in the area of Muangmuay as a possible intervention pathway for increasing community participation in landscape governance, especially land use planning processes. The initial results from the implementation of the project will be explored especially in the context of no access to web-based technologies in the district, and little or no access to telecommunications or other information communication technologies outside of the district capital. The article will also identify alternative pathways for improving communication for community participation in governance that have arisen through consultations with village, *kumban* and district level actors and their possible implementation.

FRAMEWORK

Landscape Governance: A Model of Adaptive Co-Management for Livelihoods and the Environment in Tropical, Rural, Forested Landscapes

Landscape Governance has been proposed as a model of governance that is able to effectively account for the multiple actors interacting at different scales of governance across the landscape, a territorial unit that links natural and social processes (Görg, 2007). The term landscape, as it is used in the Landscape Mosaics Project, is understood as being a multifunctional landscape. A multifunctional landscape is a territorial unit where the multiple dimensions of landscapes, which include the ecological, economic, cultural, historical and aesthetic, interact (Tress & Tress, 2000). The landscapes that have been selected as part of the project have generally been located adjacent to a protected forested area, and on a gradient from dense forest to intensive agriculture, usually within the boundaries of a single district or other adminstrative unit. These multifunctional landscapes are considered, first, in terms of the different people who live there, their aspirations, culture and livelihood activities. Second in terms of other actors who also have a claim to the management or resources found there. And, third, the complex biophysical processes that interact with these social systems.

Governance in turn is broadly understood as being "about who decides and how, and encompasses policies, institutions, processes and power (Swiderska et al., 2009, p. 1)." In the context of the project, governance is studied from the national policy level, to processes, institutions - formal and informal - and actors at the district and village levels who affect the governance of the landscape. The central hypothesis of the governance theme of the Landscape Mosaics Project is:

Overall, landscape sustainability is enhanced if public policies are informed by, allow and support customary or local rules and practices. Strengthening mutual support among levels of governance will result in better forest management and improved human well being (Pfund et al., 2008, p. xix).

To test this hypothesis, the project, through its intervention component, aims to bring together village and district level actors to discuss issues affecting the landscape and develop new collaborative institutions for managing the landscape. Ideally, the project aims to facilitate the emergence of a multi-level governance arrangement (Armitage, 2008) that provides the conditions for the successful adaptive governance and co-management (Borrini-Feyerabend, 2004) of social-ecological systems (Folke et al., 2005) for multi-functional landscapes.

Information Flows

To catalyse effective landscape governance and management, the project tests the hypothesis that effective landscape management will occur when landscape managers have access to the following forms of information:

- Local knowledge: relating to traditional and current land uses, economic activities, cultural practices and governance institutions;
- Scientific knowledge: relating to ecology, agricultural technologies, general education including literacy and other technological information such as for industrial production; and
- Systemic knowledge: relating to policy contexts, market information, and other social-ecological processes that may affect the trajectory of the landscape.

The transformation of these types of information into effective landscape governance and management requires both access to this information and strong social capital, which can be divided into the following three types:

- Bonding capital - which involves the links between individuals in the same group;
- Bridging capital - which involves the links between individuals within different groups; and
- Linking capital - which relates to the links to people and institutions of power. (Woolcock & Sweetser, 2002; cited in Dahal & Adhikari, 2008)

The focus of the intervention component is to try to build the three types of social capital through action research exercises targeted at specific groups within the village. The project would then bring those groups together with joint exercises. Finally, village level actors together with representatives from other more powerful institutions at the landscape level would be brought together to facilitate the emergence of co-management of the landscape. The activities would be enhanced through longer-term PAR group activities at the village and district levels. Effective co-management, and consequently landscape management, has been described as occurring when social networks are centralised and cohesive internally, for effective decision-making, and heterogeneous externally, for facilitating greater resource mobilisation (Carlsson & Sandström, 2008). The intervention component of the project relies on the ability of the project to include sufficient numbers of people at the village level in the activities, and then to bring village level actors into contact with sufficiently enabled representatives of institutions of power together at the same time in a relatively equal negotiating platform. Drawing together actors in a participatory platform presents enough challenges of its own. Enabling the actors to effectively and adaptively negotiate, plan, implement and manage their landscapes in a way that addresses their visions for the landscape also requires regular modes of access to relevant information and technologies. The challenges of facilitating the emergence of this model of governance and the relationship with lack of access to information technologies will be discussed later in the article.

STUDY SITE

The Vieng Kham Landscape

The study site of the Landscape Mosaics Project in Laos is located in Vieng Kham District, Luang Prabang Province, in Northern Laos. The landscape area assessed by the project follows a north-south axis of lands between Phou Loey National Protected Area and the National Road that goes from Luang Prabang to Vietnam, via the neighbouring Huapan Province. Three villages were selected that represented the ethnic-linguistic heterogeneity of the landscape and according to a gradient corresponding to elevation and access to the national road.

The village of Phadeng, almost exclusively composed of ethnic Hmong people, is situated at an elevation of 1100 meters above sea level, and three hours walk to the nearest village, Phoukong, that has semi-permanent road access. This walk turns into a five-hour walk to the main road during the wet season as the dirt road to Phoukong becomes inaccessible to vehicles other than motorbikes. The inaccessibility of Phadeng, and consequently, the lack of access to basic services such as education, water and health, was the official rationale of the district of Vieng Kham for ordering the resettlement of the villagers to a site nearer to the main road. The village resettlement was scheduled to be completed by the end of 2008. At the time of writing, however, villagers were still in the process of moving and it was anticipated that the villagers would move by the end of 2009.

The second village, Bouammi, is comprised of two hamlets: Bouammi and Vang Mat. The villages were officially consolidated in 1998, but still remain separated by half an hour walk on a semi-permanent road. The old sub-village of Bouammi, is predominately ethnically Lao Lum, which nationally is the largest ethnic group and native speakers of the national language, but has the smallest population of the three ethnic groups in Vieng Kham District. The population of the sub-village of Vang Mat is more evenly distributed between ethnic Khamu and Lao Lum, with slightly more Khamu people in the sub-village. The village, at an elevation of 800 meters above sea level, is linked to a semi-permanent road with all year access by motorbike, or with all vehicle access during the dry season access after a thirty-minute walk from the main Bouammi village. During the wet season, this transforms into a one-hour walk to the main road.

The third village, Muangmuay, is located on the national road, at an elevation of 600 meters above sea level, the largest of the three villages and ethnically dominated by Khamu families, with a smaller percentage of Lao Lum families. It is by far the largest village of the three and its proximity to the road means that it has greater access to markets and is more likely to be the focus of development projects.

Information Communication Technologies in the Vieng Kham Landscape

The town of Vieng Kham, the capital of Vieng Kham District, is a riverside town of around 1110 inhabitants. The town now has access to two mobile phone networks. According to three district officials interviewed, they have never had any experience in using the Internet and Vieng Kham has no access to the Internet. Aside from mobile phone access, the residents of Vieng Kham have access to television via satellite dishes - predominately Thai content with two Lao channels - and to radio. Beyond the district capital, access to information communication technologies is more restricted with mobile access limited to the area around Vieng Kham. The three villages along the main road, Muangmuay, Vang Kham and Don Keo will get access to a mobile phone network later in 2009. Access to television in the villages is contingent on a regular electricity supply, which for most villages comes from micro-hydro turbines in the adjacent rivers, if they have a sufficient flow of water. The main source of information for most villagers, aside from direct, interpersonal communication, is via the radio (see Table 1 for a summary of each of the villages in the Muangmuay *Kumban*).

Table 1. Villages of the Muangmuay Kumban

Village	Population	Access to all season road	Access to electricity	Ethnic groups
Muangmuay	882	Y	Y	Majority Khamu, minority Lum
Don Keo	378	Y	N	Khamu
Vang Kham	262	Y	Y	Khamu
Hoey Khone	315	N	Y	Khamu
Paklao	358	N	N	Khamu
Bouammi	349	N	Y	Majority Lum, minority Khamu

Source: Village committee interviews - April 2009

METHODS

Initial Steps for Improving Communication between Local and Landscape Level Actors

In the first steps of the intervention process, the project sought to facilitate an understanding within the three villages of the future that they wanted for their landscape, using visioning exercises that asked villagers to imagine a vision of their landscape twenty years in the future and the things that they would like to see changed for the better (Evans et al., 2006; Wollenberg et al., 2000). The sustainable livelihoods framework was used to encourage villages to think about the present landscape and the desired future changes of the landscape in terms of the five capital assets - natural, human physical, social and financial (DFID, 1999). These activities were conducted with groups of men, women and young people in the village with normally less than ten per group, and then a final joint activity together.

This same exercise was undertaken at the district level with a range of actors who have influence over the landscape including: the district agriculture and forestry office (DAFO), the district planning office, the district land management office, a representative of the Wildlife Conservation Society (WCS) and local traders and business people.

A landscape level workshop was held in February 2009 that brought together representatives from the villages, district and other stakeholders from government and NGOs. The objectives of this workshop was to present the initial results of the project, define common indicators for the landscape as well as defining an intervention pathway for the project based on village, district and other stakeholders' priorities. The indicator exercises used were based on the Landscape Outcomes Assessment Methodology (LOAM) developed by WWF (WWF, 2007; Sayer et al., 2007).

The project team had additional focus group discussions in each of the six villages of the Muangmuay *Kumban* with village representatives, including the women's union representative, as well as representatives of district government agencies in late April and early May 2009. The objectives of the discussions were to:

1. Explain the purpose and discuss potential activities of interest for the intervention component of the project,
2. Gather preliminary information on livelihood activities, communication and governance processes in the new villages, and
3. Gather additional information on communication processes from representatives of district agencies and the project villages of Bouammi and Muangmuay.

This data has been complemented by the results of focus group discussions with district officers and villagers conducted in 2008.

RESULTS

Intervention Pathway

From the village level visioning exercises, the primary focus for the villagers was on infrastructure developments such as water, electricity and schooling facilities, and in the more remote villages such as Bouammi and Phadeng, permanent road access was a high priority. Shaping the discussions around the five capital assets helped to elicit other priority areas such as designating a protected area in Muangmuay, improved livestock management in Bouammi or improved cropping techniques in Phadeng. Exercises undertaken at the district level had a distinct focus on infrastructure and services, such as health and education, but also policy related measures such as land allocation and land use planning. These priority areas developed by the exercises were used as the basis for indicators to be used in later exercises.

In order to refine and negotiate the priority areas developed into a set of indicators, as well as develop strategies for achieving these shared visions, a workshop was held in Luang Prabang, the provincial capital. Representatives of all the actors with an interest in the landscape were invited, ranging from village representatives, who included the village head and sub-head as well as the women's union representative, district level officials and traders, and representatives from conservation, development and research organizations. The participants were presented with the results of the exercises held in each of the villages and the district, and then asked to develop, in small groups, relevant indicators for the landscape that fitted within each of the asset groups. From the indicators developed in these groups, a broader set were synthesized from the results that reflected the change that participants wanted to see for the landscape.

The other discussions centered on what work has been undertaken in the landscape, where greater coordination was possible, and how the Landscape Mosaics Project could make its intervention component more relevant to local actors. The proposition presented to the participants was for the Landscape Mosaics Project to focus its intervention on:

1. Improving communication and decision-making processes within villages through facilitating the development of more participatory processes that are more inclusive of women and ethnic minorities; and
2. Improving communication and negotiation skills among villages, and between villages and the district through capacity building of actors involved in village cluster structure known as the *kumban pattana*.

The chosen *kumban* (village cluster) for the intervention was the Muangmuay *Kumban* comprised of six villages, including the two project villages of Muangmuay and Bouammi. For the village of Phadeng a separate set of participatory activities was proposed that better addressed their current situation as a village in the process of resettlement. Participants also suggested that the activities directly link with the new national policy process of Participatory Land Use Planning at the village and *kumban* levels in order to more effectively link landscape governance activities with land planning and management processes.

The *kumban* was selected as the intervention focal point, for a variety of reasons. The first was that the scale of the Muangmuay *kumban*, composed of six villages and their agricultural lands, was conducive for catalysing effective landscape management. The proximity of the *kumban* to the Phou Louey National Protected Area, with three of the villages having lands bordering the park, also made it a relevant case study for landscape approaches to conservation.

The second related to the project's aim to facilitate the emergence of multi-level governance and communication platforms. The *kumban*, in addition to its political and security mandates, has the objective of economically, culturally and socially improving the livelihoods of villagers in the *kumban*. These are to be achieved through measures such as establishing cooperative or development funds, land allocation, increasing agricultural production especially for export markets, improving education and reducing forest degradation resulting from shifting cultivation (Lao PDR, 2004). To achieve these goals, district staff will support the *kumban* in order to provide relevant expertise. One of the official purposes of the *kumban* then is to draw village level and district actors together around development and land use issues, which matched both the project's desired intervention focus and the visions that arose from the exercises with the villagers.

The third rationale was that the *kumban* is a relatively new structure, decreed in 2004, but only recently established for the Muangmuay *kumban*. The district government welcomed the intervention to support its goals of improving rural development and natural resource management via the new political structure of the *kumban*.

CHALLENGES FOR PARTICIPATORY LANDSCAPE GOVERNANCE

Mobilising Village Level Actors

Participation in governance requires varying degrees of commitment to the process, especially in terms of time. In developing rural contexts, the ability to mobilize village level actors for a participatory process is also complicated by trade-offs between sustaining agricultural livelihoods and information sharing techniques. For sustaining these processes, seasonal variations especially relating to agricultural practices, such as harvesting, planting or NTFP collection seasons as well as challenges to mobility presented by the wet season, further restrict the times and places available for broad level participation. Mobilizing actors for participatory processes at the village level requires actors who are close enough and have enough available time to take part. In some villages, such as Muangmuay, this problem is addressed through village level regulations that require a representative of the household to return to the village every ten days to participate in village meetings (Fitriana, 2008). Similarly, dissemination of results is dependent on direct attendance or word of mouth.

Bringing village representatives together for *kumban* meetings also presents additional issues. While village heads officially will be obliged to attend *kumban* meetings, there are many challenges in mobilizing them for such events. In the absence of telecommunications, village representatives are invited to the meetings via letters that are sent to the villages. Those villages located along the road are personally invited to the meetings (Don Keo, Muangmuay and Vang Kham), while for those villages located further away along the seasonal roads (Paklao, Bouammi and Hoey Khone) the letter must be passed indirectly to the villages. District officials reported that often the letters do not arrive. Attendance at the meetings is also affected by seasonal variations, as during the height of the wet season even motorbike access to the villages is limited so village representatives may be required to walk several hours in order to attend the meeting. So far, villages located along the main road have only attended the meetings of the *kumban*. Villages also located along the main road have the additional obligation of reporting monthly to the district. Encouraging villages to participate in more regular meetings, with more participation from mass organizations of the villages, such as the women's union, will require that meetings are more relevant to village concerns and consequently, villagers have more incentives to attend.

Sharing information that results from the meetings of the *kumban* is also constrained by access, and other than by word of mouth, the only method of disseminating information is a *kumban* information board located in Muangmuay.

Enabling the Participation of Mass Organisations through Networking

From the project's perspective, increasing participation in landscape governance also requires greater participation of normally excluded groups, such as women and ethnic minorities. Participation is viewed not only as attendance and representation at decision-making forums, but also enabling such groups to more effectively manage and articulate the specific issues relating to their livelihoods. In the cases of women from ethnic minority groups, specifically the Khamu villages in the Muangmuay *Kumban*, they are presented with several disadvantages which result from the lower abilities to speak Lao (a language quite similar to Thai), the official national language and language used in official communication, radio and television, and the related problem of lower levels of literacy and education.

Formally, the government of Lao provides avenues for empowering traditionally disadvantaged groups. Throughout all tiers of Lao government - from the national to the village level - are the mass organizations, which including in the villages where we work with women's and youth unions. While all villages are officially required to have a women's union and women's union representative, there was generally a lack of activity and understanding of the role of the union. Focus group discussions with village representatives in the six villages of the Muàngmuay *Kumban* found that women's union representatives described their unions as not active; an unclear understanding of the potential and function of the union; and a lack of communication and networking both with other village organizations and with higher levels of the women's union, especially at the district and provincial level. During the discussions, women's union representatives at some villages mentioned that they had heard of training exercises in weaving being held in the district, although none had attended these events. In general, the women expressed a desire for greater interaction with other women's unions, especially at the district and higher levels, as well as training for typically women's activities such as weaving. Although there are such activities at the higher levels, and available information for women's unions at the provincial level, this information has not been disseminated to these remoter, rural village organizations.

DISCUSSION

Landscape Governance - Informed and Adaptive Decision-Making for Complex Social-Ecological Systems

Attempting to bring together actors for participatory governance presents several challenges. En-suring that villagers and other actors in multi-level governance forums have access to the relevant information in order to adaptively manage their landscape presents several more. The types of information that can assist actors to collaboratively and adaptively manage their landscapes in order to sustainably achieve their visions are listed below, as well as the constraints on access to them are described below.

Local Knowledge for Decision-Making

Local knowledge, in this case referring to livelihoods, which includes the broad range of land uses, from Non-timber Forest Product collection for local use including consumption and medicine, to other agricultural activities, the knowledge of the functional uses of forests and other natural resources, as well as the needs and aspirations of villagers, that are naturally embodied in their daily cultural practices and livelihood choices. Often, however, this knowledge is orally communicated and not properly accounted for in the formal institutions of village governance. Local people, especially traditionally disadvantaged groups such as women and ethnic minorities, may also be more reluctant to articulate their own needs and traditional practices to more dominant groups, official government representatives or representatives of scientific organisations, especially when they run counter to dominant narratives (Colfer, 1983). The consequence is that often when challenged by alternative narratives of how their landscapes should be used, configured and for what objectives, villagers do not have a resource for negotiation that encapsulates this knowledge and aspirations.

Various research, conservation and development agencies have developed a wide variety of participatory, catalytic tools that can help villagers develop a consensus and then document their current practices, as well as developing visions and indicators for the development of their village (Evans et al., 2006). One such valuable tool is participatory mapping (Anau et al., 2004). Through using a base map, normally generated from a Geographical Information System (GIS) application, villagers can define the boundaries of their village territory, as well as the multiple traditional land uses and settlements within it. The final product, usually a combination of the maps of different groups drawn in the village, is a valuable negotiating tool for villagers in areas such as tenure, access to resources and land use planning. The problem of such a participatory technique is that it is often contingent on access to GIS technologies (although topographic maps, if available can be used), in addition to the intervention of a project or trained local extension or other staff, who can facilitate the participatory mapping exercise. Transforming local knowledge into a format that can be effectively used for negotiation is a difficult process.

Agricultural Information and Technologies as a Pathway for Development and Realizing Visions

Improving agricultural technologies has been raised as one of the central pathways for improving village livelihoods. These types of technologies have ranged from new crops, cultivation techniques to improved animal husbandry, for instance. For villagers dependent on shifting cultivation of upland rice, they also face additional policy pressure from the central government that seeks to stabilize shifting cultivation by 2010, through encouraging upland villagers to switch to cash crops. While research on new technologies, as well as the development of seed banks, has been undertaken at the national and provincial level, with trials in specific districts, there is not a consistent flow of information and resources to the District Agricultural and Forestry Office in Vieng Kham. In addition, resource scarcity in the office often has the result that most extension work is undertaken under the auspices of an externally funded project. Alternative ways of improving

the hierarchical flow of information and agricultural resources, from the national to village level are needed, if villagers are to move away from traditional shifting cultivation to more profitable crops. Similarly, participatory methods have been demonstrated to be effective in improving agricultural technology adoption if used by extension workers or research organizations as they more effectively address the context and demands of villagers (Linquist et al., 2005).

Market Information for Adaptive Management and Planning

For villagers, making an effective transition from upland rice cultivation to cash crops requires not only knowledge of new agricultural technologies and techniques, but also market information and sufficient bargaining power with traders (Fujita, 2006). While there exist initiatives in Laos, at the provincial and district levels, for the provision of market prices through media such as mobile phones (see for instance www.laotrade.org.la/mis), district officials in Vieng Kham stated that they have not as yet been used in the district. The absence of such technologies means that the district and villagers are dependent on traders for price information. Mobile phones, however, have been used by key DAFO staff receive information regarding important agricultural and forestry events from the National Agriculture and Forestry Extension Service (NAFES). This example demonstrates that there are existing communication mechanisms that district staff could build upon in order to participate in provincial and national level market information systems.

Village officials have described how traders, often from neighboring countries, typically approach villages individually in order to purchase their agricultural produce and NTFPs. Early experiments by farmers with contract farming for cash crops have left farmers in the Muang-muay *Kumban* disenchanted. Often the prices they were told initially that they would receive for the crops was significantly higher than the amount paid by the same traders when farmers were selling the harvested product back to them. In one instance, a district official described the price discrepancy was due to fluctuations in the exchange rate between the US dollar and Lao Kip, however, villagers were unaware that their contracts would be subject to such price fluctuations. These issues have highlighted the need for access to both market information and improved negotiation capacity for farmers if they are able to effectively manage their landscapes for improved agricultural production.

Scientific Agro-Ecological Knowledge for Enabling Adaptive Planning and Management

Traditional farming systems have often developed methods for understanding the impacts of farming practices on ecosystem services, such as soil quality, water quality or NTFPs. These systems may be challenged by increasing population sizes, infertile soils or new technologies, such as new crops or farming techniques, which may present unanticipated difficulties or surprises. Successful landscape management, for both improved agricultural production and ecosystem management, requires that agro-ecological information is available to landscape managers for planning, managing and monitoring. While much research has been undertaken at higher levels, relating to agro-ecosystems analysis and agro-ecological zoning (Land Management Component, 2006) ensuring that the information flows to the actual villages that are the implementing agents is also contingent on the information being in a format accessible to villagers. In addition, the availability of spatial planning and monitoring technologies, such as GIS and remote sensing, greatly enhances the ability of landscape managers to more adaptively manage their landscapes. In the context of the resource scarcity of district offices, these technologies are often not readily available.

Policy Knowledge for Understanding, Anticipating and Planning for Change

While in other districts in Laos, market pressures and major infrastructure developments such as hydroelectric dams, shape the trajectories of rural landscapes, in Vieng Kham District the major shaping influences on the landscape have resulted from government policies. Three major policy initiatives have had significant impacts on the villages and their territories in the district - land use planning and land allocation, eradication of opium and village consolidation (Fitriana, 2008). The effects of these policies have had wide-ranging impacts on rural livelihoods ranging from the re-settlement of villages, introduction of new crops and additional pressures on traditional farming systems (Baird & Shoemaker, 2005; Bestari et al., 2006; Fujita & Phengsopha, 2008). Interviews conducted with district officials in 2008 and 2009 have revealed various challenges of implementing these policies. These challenges range from an inability to implement land use plans once the process is complete or find suitable alternatives to shifting cultivation. A scenario presented by DAFO officers, similar to that described by the villagers, was where investors approach DAFO to cultivate a particular cash crop. DAFO representatives relay the information to villagers who grow the crop but have no one to sell it to at the time of harvest. Despite being conscious of the difficulties of finding viable livelihood alternatives, the district is required to implement these national level policies in villages.

Planning, implementing and monitoring sustainable landscape management will require that landscape managers have access to relevant policy information that can affect the trajectory of their landscapes. In addition, village level landscape managers will need to have both regular communication and capacity to negotiate with decentralized levels of governance to ensure that policies are implemented in a way that is relevant and not detrimental to the livelihoods of villagers. At present, district and village level authorities described the District Agricultural and Forestry Office as the primary disseminator of policy information to villagers and less so from other district offices, who in turn receive their information from higher-level institutions.

RECOMMENDATION

One Approach to Information Communication Technologies for Landscape Governance

There are multiple challenges in facilitating the emergence of landscape governance for rural areas that could be overcome through better use of information communication technologies for development. In the case of the Muangmuay *Kumban*, the choices of technologies are limited. Although mobile phone access will be available in the villages located along the main road by the end of the year, villages located further away will still depend on radio and television as the major sources of mass media, and of course, direct communication. Hybrid solutions, that can link village level actors to more advanced technologies like the Internet or mobile phones through intermediary technologies such as the radio, could be a potential way to overcome these issues. These solutions could take advantage of the technological capacities of different levels of governance and geographical areas, for example district level actors having greater access to more advanced technologies could be utilized for achieving better landscape governance and adaptive management. The lack of access to the Internet at the district level, however, places further constraints on the type and volume of information that is available for district level actors. Taking this into account, however, there appears to be several possible solutions. We describe one potential solution below which we have developed based on critical information gaps described by village and district representatives. The potential and sustainability of such a solution has not yet been explored with village and district actors.

A. Community Radio for Landscape Governance

Villagers reported using the radio on a daily basis in all villages as a source of information. In contrast to television, which mainly broadcasts Thai channels, radio provides a good opportunity for delivering local content. The potential of community radio to support landscape governance could have two potential aspects:

- As a method of mobilizing actors for participatory landscape governance, networking among mass organizations and disseminating results; and
- Sharing information that supports effective landscape management.

While there have been numerous examples of using radio for Market Information Systems with their positive aspects and limitations described (see Shepherd, 2001), a similar approach that seeks to address the broader information needs for landscape management could be effective. By positioning the broadcast station in the district capital, with better linkages with other communication technologies as well as access to actors from higher levels of governance, there would be more chances of relevant information being shared across the district. The challenge of positioning a broadcast station there would be the distance from and between villages and trying to ensure that villagers had some level of influence on the content broadcast. This would be a critical challenge to overcome in order to ensure that the radio content did not replicate the unidirectional flows of information that the PAR activities sought to address. Actively incorporating village groups into the design, production and performance of the radio shows could be one significant step to overcome this challenge.

CONCLUSION

Initiating the process of facilitating the emergence of participatory landscape governance in the Muangmuay *Kumban* of Vieng Kham District in Laos has revealed several constraints, many of which are directly related to lack of access to information communication technologies. The lack of advanced infrastructure at the district level, and in turn, *kumban* and village level, restricts the flow of relevant information from higher levels, from the provincial to global. While satellite television does exist at all levels within the district, the utility of the information broadcast for improving landscape management is minor. Facilitating and improving landscape governance requires strengthening the linkages of villagers, as landscape managers, to relevant flows of information. Access to two broad categories of information has been identified as important for landscape governance: that relating to the actual processes of governance and that relating to informing the processes of governance and management. Hybrid information communication technology solutions, such as that described in relation to community radio, could be used for ensuring the sustainable and adaptive management of the Muangmuay *Kumban* landscape in the context of limited direct access to information communication technologies. The major challenge of using such technologies would be to ensure the adequate participation of villagers in the broadcasts.

ACKNOWLEDGMENT

We would like to thank Carol J. Pierce Colfer and Jean-Laurent Pfund for their comments on an earlier version of this draft. In addition, we would like to thank the two anonymous reviewers for their suggestions for improving the article. Also, we would like to thank the editor of this special edition, Carlos Nunes Silva, for his support. The research was made possible through funding from the Swiss Agency for Development Cooperation (SDC), however, the views expressed in the article do not necessarily represent those of SDC.

REFERENCES

Anau, N., Iwan, R., van Heist, M., Limberg, G., Sudana, M., & Wollenberg, E. (2004). Negotiating more than boundaries: conflict, power and agreement building in the demarcation of village borders in Malinau. In Colfer, C. J. P. (Ed.), *The equitable forest: diversity, community and natural resources*. Washington, DC: Resources for the Future/CIFOR.

Armitage, D. (2008). Governance and the commons in a multi-level world. *International Journal of the Commons*, *2*(1), 7–32.

Baird, I. G., & Shoemaker, B. (2005). *Aiding or Abetting? Internal Resettlement and International Aid Agencies in the Lao PDR*. Toronto, Canada: Probe International.

Bestari, N. G., Mongcopa, C., Samson, J., & Ward, K. (2006). *Lao PDR: Governance Issues in agriculture and natural resources: A Case Study from the 2005 Sector Assistance Program Evaluation for the Agriculture and Natural Resources Sector in the Lao People's Democratic Republic. ADB - Governance Issues in Lao PDR*. Manila, Philippines: Asian Development Bank.

Borrini-Feyerabend, G., Pimbert, M., Farvar, M. T., Kothari, A., & Renard, Y. (2004). *Sharing Power: Learning by doing in co-management of natural resources throughout the world*. Tehran, Iran: IIED and IUCN/ CEESP/ CMWG.

Carlsson, L., & Sandström, A. (2008). Network governance of the commons. *International Journal of the Commons*, *2*(1), 33–54.

Colfer, C. J. P. (1983). Communication among "unequals". *International Journal of Intercultural Relations*, *7*, 263–283. doi:10.1016/0147-1767(83)90033-0

Dahal, G. R., & Adhikari, K. P. (2008). *Bridging, linking, and bonding social capital in collective action: The case of Kalahan Forest Reserve in the Philippines* (CAPRi working paper 79). Washington, DC: International Food Policy Research Institute (IFPRI).

DFID (Department for International Development). (1999). *Sustainable guidance sheets: framework*. London: Department for International Development.

Evans, K., Velarde, S. J., Prieto, R., Rao, S. N., Sertzen, S., Dávila, K., et al. (2006). In E. Bennett & M. Zurek (Eds.), *Field guide to the Future: Four Ways for Communities to Think Ahead*. Nairobi: Center for International Forestry Research (CIFOR). Retrieved from http://www.asb.cgiar.org/ma/scenarios

Fitriana, Y. R. (2008). *Landscape and Farming System in Transition: Case Study in Viengkham District, Luang Prabang Province, Lao PDR*. Montpelier, France: Agronomy and Agro-Food Program, Institut des Regions Chaudes-Supagro.

Folke, C., Hahn, T., Olsson, P., & Norberg, J. (2005). Adaptive Governance of Social-ecological Systems. *Annual Review of Environment and Resources, 30*, 441–473. doi:10.1146/annurev.energy.30.050504.144511

Fujita, Y. (2006). Understanding the History of Change in Laos. *Mountain Research and Development, 26*(3), 197–199. doi:10.1659/0276-4741(2006)26[197:UTHOCI]2.0.CO;2

Fujita, Y., & Phengsopha, K. (2008). The Gap between Policy and Practice in Lao PDR. In Colfer, C. J. P., Dahal, G. R., & Capistrano, D. (Eds.), *Lessons from Forest Decentralization: Money, Justice and the Quest for Good Governance in Asia-Pacific*. London: Earthscan/CIFOR.

Görg, C. (2007). Landscape governance: The "politics of scale" and the "natural" conditions of places. *Geoforum, 38*(5), 954–966. doi:10.1016/j.geoforum.2007.01.004

Komarudin, H., Siagian, Y., & Colfer, C. J. P. (2008). *Collective action for the poor: A case study in Jambi Province, Indonesia* (CAPRi Working Paper No. 90).

Land Management Component. (2006). *Agro-ecosystems analysis and agro-ecological zoning, a handbook. Lao-Swedish Upland Agriculture and Forestry Research Program*. Vientiane, Laos: National Agriculture and Forestry Research Institute.

Lao People's Democratic Republic. (2004, June 8). *Advising Order on Establishing Village and Developing Villages Groups* (No. 09/PB.CP). Lao People Revolutionary Party Political Bureau of Central Party.

Linquist, B., Keoboualpha, B., Sodarak, H., Horne, P., & Lai, C. (2005). Upland Research in Lao PDR: Experiences with Participatory Research Approaches. In J. Gonsalves, T. Becker, A. Braunet, A. Laguna, A. Braun, D. Campilan, H. de Chavez, E. Fajber, M. Kapiriri, J. Rivaca-Caminade, & J. Vernooy (Eds.), *Participatory Research and Development for sustainable Agriculture and Natural Resource Management: A Sourcebook. Volume 3: Doing Participatory Research and Development* (pp. 58-65). Ottawa, Canada: International Potato Center-Users' Perspectives with Agricultural Research and Development (CIP-UPWARD) and International Development Research Centre (IDRC).

Pfund, J., Watts, J. D., Boffa, J., Colfer, C. J. P., Dewi, S., & Guizol, P. (2008). *Integrating Livelihoods and Multiple Biodiversity Values in Landscape Mosaics: Research Guidelines*. Bogor Barat, Indonesia: CIFOR.

Sayer, J., Campbell, B., Petheram, L., Aldrich, M., Ruiz Perez, M., & Endamana, D. (2007). Assessing environment and development outcomes in conservation landscapes. *Biodiversity and Conservation, 16*, 2677–2694. doi:10.1007/s10531-006-9079-9

Shepherd, A. W. (2001). *Farm Radio as a Medium for Market Information Dissemination*. Rome, Italy: FAO-Marketing and Rural Finance Service.

Swiderska, K., Roe, D., Siegele, L., & Grieg-Gran, M. (2009). *The Governance of Nature and the Nature of Governance: Policy that works for biodiversity and livelihoods*. London: IIED.

Tress, B., & Tress, G. (2000). Second draft for Recommendations for interdisciplinary landscape research. Workshop no.1. The landscape – from vision to definition. In J. Brandt, B. Tress, & G. Tress (Eds.), *Multifunctional landscapes. Interdisciplinary approaches to landscape research and management. Conference material for the international conference on multifunctional landscapes*. Denmark: University of Roskilde, Centre for landscape research.

van Noordwijk, M., Tomich, T. P., & Verbist, T. P. (2001). Negotiation support models for integrated natural resource management in tropical forest margins. *Conservation Ecology, 5*(2), 21. Retrieved from http://www.consecol.org/vol5/iss2/art21/

Wollenberg, E., Edmunds, D., & Buck, L. (2000). *Anticipating Change: Scenarios as a tool for adaptive forest management - a guide*. Bogor Barat, Indonesia: Center for International Forestry Research.

Woolcock, M., & Sweetser, A. T. (2002). Bright Ideas: Social Capital—The Bonds That Connect. *ADB Review, 34*(2).

WWF. (2007). *Landscape Outcomes Assessment Methodology in Practice*. Gland, Switzerland: WWF Forest for Life Programme. Retrieved from http://assets.panda.org/downloads/ loaminpracticemay07.pdf

This work was previously published in International Journal of Information Communication Technologies and Human Development, Volume 2, Issue 3, edited by Susheel Chhabra and Hakikur Rahman, pp. 19-32, copyright 2010 by IGI Publishing (an imprint of IGI Global).

Chapter 11
Tlowitsis Re-Imagined:
The Use of Digital Media to Build Nation and Overcome Disconnection in a Displaced Aboriginal Community

Jon Corbett
University of British Columbia, Canada

Raquel Mann
University of British Columbia, Canada

ABSTRACT

Using the case study of the Tlowitsis, a dispersed indigenous community in British Columbia, Canada, this paper explores the role of ICTs, and in particular participatory video, in nation building. Also, the paper identifies factors that affect both the involvement and exclusion of the membership and addresses the challenges faced and lessons learned. ICTs, in particular new media technologies, offer great potential to overcome the geographic barriers caused by dispersal. However, it remains uncertain how they might contribute to the process of nation building. In this regard, the authors present six fundamental requirements for nation building, and then use these requirements to structure an analysis of the Tlowitsis case study.

INTRODUCTION

The territory of the Tlowitsis Nation[1] spans the coastal area of Northern Vancouver Island, British Columbia (BC), Canada. These lands have been occupied and used by members of the Nation since time immemorial. Seasonal travel routes, food processing spots, burial and cultural sites and other named places extend across the entire territory. Karlukwees, located on remote Turnour Island, became a central settlement for the Tlowitsis Nation since the turn of the 20th century. In the early 1960's, the provincial government halted essential services to Turnour Island. With little prospect of schooling and access to health care, the Tlowitsis community began to leave the island. In the ensuing diaspora, community members have become

DOI: 10.4018/978-1-4666-0047-8.ch011

culturally, as well as physically, removed from their traditional territories. A rapidly rising urban population with little attachment to these lands has dramatically reduced the opportunity, as well as ability, for community members to take an active and informed role in community governance and planning. As a consequence of this displacement, the Tlowitsis Nation, now numbering 400 members and administered out of offices in Campbell River on Northern Vancouver Island, faces a set of unique challenges as they engage in land-related negotiations as a part of the BC Treaty process.

Since 2006, the Tlowitsis Nation in collaboration with the University of British Columbia Okanagan have developed and begun to deploy a number of information communication technologies (ICTs) that seek to directly address these issues. Ranging from Participatory Video (PV) production through to the development of a web portal, all of these tools emphasize and support virtual community connection and interactivity, as well as explicitly tie much of the material back to the land-base. This paper provides an empirical case study that explores the role of ICTs, and in particular participatory video, in nation building. It identifies factors that affect both the involvement and exclusion of the membership and address the challenges faced and lessons learned through these ongoing projects and partnership. ICTs, in particular new media technologies and PV, offer great potential to overcome some of the geographic barriers caused by dispersal. Yet it remains uncertain how they might contribute to the process of nation building.

THE TLOWITSIS NATION

The Tlowitsis Nation's traditional territories spanned a large area of northern Vancouver Island from ancient history until the early 20th Century. Prior to this time, Tlowitsis members engaged in a range of land-related subsistence activities such as gathering plants, fruits and berries, hunting and trapping fish, elk, deer and moose, and clam digging. They occupied a number of seasonal village sights scattered across islands along Johnson Straight and on Vancouver Island. Seasonal travel routes, food processing areas, burial and cultural sites and other named places extended across the entire territory. Most of their activities were concentrated along waterways, marine channels and passages, river systems and freshwater lakes (Galois, 1994).

In the 18th Century British and Spanish explorations occurred in the area simultaneously. In July 1791, the ships *Santa Saturnina* and *San Carlos* explored the Strait of Georgia, identifying places along the east coast of Vancouver Island (Wagner, 1933; cited in Kennedy & Bouchard, 2008). This contact heralded the era of colonization that continues to influence Tlowitsis governance and decision-making until today. During the fall of 1879 the Indian Reserve Commission began to designate reserve lands for Tlowitsis. Despite the range of territories and resources utilized by the Nation prior to contact, only 11 reserves were allocated through an exclusionary process that did not consult Tlowitsis leadership. Many of these reserves are tiny in size (less than a few hundred square metres) and in remote and inaccessible locations (see map below). In 1914, Tlowitsis Chief Johnnie Clark petitioned the Royal Commission on Indian Affairs for the Province of British Columbia arguing the inability of reserve lands to meet the needs of the Nation and the failure of the Crown to consult his people.

No one has been to my Band or my land to sell them; no one has asked me how much, how big or where we want a reserve... I and my people were born on this land and our people before us, from the beginning. We have not come from a strange country; we are not foreigners. This country is ours. Chief Johnnie Clark, 1914 (cited in Kennedy & Bouchard, 2008)

Figure 1. Map of the location of Tlowitsis reserves. © 2009, Jon Corbett.

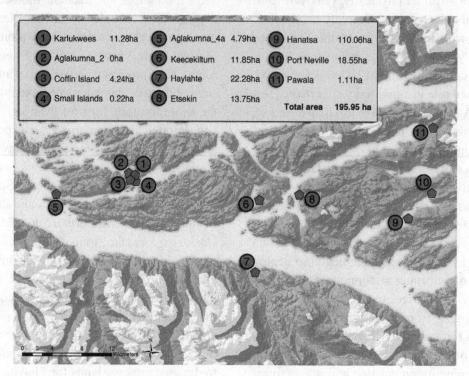

However, these reserves still remain today as isolated parcels of land comprising a fraction of the traditional territory used for generations by the Tlowitsis Nation (Figure 1).

By the 1920's Karlukwees, located on Turnour Island, had become the primary residence of the Tlowitsis and was a hub of trade and social networking for the Nation's members. However, in the late 1960s, the provincial government closed down the school on Karlukwees, stopped the hospital ship and relocated many of the children to residential schools in surrounding centralized towns and cities. This provoked the emigration of members and their families out of the territory. Karlukwees was last occupied as a permanent village site in the early 1970s.

As a consequence of this diaspora, the Nation has had great difficulty in maintaining communication and participation of its members in Tlowitsis activities and culture. A large portion of the Nation's members has limited knowledge and experience of their territories and resources and lack traditional, historical and contemporary cultural knowledge. Kwak'wala, the language of the Tlowitsis, is spoken fluently by only a small number of elders. Many Tlowitsis members lack a deep sense of their national identity and are most often poorly acquainted with their relatives and other members of the Nation; furthermore they are disengaged and disconnected from the Nation's political and decision-making activities and a general sense of apathy towards engaging in these processes pervades. A large proportion of Tlowitsis membership has embraced membership in other First Nations, internalized a multiplicity of identities or become immersed in modern urban lifestyles. As a result, feelings of indifference, frustration, hurt and anger have manifested themselves throughout the community. One member expressed these feelings in a small group discussion during the 2006 Tlowitsis Nation Homecoming Meeting:

It's kind of hard to say where I come from because I don't come from anywhere. To say that, being First Nations is important, but to say that I'm Tlowitsis doesn't really have any significance for my family ... I went there as a child - but for me to pass anything on to my children, its really hard to explain to them where our extended family came from because there's nothing, there's no land, there's nothing to go to.

These circumstances pose great challenges to the Tlowitsis Nation, both in terms of member engagement and nation building. It is hard to cultivate relationships of trust and reciprocity between community members when they do not know each other. The lack of a physical community location in which to gather, discuss and bring forward the voice of their community is a fundamental hindrance to the Nation's development. The urgency to overcome these constraints is exacerbated by the Tlowitsis' Statement of Intent being accepted by the BC Treaty Commission in June 2006. The Nation is currently engaged in substantive negotiations and is positioned at stage four of a six stage treaty process. Swift progress has been made during negotiations to date and the parties anticipate reaching an 'agreement in principle' in 2010. Identification and acquisition of community settlement lands is a key priority of those negotiations and a major focus for the Nation. However, in order to inform the decision-making process the Nation needs to seek and employ tools that facilitate the participation of community members. Various initiatives have begun to revitalize language and culture, track down members who have lost contact, motivate participation of members in community gatherings and the treaty negotiations processes, and acquire consensus on concerning land claims and resources.

These initiatives have proven effective; a number of members have expressed a desire to be better informed about the treaty negotiation as well as to contribute their knowledge and assume a role in the process. In response, the Tlowitsis Nation in collaboration with UBC Okanagan have developed and implemented two action-research projects using ICTs that seek to directly address members' appeal for a platform that supports information exchange and their participation in the Nation's decision-making processes. The first project involves participatory video production and will comprise of the substance of this paper, the second project involves the development of a Tlowitsis web-portal. Both of these projects emphasize and support virtual community connection and interactivity, as well as explicitly tie much of the material back to the land-base – a key cohesive force within this process of nation building.

NATION BUILDING

For the purposes of this paper, nation building is the process of (re)developing a national identity, sentiment and ambition that supports the establishment of a community capable of maintaining internal stability, self-governance and sovereignty over a specific geographic area in the long-term (Bell & Freeman, 1974; Chambers, 2004; Delanty & O'Mahony, 2002). This paper identifies six principle requirements of nation building, which later in the paper provide a framework to examine the impact of the Tlowitsis PV project on the Nation.

National Identity

The first requirement of nation building is that the nation must have a "distinctive identity, a definite *national character*" (Smith, 1999, p. 189). The nation must encompass a combination of unique attributes—a mythology[2], symbology, language, history, culture, and affiliation with an historic landscape or ethnoscape.

Individual Sense of Nationalism

Smith (1999) suggests that national identity is "a matter of sameness through time, of persistence through change ... and of reflective conscious of personal connection with the past" (p. 208). However, in the case of diasporic communities, members are physically removed from territory, and are concomitantly disconnected to some degree from their socio-cultural core. In such cases, an individual's identity might no longer be tied to that of the nation, and/or they might identify with a multiplicity of nationalities. This plurality might cause a dilemma of conflicting alliances where the individual will feel that their current life and identity constrains the ability to cultivate an affiliation for, and thus become actively engaged in, another identity and its accompanying lifestyle (this dilemma is particularly strong among urban First Nation community members, see Evans et al., in press). Nation building processes require that the individual feel emotionally invested in the nation, and identify a need for the nation's continued existence.

Community Organization

Community cohesion is integral to nation building. As Smith (1999) stresses, "the nation must be unified. It cannot tolerate internal divisions, territorial or social" (p. 189). If the community is not aligned and organized, they cannot mobilize and make decisions concerning the future of the nation. The development of a common vision of the past, present and future by a community, requires on some level that members gather together and engage in dialogue. If there is a lack of trust and/or community members do not feel that they are implicated on some level in the lives of the others, these gatherings will prove unproductive, and possibly dysfunctional.

Nation building is largely dependent on a solid foundation of effective communication infrastructures. Knowledge cannot be exclusive to an elite group. Rather, knowledge should become a "basic information pool possessed collectively by all members of society" (Naveh, 1998, p. 138). Therefore, structures need to be established that enable all members of a community to be equally informed. If they do not provide equal accessibility to all, gaps between members widen and a hierarchy might form, with those who are information-rich benefiting most, and those who are information-poor being further marginalized. These gaps can result in frustration, feelings of neglect, antagonism and/or indifference and thus serve to undermine the cohesion of the nation.

Member Participation and Engagement

The maintenance of a nationalist sentiment and community cohesion is largely contingent on member participation and engagement. In order to engage, participants must feel they have the power to transform and influence decision-making processes. Nation building processes need to create an environment that cultivates the individual's capacity to effect change through a heightened sense of self-awareness, self-confidence and an in-depth comprehension of how one fits within the larger, encompassing system. Individuals must also possess the will to transform these systems (Bery, 2003). Thus nation building requires the incorporation of laws, policies and institutions that support human and social rights and an environment that nurtures feelings of well being and stability (AFN, 2005).

Furthermore, member participation and engagement involves the continual maintenance of collective morale. When groups and/or individuals put energy into nation building processes, they want to feel appreciated by their governments and community. It is important to recognize and reward efforts (Kilvington et al., 1999). Celebration of successes, no matter how large or small, provides concrete evidence that the individual and community possess the power to transform.

Effective Government

Nation building seeks the establishment of a nation which can maintain the capacity for sustainable development, solidarity and sovereignty in the long-term. It requires that the nation's government be effective in the following four ways:

- *Government needs to be culturally grounded*: It has been argued that a good government reflects the fundamental cultural values of its people (AFN, 2005). This is essential, as nation building requires that the government advocate and affirm those attributes which form the unique character of the nation in its internal and external relations and endeavours. Formal governmental institutions and their activities must be compatible with the socio-cultural perspective of the nation's membership with respect to how authority should function (Poelzer, 2002).

- *Government must be self-aware, flexible and have vision*: A nation must continually invoke its traditional structures so it may function in a changing world. In order to successfully build nation and grow over time; governments must be responsive to modernization, sensitive to how it affects the changing needs of its populations and aware of how its current structures function in accordance with these changes (AFN, 2005).

- *Government must be resourceful, just and enact responsible governance*: The Assembly of First Nations define governance as "the process of government decision-making and law-making: it presumes jurisdiction or sovereignty" (AFN, 2005, p. 4). Essential to the stability, solidity and development of a nation is a 'capable government'. Specifically, cohesion and member engagement is dependent on a government's ability to implement a procedural framework which can settle internal and external disputes while maintaining a democratic and pluralistic framework. It is also one that implements laws and policies with social well-being in mind.

- *Government must be informed and inclusive*: In order for government to be culturally supportive and implement policies appropriate to changing conditions, it must be conversant in all internal and external states of affairs. As discussed in Requirement 3, cohesion is dependent on communication infrastructures that are two-way, accessible to all, and universally facilitate the dissemination of information. Furthermore, nation building requires member participation and engagement and so, government must both encourage and provide a forum for citizens to partake in debate and decision-making (AFN, 2005). The development of the nation is dependent on vertical and horizontal relationships of trust and reciprocity.

The Existence of a Geographic Locality over Which the Nation has Sovereignty

Nation building demands a geographic territory with which there is an affiliation for both the individual and community and that presents a viable option for the nation to establish a desirable and realistic degree of sovereign governance.

The creation of nations requires a special place for the nation to inhabit, a land 'of their own'. Not any land; an historic land, a homeland, and ancestral land. Only an ancestral homeland can provide the emotional as well as physical security required by the citizens of a nation (Smith, 1999, p. 149).

Collective experience shared in a historic and ancestral landscape helps foster a common vision of the past, present and for the future within a community. Community members need to develop a relationship in a place saturated with national history, mythology and symbology whether or not physical, human artefacts of the nation's ancestral occupation remain.

Furthermore, members need to perceive the prospect that this territory will be available for future generations and the continued growth of the nation. This need was articulated by one Tlowitsis member during a Tlowitsis Nation meeting held in September 2006, Campbell River:

Our home and our land should be our children's memories as well. But we don't have a land to show our children what we are proud of, we have nothing. We're just proud because of what we are, where we came from, and our ancestors; what they told us. My great grandma, she took the time to teach a lot of us how to can fish and although I was very young, I still remember a lot of what to do, what she taught us and how we used to live. Those are good memories, but those are my memories; those aren't my daughter's memories or my grandchildren's memories. I want them to have a land where they can have good memories like what we had. We can't teach them on white man's land.

In other words, territories are valued not simply as economic resources, but as an essential component to sustaining the cultural identity of the people and in turn act as a buffer to competing challenges from political and cultural forces from outside the community.

PARTICIPATORY VIDEO

Video and film production has until recently remained in the domain of the expert. This monopoly is now being eroded; a number of community groups and their associates are now using video with varying levels of skills and sophistication (Ferreira, 2006; Harris, 2009; Johansson et al., 2000; Lunch, 2007; Norrish, 1998; Snowden, 1987)[3]. Using video as a tool of grassroots communication is increasingly referred to as Participatory Video (PV) (Lunch & Lunch, 2006). Johansson et al. (2000) declare that PV is a:

Scriptless video production process, directed by a group of grassroots people, moving forward in an iterative cycle of shooting-reviewing. This process aims at creating video narratives that communicate what those participating in the process really want to communicate in a way that they think is appropriate (p. 35).

White (2003) further notes that no matter what becomes of the product, whether it effectively achieves a desired reaction from the audience or not, the success of PV is fundamentally dependant on how it affects the people who make it. She states that making participatory video is:

Simply a tool to facilitate interaction and enable self-expression. It is not intended to have a life beyond the immediate context...Once those purposes are achieved; the tape itself is no longer relevant (p. 65).

In reconciliation of these varying perspectives, participatory video projects, whether product or process orientated or both, are always propelled by, determined and dependent on the social circumstances of its participants (Buddle, 2005). Though there might be a body of fundamental concepts which are intrinsic and relevant to all PV projects, the goals and processes of these projects will always be particular to the needs and desires of the groups involved.

Traditional documentary on the other hand, does not have this intrinsic social focus. Its structure and process is characterized largely by a *transfer* of information. The production is most often localized in big cities, and equally often its content is most relevant to those populations. The processes involved in production usually involve a top-down hierarchical approach (Huber, 1999). The script is subject to change according to decisions made by the director. Even when filmed in smaller communities, or when the subject matter of the documentary concerns minority groups, the final product will ultimately abide the agenda of its producers.

PV is different from traditional documentary. It is inspired by Friere's (1970) belief that every human being is capable of looking critically at the world, perceiving his/her personal and social reality, and transforming it through conscious action. Huber elaborates that participatory video embraces the idea that "people should not only be receivers, but also producers of messages" (Huber, 1999). PV production revolves around concepts of democracy, inclusiveness, pluralism and transformation. PV, when used by minority, marginalized and indigenous groups, aims to counter repressive dominant forces and/or initiate internal development. This is achieved through using video to identify and expose subordinate positions, express the desire for change, showcase pre-existing values, cultivate feelings of community pride in engaging and successfully representing relevant subject matter that reclaim power, mediate conflict, advocate rights and inform policy dialogue (Johansson et al., 2000).

Participatory video projects can be initiated internally (where the community undertakes the project themselves or solicits facilitation) or be recommended by an external individual, group or institution. In either case, it is good practice to first gather the community together, consult their needs and aspirations, and educate all members and stakeholders about the potential benefits of PV in light of assisting these requests (CBNC, 2005; Lunch & Lunch, 2006). The next step involves training interested members on how to use the technology. Once sufficiently skilled, the members should then receive primary control of the filming itself. The job of the facilitator at this point is to be available for support. As PV is primarily a community based endeavour, it should

revolve around what Buddle terms "*production of locality*:" this means a community will produce actors who properly belong within a *situated* network of relationships" (Buddle, 2005, p. 9). In other words all the characters and subject matter filmed should be authentic and relevant to the narrative or message as identified by the community. Once footage is acquired, the community and facilitators should engage workshops where this footage is viewed and then a 'debrief' where any issues the members feel need to be voiced or reconciled, are discussed as a group. Both the viewing and discussion should be characterized by an environment which encourages members to *critically* think about the process and product, be fully *engaged* in the activities of the moment and assist a forum where all feel their opinions are equally valid.

The goals of the Tlowitsis Participatory Video project were to a.) promote communication and community cohesion while exploring community's knowledge of traditional territories and resources, and b.) to begin to document the members' aspirations for future land management practices in a form that can be accessible over time and despite distance. To achieve this goal, the Tlowitsis Nation purchased two Panasonic digital cameras with microphones, a computer and editing software.

RESEARCH APPROACH

In their exploration of how to assess the impact of ICTs on poverty reduction, Wakelin and Shadrach (2001) discuss Michel Menou's design of assessment techniques; Menou's approach largely mirrors our own in assessing the Tlowitsis case study. Menou's first step is to assess and acquire knowledge of the community and its key development problems as defined by the community members themselves. Before we designed the questions and topics to guide evaluation, we interviewed community members, the Chief and the Chief Negotiator to define key issues and problems the

nation faced. These individuals identified that the main challenges for the Tlowitsis were disunity within the nation, lack of member commitment, participation in the band, lack of member's socio-cultural and territorial knowledge, and lack of adequate, equal and accessible information flow. Thus, we focused our research questions towards evaluating how Tlowitsis members thought the DVD medium could aid in building a sense of nation and overcoming these challenges of engagement and dispersal.

Menou further notes that it is important for assessment processes be reflective, action-orientated, build capacity in the community and generate knowledge that leads to positive actions. Open-ended questions delivered in a conversational manner were used in semi-structured interviews and focus group discussions. The conversational approach provided an atmosphere that encouraged participants to critically reflect on the DVD process and product. The questions were largely orientated towards determining what actions people believed needed to be undertaken to overcome the challenges identified above.

In total over the course of the research project, we recorded 12 semi-structured interviews and 6 focus group discussions (each comprised of 8 – 10 participants). Members recruited for the interviews were first informed about the intent of the research, the topics to be addressed in the questions, the nature of the interviews as being dynamic and open ended, and of their options to withdraw, veto, censure information at any time and remain anonymous. They were only interviewed with their verbal consent. These interviews ranged from 15 –45 minutes during which participants were encouraged to ask questions and were not discouraged from bringing in topics of their own interests. We also took measures to interview a selection of members that were diverse in both background and degrees of involvement with the nation and its territories.

Due to the limited number of participants relative to the population of the band as a whole (350 members in total), as well as the conversational nature of the questionnaires, discussions, and interviews, the data analysis focused on qualitative and thematic analysis. Analysis involved categorizing patterns in major themes and highlighting important portions of discussions in order to understand the diversity of opinions, values, and worldviews of the participants in relation to the topics presented. It was concerned with listening to *whole* stories, reflecting on those stories, in conjunction with the storyteller and engaging in subsequent dialogue which was elicited from the telling. Seidl contends how this theme is intrinsic to all participatory processes:

It's not about quantifiable demonstrable truth; it is about relative truth....the truth of the story is as much in the 'retelling' of an actual experience. It's in the recounting of emotions and reactions. So the story is as much about what happened to people as it is about the factual sequence of events (Seidl, 2003, p. 162).

The research component of the project presented in this paper examined how digital media technologies create a platform that facilitates community members to come together, express and discuss their interests, visions and values for the Nation – as well as engage on issues related to nation building, such as the revitalization, preservation and transmission of Tlowitsis culture and knowledge.

PARTICIPATORY VIDEO AND THE TLOWITSIS NATION

The project employed a participatory methodology in which all steps of the video production, screening and dissemination were directed by community members. The project took place at several locations throughout the Tlowitsis territory. It began with a two day retreat where participants videoed their experiences and discussions, and acquired landscape footage, and continued through to the screening of a DVD product at a Tlowitsis Nation gathering. The goal of the project from the outset was to create a DVD – this was requested by the Tlowitsis Chief Negotiator who hoped to use the product in their treaty negotiations – yet the content and future usage of the DVD were defined by the participants and grew out of their involvement in the process.

Recruitment of participants was undertaken by the Tlowitsis Chief Negotiator. The selection criteria required participants possess membership in the Nation, have informed opinions and ideas concerning the Tlowitsis lands, an interest in the PV production process and willingness to answer questions pertaining to their experiences in it. The process was broadly split into five distinct stages:

Pre-Shoot

A pre-trip workshop was held in the community center in Campbell River in early June 2006. The workshop was facilitated by the Chief Negotiator. The meeting included 20 Tlowitsis members of whom 90% were elders and 10% youth. The meeting consisted of a group discussion where community members identified the issues and concerns that they wanted incorporated into the video and their desired outcomes in undertaking this project. The main themes identified during

the workshop were the need for greater community cohesion, more control over territory and resources, cultural and language revitalization, and activating member participation in the treaty process and community events. Three youths from the group displayed a strong interest in the learning how to use the equipment. They became the focus of training efforts and operated the cameras through the fieldtrip. Training was conducted in an informal 'learning by doing' approach and included the mechanics of operating the camera, issues of audio and lighting, smooth hand-holding and framing shots (Corbett et al., 2009).

The Shoot

The day after the pre-shoot workshop, 20 Tlowitsis members, the Chief Negotiator and three university members left on a two day trip to the traditional lands. The first day of the retreat the group travelled to Hiladi, a deserted village site still used by the Tlowitsis for fishing and hunting. It was also the setting of an important historic event involving the legendary Tlowitsis warrior, Siwidi. Interviews at the site included the importance of unifying the band, reclaiming the land and members' personal experiences in this particular location. These discussions revolved around an

Figure 2. Preparing and smoking fish in Hiladi. © 2006, Jon Corbett

Figure 3. Tlowitsis youth videoing elders in Hiladi. © 2006, Raquel Mann

open fire where one community member prepared and smoked fish (Figure 2).

Members appeared comfortable talking to the cameras, perhaps because other community members were operating the equipment. At times, the technical operation proved challenging, although with support and encouragement humours remained intact and the quality of the footage excellent. During this first day of videoing it proved important to reinforce the notion that this trip and the video were theirs on a personal level as well as for the community. In the afternoon, two of the participants with a background in forestry did an interview about the political and environmental concerns related to resource management in the area and how these issues held implications for the past, present and future of the Nation.

On the second day of the retreat the group travelled by boat into the island areas of the Tlowitsis territory. This includes important historic sites including burial grounds, clam digging beds and village sites. Perhaps the most significant event of the second day was the arrival at Karlukwees (on Turnour Island), a place evoking memories of the past, frustration with the present, and hope for

the future. For the eldest participant on the retreat, it was the first time that she had returned in over 30 years. Several of the other participants had spent the early years of their lives in the village. Many of the youth had never stepped foot on the island (Figure 3).

By this point in the retreat, the group felt comfortable with each other, and the interviews that ensued were open, emotional, honest and impassioned. The themes discussed were centred on the participants bonds with Karlukwees, childhood memories, anger and sadness in being relocated to residential schools, disconnection from relatives, and frustration upon seeing the overgrown state of their village. They also related an enthusiastic desire to clean up Karlukwees, and make it accessible for the Tlowitsis people in the future. One universally supported idea was the desire for an annual Tlowitsis retreat, or summer camp on Karlukwees, where their children and grandchildren could come, learn about their culture, history, traditional territories, resources and practices. The participants also discussed how the nation desperately needed gatherings such as this in order to engage the members of the community and develop relationships. A number of participants also voiced that this trip and the project itself functioned as a good start in focussing the nation's attention on the land and that perhaps the message of the video could be related to calling their people home. As the Chief Negotiator identified:

[The project] *is far more serious than holiday snapshots or home movies because it's planned to have a message and to demonstrate something far more important than a vacation. It's about bringing a group of people who have been scattered, together with shared objectives.*

Post Shoot

Upon completion of the retreat, participants had collected 18 hours of video footage and over four hundred still images. Participants also contributed archival media such as old photographs of Karlukwees and audio recordings of songs sung by relatives. These were digitized and spliced into the video.

Two weeks after the retreat (towards the end of June 2007), the group reconvened in a workshop to examine the rough video cuts that had been edited by one of the youth participants and the two authors. This became an initial moment for the participants to consider the impact of the process and provided an opportunity for introspection about the state of the community. This involved a collaborative process where participants viewed the shots and then selected which should be considered for the final video, and which should be left out. The group decided to omit controversial political material and keep the message positive. Specifically the message would be a call to the Tlowitsis people to come home and engage in the revitalization of their culture and the nation's social, political, and economic development. The rationale was that if the final product emanated a sense of negativity, it would further evoke feelings of hopelessness, anger, frustration and apathy

within the nation. The group was unanimous in their agreement that the nation's priority should now be that of encouraging member's engagement in a positive way and helping them come to understand that they have the capacity to transform the nation's present condition.

The Product

The Tlowitsis video (finished in mid August 2006), at this point named the Homecoming DVD, reflects many elements found in the Fogo Island films (see Snowden, 1987). Fogo Islanders made films about themselves, their values and concerns and distributed these films to their neighbours. These groups watched the videos, reflected on them and responded to the first group by making and sending them their own videos. Crocker relays Colin Low's observation that the Fogo films were structurally different from most documentaries, which are based on one main issue representing a myriad of sources of information stylistically spliced together. Rather, it consists of a beginning, middle and end narrative structure. The interviews are complete, and for the most are cut together as whole interviews in line with the actual chronology of events that took place during the filming; this style of editing is *naturalistic* (Crocker, 2003).

The Homecoming DVD was very much naturalistic. It was cut together in chronological order. The chapter sections read: Day 1: Hiladi; Day 2: Karlukwees; Credits. Day 1 told the story of Siwidi narrated over footage of landscape in the area and the processes of cooking salmon. The Day 2 focused on the experience of the excursion, the emotions felt by the participants and returning to Karlukwees. Emotions ranged from joy and humor to anger and sadness. For the most part feelings were celebratory in nature and full of hope for the future. The sharing of ideas concerning how to bring the people together and rebuild the community followed discussions involving disconnection or destruction. The Tlowitsis, like the Fogo Islanders, "wanted to avoid bombarding people with too much serious material that might deaden the atmosphere" (Crocker, 2003, p. 28). They critically reflected on their experiences, magnified them in film and used them as a metaphoric tool to describe the scope of development required by the Nation.

Tlowitsis Nation Gathering

A nation-wide gathering was held in Campbell River in early September 2006, all Tlowitsis members were invited to participate. It took place over two days and comprised of a screening of the Homecoming DVD and its evaluation using questionnaires, semi-structured interviews and focus group discussions. Other parts of the gathering involved presentations by guest speakers selected by the Chief Negotiator. The overall intention of the meeting was to tie these various discussions and presentations together and relate them to nation building. The gathering was attended by 75 Tlowitsis members, 12 semi-structured interviews and 6 focus group discussions were conducted during the gathering in order to evaluate the impact of the DVD.

DISCUSSION

Research materials from the gathering, as well as participant observation from throughout the project cycle, are used in the next section to explore the role of the Homecoming DVD project in building the Tlowitsis Nation and how the project supported the fulfillment of the six requirements of nation building presented in the second section of this paper.

Requirement One: National Identity

The Homecoming DVD functions as visual proof that the nation has a distinctive identity and character. The product itself presents images and narratives that concern the nation's mythology,

language, history, culture, its ancestors and current membership, and affiliation with an historic landscape. In doing so, the video elucidates how the Nation is unique. When asked what the most important message in the DVD was, the majority of the responses referred to themes of how the nation's identity is connected with its land base, cultural history, roots and traditional use of resources. One respondent replied that the video showed him/her that "we do belong somewhere." Furthermore a large number of respondents identified that the DVD could support the development of a sense of community. Another question from a focus group discussion asked to how the DVD added to member's understanding of the Tlowitsis community. One response contended that it shows that "we still exist, but have changed."

From these and other similar participant statements, we can infer that the DVD succeeded in capturing an essence of the nation's identity and how it has evolved over time. It thus functions as form of proof of national identity and so may facilitate the fulfillment of the first requirement of nation building processes. Wakelin and Basheer (2001) suggest that ICTs have played significant roles "in preserving and identifying threatened or marginalized cultural artefacts and traditions" (p. 8). The Homecoming DVD supports this idea that the creation of archival video documents allows for the opportunity of future generations to reaffirm and re-evaluate their national identity as they may draw information, image and narratives which encompass the nation's characteristics from these sources. The Tlowitsis Chief Negotiator confirmed this potential in identifying the fact that "we all know that people retain a certain amount of information and over time, it fades away. That's why people create textbooks, so we can look back and have a reference" (pers.com, 2006). Video, like textbooks, may function as a continual resource in the identification of national identity

Requirement Two: Nationalism in the Individual

Nation building necessitates that a nation's members acquire a nationalist sentiment. A precondition to this is that the individual must come to recognize that the nation's identity makes up an integral part of their own identity and thus the individual's personal growth and development is fundamentally dependent on the integrity of the nation's perseverance. If an individual does not have this sense, it must be triggered by some sort of external force or entity, whether it is an experience with an object, person, or philosophy. This stimulation can result in an inner dialogue and reflection where the individual explores if and how the national identity is relevant to her own. Freire (1970) elucidates this concept as he states that "only through communication can human life hold meaning" (p. 58). Both the PV process and product involve communicating information about the national identity through visual, audio and experiential stimuli. This communication provokes the nation's members into such reflection.

PV involves critical reflection on how participants recognize their identity. Reicken et al. (2006) conducted a research project where First Nations students were required to make a video about a topic of their own interest relating to the themes of health and wellness. They noted that these video projects triggered the students to embrace their national and cultural identities. They illustrate that when the students engaged in:

Seeing themselves, their relatives and other First Nation people on video expressing pride in their cultural teachings, speaking their language and making direct reference to their way of seeing the world absolutely and positively affirmed the identities for the students in the project (Reicken et al., 2006, p. 283).

These kinds of impacts were equally apparent in the Tlowitsis Homecoming DVD project. One member, who had not been involved in the making of the video, expressed this affirmation of his national identity during a discussion after the screening of the video at the Nation's meeting.

I am part of the Tlowitsis tribe but I never knew about it. I am from the generation that lost a lot of my culture, and having to realize that there's a place to come, to learn and recognize where my roots come from and hearing the last bit of the DVD when I came in this morning gave me an understanding that the knowledge is there, that I can try to find out where my people came from, what they're like ... its very hard to know nothing about my home.

Furthermore, nation building requires that the individual embrace a sense of obligation in terms of assisting the development of the nation. This obligation is motivated by the individual feeling that they are emotionally invested in the nation. Leuthold (2001) discusses how indigenous media creates a sense of empathy in its viewers and acts as "a form of communication intended to move the viewer to identification and ultimately agreement with the author or speaker...using emotional appeals" (p.56). Video media therefore has great power in instilling such connections. One Tlowitsis participant expressed her own emotive reaction upon the viewing the DVD:

I got chills, I was almost crying. Yeah... Just knowing that my granny live there, and my family, basically. Because when I usually go back there I just feel the power that's still there, our ancestors have never left, and they never will leave.

Nationalism requires that the individual feels not only empathy and belonging, but a need for the nation's continued existence. Thus, the individual must not only be emotionally affiliated, but see themselves as emotionally invested in the nation. Authentic engagement is a fundamental element of the PV process, in that it involves creating a space where the individual is encouraged to engage in critical thinking, reflection and dialogue about themselves, their values and how they fit in with those of the people, environment and institutions around them. In engaging with each other in the creative processes of video production, people become committed to each other. The Tlowitsis Homecoming DVD functioned to infuse this sense of obligation and need for action within the members. In response to the inquiry of how the DVD had added to member's understanding of the Tlowitsis community two reoccurring themes emerge from the questionnaires; firstly that the Tlowitsis members had acquired an understanding of urgency of the challenges ahead in regards to treaty and nation building, and secondly they recognized the need for unity among the Nation's members.

Nationalism in a contemporary context requires that the nationalist sentiment must account for and reconcile plurality within its members. People need to be shown how their present, modern lives can be integrated with that of their traditional culture and roots. Huber (1999) contends that embracing plurality is at the very heart of the PV mandate, PV "asserts that there are, in any group, nation, or community, a plurality of and within the people, and all views, ideas, values and visions are relevant" (p. 37). Upon screening the Tlowitsis Homecoming DVD, it became apparent to many of the viewers that the nation includes a diverse array of backgrounds and people with varying degrees of past connections and experiences with the nation and its territories. For some, the DVD seemed to subdue the sense that their different lifestyles and paradigms might conflict with that of the Tlowitsis traditional values. One youth participant clearly expressed this identification and comfort in seeing others who, like herself, had not had much experience with the community,

Listening to Tom talk, he's around my age, he's never been to Turnour, he's only heard our family talk about Turnour. I felt the same way, he has no connection there, he's happy to be there. But there's no real connection to the land because we've never been there, grew up there... But right now, I want to go see what it's like, even if it's overgrown. I

172

would like to see it, that happy feeling would be there because that is home.

Moreover, this comfort led to feelings of the individual's willingness to participate in the nation's activities.

In the Homecoming DVD, both the process and product served to embrace pluralism and functioned to re-enchant and reconnect the individual to the community. It supported individuals to recognize the need that to engage in the community would be beneficial to themselves, their families, and the nation as a whole.

Requirement Three: Cohesion at the Community Level

Nation building requires the capacity for community members to effectively mobilize as a cohesive group. PV processes build relationships of trust and reciprocity within the group and are dependent on the group reaching agreement on the content of the production. Without this agreement, there can be no objectives set for the final video.

For those communities that have experienced displacement from their traditional territories, digital media technologies provide a means to overcome this socio-geographical separation and be used as a tool for communication between their members. Through the production and viewing of a collaboratively produced video, community members may share experiences, advice, support and converse over the obstacles and issues they face. This has the potential to unify and support the development of intimate relationships within these groups. During the 2002 World Summit on the Information Society, David Laughing Horse Robinson, Chief of the Kawaiisu Tribe, identified how ICTs enhance the possibility of "activism from the inside". He recommends, "Indigenous peoples use new technologies to make their communities and problems known and connect to groups that support Indigenous peoples because they fight for similar principles" (cited in Birraux-Ziegler, 2003, p. 6).

When people with similar interests have the means to work together and pool their resources, it enhances the potential and scale of the desired action to be taken. "Given the propensity towards the isolation and fragmentation of aboriginal peoples and disengagement from aboriginal ways of life, connectivity offers the potential for enhanced cultural continuity and rejuvenation of community ties" (CBNC, 2005, p. 17). Essential to nation building is a collective sense of community before the nation may act upon centralized social and political forces. Crocker illustrates how the Fogo process helped isolated and dispersed communities acquire this sense.

Through film, isolated communities could imagine themselves as a part of a single community. Thus the films created an external "virtual community" that could act as a reference point for people to given them an image of themselves. This not only aided in the development of long-term community strategies, but also in smaller and important matters of community organization (Crocker, 2003, p. 132).

One Tlowitsis participant discussed her reflection on how the DVD helped her identify and empathize with members she was not familiar with:

Sitting here, watching the DVD and then having a discussion about it, you figure out what other people think about it and then talking to people who were actually in the DVD so you can get more input about it instead of just having the whole thing about them just talking.

A reoccurring theme from questionnaire was that the DVD helped Tlowitsis members to understand more about their own history and culture, and that the community *is* capable of action and reunification. In response to the question "How has the DVD added to your understanding of the Tlowitsis community?" One respondent replied, "People can come together, even if they don't know each other that well and connect because we're all one Nation!"

Developing community cohesion requires that members retain a collective national memory; they must understand their relationships with each other and within their cultural framework in order to feel that there is an 'entity' that is both of themselves and bigger than themselves. Bell (2003) discusses how externalization is intrinsic to the concept of memory. A memory becomes affirmed through social interaction and those individuals who shared the experience engage in future acts of remembrance. The national memory is anchored, and thus persists, through shared experience. As national memory is essential in nation building processes, this social interaction becomes a key element. During the DVD production, Tlowitsis members cooked, ate, traveled, taught, learned and took risks together. As a result, members came to see each other's strengths and weaknesses, and thus, responsibilities and jobs were allocated accordingly. For example, in the Tlowitsis project, the youth were most interested in the camera work, and the elders in sharing stories.

Another key theme to emerge from the research materials was that Tlowitsis members recognized the need to record and share an understanding of their collective past, present and future. Harlan (2001) explains that many First Nations communities have come from a recent time where oppressive circumstances did not allow them to practice their religion, culture, and/or language; as a result secrecy became both a strategy for the culture to survive as well as a pattern and habit that continues into the present. When community members create videos, and when relatives see other relatives on the screen sharing stories, practices and history, members begin to feel more comfortable in sharing these secrets with each other and the above patterns begin to erode. Over half of the questionnaire respondents saw the community members themselves as being the primary audience for the DVD.

Requirement Four: Member Participation and Engagement

In order to function most effectively, PV requires the enthusiasm and engagement of participants. The Tlowitsis Homecoming DVD project process was inclusive and accessible to participants. The audience at the Nation's meeting received it well. 87% of questionnaire respondents said that they would be interested in getting involved in future DVD projects. During the DVD evaluation discussion, one Tlowitsis youth expressed her desire to engage in the community affairs after seeing the video:

My mom grew up in Turnour Island and watching this DVD has encouraged me to learn more. I want to know Turnour Island and see for myself, and being here, learning more, makes me want to encourage more people because I want my nieces and nephews to be able to learn more because living in the city, we don't learn a lot.

The Tlowitsis chief negotiator confirms the success in promoting the nation's members to engage:

The whole process that we've gone through is clearly good for reducing apathy and increasing participation, [and the] desire to participate. As you say, when people can see that "That's my cousin Jarrod, I can do that, heck I want to do that"... it shows the community working together.

Working in a group, agreeing on a direction to move forward and becoming aware of the larger social, political, economical and cultural spheres, an individual begins to understand how they fit within their encompassing systems. In the context of nation building, the community has the chance to represent what they *do* know, and why this knowledge is important, thereby validating the value of the community itself. PV provides individuals with platform for gathering, listening, speaking and sharing one's successes.

White (2003) explains why acknowledgement and celebration of these accomplishments is an important element in nation building:

Small successes produce capacity, confidence and courage to tackle larger more complex development plans of action. Communication media—video, radio and the Internet—will provide the mechanisms for linking and sharing the outcomes of these projects (p. 63).

The outcome of PV involves empowerment of the individual and community as they have the opportunity to have their voices heard and acted upon, and thus contribute to the progress of the community.

Requirement Five: Effective Government

PV does not directly create a 'better' or 'more capable' government, however it does function to contribute the information that those in governing positions need to understand: their community's perspectives, aspirations and issues, including the needs of members in terms of community policy, laws, programs and services. In the case of the Homecoming DVD, community members who felt alienated from the Nation's governing bodies (the chief and council) presented a clear picture of where the community is now, as well as offered solutions of where they need to go in the future. This promotes a situation where governments become informed and are presented with the opportunity to act on the materials presented in the video.

In observing the PV process and product, governments may obtain a deeper understanding of the nation's state of affairs in general, which is integral in successful governance and decision-making. Furthermore, because PV data becomes archival material for the community, governments can refer to this information in the future. Lawrence Lewis from the Hamalta Treaty society described how "Indigenous negotiators can draw information from their own databases, for instance, to prove Aboriginal [land] title through documenting historical and present day land use" (cited in Birraux-Ziegler, 2003, p. 6).

Despite the potential for PV to directly influence decision-making within the community, it needs to be understood that its effectiveness to effect change is largely contingent on the receptiveness of the governing bodies to act on the materials presented. In the case of the Tlowitsis, initially there was little desire for the Nation's governing bodies, the chief and council, to even view the Homecoming DVD. This was likely because of the fear that the video would cast them in a negative light. This fear was well founded because of the long term dysfunctional relationship that had grown between the Tlowitsis community and the governing bodies, manifest in the membership's views that the government was not responsive to their needs and exacerbated by the disconnection caused by the dispersed nature of the Nation. However, once the chief and council members had a clearer understanding of the objectives of the DVD and they had received positive feedback from other community members, they were more openly supportive of the DVD. However, at the time of writing this paper, there remains no evidence that any of the recommendations presented have been acted upon.

The Homecoming DVD has shown greater promise at influencing government representatives at the treaty table. The video was shown to members of the BC Treaty Commission whose response was immediate. They identified that they had a much clearer understanding of the unique challenges that the Nation faced in regards to the dispersed nature of the membership and the difficulties in convening the community in one location at one time. This understanding is important for having a clearer picture of the Nation's strategy in engaging its membership in decision-making processes a well as supporting it financially through the allocation of treaty related resources.

Requirement Six: The Existence of a Geographic Locality over Which the Nation Has Sovereignty

Nation building requires that the population is directly related to a geographic territory saturated with a national history, mythology and symbology. The Tlowitsis Homecoming DVD project provided the opportunity for members to come together on their traditional lands and learn about its history, cultural significance and its past, present and potential future uses. For those who participated in the retreat, they were able to physically experience their land, while learning about it directly from the memories and storytelling of their elders. One woman expressed her feelings upon visiting Karlukwees:

You walk on that beach or that wharf you know your home, where you belong ...it's a different feeling altogether. I get this special feeling every time I step on Turnour Island on the ground, you know, it is a real nice uplifting moment for me. Joy and all the good memories, and yeah, knowing my home, a place to call home.

Even for those community members who weren't on the retreat, watching the DVD invoked emotion and a desire to see and learn more about the territory. It proved useful in engaging those who have never seen the territory and are largely disconnected from the community. When interviewed, a Tlowitsis youth expressed how useful the medium can be for inspiring the nation to be more active in the future of their territories:

A lot of people hadn't seen the territory and that was their first glimpse of it and it got them interested in being able to see the territory and it might have an effect for other people to go and visit he territory and do projects of their own.... It's motivational, cultural, but also a good visual for people, instead of just hearing about it and seeing maps its sort of a visual way for people to make a connection and actually see what their territory looks like instead of just hearing about it.

Reconciliation of Dangers: Subjectivity and Exclusion

When working with any ICT in a community setting subjectivity and exclusion pose potential risks. If media technologies are introduced to communities that are unfamiliar with their operation and lack the skills to analyze the process and product, it is imperative that they be made aware of the subjective nature of the media and of unavoidable bias (Wakelin & Basheer, 2001). The principal criticisms Tlowitsis members had of the Homecoming DVD project concerned its biased nature, sugarcoated material and exclusion.

In making the video, the original group had come to a consensus that the main message be positive, and that they wanted to avoid becoming embroiled in politics concerning the exploitation of land, conflicts within the Nation and the dysfunctionality of their governing systems. One of the members who hadn't participated in the making of the video elucidated his frustration about the nature of the editing after the screening:

There's extreme editing. They didn't show the amount of logging taking place in that territory. I've seen it, I've walked through there and it breaks my heart ... I think [the DVD] needs to be real. You just showed the prettiness of it, without the other parts. It's a falsity.

This kind of frustration and lack of understanding about objectives of the video, can potentially promote disinterest in future engagement in the Nation's activities. The Chief Negotiator responded to such complaints:

The purpose of the DVD was to help with motivation and get a sense of what is possible. And yes, we were trying to craft a positive message, but if people are saying it does seem to be a little

apple pie, I'm fine with that. But if people were saying this was deliberately crafted to create an incorrect perception, I would reject that.

Another Tlowitsis participant declared his disappointment in lack of representation of a broader representation of community members in the video:

I wasn't too impressed with the video just for the simple fact that it wasn't real there's not enough representation of the diversity of the families who used to live there. There's a lot of one point of view one-sidedness to it, which has been the case in a lot of areas in our band. Which is, if we're going to show the diversity of our people and resources we need to include everybody in this picture.

Because the Tlowitsis was a pilot project aimed at grabbing the attention of the community and instilling the desire to participate, it might be argued that in this case, exclusion might either serve to further exclude certain members of the community, or perhaps work to provoke members' to become more engaged in the future.

CONCLUSION

In conclusion, Buddle (2005) asks whether First Nations are in danger of being further influenced and assimilated through the appropriation of Western technologies. Does this possibility mean that PV and related processes might actually counter nation building? Buddle quotes Rosemary Kuptana, former president of the Inuit Broadcasting Corporation of Canada, who contends that Aboriginal participation in the media world is in fact, bringing communities together and strengthening them.

The technology may be new but the message is still very old, spoken down to us from our elders. We have produced programs that strengthen and revitalize our cultures, our languages, our his-

tory. They tell us who we are and to be proud of where we are going as a people. But it has not always been a happy journey. The generational breakdown between young and old was made worse by the arrival of television and radio. I find it ironic that those same technologies are pulling us back together (Rosemary Kuptana, in Buddle, 2005, p. 13).

The Homecoming DVD project is also proof that PV has the potential to fuel nation building. The making of the DVD, it's screening at the band meeting and the dialogue that followed stimulated members to critically reflect on their present situation and how to take on the future, which in turn has stimulated nationalism; unified disconnected members; served as a tool to educate, and inform governing bodies and community in the topics and issues that are important to the community members and their future development. This initial project has also led to further new media projects within the community. In 2009 a DVD called the Virtual Land Tour was created with elders within the community discussing the range of traditional resource management practices within the community.

It is evident that the Tlowitsis recognize these values in using PV for nation building purposes. For these reasons, a participatory video has potential for a nation to acquire the kind of community cohesion necessary for mobilization and development. The Homecoming DVD served to function as a tool to unify the community by bridging generational, cultural, social, political, economical, ideological and geographical gaps.

ACKNOWLEDGMENT

The authors would like to sincerely thank the members of the Tlowitsis community with whom this project was undertaken. We would also like to acknowledge the important role that the Tlowitsis chief negotiator, the chief and council had in supporting the project.

REFERENCES

Assembly of First Nations (AFN). (2005, March). Recognition and Implementation of First Nation Governments. *Resolve Newsletter*.

Balit, S. (2003). Forward. In White, S. (Ed.), *Participatory Video: Images that Transform and Empower* (pp. 8–12). New Delhi, India: Sage Publications.

Bell, D. (2003). Mythscapes: memory, mythology, and national identity. *The British Journal of Sociology*, *54*(1), 63–81. doi:10.1080/0007131032000045905

Bell, W., & Freeman, W. (Eds.). (1974). *Ethnicity and Nation-Building*. Beverly Hills, CA: Sage Publications.

Bery, R. (2003). Participatory Video that Empowers. In White, S. (Ed.), *Participatory Video: Images that Transform and Empower* (pp. 271–285). New Delhi, India: Sage Publications.

Birraux-Ziegler, P. (2003, December 8-11). *NGO Narrative Report on the Global Forum of Indigenous Peoples and the Information Society*. Geneva, Switzerland: Indigenous Peoples' Centre for Documentation, Research and Information (DoCip). Retrieved September 2009, from http://www.docip.org/anglais/ news_en/reportGFI-PIS_eng.rtf

British Columbia Treaty Commission (BCTC). (2002, May). Improving the Treaty Process: Report of the Tripartite Working Group. In *First Nations Summit*, BC, Canada. Retrieved December 2007, from http://www.gov.bc.ca/tno/down/tripartite_working_05_15.pdf

Buddle, K. (2005). Aboriginal Cultural Capital Creation and Radio Production in Urban Ontario. *Canadian Journal of Communication*, *30*, 7–39.

Chambers, R. (2004). *Ideas for Development: reflecting forwards* (IDS Working Paper 238). Brighton, UK: University of Sussex, Institute of Development Studies.

Corbett, J. M., Muir, K., & Singleton, G. (2009). Web 2.0 for Aboriginal Cultural Survival: A new Australian Outback Movement. *Participatory Learning and Action, 59*, 71–78.

Crocker, S. (2003). The Fogo Process: Participatory Communication in a Globalizing World. In White, S. (Ed.), *Participatory Video: Images that Transform and Empower* (pp. 122–144). New Delhi, India: Sage Publications.

Crossing Boundaries National Council (CBNC). (2005). *Aboriginal Voice National Recommendations: From Digital Divide to Digital Opportunity (Crossing Boundaries Papers)*. Ottawa, Canada: KTA Centre for Collaborative Government.

Delanty, G., & O'Mahony, P. (2002). *Nationalism and Social Theory: Modernity and Recalcitrance of the Nation*. London: Sage Publications.

Dudely, M. (2003). The Transformative Power of Video: Ideas, Images, Processes and Outcomes. In White, S. (Ed.), *Participatory Video: Images that Transform and Empower* (pp. 145–156). New Delhi, India: Sage Publications.

Evans, M., Hole, R., Berg, L., Hutchinson, P., & Sookraj, D. Okanagan Urban Aboriginal Research Health Collective. (in press). Common Insights, Differing Methodologies: Towards a Fusion of Indigenous Methodologies, Participatory Action Research, and White Studies in an Urban Aboriginal Research Agenda. *Qualitative Inquiry*.

Ferreira, G. (2006). Participatory Video for Policy Development. *Canadian Journal of Communication*. Retrieved September 2009, from http://www.cjconline.ca/ index.php/journal/thesis/view/68

Ferreira, G., Ramirez, R., & Walmark, B. (2004, September 18). *Connectivity in Canada's Far North: Participatory Evaluation in Ontario's Aboriginal Communities*. Paper presented at the Measuring the Information Society: What, How, for Who and What? Workshop, Brighton, UK.

Freire, P. (1970). *Pedagogy of the oppressed*. New York: Continuum.

Galois, R. (1994). *Kwakwaka'wakw Settlement Sites, 1775-1920: A Geographical Analysis and Gazetteer*. Vancouver, Canada: UBC Press.

Harlan, T. (2001). Editors introduction. *Wizaco Sa Revue, 16*(2), 55–73.

Harris, U. (2009). Transforming images: reimagining women's work through participatory video. *Development in Practice, 19*(4), 538–549. doi:10.1080/09614520902866405

Huber, B. (1999). *Communicative aspects of participatory video projects: an exploratory study*. Unpublished master's thesis, Sveriges Lantbruks Universitet, Sweden. Retrieved September 2007, from http://www.maneno.net/ pdfs/bernhardsthesis.pdf

Johansson, L., Knippel, V., Waal, D., & Nyamachumbe, F. (2000). Questions and answers about participatory video. *Forest. Trees and People Newsletter, 40/41*, 35–40.

Kennedy, D., & Bouchard, R. (2008, May 6). *Tlowitsis rights and title: a discussion paper*. Paper presented at the Tlowitsis Nation, Victoria, Canada.

Kilvington, M., Allen, W., & Kravchenko, C. (1999). *Improving Farmer Motivation Within Tb Vector Control* (Landcare Research Contract Report No. LC9899/110).

Leuthold, S. (2001). Rhetorical Dimensions of Native American Documentary. *Wizaco Sa Review, 16*(2), 55–73. doi:10.1353/wic.2001.0022

Lunch, C. (2007). The Most Significant Change: using participatory video for monitoring and evaluation. *Participatory Learning and Action, 56*, 28–32.

Lunch, N., & Lunch, C. (2006). *Insight's into Participatory Video: a handbook for the field*. Oxford, UK: Insight.

Naveh, Z. (1998). Ecological and cultural landscape restoration and the cultural evolution towards a post-industrial symbiosis between human society and nature. *Restoration Ecology, 6,* 135–143. doi:10.1111/j.1526-100X.1998.00624.x

Norrish, P. (1998). Radio and Video for Development. In Richardson, D., & Paisley, L. (Eds.), *The First Mile of Connectivity*. Rome, Italy: Food and Agriculture Organization of the United Nations.

Poelzer, G. (2002). *The Self-Government Landscape*. British Columbia, Canada: BC Treaty Commission. Retrieved October 2007, from http://www.bctreaty.net/files_3/pdf_documents/self_government_landscape.pdf

Reicken, T., Conibear, F., Corrine, M., Lyall, J., Scott, T., & Tanaka, M. (2006). Resistance through Re-representing Culture: Aboriginal Student Filmmakers and a Participatory Action Research Project on Health and Wellness. *Canadian Journal of Education, 29*(1), 265–286. doi:10.2307/20054156

Seidl, B. (2003). Candid Thoughts on the Not-so-candid Camera: How Video Documentation Radically Alters Development Projects. In White, S. (Ed.), *Participatory Video: Images that Transform and Empower* (pp. 157–194). New Delhi, India: Sage Publications.

Smith, A. (1999). *Myths and Memories of the Nation*. New York: Oxford University Press.

Snowden, D. (1987). Eyes See; Ears Hear. In Richardson, D., & Paisley, L. (Eds.), *The First Mile of Connectivity*. Rome, Italy: Food and Agriculture Organization of the United Nations.

Wagner, H. (1933). *Spanish Explorations in the Strait of Juan de Fuca*. Santa Ana, CA: Fine Arts Press.

Wakelin, O., & Shadrach, B. (2001). *Impact Assessment of Appropriate and Innovative Technologies in Enterprise Development*. London: Department for International Development. Retrieved August 2009, from http://www.alle.de/transfer/downloads/MD380.pdf

White, S. (Ed.). (2003). *Participatory Video: Images that Transform and Empower*. New Delhi, India: Sage Publications.

ENDNOTES

[1] An Indigenous group, referred to as First Nation in Canada, located on the West Coast of the province of British Columbia.

[2] A defining mythology means that the nation encompasses a narrative which explains where, how and why it was originally forged, how and why it has come to be the way it is today, and in what way it can develop into the future (Smith, 1999, pp. 57-96).

[3] The application of PV is increasingly widespread as video technology becomes more accessible to non-professional users - equipment is progressively more affordable, portable and easier to use (Huber, 1999); furthermore, once the equipment is bought, there are minimal additional costs (O'Farrell et al., 2000); the biggest ongoing expense is training (Johansson et al., 2000). The digitization of the video production workflow also allows for trial and error in both the filming and editing stages with little cost to the user and makes the final product transferable over the Internet, satellite, DVD, and cable.

This work was previously published in International Journal of Information Communication Technologies and Human Development, Volume 2, Issue 3, edited by Susheel Chhabra and Hakikur Rahman, pp. 33-54, copyright 2010 by IGI Publishing (an imprint of IGI Global).

Chapter 12
ICTs in Chinese Distance Higher Education:
Increased Opportunities and Continuous Challenges

Xiaobin Li
Brock University, Canada

ABSTRACT

The Chinese higher education system is the largest in the world, but distance education, using information communication technologies (ICTs), started later than in developed countries. In this paper, the author examines the benefits of education to human development and provides an overview of the recent development of distance higher education in China. The potential for further developing distance higher education with ICTs is considered. In addition, challenges are discussed and recommendations are made to improve Chinese distance higher education.

BENEFITS OF EDUCATION TO HUMAN DEVELOPMENT

Education is valued for its benefits to human development and its role in advancing social justice. However, before realizing any larger social values, most citizens have to be literate and numerate to obtain gainful employment to be financially self-sufficient in an increasingly globalized economy. Providing an adequate education, generally considered at minimum to include a secondary school diploma but ideally to have some form of

higher education, to all youth so that they become contributing citizens is a critical and challenging issue that educators and policy-makers have to work on permanently.

Education has economic values. The more education one has, the more likely one is employed, and the higher income one tends to earn (Garner, 2004; Levin, Belfield, Muennig, & Rouse, 2007; Statistics Canada, 2004, 2006). In the United States, Angrist and Krueger (1991) find that the estimated monetary return to an additional year of schooling is about 7.5 percent. In Canada, from 1951 to 2001, the skills acquired by one extra year of education resulted in an increase in per capita

DOI: 10.4018/978-1-4666-0047-8.ch012

income of around 7.3 percent. The accumulation of human capital has played a strong role in explaining relative levels of per capita income across the Canadian provinces during the past half century (Statistics Canada, 2006). In China it is also observed that there is a positive relationship between education and career development (Chai, 2009).

Investment in human capital is three times as important to economic growth over the long run as investment in physical capital. Differences in average skill levels among Organization of Economic Cooperation and Development (OECD) countries explain fully 55 percent of the differences in economic growth over the 1960 to 1994 period. This implies that investments in raising the average level of skills could yield large economic returns (Statistics Canada, 2005).

Japan and China may be considered two examples of the difference education can make. The Japanese labor force is better educated than the Chinese labor force. In 2007 the Japanese education index was 0.949 and their GDP per capita (PPP US$) was 33,632, compared with the Chinese index of 0.851 and their GDP per capita of 5,383 (United Nations Development Program, 2009). With the realization that China lags behind developed countries in education, the Chinese system has gone through the largest expansion ever seen in the world higher education community (Zha, 2009). Recently the Chinese government has allocated a significant portion of its economic stimulus money to be used in developing education (Li & Yu, 2009).

Education also has other values. Educational attainment has large and independent positive effects on most measures of civic engagement and attitudes (Dee, 2004). More education is associated with more civic engagement. Lower education levels are almost always associated with significantly lower levels of civic engagement (Statistics Canada, 2006). There is a positive relationship between these activities and the satisfaction people derive in their lives (Statistics

Canada, 2004). In other words, people with more education tend to engage in more civic and social activities. Because they engage in more of these activities, they tend to be happier. People with more education are healthier and are less likely to have law-breaking behavior (Statistics Canada, 2005). Besides, education brings external benefits to society in addition to the person who uses the service of education (Brimley & Garfield, 2005).

CHINESE HIGHER EDUCATION

In 2008 with more than 29 million students, the Chinese higher education participation rate was 23.3 percent (Ministry of Education, 2009), which can be considered mass education (Trow, 1973). The largest higher education system in the world, Chinese higher education is more accessible than before, but there are problems.

There are significant gaps in the development of higher education across regions and social groups, as well as between urban centers and rural areas. Higher education is still not available in some remote western areas. With tuitions rising rapidly, higher education is difficult for poor families to access. In addition, the increasing availability of higher education makes people pay more attention to quality, and there are concerns. When compared with universities in developed countries, domestic ones are not rated highly (National Bureau of Statistics of China, 2002).

The average Chinese education attainment of 8.5 years (Zhou, 2007a) is significantly lower than the 12 years of the OECD countries. Within China, the gap in education attainment between eastern regions and western regions is wide. The recent needs for education spending were estimated at 6-9 percent of GDP, but the actual expenditures were about 5 percent (Dahlman, Zeng, & Wang, 2007), significantly lower than the OECD average of 6.2 percent (OECD, 2007). Even with the most recent increase in education spending (Wen, 2009), expenditures in education still lag behind those in developed countries. The demand for higher education is growing, but under-funding has been a problem (Ma, 2009). In 2008 approximately 10 million Chinese took the entry examinations for higher education; only about 6 million were admitted (Ministry of Education, 2009). It seems that part of the demand for higher education is not met by the current supply.

DISTANCE HIGHER EDUCATION WITH ICTS

To provide more opportunities, Chinese started providing higher education through correspondence in 1952 (Su, 2009) and used radio and TV stations to offer various distance education programs in late 1950s. After China opened up and started a comprehensive reform in 1978, education programs provided through TV expanded significantly. In 1999, four Chinese universities started distance education using information and communication technologies (ICTs) with 2,900 students (Liu, 2007). With China's huge education needs and geographic dispersion, contemporary ICTs have considerably increased access to higher education. ICTs can play a unique and important role in connecting people at various levels in different places for the pursuit of knowledge and training (Fang, 2009). With ICTS, students can individually obtain information on the most recent scientific developments around the world. Massachusetts Institute of Technology (2009) and Cambridge University (2010) have put some of their teaching materials on the Internet. In April 2009 faculty at the Massachusetts Institute of Technology voted unanimously to make their scholarly articles available to the public for free on the Internet. An open access movement gained momentum with the creation of free online journals and institutional digital repositories making research results openly available to anyone (Canadian Association of University Teachers, 2009). Without the constraints of status, time, space, institution, and nationality, ICTs provide learning venues for anyone who has access to the Internet. The largest national academic network in the world, China Education and Research Network has covered over 200 cities, more than 2,000 universities and research institutes with over 20 million users (Lu, 2009). Although international distance education programs are not formally open in China, there are Chinese students enrolled in foreign programs while they remain in China, learning through the Internet (Huang, 2009).

In addition, ICTs can play a significant role in realizing equity in Chinese education (Sun, 2009). Zhou (2007b) points out there are three opportunity inequities in Chinese higher education: 1) inequity among students from different regions of the country, with students in the eastern part where most universities are located having an advantage over those in the western part; 2) inequity among students from different social groups, with students from rich families having an advantage over those from poor families; 3) universities are put in different categories and are funded accordingly, which has produced inequity among institutions, with some universities having an advantage over others. Zhou argues that since distance education is able to overcome the constraints of space and time, it has an important contribution to make in promoting equity. He recommends that the government provide financial support to distance education so that it can develop faster, reducing inequity in higher education. Zhou's argument is similar to Tait's (2008) contention that one of the four main functions of open universities is to provide individual opportunity.

IMPACT OF ICTS

On January 15, 2010, China Internet Network Information Centre reported that 384 million Chinese had used the Internet as of December 31, 2009. This placed China as the country with the most Internet users in the world. About 28.9 percent of the Chinese population had used the Internet, above the world average of 25.6 percent. However, when compared with developed countries where the percentage was over 70 (Miniwatts Marketing Group, 2010), the gap was still great. There was also an obvious gap within China between urban centers and rural areas. While proportionately China lags behind developed countries, the annual increase in the number of Chinese Internet users is about 29 percent in 2009. As more Chinese go online, ICTs grow in importance as tools for distance education (China Internet Network Information Centre, January 2009). In 2007 approximately 1,325,000 students were admitted into various distance education programs that mainly use ICTs to provide education. By the end of 2007, about 6,678,000 students registered in universities that had received the Ministry of Education's approval to provide distance education programs with ICTs (Li, Yan, & Yao, 2008). According to a report from Sina Corporation (2009), the value of 2008 Chinese network education market was approximately 35.2 billion yuan (about 5.2 billion US dollars). Of this market about 85 to 90 percent was in higher education.

In November 2006, the Ministry of Science and Technology and the Ministry of Education launched the Public Service Demonstration Project for Digital Education. They hoped to advance key ICTs in providing digital education to the general public, establish a new model of services, provide high quality and individualized digital degree and non-degree programs, promote equity and accessibility, and contribute to the establishment of a life long learning system (Yan, 2007). The Ministry estimates that from 2007 to 2050 about 25 million to 30 million people per year need various types of continuous education (Dahlman, Zeng, & Wang, 2007). It is impossible for the traditional means of education to meet this demand. Education ICTs should play a greater role in meeting the increasing demand. In addition, per student cost of distance education is lower than that of face-to-face programs (Zhou, 2007b).

On October 27, 2007, the International Distance Education Forum was held in Beijing, where most of the over 200 participants were Chinese, but there were also attendees from other countries. The theme of the forum was: Quality and effectiveness, two pressing issues for Chinese educators (Song, 2007). To build an information country capable of innovation, educators and ICT professionals have much to do before China can catch up with developed countries.

While ICTs have played a positive role in providing more opportunities, there is a problem of standardization; sharing resources is difficult (Lu, 2009). In addition, although they may not be as technologically savvy as American students (Glotzbach, Mordkovich, & Radwan, 2008), many Chinese students are frequent Internet users (China Internet Network Information Centre, 2009), and they expect their instructors to deliver courses in a variety of ways. Worldwide, web-based courses and programs have been increasingly developed by many academic institutions due to their benefits for both learners and educators (Nam & Smith-Jackson, 2007).

Since 1999 the 68 universities approved by the Ministry of Education to provide distance education degree programs with ICTs have admitted over 10 million applicants into various programs, which cover about 300 subjects. These programs have graduated over 5 million students and provided training to over 40 million people (Chen, 2008; Liu, 2009). Most applicants who applied to a distance higher education program were admitted (Zhang, 2007). The admission rate of distance education programs was much higher than the admission rate of face-to-face programs, which was about 60 percent in 2008 (Ministry of Education, 2009). Besides the Internet, most programs use cable television networks and satellite technology. Distance higher education is provided through ICTs in all 31 provinces, autonomous regions, and municipalities directly under the national government.

Instruction with ICTs is mainly provided through the Internet with computers, but recently a few universities started using mobile technology. With over 100,000 students of different ages, occupations, and computer competences scattered at 59 campuses, Shanghai TV University explored the establishment of a mobile campus since September 2004, hoping to provide a more interactive learning environment that serves students 24 hours a day and 7 days a week (Sun & Chen, 2007). Mainly using cell phone texting technology, the mobile campus was the extension of the real campus and online campus. Currently Shanghai TV University provides instruction to its students mostly through online teaching, with some in person and TV broadcasting instruction. The mobile campus provides more flexibility and interaction between instructors, students and administrators. By January 2007 there were 83,892 students registered at the mobile campus. Mobile students performed better than the national average in the standardized "level A university English" tests.

While the overall mobile experience was positive, there were shortcomings (Sun & Chen, 2007). Mobile learning was not always effective, because students tended to use small amounts of time for study. It was not easy for them to concentrate for a certain period of time. ICTs used in mobile learning were quite limited, and it was difficult to display multi-media information. Learning resources applicable in mobile learning were inadequate, and there was little Chinese research to inform practice. Shanghai TV University would use 3G technology in its mobile campus to increase the capacity of mobile teaching. Instructors would make efforts to develop learning resources for the mobile campus. They would connect online learning with mobile learning, increasing the mobile component.

Shen and Ding (2007) observed that mobile learning was provided only in a few disciplines, particularly in the instruction of English. The technology in both hardware and software was almost ready to further develop mobile learning. In May 2007 New Oriental Education Group reached an agreement with Nokia to build a mobile learning platform, from which students could visit specific New Oriental curriculum websites with their Nokia cell phone. Students could download English course contents and test preparation materials. These materials would be designed specifically for students to read and listen to. Shen and Ding predicted that as mobile technology improved and the cost dropped, more Chinese would use it for education and it would become an important complement of face-to-face and online education.

While online learning was gradually being made universal in China and mobile learning barely started, Xue (2007) recommended that Chinese educators consider the establishment of a ubiquitous learning environment. He believed the learning environment was changing significantly as ICTs continued to develop with new products. An environment where learners could access uninterrupted services any time anywhere could be built. He argued that online learning, mobile learning and ubiquitous learning were different development stages of education with ICTs. He thought conceptually and technologically ubiquitous learning would be more flexible and more interactive, providing opportunities to more people.

CHALLENGES IN DISTANCE HIGHER EDUCATION WITH ICTS

Although the development of Chinese distance higher education with ICTs has provided more opportunities, it has not become part of the main stream education (Su, 2009), and it has its problems. In a study comparing Chinese distance education with British distance education, Hao, Wang and Wang (2008) found that Britain had a more detailed and easier to operate system to ensure quality. The Chinese system was not as transparent as the British one. Chinese students did not receive feedback from their instructors in time. Chinese instructors tended to work in isolation, and the curricula they designed might not always be appropriate for distance education due to their lack of teaching experiences with ICTs. Hao, Wang and Wang suggested that Chinese instructors increase their net teaching competence and adopt a student-centered approach. They also suggested that governments at various levels enhance the monitoring of quality assurance.

In comparing Chinese and British policies, Tian, Wang and Wang (2007) found that there was an obvious gap between Chinese policies and British ones, with Chinese policies not as sophisticated as those in Britain. Britain started using a national learning network in January 1998, but a Chinese national system was still to be built. In addition, the British government provided more financial support to distance education, the British network was more extensive proportionately reaching more people, and British universities had more autonomy. Tian, Wang and Wang recommended that the Chinese government learn from the British system, but also consider the particular Chinese context, and construct realistic, comprehensive, and specific policies to promote distance education.

In a study comparing distance education in China and India, Gong (2007) found that its development in both countries was quite uneven, with an obvious gap between more developed areas and less developed ones. However, Indian universities were more autonomous, and India had a more established legal system regulating distance education's development and operation. In addition, unlike Chinese programs that provided certificate and bachelor programs only to Chinese students, one Indian open university extended its services to 41 teaching centers in 35 countries, providing certificate, bachelor, master and doctorate programs. The Indian government paid more attention to the development of distance education, planning to increase the portion of it in higher education from 20 percent to 50 percent. Gong believed the Chinese government should

let universities have more autonomy and provide more administrative support.

From 2001 to 2005, a few incidents happened that exposed the less than desirable quality of some distance education programs (Zhang & Wang, 2007). The Ministry of Education had to promulgate policies and adopt measures to regulate the admission of students into distance education programs. As a result of this concern over quality, the Central Radio and TV University started evaluating its open education programs. Today people still have doubt about the quality of some distance education programs (Zhou & Chen, 2009).

Since 2004, Chinese distance education students taking some general courses have to participate in standardized national examinations administered by the Ministry of Education. These examinations are necessary in improving and ensuring the quality of programs. The Ministry of Education established a national Internet registration system that acknowledges all successful distance education graduates (Li, 2007).

China's recent move to mass higher education has turned more and more to the market for needed resources (Zha, 2009). Although marketization allows distance education to develop fast, effectively providing opportunities to individuals who otherwise have no access to higher education, it has some negative consequences (Huang, 2007). Marketization leads to the drop of the quality of some programs. Since distance education is exclusively financed by student tuitions, it is often beyond the reach of poor families, actually increasing opportunity inequity. The lowering of quality and the increase in inequity weaken the characteristic of education as public good, which is against the goal of building a harmonious society in China.

Since the 1990's the gap between the rich and poor among Chinese has increased, the number of people in marginalized groups becomes larger, members of these groups are increasingly unhappy with the government's economic reform, and the government's credibility has dropped (Huang, 2007). Having a fair and just society is the basis of a harmonious society. It is obvious that developing distance education with ICTs exclusively depending on student tuition will not help to build harmony in China. Huang contends that different distance education programs need to be clearly categorized and regulated accordingly, and a fair competition and free selection system needs to be established. He recommends that a national legal system protecting the interests of the public be constructed, a fair government bidding system be set up to encourage transparent competition, the cost be kept at the minimum to provide more opportunities, government financial assistance be provided to students from poor families, tuitions be specifically capped, and the regulations protecting students' rights be improved.

Chinese distance education with ICTs is a recent and progressive phenomenon in need of continuous improvement. Although the application of ICTs in distance education has increased opportunities, it is not meeting most people's expectations. Some of the challenges are summarized in the following paragraphs.

Chinese educators have been learning from international colleagues in using ICTs, but domestic experiences have not received sufficient study they deserve. There is a lack of high quality research to inform practice (Wang, Y., 2008; Yang, Deng, & Cao, 2008). Most distance education courses stress content presentation, and instructors do not pay enough attention to the learning environment. The teaching model used most often is a mere transmission of information. A large part of distance education content is a direct video broadcasting of instructors' lectures, with little or no interaction between instructors and students. In recent years there has been some improvement in these areas, and students now have more options. Still, distance education so far is mainly a transmission of teaching resources and course content (Wang, Zhao, & Chen, 2009).

While ICTs are generally shared and there are opportunities for cooperation, educators use it at their discretion. A broad national system where educators can exchange and share teaching resources has not been established. Similar to what happens among Western European institutions (Cartelli, Stanfield, Connolly, Jimoyiannis, Magalhaes, & Maillet, 2008), some Chinese universities repeat what others have already done, which is a waste of resources (Lu, 2009). There is a shortage of Chinese educators with network teaching expertise. Most instructors using ICTs are regular instructors with little knowledge of network teaching experiences. They do not put enough time into meeting the needs of distance education students. They do not understand that in distance education with ICTs students play a more important role. Significant efforts have been put into building hardware, but attention to creating applicable software is far from enough (Fang, Zhao, & Duan, 2008). High quality coursework and relevant resources are inadequate (Li, 2008). When distance education expands quickly, quality is not assured (Wang, C., 2008; Zhou & Chen, 2009).

Since distance education students and instructors usually do not meet in person, support services provided through ICTs are vital. However, students are not provided sufficient guidance. Few of them receive feedback on their work from instructors, and there is little individualized teaching (Zhang & Zhao, 2009). In designing course materials, instructors tend to emphasize content over support (Yang, Deng, & Cao, 2008; Zhou & Chen, 2009). In addition, fees are sometimes too high and networks are not always stable.

Similar to Cambodian, Laotian and Vietnamese distance education programs (Baggaley, 2007), some Chinese programs do not meet students' needs and do not enjoy as high a reputation as face-to-face programs. Since most distance education programs are paid for mainly or exclusively by students, equity is a serious issue owing to income disparities among students (Huang, 2007).

Governments at various levels provide almost no financial support to distance education at all (Yan, 2008; Yang, Deng, & Cao, 2008).

Contemporary higher education has been influenced by two mega-trends—massification and globalization (Shin & Harman, 2009)—and China is no exception. As more Chinese go abroad to receive education, more international students are studying in China. In 2009 there were 238,184 international students from 190 countries in 610 Chinese institutions (Ministry of Education, 2010). The increase of international students going to China surpassed the increase of Chinese students going overseas (Zhang, 2008). Even under the impact of the recent economic recession, there were more international students in China in 2009 than the previous year (Ministry of Education, 2009). Education provided through ICTs should play a role in helping the world better understand China, however, overall, most Chinese distance educators have yet to recognize the benefits and challenges of internationalization (Ma, 2007).

THE WAY FORWARD

It has been over 10 years since Chinese universities started using ICT's to provide distance education. To offer more opportunities for quality education, the author makes several recommendations here, of which most are based on recent literature. Chinese distance educators need to aim at providing higher education, continuing education and life long learning opportunities to the masses. Universities need to consider what they can do to fully utilize their strengths to meet people's varied needs (Su, 2009) and to contribute to developing higher education in western China.

Chinese educators need to learn from international colleagues, reflect on their own practices, analyze their own experiences, and construct distance education theories appropriate for the Chinese context (Li, 2007; Wang, C., 2008). Universities that already provide distance education

with ICTs should promote research on it and train distance education instructors (Chen, 2008). They also need to increase cooperation, efficiency and standardization (Lu, 2009; Wang, Zhao, & Chen, 2009). It is a good thing that the Central Radio and TV University started building a national higher education network and digital learning resource center (Zhong, 2009). Resources provided through ICTs need to be evaluated. At least Chinese need a system similar to the Student Guide to Evaluating Information Technology on Campus (Educause, 2009). In improving quality, four factors have to be considered. They are: 1) Advancing network technology, 2) providing satisfactory services to students and society, 3) building rich and excellent teaching resources, and 4) offering more support to students (Qian, 2009).

Information and communication platforms need to be designed to emphasize the interaction among students, instructors, and administrators. Ideally, students should have an environment where they can easily select courses and receive support. In developing a distance education environment, universities need to design affordable high quality curriculum resources that are user-friendly (Chen, 2008). They need to build websites specifically for distance education with ICTs (Fang, Zhao, & Duan, 2008).

Since instructors and students usually do not meet in person, it is important for instructors to have a better understanding of their students. Educators need to further explore how to diagnose their students' learning and adjust their teaching accordingly (Hu, 2009). More monitoring and supporting are needed (Zhang & Zhao, 2009).

Finally, to regulate the distance education sector effectively, to develop it efficiently, and to provide equitable learning opportunities to all citizens, governments need to invest in distance education (Lu, 2009), play a greater role in the construction of a national system, and establish laws that both facilitate and monitor the development and operation of programs (Yang, Deng, & Cao, 2008; Yu, Zhang, & Zhu, 2009; Zhang & Wang,

2007). In addition to the Higher Education Act, a national statute regulating the development and operation of distance education with ICTs has to be established and enforced (Sheng, 2008). Financing and governance reforms have an important role to play in making education opportunities more equitable (United Nations Educational, Scientific and Cultural Organization, 2009).

On November 10, 2009, Distance Education and Life Long Learning Forum and Contemporary Distance Education Achievements in the Past 10 Years Exhibition were held in Beijing with over 400 participants from the 68 universities providing distance education programs and other organizations involved in distance education. The theme of the forum was: Actively developing distance education and promoting life long learning for all citizens. Participants discussed how to build effective distance education models, ensure quality, develop and share excellent teaching resources, provide support to learning, and apply and develop new technologies (Liu, 2009).

Chinese educators started applying ICTs in distance higher education later than educators in developed countries, but they are making significant progress. ICTs have made higher education more accessible, but there is much to do before we can say ICTs have made Chinese higher education more equitable. A Chinese digital divide exists and it needs to be overcome. While there are problems in development and there is so much to do before Chinese distance higher education demonstrates the three characteristics described by Spector and Merrill (2008): effective, efficient and engaging, as Chinese educators learn from international colleagues, reflect on their own practices and conduct more research on distance education with ICTs in the Chinese context, distance higher education will move forward and make its due contribution. As distance higher education with ICTs continues to develop, it will provide learning opportunities to more Chinese.

REFERENCES

Angrist, J., & Krueger, A. (1991). Does compulsory school attendance affect schooling and earnings? *The Quarterly Journal of Economics*, *106*(4), 979–1014. doi:10.2307/2937954

Baggaley, J. (2007). Distance education technologies: An Asian perspective. *Distance Education*, *28*(2), 125–131. doi:10.1080/01587910701439191

Cambridge University. (2010). *Search results of open courseware*. Retrieved March 16, 2010, from http://web-search.cam.ac.uk/ query.html?qt=Open+Courseware

Canadian Association of University Teachers. (2009, April). MIT faculty to make articles freely available to public. *CAUT Bulletin*, A4.

Cartelli, A., Stanfield, M., Connolly, T., Jimoyiannis, A., Magalhaes, H., & Maillet, K. (2008). Towards the development of a new model for best practice and knowledge construction in virtual campuses. *Journal of Information Technology Education*, *7*, 121–134.

Chai, W. (2009, March 4). Beijing University social studies center announcing the report of an investigation on life in Beijing, Shanghai and Guangzhou: Education attainment's influence on career development is obvious. *China Education Daily*, 2.

Chen, Z. (2008). *Fully utilizing the important contribution contemporary distance education makes in building a country with rich human capital*. Retrieved September 7, 2008, from http://www.moe.edu.cn/edoas/ website18/98/info1201846559236298.htm

China Internet Network Information Center. (2009). *CNNIC announces the 23rd Chinese Internet development report*. Retrieved August 31, 2009, from http://research.cnnic.cn/html/1245053573d634.html

China Internet Network Information Center. (2009). *CNNIC announces the 24th Chinese Internet development report*. Retrieved March 16, 2010, from http://research.cnnic.cn/html/1247709553d1049.html

China Internet Network Information Center. (2010). *CNNIC announces the 25th Chinese Internet development report*. Retrieved March 16, 2010, from http://www.cnnic.net.cn/uploadfiles/pdf/2010/1/15/101600.pdf

Dahlman, C., Zeng, D., & Wang, S. (2007). *Enhancing China's competitiveness through lifelong learning*. Retrieved September 10, 2008, from http://web.worldbank.org/WBSITE/EXTERNAL/WBI/WBIPROGRAMS/KFDLP/0,contentMDK:21387573~menuPK:1727232~pagePK:64156158~piPK:64152884~theSitePK:461198,00.html

Educause. (2009). *Student Guide to Evaluating Information Technology on Campus*. Retrieved December 18, 2009, from http://www.educause.edu/ studentguide

Fang, G., Zhao, C., & Duan, W. (2008). Building and utilizing post-secondary network education resources. *China Education Info, 19*, 28–32.

Fang, Z. (2009). Understanding new trends in distance education and building high quality distance higher education. *Distance Education in China, 9*, 10–14.

Garner, C. W. (2004). *Education finance for school leaders*. Upper Saddle River, NJ: Pearson-Merrill Prentice Hall.

Glotzbach, R., Mordkovich, D., & Radwan, J. (2008). Syndicated RSS feeds for course information distribution. *Journal of Information Technology Education, 7*, 163–183.

Gong, Z. (2007). Open distance education in China and India: A comparison. *Distance Education Journal, 5*, 38–41.

Hao, L., Wang, Y., & Wang, Y. (2008). A comparison of quality safeguard systems in Chinese and British network higher education. *China Education Info, 1*, 6–11.

Hu, Z. (2009). A study on the diagnosis of student learning in distance education. *Distance Education in China*. Retrieved September 2, 2009, from http://www1.open.edu.cn/ ycjy/jiaoxue.php?id=295

Huang, F. (2009). Quality assurance in cross-border distance education: An international perspective. *Distance Education in China, 3*. Retrieved December 19, 2009, from http://caod.oriprobe.com/articles/ 15993542/Quality_Assurance_in_Cross_ border_Distance_Educati.htm

Huang, W. (2007). Introduction of the market mechanism into distance higher education and legal safeguard of the public interest. *Distance Education in China*, 18-21.

Levin, H., Belfield, C., Muennig, P., & Rouse, C. (2007). *The costs and benefits of an excellent education for all of America's children*. Retrieved April 27, 2009, from http://www.cbcse.org/media/ download_gallery/ Leeds_Report_Final_Jan2007.pdf

Li, D., Yan, J., & Yao, W. (2008). Network education development in regular universities and in TV universities: A comparison. *Distance Education in China*. Retrieved January 8, 2009, from http://www1.open.edu.cn/ ycjy/indexzonghe.php

Li, J. (2007). An evaluation of the regulations in Chinese distance education. *Distance Education in China*, 25-29.

Li, J., & Yu, Q. (2009, April 18). Chinese university presidents reflect on higher education. *People's Daily Overseas Edition*, 4.

Li, Z. (2008). Current situation of Chinese network coursework and resource development, its difficulties and strategies. *China Education Info, 19*, 12–14.

Liu, Y. (2007). Presentation given at 2007 Innovation and Development in ICT in Chinese Education Forum. *China Education Info, 7*, 5.

Liu, Y. (2009). *Distance Education and Life Long Learning Forum and Contemporary Distance Education Achievements in the Past 10 Years Exhibition held in Beijing.* Retrieved December 18, 2009, from http://www.moe.gov.cn/edoas/website18/57/info1257844793253457.htm

Lu, X. (2009). Promoting comprehensive education informationization, building and perfecting a national education information management and public service system. *China Education Info, 15*, 5–7.

Ma, L. (2007). TV university distance education from the perspective of internationalization in higher education: Issues and strategies. *Distance Education in China*, 31-34.

Ma, W. (2009). The prospects and dilemmas of Americanizing Chinese higher education. *Asia Pacific Education Review, 10*, 117–124. doi:10.1007/s12564-009-9006-3

Massachusetts Institute of Technology. (2009). *MIT Open Courseware.* Retrieved April 23, 2009, from http://ocw.mit.edu/OcwWeb/ web/home/home/index.htm

Ministry of Education. (2009). *2008 Chinese Education Development Statistics.* Retrieved August 31, 2009, from http://www.moe.gov.cn/edoas/website18/34/info1247820433389334.htm

Ministry of Education. (2009). *Chinese universities receive more international students in the new academic year after overcoming the negative impact of the financial crisis.* Retrieved December 18, 2009, from http://www.moe.gov.cn/edoas/website18/21/info1257818426102421.htm

Ministry of Education. (2010). *2009 over 230,000 international students studied in China.* Retrieved April 2, 2010, from http://www.moe.gov.cn/edoas/website18/39/info1269244278510339.htm

Miniwatts Marketing Group. (2010). *Internet World Stats.* Retrieved March 16, 2010, from http://www.internetworldstats.com/stats.htm

Nam, C. S., & Smith-Jackson, T. L. (2007). Web-based learning environment: A theory-based design process for development and evaluation. *Journal of Information Technology Education, 6*, 23–43.

National Bureau of Statistics of China. (2002). *89.5% respondents interested in foreign higher education.* Retrieved September 11, 2008, from http://www.stats.gov.cn/tjfx/ rddc/t20020531_21041.htm

Organization for Economic Cooperation and Development. (2007). *Education at a glance 2007.* Retrieved September 10, 2008, from http://www.oecd.org/document/30/ 0,3343,en_2649_392632 38_39251550_1_1_1_1,00.html

Qian, X. (2009). A study of factors affecting the quality of network education services. *Journal of Distance Education, 4*, 54–56.

Shen, Y., & Ding, G. (2007). Application of mobile learning in contemporary distance education. *Distance Education Journal, 4*, 37–39.

Sheng, L. (2008). Exploring the establishment of a legal system to regulate contemporary distance education. *Modern Distance Education Research, 6*, 5–8.

Shin, J., & Harman, G. (2009). New challenges for higher education: global and Asia-Pacific perspectives. *Asia Pacific Education Review, 10*, 1-13. Retrieved September 2, 2009, from http://www.springerlink.com/content/ v1153p72h3117723/fulltext.pdf

Sina Corporation. (2009). *2008-2009 Chinese network education market research report.* Retrieved September 4, 2009, from http://blog.sina.com.cn/s/ blog_5b9aa6e30100e62w.html

Song, X. (2007). *2007 International Distance Education Forum opened*. Retrieved September 11, 2008, from http://www.yhedu.syn.cn/ycjy/ShowArticle.asp?ArticleID=67

Spector, J. M., & Merrill, M. D. (2008). Editorial. *Distance Education, 29*(2), 123–126. doi:10.1080/01587910802154921

Su, W. (2009). A study of the development of Chinese distance higher education in transformation. *Modern Distance Education, 3*, 21–23.

Sun, Y., & Chen, X. (2007). Exploring the establishment of an open university's "mobile campus". *China Education Info, 10*, 7–9.

Sun, Z. (2009). Paying attention to education equity from a technical point of view. *Modern Distance Education, 4*, 6–8.

Tait, A. (2008). What are open universities for? *Open Learning: The Journal of Open and Distance Learning, 23*(2), 85–93. doi:10.1080/02680510802051871

Tian, F., Wang, Y., & Wang, Y. (2007). What we have learnt from a comparison of Chinese and British net higher education policies. *Distance Education Journal, 4*, 28–34.

Trow, M. (1973). *Problems in the Transition from Elite to Mass Higher Education*. Berkeley, CA: Carnegie Commission on Higher Education.

United Nations Development Program. (2009). *Overcoming barriers: Human mobility and development*. Retrieved December 7, 2009, from http://hdr.undp.org/en/media/ HDR_2009_EN_Complete.pdf

United Nations Educational, Scientific and Cultural Organization. (2009). *Overcoming inequality: Why governance matters*. Retrieved September 5, 2009, from http://unesdoc.unesco.org/ images/0017/001776/177683e.pdf

Wang, C. (2008). Exploring the establishment of a distance education quality assurance system. *Distance Education Journal, 1*, 40–42.

Wang, Y. (2008). Current situation of Chinese digital education resources and its development strategies. *China Education Info, 1*, 9–11.

Wang, Y., Zhao, Y., & Chen, M. (2009). A retrospect of Chinese education informationization in the past 20 years and a look into the future. *China Education Info, 17*, 14–16.

Wen, J. (2009, March 16). The report on the work of the government. *People's Daily Overseas Edition, 1*.

Xue, W. (2007). From e-learning to u-learning. *China Education Info, 12*, 7–9.

Yan, B. (2007). Establishing a contemporary public distance education service structure. *Distance Education in China,* 12-16.

Yan, B. (2008). Cost and sustainable development of distance education. *Distance Education in China.* Retrieved September 28, 2008, from http://www1.open.edu.cn/ ycjy/indexzonghe.php

Yang, Q., Deng, K., & Cao, F. (2008). Destructive competition in Chinese network education economy. *Distance Education in China, 9*(1). Retrieved September 29, 2008, from http://www1.open.edu.cn/ ycjy/indexzonghe.php

Yu, X., Zhang, Y., & Zhu, Z. (2009). A model for measuring competitiveness of education informationalization and a comparison of international indexes. *China Education Info, 17*, 4–10.

Zha, Q. (2009). Diversification or homogenization: how governments and markets have combined to (re)shape Chinese higher education in its recent massification process. *Higher Education, 58*(1), 41-58. Retrieved August 28, 2009, from http://www.springerlink.com.proxy.library.brocku.ca/content/44217643h4322r17/fulltext.pdf

Zhang, K. (2007). An analysis of Chinese open distance higher education models. *China Education Info, 9*, 15–17.

Zhang, P., & Zhao, H. (2009). Monitoring and supporting network learning. *China Education Info, 15*, 55–58.

Zhang, X. (2008). *Deputy Minister of Education Zhang Xinsheng: Opening up and international cooperation of Chinese education*. Retrieved September 16, 2008, from http://www.moe.gov.cn/edoas/website18/83/info1218778117003283.htm

Zhang, Z., & Wang, Y. (2007). Social responsibilities of contemporary distance education institutions. *Distance Education Journal, 4*, 8–13.

Zhong, W. (2009, February 13). Distance education provides important support to promote lifelong learning. *China Education Daily*, 7.

Zhou, J. (2007a, October 17). *Continuing to develop education as a priority and striving to provide education that satisfies the people: A retrospect at the education reform and development since the Party's sixteenth congress.* Retrieved September 24, 2008, from http://www.moe.edu.cn/edoas/website18/ level3.jsp?tablename=2038&infoid=33909

Zhou, J. (2007b). Contemporary distance education, a means to realize equity in Chinese higher education. *Contemporary Distance Education, 113*, 9–13.

Zhou, Y., & Chen, Z. (2009). The problems and solutions of higher education institutions' network education. *China Education Info, 5*, 7–9.

This work was previously published in International Journal of Information Communication Technologies and Human Development, Volume 2, Issue 4, edited by Susheel Chhabra and Hakikur Rahman, pp. 1-12, copyright 2010 by IGI Publishing (an imprint of IGI Global).

Chapter 13
The Concerns of Elementary Educators with the Diffusion of Information and Communication Technology

Armin Samiei
Simon Fraser University, Canada

Daniel A. Laitsch
Simon Fraser University, Canada

ABSTRACT

In this paper, the authors use a mixed methods study, including a survey and follow up interviews, to investigate the concerns that elementary educators in a school district in British Columbia have regarding the diffusion and integration of Information and Communication Technologies (ICT) in their teaching. The research participants identified four major categories of concerns: the philosophy and pedagogy of ICT integration; accessibility of ICT (including software, hardware and resource personnel); infrastructure technical support; and educational integration of ICT in their teaching. Based on the research findings, the authors propose appropriate intervention methods to address these concerns, including targeted professional development, technical and educational support, and sustained access to proper ICT equipment.

INTRODUCTION

One of the impacts of continuous technological advances and the information technology reform movement in schools is the requirement for professional staff to adopt skills and abilities that help

DOI: 10.4018/978-1-4666-0047-8.ch013

meet challenges and pressures brought on during implementation of ICT. The concerns that individuals have regarding change implementation is known to directly impact their performance (Hall & Hord, 1987). The active support and involvement of teaching staff is essential for meaningful reform and innovation in schools (Dooley, Metcalf, & Martinez, 1999; Haddad & Draxler, 2005; Hall

& Hord, 1987). Thus, the human factor can be considered as important as hardware and software when allocating funds for integration of ICT in teaching. By identifying and understanding the issues raised by educators, district staff development departments and other change agents can better target individual concerns of teachers and design and implement appropriate models based on personal and professional needs and demands.

Research on teachers and innovations gives direction to districts' staff departments as well as teacher training programs to implement policies that are suitable to teachers' needs throughout the change process. This research helps to develop recommendations to meaningfully implement ICT in schools and looks at the future needs of teachers—specifically at the elementary level—with regard to implementing technology.

ISSUES IN ICT IMPLEMENTATION

The emergence of ICT and its growing potential in improving and transforming teaching and learning has led countries to invest significantly in integrating modern technologies and education in order to help individuals develop the skills and competencies that they require to function well in information societies (Delors et al., 1996; Guzdial & Weingarten, 1995; Haddad & Draxler, 2005; Rychen & Salganik, 2003). As a result, schools are filling with computers, printers, scanners, digital cameras and the latest technical tools and equipment. New positions and centres are created to help teachers develop professionally in the area of educational technology. University education departments implement new programs to reinforce the importance of technology, and review and research teams envision a new future of learning for children (Browne & Ritchie, 1991; Carlson & Gadio, 2005; Guzdial & Weingarten, 1995; Stuhlmann & Taylor, 1999). With the emergence of new forms of ICT and multimedia, more demands are made on professional staff to acquire the skills

and abilities to respond to the implementation of ICT in schools (Delors et al., 1996; Haddad & Draxler, 2005; Rychen & Salganik, 2003; Trewin, 2002). However, in the final analysis, it is the way technology is implemented by educators that determines its impact on student learning.

Despite the growing number of modern technical tools in schools, there is still scepticism about the way these new technologies are used by teachers (Becker, 1994; Cuban, 2001; Pelgrum, 2001; Plante & Beattie, 2004; U.S. Department of Education, 1999). Teachers learning technology skills in workshops do not always lead to the willingness and/or ability to implement those skills in the art of daily classroom teaching (Granger, Morbey, Lotherington, Owston, & Wideman, 2002). And as districts continue to infuse newer technologies into their systems, the necessity of understanding teachers' perceptions, feelings and concerns towards the integration of ICT in their practice becomes more apparent. The willingness and involvement of teaching staff is essential to integrating any innovations in schools—including educational technology (Dooley et al., 1999; Haddad & Draxler, 2005; Hall & Hord, 1987).

Canadian schools are well-equipped with computers, and students generally have access to internet at all levels of their schooling; however, Canada is no different from its counterparts in international surveys with regard to the generally weak integration of ICT by teachers (Pelgrum, 2001; Plante & Beattie, 2004;). The low percentage of teachers integrating ICT in their practice raises many questions about factors that impact the rate of adoption of ICT by many educators. Most notably, if the introduction of technology into schools can play a critical role in improving teaching and learning (Carlson & Gadio, 2005), why are educators slow to integrate technology in their teaching practice? Can well-designed teacher pre-service and district in-service programs that consider teachers' concerns toward educational technology open doors to new educational opportunities for both teachers and students?

Two major studies formed the content framework for this investigation: the internationally focused *International Association for the Evaluation of Educational Achievement (IEA)* (Pelgrum, 2001); and *The Information and Communications Technologies in Schools Survey (ICTSS)*—focused specifically on Canada (Plante & Beattie, 2004). The main objective of the IEA assessment was to investigate the obstacles that were perceived by educational practitioners as hindering the realization of their ICT-related goals, while the *ICTSS* aimed at investigating ICT accessibility and integration in Canadian elementary and secondary schools (Plante & Beattie, 2004). Regarding ICT implementation, these studies highlighted the importance of four issues: ICT accessibility, the impact of teachers' characteristics and personal responses, the impact of the school environment, and the impact of existing support systems. Within this overarching frame, this research looked specifically at the concerns of elementary school teachers related to the implementation of ICT as an innovation.

RESEARCH QUESTIONS

One way that researchers, staff departments, change facilitators and school principals can design and develop interventions to address educator needs and facilitate the process of change during the adoption of new educational technology is by identifying the concerns of elementary educators (George, Hall, & Stiegelbauer, 2006; Hall & Hord, 1987; Hall, Wallace, & Dossett, 1973). As such, the guiding question for this research was, "What are the concerns of elementary educators regarding the diffusion and integration of Information and Communication Technology in their practice?" To answer this question, quantitative data were collected from teachers through application of a survey and qualitative data were gathered through follow-up interviews. The survey focused on two sub-questions:

1. What are the proportions of self, task and impact concerns among elementary educators with regard to the integration of Information and Communication Technology in curriculum?

2. What are the relationships between elementary educators' current Stages of Concern and their demographic background?

The qualitative phase of this study expanded on the initial findings by using interviews to answer the question:

What are elementary educators' responses (views, feelings, concerns, perceptions and experiences) toward the diffusion and integration of ICT in their practice?

The interviews were conducted with a sample of educators at different stages of concern and offered an opportunity for the participants to express their views and feelings and describe their experiences and concerns in their own terms. The interview enabled greater understanding of educators' personal responses to ICT integration, and whether these responses confirmed their levels and types of concern and involvement with ICT in their teaching.

THEORETICAL FRAMEWORK

The framework for this research stems from two theories: *Diffusion of Innovations* (Rogers, 1995) and *Concerns-Based Adoption Model* (*CBAM*) (Hall et al., 1973). Rogers' *Diffusion of Innovations* and *CBAM* complement each other in the way that one defines features and characteristics of the process of diffusion of an innovation, and the other addresses the human side of the changes that are triggered as the result of this diffusion.

According to Rogers, infusion of ICT in schools is basically a diffusion process in which ICT serves as an innovation to be integrated into the current system. Within concerns-based research, these innovations then trigger different responses amongst individuals who are involved in the change process (Hall & Hord, 1987; Hall et al., 1973). If individuals' responses or concerns with regard to innovative changes can be understood, intervention methods can be designed to increase the adoption (diffusion) rate of teachers, facilitating change in schools.

Within this framework, the *CBAM* team conceptualized seven Stages of Concern that teachers might experience during a change process: Awareness, Informational, Personal, Management, Consequence, Collaboration and Refocusing. These stages fall into three larger categories: Self concerns, that evolve around general characteristics, effects, requirement of use and financial or status implications of the innovation; Task concerns, which focus on the process and task-related issues concerning the use of the innovation; and Impact concerns, that reflect a more advanced level of involvement with and application of the innovation.

The individuals' concerns about an innovation are developmental in nature, and change and vary in intensity over time as the implementation process progresses (George et al., 2006; Fuller, 1969; Hall et al., 1987). These individuals may have concerns at more than one of the Stages of Concern at any given time and with different levels of intensity, and they do not move at the same rate through the seven hypothesized Stages of Concern, nor do they exhibit the same level of intensity at different stages.

Throughout these stages, participants' foci shift to the impact of the innovation on students; cooperation and coordination with other colleagues in the use of the innovation; and finally to a mastery that leads to the exploration of more powerful alternatives to the innovation in use. This stage is in line with the *re-invention* characteristics of innovations as described by Rogers (1995).

METHODOLOGY

The purpose of this study was to examine the concerns of elementary educators with regard to the diffusion and integration of Information and Communication Technology in their practice. A sequential explanatory design (Creswell, Plano Clark, Gutmann, & Hanson 2003) was deemed most appropriate for this study as it allowed us to identify the major concerns educators had regarding ICT implementation, and then gather detailed follow-up data with key individuals to better illustrate the details regarding their concerns.

SURVEY DESIGN

Stages of Concern

In the first phase of this mixed-methods study, quantitative data were collected using The Stages of Concern Questionnaire (SoCQ), first developed by Hall, George, and Rutherford in 1979 and later revised by George, Hall, and Stiegelbauer in 2006. The *SoCQ* is a major diagnostic tool within the *CBAM* framework designed to help researchers, change facilitators and staff development departments assess the concerns of individuals during the change process, and recommend appropriate assistance. This survey provided basic research evidence in terms of teachers' Stages of Concern as well as identifying statistical relationships between Stages of Concern and different demographic factors.

Demographic Data

Demographic data were collected using a researcher-generated survey attached to the SoCQ, *The Demographic Information Questionnaire*. The 15-item questionnaire contained a range of questions related to teachers' gender, experience, degree, home access to computers and the Internet, number of computers in class and number of computers connected to the Internet, perception of computer expertise, hours of computer training/workshops, type of technology-related activities, amount of District provided technology release time, as well as a question to assess teachers' technology self-efficacy and an open-ended question with regard to ICT integration in schools.

The method of data collection for the qualitative stage of the research was based on a semi-structured interview format following the *General Interview Guide* Approach that uses pre-specified closed-form and open-form questions (Drever, 1995; Gall, Gall, & Borg, 2003; Kvale, 1996; Schensul, Schensul, & LeCompte, 1999). The closed questions in the study focused on information about demographic data on elementary teachers' professional activities and the availability and accessibility of ICT equipment in their respective schools. Information about the different aspects of ICT integration was gathered primarily through open-ended questions followed by a series of probes to elicit additional information. This style of interview allowed the elementary educators to focus on their individual world and reveal their views, feelings, concerns and experiences of the phenomenon of technology while focusing on their daily environment.

Interview Protocol Development

Two interview protocols were developed, one for teachers and one for the principal in the study sample. The principal guideline was very similar to teachers' guideline but it allowed him to express himself as a leader and a teacher when answering questions. Guided by the theoretical framework and survey construct, and a review of ICT integration and implementation literature, the semi-structured interview questions and prompts were designed to capture elementary teachers' personal responses and provide them with opportunities to describe their views, feelings, concerns, experience and perceptions regarding ICT integration. Interviewees were also able to

suggest various ways that they could be better supported in their ICT use. Kvale's (1983) 12 goals specific to qualitative interviews were used to guide protocol creation.

The protocol was conceived to help constitute a descriptive analytical framework for analysis (Patton, 2002) and was based on three major analytic categories regarding ICT integration: (a) general responses (personal views, feelings, concerns), (b) personal experience, and (c) perception of characteristics of integration. Five sets of questions were created to collect data as follows:

- The first set of questions was a background check to verify teachers' professional background documented on the *DIQ* used in the quantitative phase, as well as an exploration of other professional duties that the teachers were involved with.

- The second set of questions expanded on the *CBAM* to allow the respondents to openly express their views, feelings and concerns with regard to ICT integration.

- The third set of questions was based on the outcome of the literature review. Teachers were asked to think about the barriers they had encountered while using ICT, and suggest ways they could be better supported in this regard.

- The fourth set of questions expanded on Rogers' *Diffusion of Innovations* and explored the participants' perceptions of the characteristics of computer technology in their practice.

- The fifth and final set of questions encouraged participants to reflect on the entire interview and add final thoughts.

DATA SAMPLE

With a population of over 30,000 students and 4,000 full-time and part-time employees, School District X is a large district in British Columbia, Canada. In the school year 2006/2007, there were approximately 1,843 educators, with the number of female educators (1,213) almost double the number of male educators (629). The average years of education experience was approximately 12 years, and the average age of educators was 43 years (Ministry of Education, n.d.).

Elementary schools were purposively sampled from a list of district schools that were participating in a variety of learning teams as part of professional development activities offered by the district. The purposeful sample identified for this study represented 15 elementary schools that participated in ICT learning teams. These schools were selected because the specialized learning teams targeted a point of inquiry related to the meaningful integration of ICT into a defined curricular area as chosen by the group of individuals on the team, providing an opportunity for focused study of ICT implementation issues. The survey was administered to the entire teaching population in 14 of the elementary schools accounting for a total of 230 teachers (one school chose not participate). From the 230 elementary educators in the sample, 63 educators completed and returned the questionnaires in this phase, which represented a response rate of 27.4% for the survey.[1]

Survey participants were also asked if they were willing to be interviewed. A stratified purposeful sample of educators comprising 16 teachers and one principal were selected from this volunteer pool based on their alignment within each of the stages of concern, as follows:

- **Collaboration Stage 5:** all three volunteer respondents were interviewed.
- **Management Stage 3:** all four volunteer respondents were interviewed.
- **Personal Stage 2:** two volunteer respondents were interviewed.
- **Information Stage 1:** two volunteer respondents were interviewed.
- **Unconcerned Stage 0:** 11 teachers with a wide range of teaching assignments volunteered for an interview. Seven teachers

with a variety of teaching assignments from different schools were purposively selected for interview, five of whom agreed to participate.
- **Unconcerned Innovation Users:** Two teachers volunteered: one full-time Grade 1 and 2 teacher and one part-time teacher. The full-time classroom teacher was selected due to the teacher's full-time presence in the school.

DATA ANALYSIS

Statistical Treatment of Data

Phase one of this study used both descriptive and inferential statistics. The first stage of the statistical analysis consisted of descriptive statistics. The *DIQ* responses were tallied to represent the number of respondents and their percentiles for each question in the survey. Open-ended answers in the additional comment section of *DIQ* were classified into the main categories of concern as expressed by respondents, using qualitative methods of coding and categorizing. Guidelines included in the *SoCQ* manual for data analysis and interpretation (George et al., 2006) were applied using the SOCQ 075 Scoring Program (SAS file, George et al., 2006). This program scores the *SOCQ* and computes the raw scale scores, percentile scores, and group averages. The program is set up to construct individual and group profiles and each respondent was assigned a score for each of the Stages of Concern (awareness, informational, personal, management, consequence, collaboration, and refocusing) for which he or she had the highest percentile.

Each of the seven Stages of Concern was represented by five statements from the *SoCQ* (George et al., 2006). The raw score for each scale was the sum of the responses to the five statements for that scale. For example, Stage 0 raw score total was derived by adding the scores for questions 3, 12, 21, 23 and 30. These were then converted to percentile scores for the sample using the scoring program.

The second phase of the analysis consisted of inferential statistics used to examine the relationship between the various demographic variables and the respondent stages of concern. In this section, the appropriate measure was calculated between the stages of concern and each independent variable (gender, age, level of education, teaching experience, perception of computer expertise, number of hours of technology training during the past two years, and number of ICT skills used in teaching and for personal use). Since almost all the respondents had access to home computers and the Internet, this variable was excluded as it did not provide any useful information. A contingency table and $\chi 2$ Test of Independence and Spearman correlation coefficient were used to measure the degrees of association. An alpha 0.05 was used for all calculations.

Qualitative Interview Analysis

The interviews ranged in length from 19 to 62 minutes averaging approximately 40 minutes. After each interview, the recorded interview data were saved on a hard drive and notes added to a reflective journal focused on each respondent

and the overall process after each interview was completed. The aim of the data analysis stage was to categorize and reorganize the qualitative data and identify patterns and themes (Drever, 1995; Gall et al., 2003; Lofland, Snow, Anderson, & Lofland, 2006; Patton, 2002). Content analysis (Atkins, 1984; Burnard, 1994; Coffey & Atkinson, 1996; Graneheim & Lundman, 2004; Lofland et al., 2006; Patton, 2002; Weber, 1985) was used to analyze the data in this study, and to identify emerging categories of personal responses of elementary educators from the transcripts of the interviews.

Using HyperResearch software, meaning units were identified, tagged, and coded in an iterative process that allowed for additional refinement and the linking of larger segments of data together as well as elimination of the less useful descriptive and analytical codes. This led to creation of a dictionary of meaningful codes used to classify the responses of participants. Table 1 displays an example of this process. Once the meaning units were tagged and coded, response patterns (similarities and differences in the responses offered) were identified and regrouped into corresponding categories (Atkins, 1984; Burnard, 1994; Graneheim & Lundman, 2004).

In a sequential explanatory mixed methods study, the quantitative and the qualitative findings

Table 1. Examples of meaning units, condensed meaning units and codes (adapted from Graneheim & Lundman,, 2004)

Meaning Unit	Condensed meaning unit	code
I believe the technology and information on the computers has to be used also with other resources, library books, encyclopaedias, there has to be a balance, if you just do technology and computer and the kids don't know how to research using other places of information so there has to be a balance there.	balanced use of ICT and other resources, library books, encyclopaedias	different resources
So there are two things, there is excitement there and the vision and yes I can see where we can go with it but then the reality comes in, as oh, I don't have enough time or materials or my own knowledge isn't where I need to so I have got two conflicting sort of feelings, frustration and excitement, worrying away which I suppose it's in anything that happens when you learn.	mixed feelings of excitement of what can be done and frustration due to lack of resources and knowledge concerning the integration of ICT	mixed feelings

are connected and talk to each other to build a negotiated account of what they mean together (Creswell, 2003; Tashakkori & Teddlie, 2003). By consolidating the quantitative and qualitative findings from the four data sources (the *SoCQ*, the *DIQ*, the open-ended statements in *DIQ* and the interviews) the independent conclusions from each phase built a shared meaning together that answered the major research question.

FINDINGS

SoCQ

Using data gathered with the *SoCQ*, the 63 elementary educators who participated in this study were grouped into the three main categories of concern in the *CBAM* framework: Self, Task and Impact (see Figure 1). These different types of concerns indicated where educators were in their

personal and professional involvement with the use of ICT. Seventy-one point four percent of educator concerns were self oriented, 22.2% were task oriented, and just 6.4% were impact oriented. These results are similar to those of some other concern studies (Askar & Usley, 2001; Liu & Huang 2005; Rakes & Casey, 2002), where a large proportion of teachers examined were still at the self-oriented Stages of Concern. Based on some national and international survey results (Pelgrum, 2001; Plante & Beattie, 2004; U.S. Department of Education, 1999), this survey matches similar findings where large proportions of teachers still do not feel comfortable using ICT in their teaching.

SoCQ and DIQ

The statistical analyses of degree of association of the Stages of Concern and Demographic Data suggested that there was no relationship between an elementary educator's gender, age, teaching

Figure 1. Statistics of the stages of concern about ICT integration in curriculum

IMPACT	Successful	Users	Refocusing		0 (0%)
			Collaboration		4 educators (6.4%)
			Consequence		0 educator (0%)
TASK	Management	Explorers	Management		14 educators (22.2%)
SELF	Nonusers or Low Users	Typical Nonusers		Personal	3 educators (4.8%)
				Informational	9 educators (14.3%)
				Unconcerned	27 educators (42.8%)
		Unconcerned Innovation Users			6 teachers (9.5%)

Table 2. Summary of findings concerning the degree of association of Stages of Concern and the demographic data (P=0.05)

Demographic Variables	X²	Threshold Value	Degree of Freedom	Relation between respondents' demographic variables and their stages of concern
Gender	5.77	9.49	4	No relationship
Age	10.51	21.03	12	No relationship
Level of Education	20.66	15.51	8	Yes relationship
Teaching Experience	23.52	31.41	20	No relationship
Years of computer use in teaching	11.30	31.41	20	No relationship
Number of hours of technology training during the past two years	43.24	26.30	16	Yes relationship
Number of ICT skills used in teaching	35.20	39.25	16	Based on Spearman rank correlation coefficient of 0.47: Yes relationship
Number of ICT skills used for personal use	43.61	39.25	16	Yes relationship
Perception of Computer Expertise	20.51	15.51	8	Yes relationship

experience and length of computer use in teaching and their Stages of Concern about integrating ICT in curriculum (see Table 2). The change process that involves integrating ICT in curriculum is one that all educators of both genders and all ages and with different teaching experience might go through. In fact, all the educators in the sample had access to computers and Internet at home, which suggests that these educators had already become involved with ICT on a personal basis despite the fact that they might be minimally involved with ICT integration in curriculum at school. These findings are similar to previous research that found no relationship between teachers' Stages of Concern and variables such as age, gender, and teaching experience (Atkins & Vasu, 2000).

The lack of relationship between the Stages of Concern of the responding educators in this study and the number of years they had used computers in teaching was another indicator that the simple fact of using computers by teachers does not reflect its meaningful integration in curriculum, as some teachers might only use computers for clerical tasks such as attendance, report cards and typing assignments and tests. These

findings support previous research where Canadian school principals reported that their teachers possess the required technical skills for administrative purposes but are still not adequately prepared to effectively engage students in using ICT (Plante & Beattie, 2004).

The statistical analyses did show a positive relationship between educators' Stages of Concern and the number of hours of technology training/ workshops taken over the past two years, their perception of computer expertise, number of ICT skills used in teaching and for personal use, and their education level. These findings support the argument that concerns will vary depending on the amount of one's knowledge about an innovation and one's experience with that innovation (Hall et al., 1979), and are in line with Atkins' and Vasu's work (2000) where a relationship between middle school teachers' Stages of Concern and computer confidence level and number of hours of technology training was reported.

The analysis of the concerns profile of educators and the open-ended statements included in questionnaires in phase one of the mixed methods study identified five categories of concerns and challenges that might have created barriers to ICT integration in curriculum: concerns related to time constraints; concerns related to proper technology equipment; concerns related to lack of information and/or proper technology training; concerns related to onsite contact people; and concerns related to ICT literacy and integration. These concerns reflected the respondents' self and task type anxiety and preoccupation with regard to the logistics and management issues related to the integration of ICT in their teaching.

Interviews

Educators in the study sample expressed three major types of feelings with regard to the integration of ICT in their practice. Of the 17 interview participants, five either had positive and proactive feelings of comfort and excitement, and welcomed any change that allowed them to approach their teaching differently; four reflected reactive and negative feelings of nervousness, anxiety and frustration and lack of confidence concerning ICT integration; and eight expressed mixed feelings of both proactive and positive feelings and negative feelings with regard to the integration of ICT in teaching. In general, the more these teachers became involved with ICT integration, the more they felt comfortable, excited and pleased with the outcomes. However, they were also frustrated, uncertain and concerned by the limitations and the constraints that they were discovering as a result of their increasing involvement with ICT.

Specifically, the educators identified a range of barriers to the integration of ICT in their practice: accessibility, as defined by the lack of adequate ICT equipment and educational resources; technical issues related to the use of software and hardware; a lack of support; time limitations; constraints caused by level of expertise and knowledge; and a slow shift toward using ICT-supported pedagogies. Elementary educators were also concerned with ICT safety for their students as they were generally uncertain how to monitor students' access to the Internet and online communication in

schools. These findings are similar to the barriers identified in prior research (Pelgrum, 2001).

The interviews also highlighted the perceptions of teachers concerning the characteristics of implementation suggested by Rogers—its relative advantage, compatibility, complexity, trialability and observability (1995). Almost all the elementary educators (16) perceived ICT integration as advantageous. A large proportion (14) perceived ICT integration as compatible with what they did at their schools. Almost half of the educators (nine) did not perceive ICT integration as complex and difficult to understand; among the remaining teachers, five found ICT difficult to understand and integrate, and three mentioned that the complexity was relative depending on different projects. A large proportion of educators (14) felt that they had meaningful opportunities to try out and experiment with ICT, and learn about this innovation and reduce their uncertainty, especially through learning teams. Many elementary educators (11) felt that they did not have established structures in their schools to share and view the work of other educators working with ICT. The remaining six educators were able to observe ICT-related work and projects during the staff meetings or through the school website.

In this sample, two of the key characteristics identified by Rogers—complexity and observability—were areas still requiring support in order to help educators to adopt ICT practices.

Synthesis

The findings based on *SoCQ* data revealed that the responding elementary educators exhibited mostly self-oriented concerns, with a smaller group showing task-oriented concerns and a few demonstrating impact-oriented concerns as evident from their highest peak-SoC scores. The interviews offered the opportunity to focus on personal responses, and build a foundation for analyzing the relationship between teachers' stages of concern and their responses. The integration and interpretation of the quantitative and qualitative findings confirmed a consistent pattern of association between the stages of concern and personal responses to ICT integration in teaching. Across each stage of concerns, interviewees expressed similar concerns and implementation patterns.

In order to fully answer the research questions, a three-dimensional analysis was used to integrate the quantitative and qualitative findings: First, the findings across each SoC were examined to verify trends at each level; second, findings across all Stages of Concern were examined to compare and contrast the general trends and specific characteristics of the different stages; third, the findings were analyzed within the concerns-based framework, enabling construction of a detailed profile of the concerns expressed by elementary educators.

Based on the integrated findings the concerns of elementary educators can be summarized across the following four categories (see Figure 2):

- Concerns related to the philosophy of education and pedagogy including issues related to the teaching and learning philosophies of educators in general with regard to ICT integration, the autonomy of teachers with regard to ICT implementation policies, and the role of leadership in the process of ICT implementation;

- Concerns related to accessibility that include concerns with regard to the accessi-

bility of hardware, software and resource people;

- Concerns related to the technical infrastructure support including technical issues and building compatibility and proper setups; and

- Concerns related to educational technology integration including issues related to ICT safety, level of educators' expertise and knowledge, time for coordination with others and professional development, and integrated curriculum and age-appropriate ICT expectations.

CONCLUSION

This study looked at the concerns educators had about implementation of education innovations, in this case the implementation of ICT to improve educational practice and student learning, in one urban school district in British Columbia, Canada. While the findings are unique to the context of the district, the similarity to findings identified in prior research, as well as similarity of concerns across participants within each stage and across the data collection methods, suggests there are useful lessons from this research that can be used to inform decision making in other contexts. Ten recommendations stem from this work.

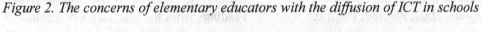

Figure 2. The concerns of elementary educators with the diffusion of ICT in schools

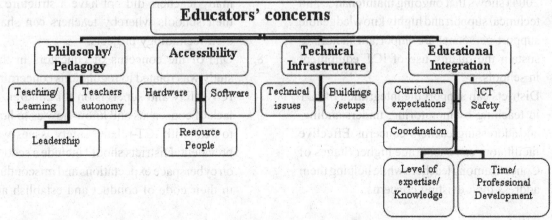

1. Districts implementing ICT should prioritize and implement learning through technology as part of their strategic direction. The ultimate goal should be to train every teacher to use ICT in their teaching. According to World Link program (Carlson & Gadio, 2005), teachers require a minimum of 80 hours of professional development in order to start integrating technology into their practice.

2. Districts should optimize the use of the available equipment. When possible, schools should be equally and similarly equipped with ICT-based equipment. Many respondents complained about old, inadequate, and scarce equipment in their schools. It is important for districts to ensure that their elementary schools do not become a haven for old and donated technology equipment as elementary years build the foundations for future learning. Training teachers to work with the technology they might not have access to in their own schools is both inefficient and frustrating for the trainee.

3. Schools should have a knowledgeable and skilled part-time or full-time technology resource teacher (or teachers) on staff who can model ICT-related activities and support teachers in integrating ICT in their teaching. Accessibility to technology tools is not sufficient by itself to persuade teachers to use and integrate them in their practice. Research (Pelgrum, 2001; Plante & Beattie, 2004) shows that ongoing maintenance and technical support and highly knowledgeable support personnel are important factors to sustain the quality use of ICT equipment in schools.

4. Districts can support the integration of ICT in teaching by monitoring, understanding, and addressing teachers' concerns. Effective facilitators can encourage higher Stages of Concern among teachers while helping them address their existing concerns.

5. In light of the findings of this study (and others) where most teachers experienced personal concerns, districts should strengthen professional development through incorporating intervention guidelines by: offering sharing sessions where teachers with early stages of concern can discuss and make decisions about ICT and its integration; receiving information that arouses their interest without being overwhelmed; seeing how ICT integration relates to their current practices; and seeing how the process of integration can be implemented gradually by establishing attainable expectations (Hord, Rutherford, Huling, & Hall, 1987).

6. One of the concerns of the elementary educators in this study was related to the provision of proper and needs-related ICT-based professional development. One way to resolve this issue is to organize professional development based on concern level. This could be done through the use of *SoCQ* or other needs-assessment tools, such as the *Teaching with Technology Instrument* (Atkins & Vasu, 1998). Another alternative is to offer learning teams for novice, intermediate and advanced ICT users and have teachers apply to these groups based on their perceptions of their own ICT expertise.

7. School principals should provide their staff with plenty of opportunities to share technology-related work and projects. Findings from the interviews revealed that many teachers did not have a structure in their schools whereby teachers can share their technology projects.

8. One of the concerns of educators in this study was related to regulations concerning ICT safety and supervision for children. A lack of consensus and know-how as to how to deal with ICT-related safety issues was prevalent. Districts should include a section on cyberspace expectations and misconduct in their code of conduct and establish ap-

propriate network and Internet use policies and procedures.

9. Another concern of the educators interviewed in this study was in relation to the lack of educational, age-appropriate and curriculum-relevant technology-based resources. Districts should establish resources to help educators assess and evaluate educational software and online websites, and review and adopt standards such as the International Standards for Technology in Education, or the standards developed by the Open Learning Agency in British Columbia.

10. Teachers should be informed of the changing district policies and be included in technology decision-making on a wider scale. Research has proved that the complicity and cooperation of teachers is necessary to sustain any innovative change (Dooley et al., 1999; Haddad & Draxler, 2005; Hall & Hord, 1987), and the inclusion of teachers in the design, development and delivery of programs can have a positive impact on their level of successful implementation.

REFERENCES

Askar, P., & Usley, Y. (2001). Concerns of administrators and teachers in the diffusion of IT in schools: A case study from Turkey. In McAlister, K., & Reagan, C. (Eds.), *Research: SITE 2001 Section* (pp. 8–9).

Atkins, E., & Vasu, E. S. (1998). Teaching with technology instrument. *Learning and Leading with Technology, 25*(8), 35–39.

Atkins, M. J. (1984). Practitioner as researcher: Some techniques for analyzing semi-structured data in small-scale research. *British Journal of Educational Studies, 32*(3), 251–261. doi:10.10 80/00071005.1984.9973691

Atkins, N. E., & Vasu, E. S. (2000). Measuring knowledge of technology usage and stages of concern about computing: A study of middle school teachers. *Journal of Technology and Teacher Education, 8*(4), 279–302.

Becker, H. J. (1994). How exemplary computer-using teachers differ from other teachers: Implications for realizing the potential of computers in schools. *Journal of Research on Computing in Education, 26*(3), 291–321.

Browne, D. L., & Ritchie, D. C. (1991). Cognitive apprenticeship: A model of staff development for implementing technology in schools. *Contemporary Education, 64*(1), 28–34.

Burnard, P. (1994). Searching for meaning: a method of analysing interview transcripts with a personal computer. *Nurse Education Today, 14*(2), 111–117. doi:10.1016/0260-6917(94)90113-9

Carlson, S., & Gadio, C. T. (2005). Teacher professional development in the use of technology. In Haddad, W., & Draxler, A. (Eds.), *Technologies for education: potentials, parameters, and prospects* (pp. 119–132). Paris: UNESCO.

Coffey, A., & Atkinson, P. (1996). *Making sense of qualitative data: Complementary Research Strategies*. Thousand Oaks, CA: Sage.

Creswell, J. W. (2003). *Research design: Qualitative, quantitative, and mixed methods approaches*. Thousand Oaks, CA: Sage.

Creswell, J. W., Plano Clark, V. L., Gutmann, M. L., & Hanson, W. E. (2003). Advanced mixed methods research designs. In Tashakkori, A., & Teddlie, C. (Eds.), *Handbook of mixed methods in the social and behavioral sciences* (pp. 209–241). Thousand Oaks, CA: Sage.

Cuban, L. (2001). *Oversold and underused: Computers in the classroom*. Cambridge, MA: Harvard University Press.

Delors, J., Al Mufti, I., Amagi, I., Carneiro, R., Chung, F., & Geremek, B. (1996). *Learning: The treasure within*. Paris: UNESCO Publishing.

Dooley, L. M., Metcalf, T., & Martinez, A. (1999). A study of adoption of computer technology by teachers. *Educational Technology & Society, 2*(4). Retrieved March 10, 2006, from http://ifets.massey.ac.nz/ periodical/vol_4_99/Idooley.html

Drever, E. (1995). *Using semi-structured interviews in small-scale research: A teacher's guide*. Glasgow, UK: The Scottish Council for Research in Education.

Fuller, F. F. (1969). Concerns of teachers: A developmental conceptualization. *American Educational Research Journal, 6*(2), 207–226.

Gall, M. D., Gall, J. P., & Borg, W. R. (2003). *Education research: An introduction* (7th ed.). Toronto, ON, Canada: Pearson Education Incorporation.

George, A. A., Hall, G. E., & Stiegelbauer, S. M. (2006). *Measuring implementation in schools: The Stages of Concern questionnaire*. Austin, TX: Southwest Educational Development Laboratory.

Graneheim, U. H., & Lundman, B. (2004). Content analysis in nursing research: concepts, procedures and measures to achieve trustworthiness. *Nurse Education Today, 24*(2), 105–112. doi:10.1016/j.nedt.2003.10.001

Granger, C. A., Morbey, M. L., Lotherington, H., Owston, R. D., & Wideman, H. H. (2002). Factors contributing to teachers' successful implementation of IT. *Journal of Computer Assisted Learning, 18*(4), 480–488. doi:10.1046/j.0266-4909.2002.00259.doc.x

Guzdial, M., & Weingarten, F. W. (Eds.). (1995). *Setting a computer science research agenda for educational technology*. Washington, DC: Computer Research Association.

Haddad, W. D., & Draxler, A. (Eds.). (2005). *Technologies for education: potentials, parameters, and prospects*. Paris: UNESCO. Retrieved May 1, 2005, from http://unesdoc.unesco.org/images/0011/001191/119129e.pdf

Hall, G. E., George, A. A., & Rutherford, W. L. (1979). *Measuring Stages of Concern about the innovation: a manual for use of the SoC questionnaire* (Tech. Rep. No. 3032). Austin, TX: Research and Development Center for Teacher Education, University of Texas.

Hall, G. E., & Hord, S. M. (1987). *Change in schools: Facilitating the process*. Ithaca, NY: State University of New York Press.

Hall, G. E., Wallace, R. D., Jr., & Dossett, W. A. (1973). *A developmental conceptualization of the adoption process within educational institutions*. Austin, TX: Research and Development Center for Teacher education, University of Texas.

Hord, S. M., Rutherford, W. L., Huling, L., & Hall, G. E. (1987). *Taking charge of change*. Alexandria, VA: Association for Supervision and Curriculum Development.

Johnson, D. R. (2005). *Addressing the growing problem of survey nonresponse*. University Park, PA: Survey Research Center, Penn State University.

Kvale, S. (1983). The qualitative research interview; a phenomenological and a hermeneutic mode of understanding. *Journal of Phenomenological Psychology, 14*, 171–196. doi:10.1163/156916283X00090

Kvale, S. (1996). *InterViews: An introduction to qualitative research interviewing*. Thousand Oaks, CA: Sage.

Liu, Y., & Huang, C. (2005). Concerns of teachers about technology integration in the USA. *European Journal of Teacher Education, 28*(1), 35–48. doi:10.1080/02619760500039928

Lofland, L. H., Snow, D., Anderson, L., & Lofland, J. (2006). *Analyzing social settings* (4th ed.). Wadsworth Publishing Company.

Ministry of Eduction. (n.d.). *British Columbia District Data Summary*. Retrieved October 17, 2009, from http://www.bced.gov.bc.ca/ reporting/ enrol/teach.php

Patton, M. Q. (2002). *Qualitative research and evaluation methods* (3rd ed.). Thousand Oaks, CA: Sage.

Pelgrum, W. J. (2001). Obstacles to the integration of ICT in education: results from a worldwide educational assessment. *Computers & Education, 37*, 163–178. doi:10.1016/S0360-1315(01)00045-8

Plante, J., & Beattie, D. (2004). *Connectivity and ICT integration in Canadian elementary and secondary schools: First results from the Information and Communications Technologies in schools survey, 2003-2004*. Retrieved January 3, 2008, from http://www.statcan.ca/english/ research/ 81-595-MIE/81-595-MIE2004017.pdf

Rakes, G. C., & Casey, H. B. (2002). An analysis of teacher concerns toward instructional technology. *International Journal of Educational Technology, 3*(1). Retrieved June 1, 2006, from http://www. ao.uiuc.edu/ijet/ v3n1/rakes/index.html

Rogers, E. M. (1995). *Diffusion of Innovations* (4th ed.). New York: The Free Press.

Rychen, D. S., & Salganik, L. H. (2003). *Key competencies for a successful life and a well functioning society*. Gottingen, Germany: Hogrefe & Huber.

Schensul, S., Schensul, J., & LeCompte, M. (1999). *Essential ethnographic methods: Observations, interviews and questionnaires*. Walnut Creek, CA: Altamira Press.

Stuhlmann, J. M., & Taylor, H. G. (1999). Preparing technically competent student- teachers: A three year study of interventions and experiences. *Journal of Technology and Teacher Education, 7*(4), 333–350.

Tashakkori, A., & Teddlie, C. (Eds.). (2003). *Handbook of mixed methods in the social and behavioral sciences*. Thousand Oaks, CA: Sage.

Trewin, D. (2002). *Measuring a knowledge-based economy and society*. Canberra, Australia: Australian Bureau of Statistics. Retrieved March 1, 2006, from http://www.abs.gov.au/ausstats/abs@.NSF/ 66f306f503e529a5ca25697e0017661f/ fe633d1 d2b900671ca256c220025e8a3!OpenDocument

U.S. Department of Education. (1999). *Preparing tomorrow's teachers to use technology*. Retrieved March 1, 2006, from http://www.ed.gov.teachtech

Weber, R. P. (1985). *Basic content analysis*. Beverly Hills, CA: Sage.

ENDNOTE

[1] The expected response rate for mail surveys of special populations ranges from 20% to 80% (Johnson, 2005). While on the low end, this sample of 63 educators was still reasonably large, and sufficiently diverse to provide important findings for informed decision-making with regard to the concerns of these educators with ICT integration. The average age and years of experience of the study sample are similar to the district averages, which adds to the credibility of findings from this research. Even so, the low response rate suggests that results should be interpreted with caution and not directly generalized to the larger population of educators.

This work was previously published in International Journal of Information Communication Technologies and Human Development, Volume 2, Issue 4, edited by Susheel Chhabra and Hakikur Rahman, pp. 13-26, copyright 2010 by IGI Publishing (an imprint of IGI Global).

Chapter 14

Examining the "Digital Divide":
A Study of Six Pre-Service Teachers' Experiences with ICTs and Second Language Education

Francis Bangou
University of Ottawa, Canada

ABSTRACT

Since the concept of "digital divide" first appeared, many researchers have argued for a more nuanced definition that highlights its complexities and better reveals its impact on the appropriation of ICTs. In this paper, the author analyzes the experiences of six Master of Education (M.Ed.) pre-service teachers learning to integrate ICTs into their practice. These case studies demonstrate how novice teachers' learning processes can be impacted by the unequal distribution of the temporal, material, mental, social, and cultural resources available (van Dijk, 2005). A number of pedagogical and curricular recommendations for the M.Ed. program are then provided.

INTRODUCTION

In recent years, Information and Communication Technologies (ICTs) have become an intrinsic part of our everyday lives. In this paper the term ICTs will refer primarily to computers and their networks. There is an increasing belief among the general public and educational leadership that computer literacy is essential to functioning properly in today's society. According to Eteokleous (2007), such perception "is warranted because

the computer represents not only an excellent curricular tool, but also a revolutionary classroom approach that can help students achieve important gains in learning and understanding" (p. 670). Consequently, many countries such as the United States have developed new policies and invested large sums of money to ensure that ICTs are integrated into the classroom. In the 1990s, the concept of a "digital divide" came to the forefront of political debates highlighting inequality of access to ICTs. At the time the digital divide referred mainly to the gap between those who had physical access to ICTs and those who did

DOI: 10.4018/978-1-4666-0047-8.ch014

not (Kim, Lee, & Menon, 2009). Consequently, in the United States many programs were developed at a federal and state level to place more computers in schools and homes with limited access to ICTs and to enhance their connections to the Internet (Egbert & Yang, 2004). In fact, schools were perceived as agents of change that would help minimize generational inequalities and close the digital divide (Holloway & Valentines, 2003; Stevenson, 2008). Large sums of money were then invested to promote the integration of ICTs into the classroom as a teaching tool and to ensure all students' access to a computer and an Internet connection (Warschaurer, 2004). ICTs are also used in the field of Second Language Education (SLE) and it is now imperative for second language teachers to acquire the necessary technological skills to use computers as an integral part of their teaching (Tognozzi, 2001).

Since the concept of a digital divide first appeared many researchers have discussed its limitations and have argued for a more nuanced definition that highlights its complexities and better reveals its impact on the appropriation of ICTs (Selwyn, 2006; van Dijk, 2006; Warschauer, 2004). The goal of this article is to examine the integration of computers and their networks into second language teacher education programs and pre-service teachers' knowledge-base development. More precisely, in this paper I will analyze the experiences of six SLE Master of Education (M.Ed.) pre-service teachers who were learning to integrate ICTs into their practice. These case studies demonstrate how pre-service teachers' knowledge-base development related to technology-enhanced second language education can potentially be impacted by the unequal distribution of temporal, material, mental, social and cultural resources (van Dijk, 2005).

After reviewing the literature on the subject and reframing the digital divide I will discuss the experiences of six SLE pre-services teachers and provide a number of pedagogical and curricular recommendations for the SLE M.Ed. program.

REVIEW OF THE LITERATURE

In the mid 1990s, the expression "digital divide" was first "used in a publication by the US Department of Commerce's National Telecommunication and Information Administration" (van Dijk, 2006, p. 221). This study placed the issue of unequal access to computer technologies at the forefront of the political and academic agenda by questioning whether ICTs were widely available to everyone. Earlier research on the digital divide focused more on physical access, considering demographic factors such as age, race, and income (Selwyn, 2004). For instance, Hoffman et al. (2000) conducted a systematic investigation of the differences between whites and African Americans in the United States with respect to computer access. They wanted to examine whether observed racial differences in access and use could be accounted for by the differences in income and education, how access influenced use, and when race affected equal access. The study revealed that people with a college degree were more likely to own and use a computer, but even with a college degree, African Americans were less likely to own and use a computer than their white counterparts. According to the researchers, one of the factors that could explain such a phenomenon was the lack of economic access to computers for many African Americans.

Although many studies still focus on physical access, in recent years scholars have increasingly argued for an expansion of the concept of the digital divide that would take into consideration "social, psychological and cultural backgrounds" (van Dijk, 2006, p. 221). It became clear that "meaningful access to ICT comprises far more than merely providing computers and Internet connections" (Warschauer, 2004, p. 6) and that access is "woven in a complex manner into social systems and processes" (Warschauer, p. 8). Many researchers started to focus on users' practices with ICTs and the ways that these technologies were appropriated and intrinsically connected to social, economical, cultural and political systems (Lally, 2006; Livingstone & Helsper, 2007; Selwyn, 2004, 2007; Stevenson, 2008; Warschauer, 2004). For instance, Noce and McKeown (2008) explored the extent to which demographic factors had an impact on people's use of the Internet in Canada. In particular, using data from the Canadian Internet Use Survey, they analyzed whether location, age, income area of residence, sex, education, language and age of children were still significant variables that would impact one's use of the Internet. They concluded that all variables except for children's age had a significant impact on the use of the Internet. Hassani (2006) conducted a study to explore whether the location of use had an impact on people's use of the Internet to search for product and health information online, to make purchases and to bank online. The study concluded that users who could connect to the Internet from multiple locations including home were more likely to engage in the four beneficial activities highlighted above.

Many studies have highlighted the fact that certain social groups are still less likely than others to engage with ICTs (Dutton, 2005; Roe & Broos, 2005). Selwyn (2006) argues that it is important to "know more about the social circumstances underlying people's disengagement from new technologies" (p. 275). It is also an opinion shared by Stevenson (2008), who conducted a study exploring ICT use in privileged families which emphasized the role of social networks in facilitating access to computers. This study had direct implications for policies on technology education and integration.

It is true that schools have often been perceived as the ideal setting to equip learners with the necessary technological skills and knowledge to function effectively in the new information age and "the availability of ICT technologies within the schools has been an important topic of investigation" (Hohfield et al., 2008, p. 1650). Consequently, numerous studies related to equal access to ICTs in schools have been conducted (Hawkins &

Oblinger, 2006; Yu, 2006). For instance, Hohlfield et al. (2008) conducted a study that examines the accessibility of software and technical support in Florida's public schools in relationship to Social and Economical Status (SES). The study revealed significant discrepancies between high and low SES schools in both accessibility to software and support and the frequency of use of ICTs.

Many studies have also been conducted on the integration of ICTs into the classroom (Vannata & Froddam, 2004; Wells, 2007; Wozney, Venkatesh, & Abrami, 2006). Both contextual factors and personal characteristics have been identified as possible barriers to the integration of computers into the classroom (Erlt & Plant, 2004). Mueller et al. (2008) conducted a study on teachers who fully integrated computers into their practice and those who did not. More precisely, this study sought to identify the "teachers' characteristics and variables that best discriminate between teachers who integrate computers and those who do not" (p. 1523). The authors concluded that both experience with computers and attitude towards ICTs were important variables affecting teachers' willingness to use ICTs in their classrooms. The authors argued for professional development tailored to teachers' individual needs. One of these needs might be to acquire the skills and knowledge that would enable a teacher to effectively integrate computer technology into an environment with limited technology. According to Egbert and Yang (2004), "optimal language learning activities can be supported by the use of 'limited' technologies" (p. 280). Considering the gaps in access to ICTs in schools, I also believe that it is important for pre-service teachers to have effective language learning experiences in language classrooms with limited access to technologies.

While research on the digital divide has covered a large range of topics and issues, many questions have yet to be addressed. For instance, I could not find any studies that focused on the influences of the digital divide on pre-service teachers' knowledge-base development as it relates to the use of ICTs in teaching second languages. As van Dijk (2006), I believe that the existing research suffers in part from a lack of qualitative research based on a strong conceptual elaboration of the digital divide. This is why I decided to base this qualitative study on this conceptual framework.

A RE-CONCEPTUALIZATION OF THE DIGITAL DIVIDE

Van Dijk (2005) argues that we need to part with traditional views on the digital divide that are based on individual notions of inequality and adopt instead a relational perspective that focuses more on the causes and consequences of such a divide. His framework is based on the following assumptions: unequal distribution of resources is caused by categorical inequalities in society; such unequal distribution lead to unequal access to ICTs; the characteristics of ICTs have an impact on their access which, in turn, affects one's participation in society; and one's participation in society impacts categorical inequalities and the distribution of resources. According to van Dijk there are five types of resources - *temporal* (time); *material* (income and properties); *mental* (knowledge, social and technical abilities); *social* (networks, relationships); and *cultural* (assets, status, credentials). These five resources will have an impact on four successive types of access - *motivational* (desire to use technology); *material or physical* (possession of ICTs and connections); *skills access* (operational, informational and strategic skills); and *usage access* (variety of application and time to use them). Within this framework, digital skills refer to the ability to a) operate ICTs and digital connections; b) effectively search and select the information, and c) use the information to improve one's status in society. According to van Dijk's model, the four types of access are cumulative stages where the motivational access always comes first and leads

to the subsequent types of access. In this article, I will argue that motivational access does not always precede the other types of access. On the contrary, the connection between the different types of access is not linear but more complex. In fact, each one influences the others.

RESEARCH QUESTIONS

This study was based on the assumption that within the SLE M.Ed. program, unequal distributions of resources caused by categorical inequalities in society led to unequal access to ICTs. This, in turn, impacted teacher candidates' construction of a knowledge base related to technology-enhanced second language education. The research questions that guided this article were:

1. How did the distribution of temporal, material, mental, social, and cultural resources affect the pre-service teachers' motivational, material, skill and usage access to ICTs?
2. How did access affect the development of a knowledge-base related to technology-enhanced second language education?
3. What are the pedagogical and curricular implications for the SLE M.Ed. program?

THE RESEARCH PROJECT

Context

The data discussed in this article were collected as part of a broader study that investigated the ways that a group of six pre-service teachers constructed a knowledge base related to using technology to improve their professional practice. This research took place in a SLE M.Ed. program at a large North American university. In 2000, the College of Education was the recipient of a three-year grant entitled Preparing Tomorrow's Teacher to Use Technology (PT3). The purpose of the grant was to ensure that pre-service teachers were able to use ICTs appropriately in their classrooms. I was hired as a technology assistant to infuse the use of ICTs into the SLE M.Ed. program (Bangou & Waterhouse, 2008; Bangou & Wong, 2009).

I started working with the SLE M.Ed. program in January 2001 and the Methods of Teaching Foreign Languages course was used to provide the pre-service teachers with a theoretical and practical framework and familiarize them with the use of ICTs in the classroom. The objective was for the pre-service teachers to have a practical experience with ICTs and to design something that they would be able to use in their future classrooms. Moreover, it was crucial that these novice teachers be made aware that ICTs could enhance and facilitate their teaching practice and promote their professional careers. As part of the program requirements, the pre-service teachers had to design from scratch an electronic portfolio that included their resume, teaching philosophy, biography, lesson plans, teaching videos and a web-based unit plan which was meant to be taught entirely online.

The Participants

Twenty-six students were enrolled in the M.Ed. program. It was important to have a diversity of languages and experiences represented and to establish a comfortable relationship with the research participants. The pre-service teachers who allowed for a greater variability and balance were invited to be part of the study.

The participants in this study were six full-time novice teachers who wanted to teach French, German, Spanish, Latin, or Japanese. All the names in this article are pseudonyms to protect the confidentiality of the participants and the institutions.

Michaela

She was a twenty-two year old Venezuelan born in England, planning to teach Spanish. She was a single mother of a two year old boy and did not have a personal computer. Before enrolling in the M.Ed. Program she used computers primarily for word-processing and email. She had never attended a class where ICTs were used as an integral part of instruction.

Andrea

She was a twenty-nine year old African-American female who wanted to teach Spanish. Prior to enrolling in the M.Ed. program she had worked as a nurse and she decided to attend the M. Ed. Program to change careers. As a nurse she had used computers to do her "charting." At the time of the research she was living with her parents and had access to three computers and the Internet at home. Before the M.Ed. she used computers mostly to do word-processing and use email. She had never taught or attended a class where ICTs were used to teach.

Babette

Babette was a twenty-three year old Caucasian female who wanted to teach French. She said that she started college thinking that she would major in Computer Sciences. She also enjoyed using her personal computer at least once a day to do word-processing, type emails, use PowerPoint, or browse the Internet. Once, she started a chat room on Yahoo to be able to communicate with one of her friends who was living abroad. She had never taught or attended a class where computers were used to teach.

Pam

She was a twenty-four year old Caucasian female who wanted to teach German. Her father was a professor at a private university where he taught computer classes and she acknowledged that she had always been surrounded by ICTs. Pam also had the opportunity to be a substitute teacher at a middle school for one semester. She declared that she was surprised to see that students at the middle school were "more into" the computer than she was. At the time of the research she did not have a personal computer but sometimes she would borrow her parents' laptop. She would mainly use the computer for word-processing, email, and Internet use.

Nathalie

She was a thirty-six year old Caucasian female who wanted to teach Japanese. She taught English in Japan for three years. She had to quit a tenured job to attend the M.Ed. program and during the research she was working four jobs. When she was teaching Japanese she enjoyed using the textbook's CD-ROM. Nathalie bought her first personal computer at the beginning of the M.Ed. Program.

Tim

Tim was a twenty-five year old Caucasian male who wanted to teach Latin. Before the M.Ed. program he taught Latin for two years as a teaching assistant. He "had never had a computer growing up or anything." Through junior high school he used a typewriter to type his essays. At the time of the research he did not have a personal computer. Before the M.Ed. program he used computers only to type his assignments and for email. He had never attended a class where ICTs were used to teach.

Data Collection and Analysis

A qualitative multiple case study methodology was used to conduct an in depth analysis of the pre-service teachers' experiences with ICTs within the M.Ed. program. A multiple case study has been described as an empirical inquiry that enables one to analyze complex real-life activities using a diversity of sources of evidence (Anderson, 1993; Yin, 2009). Case studies focus on how and why

things happen, which is why I believed that this methodology was most appropriate to address the research questions.

To ensure credibility when using a multiple case study methodology, it is important to study processes from different lines of inquiry (Yin, 2009; Creswell, 2008). In this study, four data collection strategies were used: 1) observation field notes, 2) interviews, 3) chat room discussions and 3) document analysis.

For an entire year the research participants were observed both at the university and in their field placements. Through these intensive observations and detailed field notes, participant's behavior towards ICTs was described. I also highlighted participants' teaching strategies and how ICTs were integrated.

Each participant was also interviewed once during the fall, the winter and the spring quarters. The goal of the interviews was to understand participants meaning-making of their experience and feelings and not trying to control or predict their behavior. Therefore, semi-structured interviews were used in talking with research participants to probe different subjects with different questions, depending on the participants' responses. The interviews had three major themes: the technological tools used in their field placements and at the university, the curriculum both in schools and at the university, and students' relationships with their peers, instructors, mentor teachers and field educators. The mentor teachers were also interviewed.

Moreover, I met with the participants seven times to discuss collectively, in a chat room, issues related to technology and education. The purpose of the chat room discussions was to encourage discussion of common experiences and the expression of differing opinions.

I also collected participants' final projects and looked at their electronic portfolios and their web-based unit plans. Written documents, such as position papers or journals are "rich in portraying the values and beliefs of participants in the settings" (Marshall & Rossman, 1995, p. 85). Participants' teaching philosophy and pedagogy as they were expressed in these documents were highlighted.

Although qualitative multiple case studies are context bound and commonly deal with small samples of participants, trustworthiness can be ensured through the use of multiple sources of evidence as well as cross-case examination and within-case examination in parallel with a review of the literature (Johnston, 1994; Yin, 2009). For each participant, I went through the field notes and interview transcripts and an initial list of codes was derived from the research questions and van Dijk's framework (e.g. material, mental, cultural resources, etc.) Afterward, I conducted a content analysis and highlighted the emerging themes (e.g. time management, classmates. etc.). This procedure was repeated across participants to identify the shared themes. Taking a developmental approach, I also looked at how the themes and patterns changed over time (Bangou & Wong, 2009). Through this analysis of the participants' experiences with ICTs I was able to highlight the ways that the distribution of temporal, material, mental, social, and cultural resources affected the pre-service teachers' motivational, material, skill and usage access to technology and how such access contributed to the development of their knowledge-base related to technology-enhanced second language education. In this study we looked for patterns but we also highlighted the unique experiences we thought were relevant to the study because the most serious threat to trustworthiness is "not collecting or paying attention to discrepant data, or not considering alternative explanations or understandings of the phenomena you are studying" (Lawrence-Lightfoot & Hoffmann, 1997, p. 192).

RESULTS

The Distribution of Temporal Resources and Pre-Service Teachers' Access to ICTs

The M.Ed. program was an intensive one-year program and all the participants admitted that one of their biggest challenges was time management. For these novice teachers learning to teach was already a time consuming process and they felt that learning simultaneously to integrate ICTs into their practice accentuated the challenge. For instance, all of the participants declared that they would spend hours planning their classes and expected the integration of technology to prolong their preparation. Michaela said: "I think right now it takes me longer to plan for technology than just plan using the textbook and stuff." One of the strategies used by the participants to survive was to select the activities and requirements they felt were more deserving of their time. For these novice teachers, learning to teach was more important than learning to integrate technology. They would not integrate ICTs in their lessons if they felt that it was a threat to their teaching practice. For instance, Andrea declared: "I don't really like those [classes with technology] as much because it requires a whole lot more preparation than anything else." Most of the participants became more motivated to integrate ICTs into their teaching when they realized that these technologies could help them save time. For instance, when the participants realized that they were able to quickly and easily find a plethora of pedagogical resources on the Internet it had an impact on their motivational and usage access. For instance, Michaela told me during an interview: "I realized that there are many resources on the Internet. All you have to do is type something and you have a web site that you can do a whole class with. So, I feel much better about technology now."

Unfortunately, time was not equally distributed among the research participants and it influenced their access to technology. For instance, Nathalie was working part-time at four different places and it was difficult for her to find the time to go to the computer lab and work on her assignments. Once a week, as part of the methods course, the novice teachers could work on their assignments in the computer lab for one hour. Nathalie admitted that she needed more time in the computer lab in part because these lab sessions forced her to take time out of her full schedule to work on her electronic portfolio. She said: "Because it [the lab] provided a separate part of time that we had to have in our schedule to go and do this." Nathalie also admitted that because of her schedule she would use the lab sessions to work on assignments for other courses. Her situation was worsened by the fact that the computers on campus did not recognize Japanese typescripts; to overcome this handicap Nathalie spent hours scanning and formatting all the authentic documents she wanted to use in her web-based unit plan: She once declared: "Technologically speaking the biggest problem, is we're using computers whether or not they would recognize Japanese typescripts." Because of time constraints, Nathalie had less usage access than other participants and within the context of the M.Ed. program such access was crucial to developing the necessary technological skills and knowledge. Indeed, all the participants declared that it was through the use of ICTs that they were able to develop their technological skills. For instance, Nathalie reported during an interview: "I think it [using ICT] provided me with this training and chance to develop skills and become more comfortable with a computer;" and Andrea said: "The repetitive use of having to use the technology, the computer, the Internet, the programs it does lessen that anxiety of having to do that stuff."

The Distribution of Material Resources and Pre-Service Teachers' Access to ICTs

In order to attend the program most of the pre-service teachers had to quit their full-time jobs and borrow money to pay the mandatory tuition. Two of the participants lived with their parents, one participant had to work multiple part-time jobs, and one was on welfare. For all of the participants, a great deal was at stake and failing the program was not an option. However, the pressure seemed to be higher for some participants, with a direct impact on their motivational access. For instance, at the time of the research Michaela was the single mother of a baby boy and was going through a difficult divorce. When I started talking about the technological requirements at the beginning of the M.Ed. program, she had the strongest reaction of all the pre-service teachers. She verbally expressed her disagreement and almost cried. She later declared that she had such a reaction in part because of her past learning experiences with technology and because of her son. She could not afford to fail the program for her baby's sake:

I'm putting my life on hold for this program because I have chosen to do so.

But at the same time I'm affecting my son's life because I'm choosing to do this. So you know our financial level is lower, we live in subsidized housing; we do the food stamp thing and stuff like that. You know that tells me that I have to give my very best effort in everything I do.

Prior to the M.Ed. program, Michaela's learning experience with ICTs was not very successful and in her eyes, learning to integrate ICTs into her teaching was a serious threat to her success in the program: "I took a computer class in Venezuela and it was terrible. I got terrible grades and I barely passed, and I didn't want to do that. Yeah, it could be a threat."

To do their practicum the pre-service teachers were placed in school districts with an unequal distribution of material resources, which impacted their motivational, material, skills and usage access. Some pre-service teachers were placed in wealthy schools with a high degree of material access to ICTs. For instance, Babette's room had wireless Internet access and each student could use a laptop if they wanted. Others were placed in poorer schools where such rudimentary technology as a VCR was not always available. Consequently, some participants felt that the way that ICTs were introduced in the M.Ed. program was unrealistic and unsuitable to the environment of every school. They felt that it would be more difficult for some people to fulfill the program's technological requirement. For instance, Andrea declared during an interview:

There are some of the schools systems that some of the interns are in now that don't have as nice of a program as some of the other students. So they're not going to be able to do some of the things that you would like for us to do.

Each setting had different technology available to the teachers and it seemed that it had an impact on the participants' learning process. Tim reported that he did not use technology as much as some of the other participants in part because there was not as much technology available to him. Babette found it difficult to bring her students to the computer lab but thanks to the wireless laptops it was easier for her to implement technology into her teaching. Because of the material resources of her schools Babette had more motivational, material, skill and usage access than Tim and more opportunities to develop her technological skills.

The Distribution of Mental Resources and Pre-Service Teachers' Access to ICTs

At the beginning of the M.Ed. program most of the participants agreed that ICTs could be beneficial in their classroom but they also agreed that ICTs were not necessary and not always compatible with their pedagogical objectives. Once, Michaela told me that completing the technological requirements of the program made her feel that she was passing a required mathematics class to be a language teacher. Most participants did not have previous teaching experience and they never attended a class where ICTs were used to teach the target language. For them, it was conceptually difficult to connect both teaching the language and using ICTs. For instance, Babette declared during an interview: "When I was taught French we didn't use a lot of technology. We used the VCR and the TV but that was it. So for me to adapt to that; I'll have to integrate it in my thinking." Her comment suggests that mental resources had an impact on participants' motivational and usage access.

Unlike the other participants, Pam had taught in a school where ICTs were highly integrated into the classroom. Because of this experience, she was convinced that teachers could not afford any longer to teach without the use of ICTs and she was happy to receive such training in the M.Ed. program: "I think that we gonna need that stuff [computer training] so. I'm glad to have that. Cause I see it in the classroom, like all the teachers have a home page now."

Mental resources influenced participants' motivational access as well as their material, skills, and usage access. Some participants did not integrate ICTs into their teaching in part because of their teaching philosophy. For instance Andrea agreed that technology could be beneficial but she was from a generation which did not use technology as much as today's students to learn and she believed that learners should also be able to learn without the help of ICTs: "It's great to have technology and the computer and all the Internet, but if that goes down what you gonna do, if you don't know how to use a library." Andrea's conviction had an impact on her willingness to integrate ICTs into her teaching. As she said she liked to "teach the old fashioned way and maybe enhance it with technology." Tim also believed that ICTs were not necessary to learn a language. This belief was accentuated by the fact that as a Latin teacher, his main goal was to enable students to read and translate the target language and not so much to communicate in the language. In the M.Ed. program the focus was placed on the development of a communicative competence, which he saw as irrelevant for a Latin teacher: "The program focuses on being able to go to the country where a language is spoken and function, it is not something that as a Latin teacher I would teach my students; I would focus on trying to read text." Tim's motivational, material, skill and usage access were influenced by the nature of the language he wanted to teach and his pedagogical objectives. Throughout the year Tim mostly used ICTs to introduce the culture of ancient Rome. He said during an interview: "I think technology can be good to introduce culture because looking through the web sites lists there's a lot of neat stuff." However, for Tim, teaching culture was not the main objective of teaching Latin. It seems that it is not solely material access to ICTs that determines a teacher's willingness to use technology in the classroom.

Conversely, limited material access to ICTs does not necessarily mean that a teacher will not try to integrate as much technology as possible into her/his practice. Prior to the M.Ed. program Babette wanted to be a computer scientist and she enjoyed playing with computers. During an interview, she admitted: "If I do not know a program just give me a couple of days to get used to it. I like to play, find out little things about a program and spend hours to find something." During her practicum, Babette was struggling to find the material she needed on the Internet because of the firewalls that were installed on the computers. Because she enjoyed playing with the computers, she eventually was able to go around them and have access to what she needed. She once said: "I have different strategies now to get around firewalls." Because of their backgrounds and experiences the research participants came to the M.Ed. program with diverse mental resources that impacted their motivational, skill and usage access to ICTs in different ways.

The Distribution of Social Resources and Pre-Service Teachers' Access to ICTs

Within the M.Ed. program the social resources were mainly family, classmates, and mentor teachers. Most participants reported that working in a group to design their web-based unit plan was an enjoyable experience, largely because of the support that the other members of the group provided. It seems that working in a group had an impact on the participants' motivational access. For instance, although Tim was skeptical about using ICTs as learning tools, he invested a lot of effort into the design of his group's web-based unit plan because he did not want his performance to reflect poorly on the group and he admitted that working in a group made the experience enjoyable: "with the web unit plan especially since it was a group effort you know I wanted to make my part good so that the group as a whole wouldn't suffer and you know it was actually enjoyable making that web page." In contrast to the other group members, Nathalie could not be part of a group to design her web-based unit plan because she was the only pre-service teacher who wanted to teach Japanese. She admitted that working alone on the web-based unit plan was a tremendous challenge. During an interview she declared that she was grateful that her classmates offered their help when she was pressed with time and could not meet the deadlines: "I can't tell you how many people when I was pressed for time at the end of the unit who said tell me what I can do to help you, to offer to help me 'cause it was great."

Family also influenced participants' motivational and material access to ICTs. At home, most participants did not have access to the software they needed to complete the technology requirements of the program. Most of them would spend hours in the computer labs to complete their assignments. Although Babette enjoyed using the computer, she reported that her motivation was affected by her lack of material access at home:

I don't mind doing anything on the computer. My problem is that at home my laptop the keyboard set is hard to type because it's older and when I want to work on FrontPage I have to come to school and go to the lab and sit in the boring lab for hours and hours and do it.

Fortunately, during the winter quarter, her mother gave her a newer laptop equipped with the latest software and she reported that it did make a difference: "I can go on FrontPage, sat there on Friday night and in 10 minutes I even didn't have to leave my bed. It was awesome, I love it now."

As part of their practicum the research participants were placed in primary and secondary schools where they observed and taught the class of their mentor teachers. In each placement, the integration of technology depended on; a) the mentor's and the pre-service teacher's relationship; b) the mentor's and the pre-service teacher's methodological orientations; c) the mentor's attitude towards ICTs; and d) the pre-service teacher's management of her/his learning process (Bangou, 2006). In some cases, the pre-service teachers did not feel welcome in the mentor teacher's classroom. After her practicum at one of the elementary schools, Pam told me: "My mentor was nice but I don't think she really wanted me to be there, or she just didn't like me." In this context, if the mentor teacher did not use ICTs to teach the target language, the pre-service teacher did not feel comfortable doing so. Pam did not

use ICTs when she was working in this school. Babette reported that she did not use computer technology in one of her elementary placements in part because she was doing what the mentor wanted her to do. The participants who most often integrated ICTs into their practice were placed with mentor teachers who either used ICTs to teach the target language or were very encouraging. For instance, Pam's mentor in her secondary placement was very enthusiastic about ICTs and she provided Pam with multiple opportunities to integrate it into her teaching. Once, Pam told me "My mentor today found a site on Discovery.com where you can…puzzles like a puzzle make. [?] She was like "it's so much fun you should do it." They collaborated on many Internet projects and the mentor wanted Pam to teach her what she was learning in the program: "Yes, I taught her about technology, that's funny." Pam was the pre-service teacher who used ICTs the most in her classroom during her practicum in the secondary school. From these examples, it seems that the distribution of the social resources within the M.Ed. program had an impact on the participants' motivational, material, skill and usage access.

The Distribution of Cultural Resources and Pre-Service Teachers' Access to ICTs

The pre-service teachers who attended the M.Ed. program were predominantly white and middle class. As students of color, both Andrea and Michaela were aware of their status as racial minorities within the M.Ed. program. Once during an interview Andrea told me: "You know sometimes it gets old to be the only one of an only race."

Both Michaela and Andrea complained about the lack of diversity and racial awareness in the M.Ed. program and in their school placements. Once, Michaela told me that students in her field placement "are just so far away from reality. So even like in France you do your own stuff but you're so aware of the rest of the world. Here, you are aware of Galburns [a neighboring town] and that's it." At the beginning of the program both Michaela and Andrea were not enthusiastic about learning to use ICTs to teach a second language. However, it seems that their motivation was enhanced in part because they were able to use the available technology to break racial stereotypes and empower themselves as women and teachers of color (Bangou & Wong, 2009). For instance, it was important to Andrea to represent who she was racially in her electronic portfolio: "There's a part where I have my students' handbook and it's a little black teacher at the board and I love it because that is me. I don't think many people would expect to see that."

Michaela was among the pre-service teachers who used ICTs the most during her practicum in the secondary school, in part because she realized that the computer allowed her to broaden students' world views. She said during an interview: "The main conclusion that I came to was that I can use it [the computer] to do what I wanna do in the classroom which is ... to make them have a little bit of awareness of the world we live in." Andrea's and Michaela's cultural resources within the program had an impact on their motivational, skill, and usage access to ICTs (Bangou & Wong, 2009).

DISCUSSION

In response to the first question, the results suggest that the unequal distribution of temporal, material, mental, social and cultural resources did lead, in complex ways, to unequal motivational, material, skill and usage access to ICTs. Depending on context and pre-service teachers' experiences, it appears that:

1. The distribution of a resource may affect all of the participants or only some of them. For instance, within the M.Ed. program, the unequal distribution of social resources seemed to affect all participants, whereas the unequal

distribution of cultural resources appeared to affect only Andrea and Michaela.

2. The unequal distribution of a specific resource may affect a specific type of access or all of them. For instance, in the case of Nathalie, the unequal distribution of time seemed to affect her usage access in particular, whereas the unequal distribution of material resources affected other types of access.

3. The distribution of one resource may have an impact on how another resource affected a participant's access. For instance, as a Latin teacher, Tim was not convinced that ICTs could be beneficial to teaching Latin and it negatively affected his motivational access. However, he also acknowledged that working in a group to design the web-based unit plan did increase his motivational access. In this case, the distribution of social resources altered how the distribution of mental resources affected Tim's motivational access.

4. Access may change the distribution of resources. For instance, thanks to her motivational, skill and usage access, Babette was able to go around the firewalls installed on the computers at her school and improve how mental resource was distributed.

5. Van Dijk's framework suggests that motivational access precedes the others and can only be affected by usage access. However, the data analysed here suggest that the distribution of resources within specific contexts may affect how different types of access interact with each other. For instance, throughout the program, Tim and Andrea increased their usage access. However, at the end of the program they were still convinced that ICTs were beneficial but not necessary to teach a second language. In these cases, it seems that usage access did not affect motivational access, partly because of the distribution of mental resources. Moreover,

within the M.Ed. program, a majority of participants admitted that they started using the available technology not because they wanted to, but because of program requirements. In one instance, Nathalie declared that at the beginning of the program, learning to integrate ICTs into her teaching was like pulling teeth. It appears that within the M.Ed. program, for a majority of participants, material, skill and usage accesses preceded motivational access.

In response to question two, if we consider that second language teachers' construction of a knowledge base is grounded within specific sociocultural contexts and is impacted by teachers' background experiences and beliefs (Freeman & Johnson, 1998), the data clearly show that access had an impact on pre-service teachers' knowledge-base construction. The six pre-service teachers' experiences can be considered successful since, at the end of the program, all reported having gained more confidence as well as practical knowledge about using ICTs to teach the target languages. All of them had integrated ICTs into their practice to some extent and they viewed positively the development of their technological skills. However, through analysis of the six pre-service teachers' experiences in the M.Ed. program, I was able to specify how the distribution of resources affected access to technology and impacted the participants' learning experiences. Because of the participants' backgrounds, field placements, mentor teachers and beliefs, each experience was unique and the outcomes of the program were in fact more nuanced. Some participants had more opportunities than others to gain more skills and knowledge related to technology-enhanced second language education.

CURRICULAR AND PEDAGOGICAL IMPLICATIONS FOR THE SLE M.ED. PROGRAM

The findings of this study have pedagogical and curricular implications for the SLE M.Ed. program. Because of the contextualized nature of this research and the number of participants, the results cannot be universally applied in different settings. However, the findings of this study echo previous research on second language education and ICT.

The findings of this study suggest that within the M.Ed. program, the participants' mental resources had an influence on their motivational, skill and usage access to ICTs. By asking pre-service teachers to reflect on their experiences and to identify their resulting beliefs, teacher educators may begin to help their students deconstruct their current understanding of technology and language teaching and learning (Johnson, 1994; Richardson, 1996). Some of the tools that students might use to reflect are journals, classroom discussions, and reflection papers. It is critical to encourage pre-service teachers to reflect on equity issues and how they impact their knowledge and teaching practice. According to Igoa (1995), personal narratives are powerful tools for students to explore and understand their surroundings as well as deal with a variety of problems and dilemmas.

Moreover, the research findings highlight the fact that some participants felt that their needs were not addressed in the program. These participants reported that they became less engaged with and less motivated to use ICTs. Examples from diverse languages need to be provided while teaching about ICTs and second language teaching so that every student in the cohort feels that computer technology can be applicable to their language - particularly for classical languages or languages that use other alphabets such as Japanese.

Within the M.Ed. program, time was an important resource that facilitated or hindered the participants' learning experiences with ICTs. Technology should be included as an integral part of the program during the course work as well as during the internships, making technology part of the program requirements pre-service teachers must complete before graduating. Moreover, in parallel, more lab sessions need to be included in the curriculum. Because of the intensity of the program, these additional sessions should not increase the total hours, but made a part of the existing curriculum.

The social resources within the M.Ed. program were varied and a majority of research participants appreciated working in groups on their web-based unit plan, mostly because of the help that they received from the other group members. It is important to include collaborative projects in the curriculum when teaching about ICTs, in part because it provides students with opportunities to help their peers, and fosters their knowledge and confidence. Putman and Borko (2000) argue that the relationship of the pre-service teachers with their students and mentors influenced their learning process. The research findings indicate that the mentor teachers played a role in participants' learning process as models, hosts, and supporters. Pre-service teachers typically want to please their mentors and be successful with their students (Weber & Mitchell, 1996). In order for pre-service teachers to benefit from their practicum, they need to be placed with mentors who regularly implement ICTs into their teaching and would encourage pre-service teachers to do so.

The research findings indicate that participants' learning experience was impacted by their material access to technology in the schools and on campus. Raymond (1999) suggests that "in addition to careful screening of mentor teachers, teacher educators may address some of the challenges of specific classroom contexts by incorporating case studies in methods courses" (p. 226). For instance, pre-service teachers could discuss in class the strategies they might use if they only had one computer in the classroom. Pre-service teachers could also discuss the strategies they would use if they were teaching a less commonly taught language such as Japanese.

CONCLUSION

Through this study I was able to problematize the notion of digital divide by showing that its effect on one's construction of a knowledge base is rooted in intricate and context-bounded interactions between diverse distributions of resources and types of access. Due to participants' experiences with ICTs, beliefs, relationships with their peers and mentors, socio-economical and cultural background, some pre-service teachers had more opportunities than others to develop their knowledge base associated with technology-enhanced second language education. To keep improving access to technology as well as its integration into second language teacher education programs, we need further research that focuses on the impact of the digital divide on one's learning in diverse settings and with larger numbers of participants. We also need more research on the decision-making process of pre-service teachers as well as the intersections of various dimensions of social inequality and power. More research on the way that ICTs can support those who traditionally are excluded from the educational system is also needed (Bangou & Wong, 2009).

REFERENCES

Anderson, G. (1993). *Fundamentals of educational research*. London: Falmer Press.

Bangou, F. (2006). Intégration des TICE et apprentissage de l'enseignement: Une approche Systémique. *ALSIC*, *9*, 145–159.

Bangou, F., & Wong, S. (2009). Race, and Technology: Where is the Access? In Kuboka, R., & Lin, A. (Eds.), *Race, Culture, and Identities in Second Language Education: Exploring Critically Engaged Practices* (pp. 158–176). London: Routledge.

Creswell, J. W. (2008). *Qualitative inquiry and research design*. Thousand Oaks, CA: Sage.

Dutton, W. (2005, February). *The social dynamics of the Internet.* Paper presented at the International Knowledge and Society Conference, Berkeley, CA.

Egbert, J., & Yang, Y. F. (2004). Mediating the digital divide in CALL classrooms: Promoting effective language tasks in limited technology contexts. *ReCALL, 16*(2), 280–291. doi:10.1017/S0958344004000321

Ertl, H., & Plante, J. (2004). *Connectivity and learning in Canada's schools* (Research Paper No. 56F0004MIE –No. 011). Ottawa, ON: Science, Innovation and Electronic Information Division, Statistics Canada.

Eteokleous, N. (2008). Evaluating computer technology integration in a centralized school system. *Computers & Education, 51*, 669–686. doi:10.1016/j.compedu.2007.07.004

Freeman, D., & Johnson, K. (1998). Reconceptualizing the knowledge-base of language teacher education. *TESOL Quarterly, 32*(3), 397–416. doi:10.2307/3588114

Hassani, S. N. (2006). Locating digital divides at home, work and everywhere else. *Poetics, 34*, 250–272. doi:10.1016/j.poetic.2006.05.007

Hawkins, B. L., & Oblinger, D. G. (2006). The myth about the digital divide. *EDUCAUSE Review, 41*(4), 12–13.

Hoffman, D. L., Novak, T. P., & Schlosser, A. E. (2000). The Evolution of the Digital Divide: How Gaps in Internet Access May Impact Electronic Commerce. *Journal of Computer Mediated Communication, 5*(3). Retrieved October 6, 2009, from http://jcmc.indiana.edu/ vol5/issue3/hoffman.html

Hohlfeld, T. N., Ritzhaupt, A. D., Barron, A. E., & Kember, K. (2008). Examining the digital divide in K-12 public schools: Four-year trends for supporting ICT literacy in Florida. *Computers & Education, 51*, 1648–1663. doi:10.1016/j.compedu.2008.04.002

Holloway, S. L., & Valentine, G. (2003). *Cyberkids: Children in the information age.* London: Routledge Flamer.

Igoa, C. (1995). *The Inner World of the Immigrant Child.* Mahwah, NJ: Lawrence Erlbaum.

Johnson, K. E. (1994). The emerging beliefs and instructional practices of preservice English as a second language teachers. *Teaching and Teacher Education, 10*, 439–452. doi:10.1016/0742-051X(94)90024-8

Kim, E., Lee, B., & Menon, N. (2009). Social welfare implications of the digital divide. *Government Information Quarterly, 26*, 377–386. doi:10.1016/j.giq.2008.11.004

Lally, E. (2006). Compputing in domestic pattern of life. In Bell, D. (Ed.), *Cybercultures: Critical concepts in media and cultural studies* (pp. 219–241). Abingdon, UK: Routledge.

Lawrence-Lightfoot, S., & Hoffmann, D. J. (1997). *The art and science of portraiture.* San Francisco: Jossey-Bass.

Livingstone, S., & Helsper, E. (2007). Gradation in digital inclusion: Children, young people and the digital divide. *New Media & Society, 9*(4), 671–696. doi:10.1177/1461444807080335

Marshall, C., & Rossman, G. B. (1995). *Designing Qualitative Research* (2nd ed.). Thousand Oaks, CA: Sage.

Mueller, J., Wood, E., Willoughby, T., Ross, C., & Specht, J. (2008). Identifying discriminating variables between teachers who fully integrate computers and teachers with limited integration. *Computers & Education, 51*, 1523–1537. doi:10.1016/j.compedu.2008.02.003

Noce, A. A. (2008). A new benchmark for Internet use: A logistic modeling of factors influencing Internet use in Canada, 2005. *Government Information Quarterly, 25*, 462–476. doi:10.1016/j.giq.2007.04.006

Putman, R. T., & Borko, H. (2000). What do new views of knowledge and thinking have to say about research on teacher learning? *Educational Researcher, 29*(1), 4–15.

Raymond, H. (1999). *Learning to Teach Foreign Languages: Case Studies of Six Preservice Teachers in an Education Program.* Unpublished doctoral dissertation, The Ohio State University.

Richardson, V. (1996). The role of attitudes and beliefs in learning to teach. In Sikula, J. (Ed.), *Handbook of Research on Teacher Education* (2nd ed.). New York: Association of Teacher Educators.

Roe, K., & Broos, A. (2005). Marginality in the information age: The socio-demographics of computer disquietude. *European Journal of Communication, 30*(1), 91–96.

Selwyn, N. (2004). Reconsidering Political and Popular Understandings of the Digital Divide. *New Media & Society, 6*(3), 381–361. doi:10.1177/1461444804042519

Selwyn, N. (2006). Digital division or digital decision? A study of non-users and low-users of computers. *Poetics, 34*, 273–292. doi:10.1016/j.poetic.2006.05.003

Selwyn, N. (2007). New technologies, young people and social inclusion. In Kutscher, N., & Otto, H. (Eds.), *Grenzenlose cyberwelt? Um verhaltnis von digitaler ungleichheit und neuen bildungszugangen fur jugendliche* (pp. 31–45). Aachen, Germany: Shaker.

Stevenson, O. (2008). Ubiquitous presence, partial use: The everyday interaction of children and their families with ICT. *Pedagogy and Education, 17*(2), 115–130. doi:10.1080/14759390802098615

Tognozzi, E. (2001). Italian language instruction: The need for teacher development in technology. *Italica, 78*(4), 487–498. doi:10.2307/3656077

van Dijk, J. (2005). *The deepening divide: Inequalities in the information society.* Thousand Oaks, CA: Sage.

van Dijk, J. (2006). Digital divide research, achievements and shortcomings. *Poetics, 34*, 221–235. doi:10.1016/j.poetic.2006.05.004

Vanatta, R. A., & Fordham, N. (2004). Teachers disposition as predictors of classroom technology use. *Journal of Research on Technology in Education, 36*, 253–271.

Warschauer, M. (2004). *Technology and Social Inclusion: Rethinking the Digital Divide.* Cambridge, MA: MIT Press.

Weber, S., & Mitchell, C. (1996). Betwixt and between: The culture of student teaching. In Moore, Z. (Ed.), *Foreign language Teacher Education: Multiple Perspectives* (pp. 301–316). Lanham, MD: University Press of America.

Wells, J. G. (2007). Key Design factors in durable instructional technology professional development. *Journal of Technology and Teacher Education, 15*(1), 101–122.

Wozney, L., Venkatesh, V., & Abrami, P. C. (2006). Implementing computer technologies: Teachers' perceptions and practices. *Journal of Technology and Teacher Education, 14*, 120–173.

Yin, R. K. (2009). *Case Study Research: Design and Method* (4th ed.). Thousand Oaks, CA: Sage.

Yu, L. (2006). Understanding information inequality: Making sense of the literature of the information and digital divides. *Journal of Librarianship and Information Science, 38*(4), 229–252. doi:10.1177/0961000606070600

This work was previously published in International Journal of Information Communication Technologies and Human Development, Volume 2, Issue 4, edited by Susheel Chhabra and Hakikur Rahman, pp. 27-41, copyright 2010 by IGI Publishing (an imprint of IGI Global).

Chapter 15
Leveraging Technology to Promote Assessment for Learning in Higher Education

Christopher DeLuca
University of South Florida, USA

Laura April McEwen
Queen's University, Canada

ABSTRACT

Assessment for learning (AFL) is a highly effective strategy for promoting student learning, development and achievement in higher education (Falchikov, 2003; Kirby & Downs, 2007; Nicol & Macfarlane-Dick, 2006; Rust, Price, & O'Donovan, 2003; Vermunt, 2005). However, since AFL relies on continuous monitoring of student progress through instructor feedback, peer collaboration, and student self-assessment, enacting AFL within large-group learning formats is challenging. This paper considers how technology can be leveraged to promote AFL in higher education. Drawing on data from students and instructors and recommendations from an external instructional design consultant, this paper documents the process of pairing technology and AFL within a large-group pre-service teacher education course at one Canadian institution. Recommendations for the improvement of the web-based component of the course are highlighted to provide practical suggestions for instructors to evaluate their own web-based platforms and improve their use of technology in support of AFL. The paper concludes with a discussion of areas for continued research related to the effectiveness of this pairing between assessment theory and technology.

INTRODUCTION

Given increased demands for higher education across Canada, the United States and many parts of Europe, large-group learning formats continue to dominate as a mode of education delivery (Weber,

1999). As such, innovative pedagogical strategies are needed to maintain educational quality within this climate. Assessment for learning (AFL) has been identified as a highly effective strategy for improving student learning and achievement in higher education (Falchikov, 2003; Hargreaves, 2005, 2007; Kirby & Downs, 2007; Nicol &

DOI: 10.4018/978-1-4666-0047-8.ch015

Macfarlane-Dick, 2006; Rust et al., 2003; Vermunt, 2005). AFL involves the ongoing monitoring of student progress through non-graded assessment activities. This form of assessment has been characterized as the assessment that occurs between summative tasks to promote student learning (Black & Wiliams, 1998). As AFL typically involves instructor feedback, peer collaboration, and student self-assessment, enacting AFL within a large-group structure is challenging. This paper considers how technology can be leveraged to promote assessment for learning in higher education. Drawing on data from students, instructors, and recommendations from an external instructional design consultant, this paper documents the process of pairing technology and assessment for learning within a large-group pre-service teacher education course at one Canadian institution.

Specifically, the site for this research was a required module for teacher candidates at the Faculty of Education, Queen's University in Ontario. The Assessment and Evaluation Module (AEM) was one of four components of a larger course on *Concepts in Teacher Education*. The module was developed in response to recommendations by the Ontario College of Teachers (2004) for greater emphasis on assessment education in pre-service programs. Given the increased reliance on assessment and testing in Ontario schools, the goal of the module was to enhance the development of teacher professional knowledge on issues of assessment language, policy, theory (i.e., concepts of assessment for and of learning), and large-scale testing. The purpose of the module was to enable teacher candidates to examine the inherent complexities of (a) measuring change in learning, (b) making judgments about individual growth and achievement, and (c) making justifiable decisions about grading. The module consisted of two streams, one for elementary teacher candidates (PROF 150) and the other for secondary (PROF 155), and involved nine hours of lecture-based instruction spanning a three-week period. It was first offered in the fall of 2006 with enrollment of approximately 700 students divided evenly between the two streams.

Members of the Assessment and Evaluation Group (AEG), responsible for the module's design and implementation, assumed a developmental-orientation and anticipated continual modification and improvements to course structure and content. In order to inform changes for the second year iteration of the module, members of the AEG undertook an evaluation of the module's first year implementation. One of the central aims of the evaluation was to examine the use of technology to support learning and, in particular, to evaluate the adoption of assessment for learning principles within this context.

This paper presents findings from the module's first-year evaluation as they relate to the use of technology in supporting AFL. In order to contextualize these results, this paper begins with an overview of the instructional design of the AEM followed by a description of the evaluation framework and evaluation plan. Recommendations for the improvement of the web-based component of the module are then highlighted. These recommendations are offered to provide practical suggestions for readers so that they may evaluate their own web-based platforms and improve their use of technology in support of AFL. The paper concludes with a discussion related to areas for continued research.

INSTRUCTIONAL DESIGN OF THE AEM

In the first phase of development, members of the AEG conducted an extensive needs analysis to inform content selection for the module. According to these findings, course content was organized around four main units for assessment literacy development including: (a) assessment language and policy, (b) assessment theory and practice (specifically concepts of assessment for and of learning), (c) links between assessment and learning theories, and (d) large-scale testing programs. Initial module development was focused on identifying and collecting appropriate learning resources and initiating a web-presence for the course. The intent of the website component was to provide beginning learners with level-appropriate materials related to the four main units. These materials served as a primary support for teacher candidates as they engaged in learning about assessment. Further, in an effort to leverage technology to promote AFL, the website was designed to provide teacher candidates with feedback on their learning. A prior-learning assessment was available which served as a diagnostic assessment whereby teacher candidates could identify areas for further study and focus throughout the module. Each of the four units of study had open learning activities so that candidates could practice their learning throughout the module. Finally, at the end of each unit of study was a formative multiple-choice quiz targeting key concepts, which provided candidates with instant feedback on their learning. In addition to the website being used as a course support, the site was also seen as a resource for teacher candidates once they had completed the module and started their careers as teachers. Given the developmental approach towards the module, it was anticipated that the website would continue to evolve in response to teacher candidate feedback and to developments in the field of assessment and evaluation.

The instructional design of the initial iteration of the module was grounded in a self-regulated learning approach. Teacher candidates (TC) were required to attend lectures in a large auditorium and complete six learning tasks within a three-week period in order to pass the compulsory module. The six tasks involved: a) completing a multiple choice prior-learning assessment, b) setting personal learning goals based on the results of their prior-learning assessment, c) establishing a personal learning plan, d) selecting appropriate content from the website to address individual learning needs, e) completing a multiple choice summative assessment with a minimum score of 80%, and f) submitting a final assignment (selected from a range of options). The design and ordering of the six tasks was intended to scaffold learners through the self-regulated learning process by drawing on AFL principles.

The module endeavored to reflect newer notions of assessment by bringing together principles of assessment for learning with assessment of learning (AOL). Conventional notions focus on assessment as a mechanism of certification, accreditation, accountability, and summative measurement of learning (i.e., AOL). Although a necessary component of education, this narrow conceptualization generally fails to leverage assessment as a tool for learning because information gained from assessment comes too late to inform the learning process (Shepard, 2000). Newer notions of assessment argue for an integrative approach where assessment is regularly interspersed with instructional activities and learners are actively encouraged to self-monitor their learning (Taras, 2002). This reconceptualization of assessment represents a blended approach of AFL and AOL.

Empirical evidence supports the influence of including AFL within course design with typical effect sizes achieved for interventions of this nature ranging between 0.4 and 0.7 (Black & Wiliam, 1998). AFL strategies can be understood to fall into two broad categories. The first involves methods focused on making learning and assessment explicit to students (e.g., presenting learning outcomes in advance and sharing assessment criteria). The second category aims to promote learner autonomy, e.g., having learners set personal learning goals, chart learning paths and negotiate assignment requirements (James & Pedder, 2006). Although instructors have generally become quite proficient at making learning and assessment explicit for students, promoting learner autonomy is more challenging (James & Pedder, 2006). It was this latter category of AFL methods that the design team of the AEM sought to leverage in support of learners' self-regulated learning processes through the use of a computer based self-assessment tools and online open-ended learning activities.

EVALUATION FRAMEWORK

A developmental-orientation was used as the central framework throughout the evaluation process to compliment the developmental design of the AEM. This framework was further supported by a participatory approach. Developmental evaluation utilizes an indeterminate approach to evaluation planning and recognizes that goals and outcomes are not pre-set but rather evolve as an evaluation unfolds (Patton, 1997). In this way, a developmental approach allows the evaluation to be responsive to emerging circumstances, new information, and changing stakeholder needs. The flexibility in this approach was thought to more fully capture the complexities inherent to the module's first year implementation in which changes constantly occur. The evaluation also employed a participatory approach involving collaboration with various stakeholders (i.e., two instructors, teaching assistants, and the Faculty's Associate Dean) throughout the evaluation planning phase. This approach led to an iterative planning process further complimenting the developmental orientation (Cousins & Earl, 1992).

EVALUATION PLAN

As an initial starting point for the evaluation, the module content, requirements, and structure were reviewed by the evaluation team. A curriculum mapping process was used to identify areas in which structure, content, and requirements overlapped. This process led to the identification of gaps amongst module elements. Subsequently, interviews were conducted with the two instruc-

tors and with the Associate Dean of the Faculty. These interviews focused specifically on areas of the module that were perceived as challenging or problematic. This data provided the basis for structuring evaluative questions and led to the development of an evaluation plan. Once agreed upon by team members, the questions were forwarded to the two instructors and the Associate Dean to ensure that the evaluation questions fully captured their concerns about the module. Revisions to the questions were made based on this stakeholder feedback. Once the evaluation questions were established, the evaluation team created an evaluation plan which identified for each evaluation question the source of evidence (i.e., teacher candidates, instructors, teaching assistants, etc.) and the proposed data collection method (i.c., focus group, survey, etc.). In addition, the evaluation questions were thematically categorized as a means of organizing the evaluation. These initial broad thematic categories included: impact, assignments, website, large-group format, teaching assistants, and student support. The evaluation plan was forwarded to stakeholders for feedback and based on their comments changes were made to the evaluation plan.

The evaluation occurred over a four month period and involved three forms of data collection: (a) three focus groups, (b) a survey of teacher candidates' experiences in the AEM, and (c) a website review from an external educational technologist. Each focus group was 45 minutes in duration and conducted by two members of the evaluation team. The first focus group involved the two instructors, the second included instructors and three teaching assistants, and the third focus group was limited to the three teaching assistants. Focus group questions targeted the thematic evaluation categories of: assignments, website, large-group format, and teaching assistants. Questions related specifically to their perceptions on the effectiveness and challenges in each of these areas. Results from the focus groups were analyzed using a standard theme analysis strategy (Patton, 2002).

Transcriptions of the three focus groups were imported into *Atlas.ti* software to enable coding and analysis of qualitative data. Initial codes were derived from the thematic categories of the evaluation questions. Upon reading through the transcripts, additional codes were created to more accurately classify data. Initially, the following 14 codes were used: assessment for Learning (AFL); assignments; content; module structure; impact and engagement; instructors' perceptions; interaction/contact with teacher candidates; large-group format; lectures; links between in-class and online; student supports; teaching assistants' perceptions; teaching assistants; and website. After the first level analysis, some of the co-occurring codes were collapsed into broader codes with redundant codes eliminated. For example, given the high degree of co-occurrence between "large-group format" and "module structure", these codes were collapsed into the code "large-group format". As the codes "instructors' perceptions" and "teaching assistants' perceptions" did not have any distinct data (i.e. data co-occurred across other code categories), these codes were eliminated. This paper is specifically concerned with data coded as: assessment for learning, large-group format, links between in-class and online, and website.

The survey of teacher candidates' experiences with the AEM was administered online. The survey was constructed with feedback from stakeholders and consisted of 20 items that considered demographics, impact, assignments, website design and utility, and support mechanisms. All items were quantitative with the exception of the final question: "please provide any additional comments that you feel may help improve the Assessment and Evaluation Module for future teacher candidates". Further, 9 of the 20 items used a Likert-scale format. A pilot was conducted with 10 teacher candidates who were conveniently selected based on their enrollment in an elective assessment course. Modifications were made to items based on feedback from the pilot trial.

All teacher candidates enrolled in the 2006-2007 pre-service teacher education programs at Queen's University who completed the Assessment and Evaluation Module were invited to participate in the survey via an e-mail request (N=674). A total of 170 teacher candidates responded to the survey resulting in a 25.2% response rate. Results were electronically collated for all respondents. Quantitative survey data were analyzed using SPSS statistical software. Frequencies and descriptive statistics including mean, standard deviation, skewness, and kurtosis values were computed where appropriate for each survey item. Analysis of variance (multi-way) was conducted for each of the Likert-based items. Factors for ANOVAs were derived based on the demographic section of the survey and included groupings of gender, age, teaching division (i.e., primary/junior, Grades 1-6 or intermediate/senior, Grades 7-12), and level of technology usage. As an exploratory approach was used in this analysis, all factors were included for all ANOVAs conducted. A Tukey post-hoc test was used to discern significant results from omnibus ANOVAs. Significant scores were based on a probability value of 0.05.

In response to findings from the focus groups and teacher candidate survey, a senior educational technologist with extensive experience in higher education contexts was commissioned to review the module's web-based component. The educational technologist systematically analyzed each page of the website and identified areas for improvement. A report was submitted to the evaluation team that included detailed comments and recommendations about content organization, presentation, website structure, and navigation. Findings from the three data sources ultimately led to significant revisions to the module's web-based component and its promotion of AFL principles.

EVALUATION FINDINGS AND RECOMMENDATIONS

In this section, we report evaluation results solely related to the use of technology within the module. Hence, three central findings are discussed that impact the way in which AFL was promoted via the module's web-based component. Specifically these three findings relate to: (a) the perception of the website as informational rather than instructional, (b) access and navigability of website, and (c) use of website in supporting AFL.

Finding 1: The web-based component of the AEM was viewed primarily as a course-specific informational resource.

This finding was consistently observed between the two data sets (i.e., focus group and survey). Focus group participants agreed that the website was the principal resource (outside of class lectures) for teacher candidates and provided information on both course structure (timetable, requirements, and assignment information) and course content (resources on assessment and evaluation). Further, several participants commented on the quality of information provided on the website, indicating that they felt the site was a strong resource base for novice teachers to explore issues in assessment and evaluation. When asked to indicate the value of various website components on their learning, teacher candidates highlighted the informational units of study over instructional activities, self-assessments, and feedback mechanisms. This suggests that the website was perceived as a course-based tool for information on course content, assignments, and policies. There was little indication that teacher candidates were using the website beyond the confines of the course or that they perceived the website as a pedagogical tool to help promote AFL.

In addition, teacher candidates were asked how many times they had visited the website to further explore and/or clarify issues in assessment and evaluation since completing the AEM. Based on the 158 respondents, 89 (56.3%) indicated that they had never returned to the website. Of the remainder, 29.1% reported that they had visited the website once or twice, 13.3% indicated three to five times, and only 1.3% reported that they had used the website more than five times. A significant, negative skewness value of -1.53 and a significant positive kurtosis value of 1.70 were observed for this item reinforcing that the vast majority of respondents had not visited the website since the completion of the module. The analysis of variance for this item revealed no significant differences between groups. Again these data point towards the website being perceived as a course-specific informational resource rather than a site for instruction and learning feedback.

Finding 2: Navigability of the web-based component of the AEM could be improved especially to assist students with lower technology proficiency. This is viewed as critical if the web-based component is promoted as a key to the implementation of AFL in large-group formats.

Navigability refers to the ease with which users can locate information of interest and move around the website (e.g. revisiting pages visited during a session). Reactions to the navigability of the website were mixed. Although 42% (72 of 170) rated the site as 'easy' or 'very easy' to navigate and only 28 individuals indicated a need for support in website navigation, this result is somewhat discouraging. As the primary resource for the module, the structure and organization on the site must accommodate the full range of learners enrolled. The fact that 29% of respondents were neutral and 22% rated the site as 'difficult' or very difficult to navigate underlines a need to rethink the layout of the site. A further caveat is that questionnaire respondents could be considered as members of a special sub-group of the general student population who possess a more developed set of technology skills as data were collected via an online (i.e., technology-based) survey instrument; a total of 61% of respondents indicated that they frequently used meta-search tools to retrieve information from the Internet with an additional 33.7% indicating that they have used information located on the web to complete course assignments. Unsurprisingly, the analysis of variance and post hoc revealed that teacher candidates with greater Internet proficiency found the website easier to navigate.

Concerns related to the website and the heavy reliance on technology were also raised in focus group sessions. There was repeated concern for teacher candidates who had minimal prior experience with technology and experienced difficulty navigating the website. Further, several comments regarding the structure of the website and difficulties in retrieving information were documented. One teaching assistant commented that "the resource material that was on the Internet was really good, but it was just hard to access". In addition to navigability, there were concerns about functionality of the prior-learning assessment and summative assessment. As completion of these tests were initially outlined as required components in order to pass the module, the fact that teacher candidates encountered technical difficulties led to confusion about expectations and what they were required to do. Further, a lack of access to the self-assessment tool could well have hindered the quality of learning for teacher candidates as they lacked guidance in determining assessment literacy levels at the on-set of instruction.

Finding 3: Significant gaps in the implementation of AFL were identified by focus group participants and teacher candidates. The web-based component of the AEM could be used more effectively to promote principles of AFL.

Based on focus group data, there were specific concerns regarding how well the assessment for learning approach was employed during the first module implementation. One instructor commented that, "if we talk about assessment for learning as having three main components: self assessment, peer assessment, and instructor assessment, then we were heavy on the self assessment, we were light on the peer assessment, and we were almost non-existent on the instructor assessment". However, given the structured emphasis on self-assessment, having teacher candidates understand that their learning in this module was self-regulated and based on what they were seeking to learn about assessment was perceived as a significant challenge. One of the professors commented that "the biggest challenge was getting them [teacher candidates] to understand the 'self' piece". The concern over the AFL orientation was also identified by teaching assistants who added that when marking the final assignments, they tried to provide descriptive feedback on student learning but this was problematic because: (a) the number of assignments that needed marking (i.e., approximately 175 assignments per teaching assistant); (b) they had little interaction with teacher candidates and were only basing judgments on their submitted assignments; and (c) they had no sense of whether or not the feedback was meaningful to teacher candidates in helping them deepen their thinking about assessment and evaluation issues. This final point was highlighted as being essential for promoting an AFL approach by "completing the learning loop".

To gain the perspective of teacher candidates on issues related AFL implementation and effectiveness, candidates were asked to rate the degree to which five components of AFL (questioning during lectures, focused feedback, clear assessment and learning criteria, self-assessment tools, and peer-assessment opportunities) were incorporated within the module using a five-point scale (1=almost never, 2=seldom, 3=sometimes, 4=often, 5=very often). The components of *questioning* during lectures, clear assessment and learning criteria, and *self-assessment tools* received mean scores positioned in between response options, 'sometimes' and 'often' (3.54, 3.36, and 3.32, respectively). The components, *focused feedback provided* and *peer-assessment opportunities*, scored lower with mean values between 'seldom' and 'sometimes' (2.43 and 2.19, respectively). These data parallel the concerns expressed by focus group participants with instructor and peer feedback identified as particularly problematic to implement in large-group settings. However, technology was identified as a potential aid to improving the implementation of AFL in the module. Specific suggestions from focus group data included creating a: (a) peer-based discussion board, (b) question forum for teacher candidate's to interact with professors, and (c) technology resource lab that provides a space for candidate's to use computer-based resources and complete prior-learning and summative assessments alongside teaching assistant support and feedback.

Recommendations from External Review

In response to findings from the focus groups and the teacher candidate survey, an educational technologist was commissioned to review the web-based component to begin to address concerns over the user-friendliness of the website. Specifically the following recommendations were made to increase accessibility, navigability, effectiveness, and use of the AEM website. Recommendations and their rational are grouped into four categories: (a) overall structure, (b) navigability, (c) accessibility, and (d) organization of content.

Overall Structure

Several modifications to the structure and design of the website were suggested to improve page layout and user experience. These included:

- Moving primary menu bar from left margin to the top of page
- Adjusting outer frame colour to match background of webpage
- Minimizing the size of the headers

In all cases these adjustments increased the amount of space that could be dedicated to content presentation. Central concerns in web design are the amount of scrolling required by users and the amount of white space occupying each page. Specially, scrolling refers to the users' movement down a web-page and is commonly measured in screen lengths. White space refers to area of the screen that is clear of text and graphics, most frequently but not limited to the margins on either side of the screen. Achieving a balance between these two design elements is crucial to effective web-page design. Research recommends limiting scrolling to a maximum of two screen lengths to avoid disorientating readers (Lynch & Horton, 2001). This disorienting effect is the consequence of a user's loss of context when navigation buttons are not longer visible on the screen. However, the impact of white space is not so straight forward. Eye tracking studies suggest that the amount of white space on a web-page has both physical and cognitive implications for website users (Johnson, 2007). A lack of white space has been associated with eyestrain; thus, increasing white space has been found to both improve reading speed and comprehension. Providing ample white space reduces cognitive load and when used effectively serves to focus a user's attention on content (Mariger, 2006). Moving the menu bar to the top of the page created screen space that could then be better allocated between content and white space. Adjusting the outer frame colour to match background of the web-pages meant that margin width of each web-page could be further reduced without overburdening users. Finally, minimizing the size of headers on web-pages freed screen space affording the placement of more content in this optimal position.

Navigability

The aim of the following recommendations was to help students identify needed information in a prompt manner and enable easy movement throughout the website. Specifically, the external reviewer highlighted the following areas for amendment:

- Provide a hot-linked table of content so users could easily jump to sections of interest
- Graphic embellishments should be used sparingly and purposefully to signal the presence of hot-links including other web-pages, resources, or portable document files (PDF) documents
- Avoid redundancy in links and clearly mark a link within text with a graphic or underline (where appropriate)

The goal of navigation within a website is to allow users to easily identify and quickly locate information of interest. Given the dynamic nature of the web and diversity of site design, providing users with a consistent approach to navigation facilitates orientation (Lynch & Horton, 2001). Establishing conventions in the format and location of navigation buttons helps accomplish this goal as can the provision of a table of contents.

In addition, graphics can be easily incorporated on websites to signal navigability cues helping users to move between pages. However, although visual markers can be effective in drawing users' attention, they can easily become distracting elements when overused (Lynch & Horton, 2006). Their inclusion should be restricted to purposeful indicators of hotlinks as opposed to superfluous clipart. Such overuse serves to limit the impact they might otherwise lend in terms of emphasizing the presences of additional resources.

Accessibility

The goal of the following recommendations was to ensure accessibility for users with special needs.

The external reviewer provided the following guidelines for improvement towards accessibility:

- Avoid the use of layout tables in the site design
- Provide links to printable versions of website content

Website construction can pose a significant challenge for users dependent upon adaptive technology. Specifically, the use of layout tables for visually impaired users can render a site almost impossible to access (Lynch & Horton, 2001). Individuals with visual impairments commonly rely on software to read web-pages and much of this software reads HTML code in a linear fashion ignoring the divisions of embedded tables often used to separate columns of content. The result would be akin to reading across two columns of the classified section of a news paper. Since the text is read out of sequence, comprehension is greatly reduced.

Further, an underlying principle of web accessibility is the potential to provide content in alternative formats whenever possible (Lynch & Horton, 2001). Many users including those with low technology proficiency prefer to read large amounts of text in hard copy as opposed to on screen. Providing access to PDFs of entire sections of a site can be advantageous for a wide range of users. Preparing such alternative versions for easy download ensures users a comprehensive document of website content. This also affords more control over content presentation as web-page content can be optimized for presentation in print.

Organization of Content

Organizing information in web-format is critical to promoting information use and engaging in meaningful learning. The following recommendations for organizing content were suggested:

- Homepage should begin with a statement of the purpose of the site, contact information, description of website layout and instructions for website use

- Subsequent pages should avoid presenting large blocks of text and strategically chuck information providing links to additional information in PDF format
- Irrelevant and/or redundant information should be eliminated
- Downloadable forms and documents should clearly indicate that they are downloadable
- Terminology should be standardized across site and correct use of terms should be emphasized. For example, a webmaster is commonly the individual to contact in cases of technology malfunction (e.g., page fails to load, broken link, etc.) not for information or guidance on course content.

This is important in large-group formats because students will inevitably have various preferences (reading online versus hardcopy) and levels of technology proficiency.

REDESIGNING TECHNOLOGY FOR LEARNING

Appropriately, the first phase of the redesign process involved incorporating data from across sources and developing a new structure for the website. Informed by the recommendations from the expert reviewer, a new website structure was established. The new structure moved the menu bar to the top of the page, removed large headers and eliminated redundant content. This process served to focus the design team's attention on reorganizing website content leading to the second phase of the redesign process.

The second phase of the design process involved discussions among design team members about the purpose of the website. Since teacher candidates had signaled their value of three units of study (Assessment for learning, Assessment of learning, and Large-scale assessment), these were

defined as a priority for further development. A forth unit entitled *What does learning look like* was also added as a basis for linking assessment practices with contemporary learning theories. A standardized format was developed for these units of study which was intended to improve the transparency of the site as learners could anticipate format consistency between units. Each unit opened with an introduction of the essential objectives of the unit, followed by content with appropriately interspersed graphics and links to further resources. Although somewhat linear in form, this model served to ensure exposure to critical content. Individual learning activities were developed for each unit and answer sheets were provided to scaffold candidates' self-monitoring skills, a crucial aspect an AFL approach.

In addition to changes made in website design and units of study, module developers also reconsidered module expectations. Given the short duration of the module (three weeks) and teacher candidates' responsibilities to other courses, expectations were revised so that candidates could focus their learning on one (or more) unit of study based on personal interest and learning need. This more individualized approach aligned with the self-regulated learning orientation assumed in the module and further promoted principles of AFL.

However, increasing learner autonomy in large-group setting poses addition challenges particularly relating to supporting students in selecting appropriate learning tasks for their individual needs and structuring a learning plan that addresses those needs.

As suggested by Zimmerman (2008), a critical first step in autonomous learning is defining learning needs and setting learning goals. However, the appropriateness of defined learning needs depends to a large extent on learners' ability to assess their current level of knowledge and understanding. Empirical evidence indicates that this is a particularly challenging task for novice learners in any domain as they tend to over estimate their abilities due to deficient metacognitive skills (Kruger & Dunning, 1999). Consequently, the development of a prior-learning assessment that could support candidates through the self-assessment process and point them towards areas for further study was seen as a useful pedagogical strategy.

The twelve item prior-learning assessment was constructed as a scenario based assessment which mapped onto the content of the four units of study. Each item presented a short scenario depicting a central concept with subsequent multiple choice questions. Each unit of study had three scenario questions. Conceptualized as a diagnostic tool, effort was made to include items ranging in cognitive complexity for unit questions. The ICE model was used as a framework for defining the level of cognitive complexity of individual items (Fostaty-Young & Wilson, 2000). This model identifies three broad categories of cognitive complexity: (a) Ideas, (b) Connections, and (c) Extensions. According to the model, at the most simplistic level, questions deal with basic ideas (e.g., names, definitions of terms) and key concepts (e.g., conventions, principles). In the connections level, students are asked to connect ideas and key concepts together and may draw links to their prior knowledge and experience. Finally, extensions level items require students to extrapolate their understanding of a concept to new contexts and propose solutions, offer justification for their position, and evaluate outcomes. Given the nature of the prior-learning assessment as a diagnostic instrument for novice learners, items were limited to the ideas and connections levels. Therefore, each set of three scenarios associated with each of the four units of study included one item at the ideas level and two items intended to assess the candidate's ability to make connections.

In order for the prior-learning assessment to function effectively and help candidates structure a learning plan, candidates were instructed to complete the task at the very beginning of the module. In addition, a key feature of the assessment was that it provided candidates with immediate feedback on their learning. This feedback not only indicated whether the candidate had selected the correct response but also justified incorrect re-

sponses and suggested areas for additional study. The prior learning assessment was mounted in WebCT so that candidates could continue to access it throughout their learning and revisit questions and scenarios as needed. Further, it was anticipated that additional items similar in format would be included at the end of each unit of study and on the summative quiz to maintain congruency in item format. In this way candidates would have extensive exposure to assessment items in preparation for the summative task while simultaneously using AFL principles to scaffold their learning over the three week module.

In order to further support teacher candidates throughout the module, a computer lab was established specifically dedicated to the AEM. Staffed by AEM teaching assistants and equipped with multiple computer stations and assessment resources, this space was envisaged as a one-stop support hub for students. It served to not only provide technical support for students but also an opportunity for instructor/teaching assistant feedback on candidates' learning. The addition of a learning lab was seen as an initial step in addressing concerns over a lack of instructor-student interaction while providing continuous support for low level technology users.

DISCUSSION

Course development is never a one-off event; it requires continuous curricular revisions upon subsequent iterations. Assuming a developmental approach paired with a program of evaluation promotes curricular modifications that address emerging needs. Admittedly novices to the large-lecture format and with limited technology integration experience, the AEG strategically assumed a developmental orientation toward the design of the AEM. As such, plans to formally evaluate successive iterations of the module was anticipated early in the design process with the expectation that recommendations from these evaluations would be integrated (where possible) across module components.

A central aim of the AEG team was to introduce teacher candidates to the notion of assessment as a means for learning. As such, it was imperative that instructors actively modeled and integrated AFL principles within the course. Given the large class size and limited resources, this goal was formidable. However, the utilization of technology was seen as a potential mechanism to facilitate this aim. Through the module evaluation and an external website review, redesign of web-based content and structure moved technology towards learning by supporting AFL. The central change was a reconceptualization of the website from strictly informational to instructional. Learning activities within units of study provided students with immediate feedback on their learning, content was organized to enable students to select appropriate learning areas, and guided self-regulated learning opportunities helped students chart and plan their assessment literacy development. Further, the prior-learning assessment and summative assessment served to benchmark students' growth throughout the module. Embedded within these two assessments were feedback mechanisms that encouraged continued learning and provided content and learning support for students.

The case of the AEM is presented here as an example of course development and evaluation in which technology has been redesigned from a site of information to a site of learning. The bringing together of AFL principles and the functionality of technology seems an area worth pursuing especially in light of increased large-group teaching formats in higher education. However, more research is needed. This case reflects initial modifications but more sophisticated uses of technology and increased diversification of assessment structures within this context are possible.

Further, research is required into the effectiveness of this pairing between assessment theory and technology with an examination of its impact on student learning. Although empirical support for the positive impact of AFL in higher education is fast accumulating (Falchikov, 2003; Kirby & Downs, 2007; Nicol & Macfarlane-Dick, 2006; Rust et al., 2003; Vermunt, 2005), such approaches are typically associated with costly, intensive instructional support (e.g., decreased student-teacher ratio), which few institutions can afford. Technology enhanced alternatives could enable faculty to leverage assessment as a pedagogical tool to enhance learning. Movements in this direction will require that we better understand the impact of various forms of automated feedback mechanisms as well as develop individualized learner tracking systems that integrate AFL procedures. Theoretically, these innovations and developments will allow faculty to effectively and efficiently foster the self-regulated learning skills students require in order successfully engage the emerging knowledge-based economy.

REFERENCES

Black, P., & Wiliam, D. (1998). Assessment and classroom learning. *Assessment in Education*, *5*(1), 7–74. doi:10.1080/0969595980050102

Cousins, B., & Earl, L. (1992). The case for participatory evaluation. *Educational Evaluation and Policy Analysis*, *14*(4), 397–418.

Falchikov, N. (2003). Involving students in assessment. *Psychology Learning & Teaching*, *3*(2), 102–108.

Fostaty-Young, S., & Wilson, R. J. (2000). *Assessment and learning: The ICE approach*. Winnipeg, MB, Canada: Portage and Main Press.

Hargreaves, E. (2005). Assessment for learning? Thinking outside the (black) box. *Cambridge Journal of Education*, *35*(2), 213–224. doi:10.1080/03057640500146880

Hargreaves, E. (2007). The validity of collaborative assessment for learning. *Assessment in Education*, *14*(2), 185–199. doi:10.1080/09695940701478594

James, M., & Pedder, D. (2006). Beyond method: assessment and learning practices and values. *Curriculum Journal, 17*(2), 109–138. doi:10.1080/09585170600792712

Johnson, T. (2007). *Some research and examples of white space in web design.* Retrieved September 15, 2007, from http://www.corporatewebsite.com/articles/some_research_

Kirby, N. F., & Downs, C. T. (2007). Self-assessment and the disadvantaged student: Potential for encouraging self-regulated learning? *Assessment & Evaluation in Higher Education, 32*(4), 475–494. doi:10.1080/02602930600896464

Kruger, J., & Dunning, D. (1999). Unskilled and unaware of it: How difficulties in recognizing one's own incompetence lead to inflated self-assessment. *Journal of Personality and Social Psychology, 77*(6), 1121–1134. doi:10.1037/0022-3514.77.6.1121

Lynch, P., & Horton, S. (2001). *Web style guide* (2nd ed.). Retrieved September 15, 2007, from http://www.webstyleguide.com/ index.html?/sites/site_design.html

Mariger, H. (2006). *Cognitive Disabilities and the Web: Where Accessibility and Usability Meet?* Retrieved October 11, 2007, from http://ncdae.org/tools/cognitive/

Nicol, D. J., & Macfarlane-Dick, D. (2006). Formative assessment and self-regulated learning: A model and seven principles of good feedback practice. *Studies in Higher Education, 31*(2), 199–218. doi:10.1080/03075070600572090

Ontario College of Teachers. (2006). *Foundations of professional practice.* Retrieved April 10, 2009, from http://www.oct.ca/ standards/foundations.aspx

Patton, M. Q. (1997). *Utilization-focused evaluation: The new century text* (3rd ed.). Thousand Oaks, CA: Sage.

Patton, M. Q. (2002). *Qualitative research and evaluation methods* (3rd ed.). Thousand Oaks, CA: Sage.

Rust, C., Price, M., & O'Donovan, B. (2003). Improving students' learning by developing their understanding of assessment criteria and processes. *Assessment & Evaluation in Higher Education, 28*(2), 147–164. doi:10.1080/02602930301671

Shepard, L. A. (2000). The role of assessment in a learning culture. *Educational Researcher, 29*(7), 4–14.

Taras, M. (2002). Using assessment for learning and learning from assessment. *Assessment & Evaluation in Higher Education, 27*(6), 501–510. doi:10.1080/0260293022000020273

Vermunt, J. V. (2005). Relations between student learning patterns and personal and contextual factors and academic performance. *Higher Education, 49*, 205–234. doi:10.1007/s10734-004-6664-2

Weber, L. E. (1999). Survey of the main challenges facing higher education at the millennium. In Hirsch, W. Z., & Weber, L. E. (Eds.), *Challenges Facing Higher Education at the Millennium* (pp. 3–17). Phoenix, AZ: American Council on Education and the Oryx Press.

Zimmerman, B. J. (2008). Investigating self-regulation and motivation: Historical background, methodological developments, and future prospects. *American Educational Research Journal, 45*(1), 166–183. doi:10.3102/0002831207312909

This work was previously published in International Journal of Information Communication Technologies and Human Development, Volume 2, Issue 4, edited by Susheel Chhabra and Hakikur Rahman, pp. 42-54, copyright 2010 by IGI Publishing (an imprint of IGI Global).

Chapter 16
Impact of Podcasts as Professional Learning:
Teacher Created, Student Created, and Professional Development Podcasts

Kathleen P. King
University of South Florida, USA

ABSTRACT

Until now, research on podcasting in education mostly examined teacher created podcasts in K-12 and higher education. This paper explores podcasts in professional learning across several genres of podcasts. Using a popular typology of podcasts, teacher created, student created and professional development podcasts (King & Gura, 2007), this paper compares, contrasts and reveals the potential of multiple educational contexts and instructional strategies, formative instructional design, interdisciplinary strategies, formal and informal learning, and effective uses of data gathering methods. The significance of the study extends from not only the extensive reach of the data gathering and production, but also the robust research model, formative and dynamic instructional design for staff development and recommendations for podcasting research strategies.

INTRODUCTION AND NEED

Since 2004, Internet-based new media formats have soared. Prolific Internet use has generated public desires and expectations to be *content creators*. Opportunities such as political and personal blogs and independent podcasts of all flavors as well as ever- popular YouTube® videos flash across users' screens and minds, creating the expectation of self as a new media communicator (Walch & Lafferty, 2006). It is through the recent advent of convenient and free Web 2.0 technologies, such as blogs, podcasts and vlogs, and Free Open Source Software (FOSS) (Rajendran & Venkataraman, 2009) that people of all ages and backgrounds are claiming their place and voice on the Web (Frontline, 2008). The great value of podcasting, a new media technology, for education is the ease of custom and inexpensive design, truly flexible, "anytime, anywhere" delivery format.

DOI: 10.4018/978-1-4666-0047-8.ch016

Since 2005, anyone with access to a computer, Internet and a $10 microphone can freely record, edit, and distribute audio content worldwide. Similarly, anyone with Internet access can hear these archived digital audios on computers or mobile devices, 24/7.

Widespread social and instructional adoption of podcasting has occurred since 2006, including adoption for formal and informal learning. With this increased use, educators and researchers need greater understanding of podcast-related instructional applications, data gathering opportunities, impact, scalability and scope of reach, instructional design, and research opportunities (eSchool News, 2008; King & Gura, 2007; Williams, 2008). For example, there are numerous free data gathering resources to couple with podcast use and yet no mention in the literature as to how schools might use it to demonstrate impact of their programs and services or instructors for formative improvement of curriculum, let alone recommended strategies for educators' reporting of them. Research studies may also provide recommendations for the design of additional action- based research and inquiry in robust and systematic ways (Devaney, 2008).

By analyzing findings from three related podcast studies, this paper provides a macro research perspective and recommendations in these areas. The work collectively addresses the impact of podcasts on professional learning and uses King and Gura's podcast typology (2007) as a framework for comparison and differentiation. This paper presents findings, discussion and interpretation of results for the following research questions: (1) What is the use and potential for podcasting in multiple educational contexts? (2) What instructional strategies are used in the podcast? (3) How is formative instructional design utilized in the podcasts? (4) What interdisciplinary strategies are used? (5) What is learned about uses and formats of formal and informal learning? And (6) What effective uses of data gathering methods are recommended from these studies? The popular typology of podcasts, teacher-created, student-created and professional development podcasts is used in three studies examining the following productions: UEGE, TTPOD/PFT, and DLPOD (see Figure 1).

Figure 1. The three cases: podcasts studied

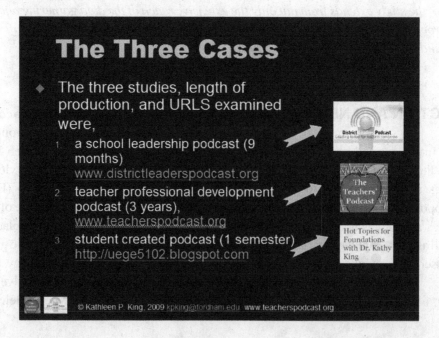

THEORETICAL BASES

Major theoretical underpinnings of this research include formative evaluation and continuous improvement of instructional design, research design and methods, podcasting and new media as instruction, podcasting typology, and informal learning.

Formative Evaluation Informing Instructional Design

Critical to the approach of this study is that educators can formatively design and evaluate instruction (Caffarella, 2001). Continuous improvement via data gathering, analysis and interpretation provides powerful means to proactively and dynamically chart the course of successful learning as many educators have demonstrated (Jonassen et al., 2003; Wlodkowski & Ginsberg, 1995). Broader and substantial research methodologies frame our thinking for instructional design, inquiry and data collection. These core frameworks include Denzin and Lincoln (2008a, 2008b) on qualitative research, Gall, Borg, and Gall (1996) on statistics and research design, and Hinchey (2008) on action research.

Research Methods (as a Theoretical Frame)

With action research as a vital model of research in many teacher education programs today, instructors engaging in instructional improvement using podcasts may go further and conduct action research inquiries. Even if research is not formally pursued, educators collect data and use student responses in informal research for guiding instructional design (Denzin & Lincoln, 2008; Hinchey, 2008). This article examines three different educational podcasting studies, therefore understanding the framework of research methodologies and decision making are important foundations for our discussion (Gall, Borg, & Gall, 1996).

In the field of instructional technology among diverse populations, action (Hinchey, 2008) and mixed-methods research (Creswell, 1998; Glaser & Strauss, 1967; Tashakkori & Teddlie, 1998) have been effective strategies across numerous studies (Jonassen et al., 2003). Analyzing the studies at hand for their research methods provides greater understanding of what educators currently do for data gathering and research in educational podcasting. In addition, it provides a basis for recommendations for more systematic and deeper inquiry, which can improve student learning, and advance the field's future.

Podcasting and Instruction

Podcasting distributes digital recordings via Really Simply Syndication–feeds (RSS-feeds). That is, individuals record audio content with computers or digital recorders, post it on the Internet on a publicly available server, create XML script RSS-feed to string it together and deliver the episodes. Teachers and students, now podcasters, visit the podcast directories on the Internet and add their information to the searchable databases (King, 2008). Potential listeners visit the search for topics on the web or visit the directories, review descriptions, select and directly listen to or download the files.

Expert authors carefully and specifically applied the technical definition of podcasts to their work (Walch & Lafferty, 2006). They define podcasts as audio (and video) new media products hosted on servers and scripted with an XML/RSS feed, utilizing push technologies. This definition distinguishes podcasts from web-based audio or video posts which are not syndicated, cannot be "subscribed" to, nor automatically delivered to listeners/learners.

Listeners may also port podcasts over to portable devices such as MP3 players, iPods, or some cell phones for mobile convenience (Richardson, 2006; Williams, 2008). This option allows listeners to choose not only *when* they want to listen, but also *where*. The rich podcasting medium reaches most people with Internet access; therefore, it provides a platform for instruction from diverse perspectives.

Essential to framing our research, design and teaching efforts are understandings of education in a pluralistic society (Greene, 1993), culturally responsive teaching (Wlodkowski & Ginsberg, 1995), and multiculturalism (Spring, 1997). When our learning space spans the globe and all 24 hours, learners may engage with people from any lifestyle who have access, thereby eliminating traditional boundaries of time, space, geography and class (Rajendran & Venkataraman, 2009). Therefore, greater skill in understanding and communicating with people different from ourselves emerges.

Podcasting Typology

King and Gura's 2007 podcasting typology provides an effective means to differentiation among and compare educational podcasts. *Podcasting for Teachers: Using a New Technology to Revolutionize Teaching and Learning* (2007) identifies three major genres of educational podcasts: *teacher-created, student-created* and *professional development podcasts.*

Teacher-created podcasts represent those developed by teachers, especially for instructional purposes. These podcasts may include lectures or presentations recorded and posted as an episode in a class or subject series. In a more creative pedagogical style, teachers may specifically plan, design and create podcasts for other instructional purposes. For example, they may develop supplementary classroom materials, distance learning, out of class or homework materials, tutorials, extension activities, etc.

Student created podcast are often developed as part of classroom assignments. From k-16 to workplace training and doctoral studies, they may be used in a plethora of ways. For instance, some teachers provide students opportunities to capture, archive and distribute their work as web-based audio or video projects, interviews, role playing or performances, historical narratives, presentations, simulations, etc. Indeed, creativity in student podcasting has been most widely seen in k-12 education, but is starting to emerge in higher education, albeit slowly. This trend may be due to different curriculum, professional development opportunities and classroom time. Nonetheless, with the growing number of Millennials or Digital Natives (Prensky, 2001) already graduating from our colleges, higher education needs to transform content expectations to be larger and in varied demanding media. Furthermore, we need post-secondary education to prepare students to be effective communicators, inventors, and analysts of digital media to guide our future. Assignments integrating critical thinking in the content area and developing innovative, creative, research grounded media exemplify the relevant learning possible with podcasts.

Professional development (PD) podcasts may be created by a variety of individuals, and organizations. These podcasting producers and hosts may include professional associations, teacher educators/professors, staff developers, schools, colleges and universities, non-profit organizations, or government agencies, and certainly teachers (that is "by teachers, *for* teachers"). Podcast-delivered PD affords much greater choice of time and space for engaging in professional learning. Indeed, the freedom shocks many educators and professionals, as they realize not only can they choose what they want to learn, but schedule it at whim or will, and much of it is free. This new generation of PD is not much like the mandatory training or staff development we sat through previously. Instead, PD on demand allows the lifelong learner to be *in control*.

All of these forms of educational podcasting create a growing archive which is freely available. Individuals and organizations alike may select formal and informal staff development resources from this rich storehouse of content. Learning must be selected with a critical eye for credentials and expertise of the presenter. In addition, the relevance of content and integration of research, theory and practice are of prime importance for educational podcasts. However, examining these characteristics creates a vibrant, relevant opportunity for situated learning including critical thinking, lifelong learning and 21st-century learning skills (King & Gura, 2007; Partnership for 21st Century Skills, 2004; Richardson, 2006; Williams, 2006). Podcasting pursued in a contextualized, learner-centered manner can be a powerful platform for education.

Formal and Informal Learning

Familiar typologies of learning include formal, nonformal and *informal learning* (Coombs, 1989). By definition, informal learning is more learner-centered, goal oriented, and flexible. Informal learning's focus on context and learner is inherent to the possibilities of the approach (Schugurensky, 2000). What distinguishes informal learning is the learners' independence and connection to the contexts of daily life, including work (Livingstone, 1999; Schugurensky, 2000). The fields of adult learning and teacher practice have done much to research (Argyris & Schon, 1974), codify (Tough, 1971), and build awareness (Dewey, 1938; Livingstone, 1999; Polanyi, 1967; Tough, 1971) of this area. Instructional technologies such as new media used for professional development provide more rich opportunities for informal learning access, use and research. Yet despite the trends of social adoption and the research opportunities, educational research has been slow to wake to this sleeping giant.

RESEARCH METHOD

This research used a cross-case, case study model, in a mixed-methods approach (Glaser & Strauss, 1967; Merriam, 1997). The case study analyzes research approaches, instructional technology innovation, and adoption. Additionally, the researcher has been podcasting for three years and thereby can be considered an expert participant observer (Creswell, 1998). She provides insight into development, use and opportunities for technology, context, and meaning of new media.

Specifically, this study was a quantitative-qualitative-quantitative sequential design (Tashakkori & Teddlie, 1998). In a Sequential Mixed Methods Analysis (SMMA), the study used 5/7 stages outlined by Onwuegbuzie and Teddlie (2003): data reduction, display, transformation, consolidation, comparison and integration. Data gathering methods included primary document examination and evaluation, collecting statistical data of podcast listener use from servers, hosting services, and statistical third-party services, blog comments, email comments, research articles and reports about the projects, website reviews, content from social networking sites, field notes, observations, and podcast directory rankings and links. Data analysis is tabulation, frequencies, and constant comparison for emergent themes pursued until theoretical saturation (Glaser & Strauss, 1967).

The three studies and length of production examined were, (1) a school leadership podcast (9 months), (2) teacher professional development podcast (3 years), and (3) student created podcast (1 semester). Figure 2 provides a comprehensive illustration of the analysis strategy. It reveals the three cases, and the sequence of data collection, and analysis.

Table 1 provides the reader with the details and table of information gathered for each podcast series. It shows the categories and results used for this study. It is provided here not only to reveal the early stages of data, but also as a model of data gathering and data display (Onwuegbuzie & Teddlie, 2003) for researchers and podcasters who desire to replicate or scaffold the methods presented in this article.

Figure 2. Analysis strategy overview

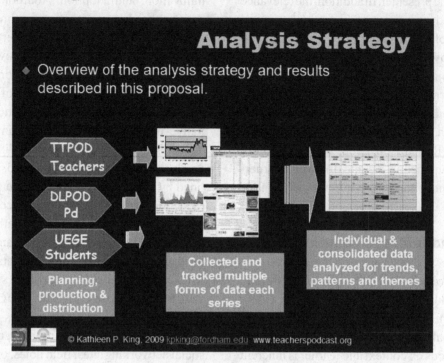

Table 1. Comparison educational podcast research

Podcast/Study	Years	Typology (K&G)	New Media Used	Stats Tools	Other Data	Research Methods
UEGE 5102 (Foundations class)	2008 (Jan-May)	Student - created	Podcast Blog Discussion Board Video	Host-Libsyn TTPOD PodPRESS	Blackboard Survey Focus group Essay	Mixed-Methods Action Research
TTPOD and PFT (Teachers Podcast™ and Podcast for Teachers ™)	(8/05-7/08-present)	Teacher -created Professional Development	Podcast Blog Discussion Board Facebook Frappr e-Mail Call-in Web-voice	Feedburner Hosts (2) Frappr.com Site counter Directories Google Analytics StatCounter PODPress Servers	Blog counts Blog posts e-Mail content Survey Focus group (NECC) Facebook	Mixed-Methods
DLPOD (District Leaders Podcast ™)	(10/07-7/08-present)	Professional Development	Podcast Website e-Mail Call-in	Feedburner Host-Libsyn Site counter Directories Google Analytics	Focus groups StatCounter Clients PODPress Server	Quantitative

FINDINGS: ANALYSIS AND DISCUSSION

Mixed methods research and action research were the predominate models describing the research methods used by the podcasts examined. Because so much data are available in quantitative format, when fully configured and accessed, many people emphasize listenership. However, many early, non-educational podcasters (2005-2007) had a strong sense of audience and rely heavily on qualitative data. When a mixed method is used, it provides a fuller realm of inquiry. Action research provides a dynamic interaction with context, learning and development. Examining Figure 2 reveals each study using a different approach: quantitative research, mixed methods, and combined mixed-methods approach for action research.

Findings and Preliminary Analysis

Perusal of the data revealed a more varied educational contexts that might be expected. Based on the podcast series descriptions, purpose, show notes, and review of their program format many indicators were found. The settings included: staff development, direct learner instruction, independent continuing professional learning, teacher education, and student research. That is, the two broad groups of users, educators and students, used the podcasts in different settings (and in different ways to be discussed later). Specifically, educators and school leaders used podcasts for their professional development through formal efforts by their schools or in degree study, but also in their informal continuing professional development. In addition, students used podcasts in completing lessons by direct instruction: as they were instructed to create or listen to a podcast, or as a solution to find additional information.

Educational podcasters were able to incorporate multiple instructional strategies in even one podcast episode. This finding was again more complex than may be expected, but encouraging

because of the possibilities for further development. Examples of incorporating new media in empowering formats for underrepresented constituencies examples include, but are not limited to, design formats of small group dialogue, peer learning, peer review, learner created media, class presentations which are designed as global resources and instructor created media; and genres of: critical reflection, historical narrative, debate, first person narrative, storytelling, performances, and role playing. These innovative educators were keenly aware of being able to use the multiple instructional strategies in order to reach a wider range of multiple learning styles and to deliver the message in multiple modes (King, 2008; Kolb, 1984; Williams, 2008).

Educators using podcasting of these varied genres demonstrate the value of using multiple instructional strategies to reach students more effectively. This example is from one teacher planning for student created podcasts,

In designing the course I tried to be especially sensitive and accommodating to access and equity issues (King & Griggs, 2000) and not make assumptions about 24/7 access or over familiarity with technology. One way I addressed these variables was to design varied technology options required for assignments (King, 2008).

Emergent Themes

Instructional Design and Monitoring Data. Major patterns in dynamic, learner-centered instructional design through monitoring data for learning benefits were revealed in this study (Caffarella, 2001; Jonassen et al., 2003). Such practices include developing a unique reporting format illustrated in Figure 3. Such reports integrate the research and instructional design thoroughly (action research) with statistics from multiple sources into one tracking file and a one-page snapshot report. The procedure of tracking the podcasts includes periodically gathering and downloading statistics, establishing an electronic filing and backup sys-

Figure 3. Consolidated statistical monthly report

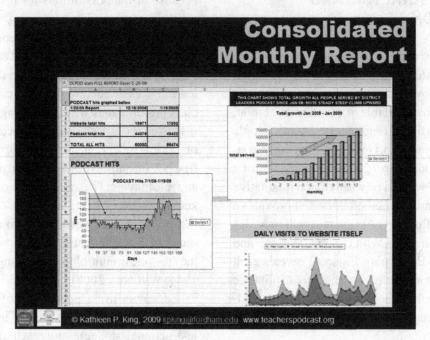

tem to archive the data, consolidating the data, and distributing reports for programmatic and instructional improvement. Certainly such extensive data gathering practices are not the norm with traditional classroom instruction. However, the podcasting distribution system and foresight to utilize it can enable educators to include the practices into their existing instructional design routines.

One project (DLPOD) benefited from extensive prior experience of the producer. This project established a statistical reporting format form the start and the ease of production tracking was significantly different. Unfortunately, to our knowledge, no one in education has discussed or published such documents previously.

- *Instructional Strategies.* The data also demonstrates educational podcasters using interdisciplinary strategies in their creations. While presenting content on educational technology professional development (the TTPOD series) for instance,

podcast hosts also discussed, in-depth, math education, literacy education and financial literacy. Alternatively a sample student created podcast (UEGE) integrated theory, research and practice from health education, government, and philosophy.

In addition, while content standards may be easily and directly addressed with podcasts, other indirect benefits are very valuable for learners. Using these learning activities, instructors can assist learners to experience greater research skills and perspectives, validation, and freedom. Furthermore, dialogue and peer learning are powerful for critical pedagogy as these new media approaches explicitly shift the classroom focus from teacher to learner (King, 2008; Wlodkowski & Ginsberg, 1995). New media enables learners to articulate their views to their classroom and distribute them worldwide if desired (King & Gura, 2007, 2009). Alternatively, instructors can create a password protected mailbox to address learners' needs and sensitive discussions (King & Gura, 2008).

Figure 4. Instructional design for educational podcasting

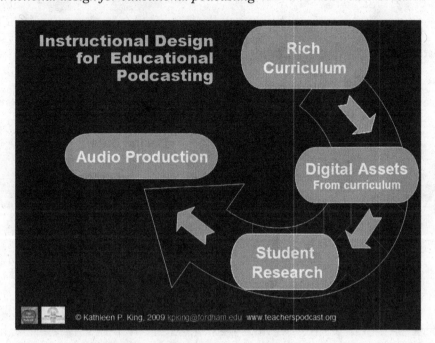

- *Emergent Model of Instructional Design.* In considering the process of instructional design, Figure 4 illustrates a simple model which conceptually and practically guides teaching preparation and practice. While most educators use a required curriculum, they may discover additional digital and supplemental publisher resources. Building upon these and other free or FOSS media (USA Library of Congress Digital media, USA National Archives, Archive. org, Teachertube.com, Schooltube.com, etc) they may scaffold student learning to develop meaningful project based learning assignments. Using the Figure 4 model, assignments focus on student created content, such as student created podcasts, and include the full cycle of curriculum-foundation, student research and student evidence of understanding through digital media.
- *Contexts of Learning and Readiness.* Podcasting for professional learning is pur-

sued both in formal and informal learning settings. Therefore, while millions of downloads have occurred as educators independently decide to pursue their continued learning, some professors use the same podcasts as part of their curriculum, aka listenings, staff developers use them to deliver or extend formal learning (for example, UEGE, TTPOD).

In addition, many young adults are Digital Natives (Prensky, 2001) and use technology to communicate, socialize, and meet most of their needs with it. Undoubtedly, Digital Natives' early adoption of this technology contributes to informal learning podcasts in general like language learning podcasts, catapulting to the tops of the charts (for example, UEGE). Incorporating digital media into formal settings provides not only authentic vehicles for learning, but also provides a model and experience in using podcasts for learning purposes. In fact, in the UEGE and TTPOD data, student essays, survey responses, and listener blog

Figure 5. Podcasting research design model

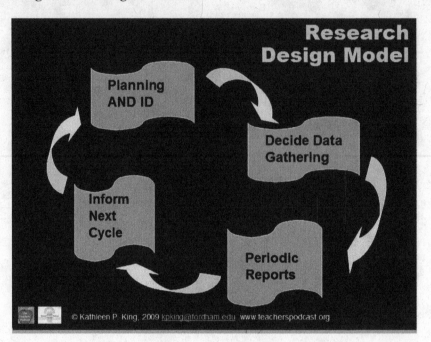

and discussion board posts reveal that learners' formal learning experience using podcast transfer (Caffarella, 2001) to informal learning practices.

Educational Podcasting Research Model

Based on review of the reports and articles, I propose a model for educational podcasting research design, Figure 5. This model includes critical characteristics that aid in research design include (1) integrate research planning and instructional design, (2), decide on data gathering methods, and reevaluate periodically, (3) plan on periodic status/data reports- at least monthly, and (4) use the information for formative evaluation and improvement. This model includes detailed essential elements of sound instructional design (Caffarella, 2001) and research methodology (Denzin & Lincoln, 2008; Gall, Borg, & Gall, 1996).

For example, qualitative data from listeners such as blog comments, emails, VOIP messages, discussion boards, and social networking provide valuable data for instructional design and should be planned for designed, data gathering routines, report protocols and analysis established from the start. TTPOD and DLPOD developed and sought these data sources vigorously to good benefit. Other formal instructional podcasts may be missing opportunities for organized research efforts in gaining direct audience feedback.

- *Podcasting Data Gathering Strategies and Sources.* Extracted from this research, examples of free statistical tracking systems include: Feedburner PRO, PODPress (through the podcast blog site), individual server statistics, Google Analytics™, and varied extents of statistics from individual hosts such as LibSyn, Podomatic, Blubrry. com, etc. Other examples of data gathered at no cost were through the use of online surveys and website statistics trackers (Statcounter, for example) (see Figure 6). When coupled with listener data this information provides podcasters and instructors

Figure 6. Gathering data on podcasting distribution

insight into how many people are listening, to what, and when (day); what content is most popular; geographical location, operating system used, time zone and URL entry point of site visitors and listeners. Such approaches and results were evident in two of the studies reviewed.

Limitations of this Study

All studies have limitations based on their design and participant thresholds. In this research project, the limitations include that although it was a diverse set of educational podcast efforts, those studied were a convenience sample. This choice was necessary to use a unifying framework. Therefore, the author's podcasts were used, albeit this identity is disclosed, documented and described.

Establishing the boundaries of this perspective, one realizes that this is an innovative educator, well versed in instructional technology and focused on learner-centeredness, formative design and instructional research. Such an orientation provides an unusual context, but a rich source for

exploring the potential of educational and research applications of podcasts with current resources. Many fields study the work of innovators in order to chart new approaches (Rogers, 2003).

Further Recommendations

Listeners engaged in using these podcasts for learning gained much from their colleagues' and podcasters' perspectives. The related blog and discussion board postings reveal impressive demonstrations of effort, depth of research, insight, public speaking, global awareness, voice, empowerment and initiative by formal and informal learners. Creating new learning communities is never easy, but using new media to support traditional classrooms can extend learning. In addition, building a virtual community of practice (Lave & Wenger, 1991; Marsick & Watkins, 2001) around a podcast resource can provide support and knowledge for educators who might have little of either. In the case of the podcasts studied here, they have variously used Facebook, blogs and now Twitter to cultivate such communities.

When using podcasts for formal and informal learning, learners are using "new media" for recreational and social uses. This technology has a great excitement and popular validation connected to it at this time. Aside from the benefits of users' flexibility and control of time and space, educators may leverage the new media as an added attraction and incentive to engage reluctant learners. In the process learners also are invested in processes which facilitate instructional improvement. They are exposed to more content; they have access to repetition via rewind and replay functions, and depending on the instructional design perhaps engage in it more, and discover new opportunities for finding and using learning resources.

In these several ways, the podcasts enable us to deftly cultivate 21st-century skills (Partnership for 21st Century Skills, 2004, 2007). Through practice, exploration and extension assignments critical thinking, research strategies, information literacy, problem solving and collaborative learning skills may be easily incorporated (ALA, 2006).

EDUCATIONAL SIGNIFICANCE AND FUTURE RESEARCH

This research has provided greater understanding of what educators do and how they engage in formative instructional design, data gathering and research in educational podcasting. Both the reflective practitioner (Schon, 1987) and teacher as researcher (Hinchey, 2008) are familiar and essential models for professional learning because they are flexible and encourage data-supported choices in their approaches. This study provides significant connections among educational podcasting, research, instructional planning and instructional improvement in the context of continuing professional learning.

Further research is needed to continue to build upon these recommendations for more systematic and deeper inquiry which can improve student learning and advance the field further. Many free resources are available for tracking podcast listeners; educators urgently need to learn how to configure and use these services accurately and to assist in instructional improvement, research and investigation. At this time, podcasters follow this basic process only inconsistently.

CONCLUSION

There are a multitude of opportunities to use podcasting for professional learning beyond the model of course casting which our universities seem to be enamored with today. Teacher-, and student-created, and professional development podcasts provide abundant opportunities for flexible learning which include many additional educational opportunities yet to be extensively explored. This study has revealed how one podcast series from each of three different genres of educational podcasts can extend learning experiences to many instructional strategies and learning contexts. It has revealed an interdisciplinary instructional design approach which can be used in formal and informal learning. Finally, the dynamic instructional design platform seen in these examples offers a foundation for research approaches, methods and recommendations. Still only four years into the world of podcasting, we know educational podcasting has only begun to explore its impact for professional learning.

REFERENCES

ALA (American Library Association). (2006). *Information literacy competency standards for higher education*. Retrieved April 23, 2009, from http://www.ala.org/ala/acrl/acrlstandards/informationliteracycompetency.cfm

Argyris, C., & Schon, D. (1974). *Theory in practice*. San Francisco: Jossey-Bass.

Caffarella, R. (2001). *Planning programs for adult learners* (2nd ed.). San Francisco: Jossey-Bass.

Coombs, P. H. (1989). Formal and nonformal education: Future strategies. In Titmus, C. (Ed.), *Lifelong learning education for adults* (pp. 57–60). Oxford, UK: Pergamon.

Creswell, J. (2003). *Research design* (2nd ed.). Thousand Oaks, CA: Sage.

Denzin, N., & Lincoln, Y. (2008). *Collecting and interpreting qualitative materials*. Thousand Oaks, CA: Sage.

Devaney, L. (2008). Schools lagging in use of digital assessments. *eSchool News, 11*(8), 22.

Dewey, J. (1938). *Experience and education*. New York: Collier Books.

DLPOD. (2008). *District Leaders Podcast*. Retrieved March 28, 2008, from http://blog.districtleaderspodcast.org

eSchool News. (2008). Schools try to reach students via podcast. *eSchool News, 11*(28), 4.

Frontline. (2008). *Growing up online*. Retrieved March 15, 2009, from http://www.pbs.org/wgbh/pages/frontline/kidsonline/

Glaser, B. G., & Strauss, A. L. (1967). *The discovery of grounded theory*. Chicago: Aldine.

Greene, M. (1993). The passions of pluralism. *Educational Researcher, 22*(1), 13–18.

Hinchey, P. (2008). *Action research*. Thousand Oaks, CA: Sage.

Jonassen, D. H., Howland, J., Moore, J., & Marra, R. M. (2003). *Learning to solve problems with technology* (2nd ed.). Upper Saddle River, NJ: Prentice Hall.

King, K. P. (2008). Introducing new media into teacher preparation. *ISTE SIGHC, 3*(4), 4–7.

King, K. P., & Gura, M. (2007). *Podcasting for teachers: Using a new technology to revolutionize teaching and learning*. Charlotte, NC: Information Age Publishing.

Kolb, D. A. (1984). *Experiential learning*. Englewood Cliffs, NJ: Prentice-Hall.

Lave, J., & Wenger, E. (1991). *Situated learning*. Cambridge, UK: University of Cambridge Press.

Livingstone, D. (1999). Exploring the icebergs of adult learning. *Canadian Journal of Studies in Adult Education, 13*(2), 49–72.

Marsick, V. J., & Watkins, K. (1990). *Informal and incidental learning in the workplace*. New York: Routledge.

Merriam, S. (1997). *Qualitative research and case study applications in education*. San Francisco: Jossey-Bass.

Onwuegbuzie, A. J., & Teddlie, C. (2003). A framework for analyzing data in mixed methods research. In Tashakkori, A., & Teddlie, C. (Eds.), *Handbook of mixed methods in social and behavioral research* (pp. 351–383). Thousand Oaks, CA: Sage.

Partnership for 21st Century Skills. (2004). *Learning for the 21st century*. Retrieved April 23, 2009, from http://www.21stcenturyskills.org/images/stories/otherdocs/P21_Report.pdf

Partnership for 21st Century Skills. (2007). *21st century skills standards*. Retrieved May 9, 2009, from http://www.21stcenturyskills.org/documents/ 21st_century_skills_standards.pdf

Polanyi, M. (1967). *The tacit dimension*. New York: Doubleday.

Prensky, M. (2001). Digital natives, digital immigrants. [from http://www.marcprensky.com/writing/]. *Horizon, 9*(5), 1–6. Retrieved April 30, 2009. doi:10.1108/10748120110424816

Rajendran, B., & Venkataraman, N. (2009). FOSS solutions for community development. *International Journal of Information Communication Technologies and Human Development*, *1*(1), 22–32.

Richardson, W. (2006). *Blogs, wikis and podcasts*. Thousand Oaks, CA: Corwin.

Rogers, E. M. (2003). *Diffusion of innovation*. New York: Free Press.

Schön, D. A. (1987). *Educating the reflective practitioner*. San Francisco: Jossey-Bass.

Schugurensky, D. (2000). *The forms of informal learning* (Working Paper #19-2000). Toronto, ON, Canada: Centre for the Study of Education and Work, Department of Sociology and Equity Studies in Education & Ontario Institute for Studies in Education of the University of Toronto.

Shor, I. (1992). *Empowering education*. Chicago: University of Chicago.

Spring, J. (1997). *Deculturalization and the struggle for equality*. New York: McGraw-Hill.

Tashakkori, A., & Teddlie, C. (1998). *Mixed methodology*. Thousand Oaks, CA: Sage.

Tough, A. (1971). *The adult's learning projects learning*. Toronto, ON, Canada: OISE.

TTPOD. (2005). *TTPOD*. Retrieved April 28, 2009, from http://www.teacherspodcast.org

UEGE. (2008). *UEGE 5102 Foundations in American Education*. Retrieved April 28, 2009, from http://uege5102.blogspot.com

Walch, R., & Lafferty, M. (2006). *Tricks of the podcasting masters*. Indianapolis, IN: Que.

Williams, B. (2008). *Educators' guide to podcasting*. Eugene, OR: ISTE.

Wlodkowski, R., & Ginsberg, M. (1995). *Diversity and motivation*. San Francisco: Jossey Bass.

This work was previously published in International Journal of Information Communication Technologies and Human Development, Volume 2, Issue 4, edited by Susheel Chhabra and Hakikur Rahman, pp. 55-67, copyright 2010 by IGI Publishing (an imprint of IGI Global).

Chapter 17
New Trends and Futuristic Information Communication Technologies for Engineering Education

Manjit Singh Sidhu
University Tenaga Nasional, Malaysia

Lee Chen Kang
University Tunku Abdul Rahman, Malaysia

ABSTRACT

Improving and enhancing education is a goal for higher learning institutions that seek to provide better learning techniques, technologies, and educators and generate knowledgeable students to fulfill the needs of industry. A field in need of significant improvement is engineering. One approach is to review the delivery and pedagogies used in the current educational system. This paper examines the problems faced by staff and students in the field of mechanical engineering. In addition, the authors explore new technologies that enhance and promote the learning process.

INTRODUCTION

Education is the driving force of economic and social development in any country (Cholin, 2005; Mehta & Kalra, 2006; Manjit, 2007). Considering this, it is necessary to find ways to make education of good quality, accessible and affordable to all, using the latest technology available (Hattangdi & Ghosh, 2009). The vast availability of tech-

nologies makes it difficult to predict if they could improve the learning process. As such it would be beneficial to research and review the options and benefits of present technologies.

This paper deals with engineering education in higher learning institutions. Our focus is mainly targeted to mechanical engineering education since it was found in the previous studies that some first year undergraduates faced problems in understanding the concepts of engineering mechanics courses (Gramoll, 2001; Katarzyna, 2002;

DOI: 10.4018/978-1-4666-0047-8.ch017

Manjit, 2007; Manjit & Ramesh, 2008; Manjit, Ramesh, & Selvanathan, 2005; Scott, 1996). This subject is chosen because a number of academicians as reported in the literatures found that the main problem faced by students is visualization of dynamic motion of particles or rigid bodies.

COMMON PROBLEMS FACED BY ENGINEERING STUDENTS

Katarzyna (2002) reported the problems that first year undergraduates face while studying the Engineering Mechanics Dynamics course is the difference in understanding with regard to what is being taught in the classroom. Undergraduate students often expect a variety of teaching methods to be used in their learning. Although, in general, the lecture method is a common way of delivering knowledge to students, it treats all students on the same level of the basic acquired knowledge. However, in general most of these students do not bring to the course the same academic preparation (do not have the same motivation, interest, and ability to learn). They come from different disciplines, some from remote regions with limited exposure to modern technology, have varying learning styles, and have different levels of proficiency in material learned at the foundation level. This results in different starting points, progress rates, and ultimately different levels of satisfaction, academic progress, and performance.

However, the aforementioned is not the only reason for the difference among undergraduate student development in the same class. Students enrolled in the same foundation program but from different institutions and cultures are taught varying degrees of basic material, which they are required to know.

Finally, some entry-level undergraduate students do not have very strong grades in science and mathematics which make certain engineering subjects difficult for them to comprehend and this discourages learning from taking place. As a result of this problem, if the lectures are too fast, this set of students may not be able to keep pace with the rest of the class, thus the gap in their knowledge will only get wider as compared to the more advanced students. In this situation, some students are left out, and often the instructors are forced to find alternative methods (for example conducting extra classes) to help these students in understanding the subject matter. Since some students may take more time to understand the problem solving techniques and may require the lesson to be repeated several times before they understand, there is a need to study and understand the availability and benefits of newer technologies that could help them visualize and understand the engineering problems better. The emerging trends and benefits of new technologies are briefly addressed in the next sections.

NEW TRENDS OF ENGINEERING EDUCATION

This section briefly describes present emerging trends in engineering education with regards to technology enhancements. In the current information society, there is an emergence of lifelong learners as the shelf life of knowledge and information decreases (Bhattacharya & Sharma, 2007).

In the past, it could take ample time to find information from traditional libraries and textbooks. Today, with the availability of these materials on-line in the form of digital multimedia, a vast amount of related information can be reached through a personal computer with Internet connection via a simple keyword search. People can easily access and gain knowledge via information and communication technology (ICT) to keep pace with the latest developments (Plomp, Pelgrum, & Law, 2007). In such a scenario, education, which always plays a critical role in any economic and social growth of a country, becomes even more important. Education not only increases the productive skill sets of an individual but also general knowledge. It gives the individual a sense of well-being as well as capacity to absorb new ideas, increases his social interaction, gives access to improved health and provides several more intangible benefits (Kozma, 2005).

The availability of digital multimedia format materials such as text, sound, image, audio, video and animation has played a significant role in the way students learn, access and interact with information (Cairncross, 2002; Manjit, 2007). In addition the various kinds of ICT products available and have relevance to education, such as teleconferencing, email, audio conferencing, television lessons, radio broadcasts, interactive radio counseling, interactive voice response system, audiocassettes and CD-ROMs have been used in education for different purposes (Sharma, 2003; Sanyal, 2001; Bhattacharya & Sharma, 2007).

Cross and Adam (2007) listed four main rationales for introducing ICT in education as shown in Table 1.

The significance of these rationales (Table 1) can also be extended to engineering education. Other powerful ICTs including laptops wirelessly connected to the Internet, personal digital assistants, low cost video cameras, and cell phones have become affordable, accessible and integrated in large sections of the society throughout the world. It can restructure the learning process, promote collaboration, make education more widely available, foster cultural creativity and enhance the development in social integration (Kozma, 2005). It is only through education and the integration of ICT in education that one can

teach students to be participants in the growth process in this era of rapid change (Bhattacharya & Sharma, 2007).

ICT can be used as a tool in the process of engineering education in the following ways:

- *Informative tool*: It provides a vast amount of data in various interactive formats such as text, graphics, audio, video, and animation.
- *Situating tool*: It creates situations, which the student experiences in real life. Thus, simulation and mixed realities such as virtual reality and augmented reality are possible.
- *Constructive tool*: It can be used to manipulate data and generate analysis.
- *Communicative tool*: It can be used to remove communication barriers such as those of space and time (Lim & Chai, 2004).

From what is discussed above, it can be seen that the use of ICT in education develops higher order skills such as collaborating across time and place and solving complex real world problems (Bhattacharya & Sharma, 2007; Bottino, 2003; Lim & Hang, 2003; Mason, 2000). Thus, ICT can be employed to prepare the workforce for the information society and the new global economy (Kozma, 2005; Manjit, 2008).

Since a variety of ICT is available to be used in education, many academicians and psychologists are trying to study and improve the pedagogies

Table 1. Rationales for introducing ICT in education (adapted from Cross & Adam, 2007)

Rationale	Basis
Social	Perceived role that technology now plays in society and the need for familiarizing students with technology.
Vocational	Preparing students with jobs that require skills in technology.
Catalytic	Utility of technology to improve performance and effectiveness in teaching, management and many other social activities.
Pedagogical	To utilize technology in enhancing learning, flexibility and efficiently in curriculum delivery.

for delivering quality education with ICT. For example, education can be improved with ICT by designing new user interfaces and patterns of interactions, employing specialized hardware and software technologies in teaching, designing teaching/learning models and creating/using new learning approaches such as blended learning (combination of face-to-face instruction with computer-mediated instruction) and game approach.

TECHNOLOGIES FOR ENHANCING ENGINEERING EDUCATION

Research has shown that the use of new technologies in engineering has the potential to enhance the learning process and provide an engaging environment for students. The following are some examples of the use of computer aided learning (CAL) packages.

The work by Vaughan (1998) in the introduction of Fluids Mechanics course contains ten modules covering topics ranging from fluid statics to boundary layers. In addition to those modules, a laboratory simulation was also developed. This simulation consisted of six sections with experiments covering measurements of basic fluid properties, pressure and velocity measurements, applications of Bernoulli equation, applications of momentum equation, and pipe friction. By using an active learning approach, instructional technology can benefit students of varying backgrounds and skill levels. Students are able to view the same information from several perspectives, strengthening connections and transferability.

The work by McMahon (2000) on Introduction to Materials Engineering CD-ROM multimedia-based course serves as a comprehensive one-semester material education course for non-materials science and engineering majors. The course employs computer-presented tutorials that can be utilized in several ways: as a replacement for classroom lectures in courses where the class meetings are devoted to studio-type active learning, as a supplement to classroom lectures that are illustrated by the animations provided, as a basic course in institutions where faculty from other branches of science or technology serve as coaches for specialized subjects such as materials science and engineering, or as a self-study course for those who must pursue the subject on their own.

The work by Callister (2003) on an Introduction to Materials Science and Engineering CD-ROM contains eight dynamic learning modules where students can view and manipulate 3-D projections and activate animations that bring these concepts to life. In addition, students have the opportunity to improve their problem-solving skills and at the same time evaluate their progress. Recent work by Manjit (2007) on the development of technology-assisted problem solving (TAPS) packages were appreciated by first year undergraduate engineering students as it could help them visualize and understand the selected engineering problems better which were otherwise difficult to understand from the textbook alone.

A part from the use of CAL packages in engineering as mentioned above, new hardware technologies also helps significantly in enhancing the interaction process between the user and the software. Some of these hardware technologies are explained in the subsequent sections.

Graphics Tablet

A graphics tablet is an input device used by artists which allows one to draw a picture onto a computer display without having to utilize a mouse or keyboard. A graphics tablet consists of a flat tablet and some sort of drawing device, usually either a pen or stylus. A graphics tablet may also be referred to as a drawing tablet or drawing pad. While the graphics tablet is most suited for artists and those who want the natural feel of a pen-like object to manipulate the cursor on their screen, non-artists such as engineering instructors may find it useful in their teaching as well. A graphics tablet may

Figure 1. An engineering learning package being used with a Graphics Tablet

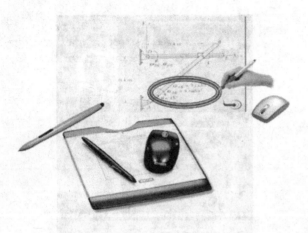

come in a range of sizes, from smaller 3" by 4" (7.6 by 10.2 cm) models to larger 7" by 9" (17.8 by 22.9 cm) ones. Even larger graphics tablets exist, up to enormous 14" by 14" (35.6 by 35.6 cm) tablets targeted towards professional designers and architects. Some well known graphics tablets include Wacom™, Aiptek™, and KB Gear™.

For the usage with CAL packages, the high pressure sensitivity of the graphics tablet allows the instructor/student to control a number of aspects of their drawing, including color and line thickness,

simply by pressing the stylus/graphics pen more or less heavily, mimicking drawing with an actual pen (Manjit, 2008). Most graphics tablets also have function buttons on the side, so that the user can perform common actions, such as switching a tool in a drawing program from paint to erase, without having to use the mouse or keyboard. This is useful for an engineering student, for example when the student needs to switch to a virtual calculator or notepad to perform calculations or make notes. Figure 1 shows a demonstration usage of the graphics pen where important engineering concepts are being highlighted directly onto an image in the learning package.

Interactive White Boards

An interactive whiteboard (IWB) is a large interactive display that connects to a computer and projector. A projector projects the computer's desktop onto the board's surface, where users control the computer using a touch sensitive pen, finger or other device. The board is typically mounted to a wall or on a floor stand as shown in Figure 2.

The use of IWBs has had a profound effect on schools, teachers, and learners (Cuthell, 2002). A

Figure 2. An engineering learning package being projected onto an interactive white board

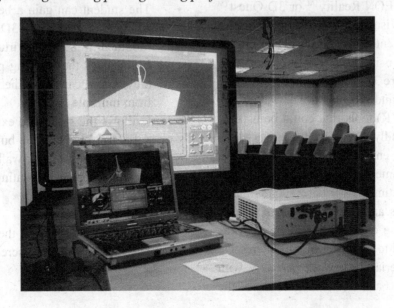

considerable body of evidence from schools across the United Kingdom has shown the transformational effect of the technology on teaching and learning (Cuthell, 2004). What the boards enable teachers to do is to support the whole range of learning styles of the learners in the class. The learners themselves feel empowered: The ability to visualize and recall the lesson supports learning; the range of resources that can be embedded within the IWB lesson software and the interactivity itself has engaged almost all of the learners and enhanced their progress (Cuthell, 2005). When using an IWB the learners see themselves engaged with the process of learning, rather than simply progressing through the scheme of work. In an interactive engineering education lab, animated engineering problems can be paused and important engineering concepts can be highlighted to help students visualize better.

Software to Interact in 3D Environments

Another alternative to allow engineering students to visualize engineering problems is to design the engineering models (i.e. a piston, rod, robotic arm) using three dimensional (3D) modeling tools such as Alias Maya™ or 3D Studio Max™ and present them in EON Reality™ or 3D Quest™ (interactive 3D visual software) as its main interface environments. An example of a jet engine being interacted using EON Reality™ software is shown in Figure 3.

EON Reality and 3D Quest are new emerging virtual reality (VR) tools that could be used to develop user friendly 3D visual interactions which allow the user to enter text, see an animation in two and three dimensions, evaluate user input, and integrate multimedia attributes such as audio, video, animations, and graphics. In addition these VR tools improve effectiveness even more, as they can be used to construct highly interactive and quality materials that work perfectly with wide and narrow band-widths, regardless of the

Figure 3. A 3D animated model being interacted using EON Reality ™

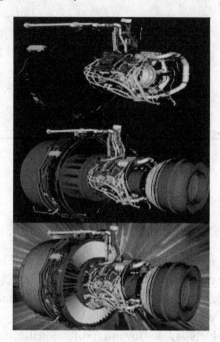

resolution of the monitors. Another powerful feature of these VR tools is that the 3D models can be interacted and visualized as stereoscopic views/images by wearing special 3D goggles.

The paradigm of stereoscopic views provides the following benefits (Manjit, 2007):

- The student can gain a better view of the path and motion of the 3D object such as a robotic arm in the 3D virtual environment.
- It enhances the learning process whereby the student can view the 3D robotic arm from multiple angles.
- It allows the student to explore the 3D robotic arm by using the built-in features in the tool (i.e. moving, walking, flying, examining, resizing, rotating and changing viewpoints).

With the above features, the user can move along any direction on the screen and have the displayed 3D robotic arm continuously and instantaneously manipulated.

Augmented Reality

In general multimedia environments have offered new ways for learners to interact with various educational resources. Since printed learning materials have been favored and used particularly for systematic study, they have been dealt with as totally different media that yield distinct learning environments and learners can only get their alternative merits at each environment. Augmented reality (AR) is an emerging technology that overlays virtual objects onto real scenes that has the potential to provide learners with a new type of learning material (Asai, 2005). The architecture of AR technology can be found in Liarokapis (2002, 2004).

AR has the ability to enhance real scenes viewed by the user, overlaying virtual objects over the real world, and works to improve the user's performance and perception of the world. Some advantages of using AR technology in teaching and learning include (1) the user can get three dimensional information based on a real scene, (2) the user can see objects from his/her viewpoint, and (3) the user can interact with both virtual and real objects wirelessly. With these advantages, some researchers have employed AR technology to develop their educational software for teaching and demonstration purposes (Asai, 2005; Lang 2004; Liarokapis 2004; White, 2001).

White (2001) presented a new approach to the teaching of top down design of hardware design language (VHDL) using a novel virtual interactive teaching environment. The environment enabled the students to learn more effectively using virtual multimedia content, while exploiting extended markup language (XML) and augmented reality. According to White, the environment can be adapted for teaching other subject areas. Asai (2005) conducted an experiment to investigate the characteristics of AR instruction and its appropri-

ate way of human computer interaction. He dealt with chemical properties of caffeine as a topic for augmented instructions and prepared a two-page document for the experiment. A handheld personal computer (PC) was compared to a head mounted device (HMD) as a presentation system for augmented instructions. The result of the experiment suggested that a handheld PC was more suitable than a HMD as a presentation system for augmented instruction in terms of long term use.

AR is now being used in engineering education, for example Liarokapis (2004) presents an educational application that allows users to interact with Web3D content using virtual and augmented reality. The study enables an exploration of the potential benefits of Web3D and AR technologies in engineering education and learning. The preliminary study finds that by employing AR technology, students can understand more effectively through interactivity and multimedia content. An example of the study by Liarokapis is illustrated in Figure 4, where the user can interact with a 3D model of the object (i.e. piston) and can compare it to real objects in a natural way.

Although AR has been used in education, its potential in education is just beginning to be explored and has not been practical enough to be used in educational environments due to its complex contents development approach (Manjit, Cheng, Der, & Omar, 2009).

NEW APPROACHES IN LEARNING ENGINEERING

Blended Learning Approach

Blended learning may be phrased as a new education pedagogical approach that combines the use of electronic learning tools (such as email, software, and web-based support) and traditional classroom components to maximize teaching effectiveness. Brown, Collins and Duguid (1989) argued that the term blended learning is used to describe a solution

Figure 4. AR Visualization of a Piston (adapted from Liarokapis, 2004)

that combines several different delivery methods, such as collaboration software, Web-based courses and knowledge management practices. Koohang (2006) and Lin (2008) claim that blended learning is a hybrid learning setting in which part of the learning activities and assignments are transferred from the face-to-face classroom to the distance learning environment. Based on these advantages, some research has stressed the importance of using a "blended learning approach", with clearly stated learning objectives and a selection of the best combination of delivery methods to meet those objectives (Smart & Cappel, 2005).

A study by Bullen and Russell (2007) on the adoption of a blended learning approach to teaching first year engineering degree students has resulted in an improved student performance as measured by final examination results. In particular the study achieved greatest benefit through:

- The use of a weekly automated assessment scheme (WATS)
- The adoption of a just-in-time teaching approach

Although blended learning becomes more and more popular among higher education institutions (Howard & Remenyi, 2006), it is still at an early stage of development. As such, further research is required to see how exactly learning competencies are to be supported and encouraged in blended learning environments.

Game Learning Approach

Games are opening up new potential for learning in formal situations and innovative ways and have been favored mainly by primary and secondary level of education. The main benefit for using a game approach in learning is motivation. Qualters, Isaacs, Cullinane, Laird, Mcdonald and Corriere (2007) pointed that the use of interactive educational games can provide students with solid learning experiences. On the other hand serious games, blended with instructor-led and e-learning training, can create high-impact social learning environments.

Today, some researchers are testing game learning approach for first year undergraduate mechanical engineering courses. For example, BEST Mechanics offers resources in statics, dynamics and the mechanics of materials. It provides interactive lessons and exercises, starting with fundamental topics and moving on to more advanced subjects. It includes Flash movies, examples and problems, games and a statics e-book. BEST Mechanics is a project from the Missouri University of Science and Technology. Its website (http://web.mst.edu/~bestmech/) states that it is a work-in-progress.

Another study by Darling (2007) on the introduction of game based learning into the first year undergraduate syllabus of Mechanical Engineering was shown to be a great success. By using existing computing resources the students were able to work both individually and as a learning community based on their tutor group to design and test a virtual vehicle. An evaluation of the students engineering knowledge before and after the activity demonstrated significant learning gains while feedback from both the students and academic staff was very encouraging.

While the benefits of employing games approach in learning has been demonstrated in a number of studies, the challenges for providing a sufficient level of institutional support both technical and pedagogic are insignificant. More studies may be required to test and see if a game based learning approach is suitable for teaching in the higher learning institutions.

CONCLUSION

Mechanical engineering course subjects, such as mechanics dynamics, combine a use of mathematics, schematic diagrams, and text descriptions. Frequently, students are unclear of basic principles of engineering mechanics dynamics, and as a result they do not know which mathematical relationships are to be applied in solving a particular problem. This paper has reviewed the feasibility of new ICTs that can be employed in teaching and learning of engineering.

ICT can enable wider access of information and knowledge, participation and interaction. Although such fundamental changes in the curriculum can take place and help transform the way students learn in many ways, this transformation may require new skills, capabilities and attitudes and questions arise such as: are students and instructors prepared to use these technologies in their teaching and learning? Are higher learning institutions committed to employ these new teaching aids?

The technologies reviewed in this paper include software such as CAL packages, virtual and augmented reality, 3D visual interactive software; hardware such as graphics tablet and interactive white board to enhance the problem solving skills and learning of students. New approaches to learning such as blended learning and game based learning are also reviewed.

It can be envisaged that the use of these technologies as replacement, or supplement to, human educators in engineering education would become widespread in the future. Such technologies can be employed to demonstrate and correlate real life application and theory thereby promoting deep learning.

ACKNOWLEDGMENT

We would like to thank Dr. Kirandeep Kaur Sidhu for her constructive comments in writing and proof reading this paper.

REFERENCES

Asai, K. (2005). Augmented Instructions – A Fusion of Augmented Reality and Printed Learning Materials. In *Proceedings of the 5th IEEE International Conference of Advanced Learning Technologies* (pp. 1-3).

Bhattacharya, I., & Sharma, K. (2007). India in the knowledge economy – an electronic paradigm. *International Journal of Educational Management, 21*(6), 543–568. doi:10.1108/09513540710780055

Bottino, R. M. (2003). ICT, national policies, and impact on schools and teachers' development. In *CRPIT03: Proceedings of the 3.1 and 3.3 Working Groups Conference on International Federation for Information Processing* (pp. 3-6). Darlinghurst, Australia: Australian Computer Society.

Brown, J., Collins, A., & Duguid, P. (1989). Situated cognition and the culture of learning. *Educational Researcher, 18*(1), 32–42.

Bullen, P. R., & Russell, M. B. (2007). *A Blended Learning Approach to Teaching First Year Engineering.* Paper presented at the International Conference on Engineering Education, Coimbra, Portugal.

Cairncross, S. (2002). *Interactive Multimedia and Learning: Realizing the Benefits.* Unpublished PhD thesis, Napier University, Scotland.

Callister, W. D. (2003). *Student Learning Resources. Materials Science and Engineering an Introduction.* New York: John Wiley & Sons.

Cholin, V. S. (2005). Study of the application of information technology for effective access to resources in Indian university libraries. *The International Information & Library Review, 37*(3), 189–197. doi:10.1016/j.iilr.2005.07.002

Cross, M., & Adam, F. (2007). ICT Policies and Strategies in Higher Education in South Africa: National and Institutional Pathways. *Higher Education Policy, 20*(1), 73–95. doi:10.1057/palgrave.hep.8300144

Cuthell, J. P. (2002). *How do interactive whiteboards enhance learning?* Retrieved February 24, 2004, from http://www.virtuallearning.org.uk/ iwb/Learning_theories.pdf

Cuthell, J. P. (2004). *Interactive whiteboards survey.* Retrieved May 22, 2005, from http://www.virtuallearning.org.uk/ 2003/whiteboards/survey.doc

Cuthell, J. P. (2005). *Seeing the meaning. The impact of interactive whiteboards on teaching and learning.* Paper presented at WCCE 05, Stellenbosch, South Africa.

Darling, J. (2007). *Investigating the effectiveness and efficiency of games and game based learning communities to support students learning.* Retrieved May, 2009, from http://www.bath.ac.uk/learningandteaching/ recognition/tdf/case_studies

Gramoll, K. (2001). An Internet Portal for Statics and Dynamics Engineering Courses. In *Proceedings of the International Conference of Engineering* (pp. 1-6).

Hattangdi, H., & Ghosh, A. (2009). Enhancing the quality and accessibility of higher education through the use of Information Communication Technology. *International Journal of Educational Management, 21*(6), 1–12.

Howard, L., & Remenyi, Z. (2006). Adaptive Blended Learning Environments. In *Proceedings of the 9th International Conference of Engineering Education* (pp. 1-6).

Katarzyna, M. (2002). *Knowledge Representation, Content Indexing and Effective Teaching of Fluid Mechanics Using Web-Based Content.* Unpublished master's thesis, Massachusetts Institute of Technology.

Koohang, A., Britz, J., & Seymour, T. (2006, June 25-28). *Hybrid/Blended Learning: Advantages, Challenges, Design, and Future Directions.* Paper presented at the Informing Science and IT Education Joint Conference, Manchester, UK.

Kozma, R. (2005). National Policies That Connect ICT-Based Education Reform To Economic And Social Development. *Human Technology, 1*(2), 117–156.

Lang, U. (2004). Virtual and Augmented Reality Developments for Engineering Applications. In *Proceedings of the European Congress on Computational Methods in Applied Sciences and Engineering* (pp. 1-16).

Liarokapis, F. (2002). Multimedia Augmented Reality Interface for E-Learning (MARIE). *World Transactions on Engineering and Technology Education, 1*(2), 173–176.

Liarokapis, F. (2004). Web3D Augmented Reality to Support Engineering Education. *World Transactions on Engineering and Technology Education, 3*(1), 11–14.

Lim, C. P., & Chai, C. S. (2004). An activity-theoretical approach to research of ICT integration 13 in Singapore schools: Orienting activities and learner autonomy. *Computers & Education, 43*(3), 215–236. doi:10.1016/j.compedu.2003.10.005

Lim, C. P., & Hang, D. (2003). An activity theory approach to research of ICT integration in Singapore schools. *Computers & Education, 41*(1), 49–63. doi:10.1016/S0360-1315(03)00015-0

Lin, K. (2008). Building on Components into Traditional Instruction in Pre-Service Teacher Education: The Good, the Bad and the Ugly. *International Journal for Scholarship of Teacher and Learning, 2*(1).

Mason, R. (2000). From distance education to online education. *The Internet and Higher Education, 3*(1-2), 63–74. doi:10.1016/S1096-7516(00)00033-6

McMahon, C. J. (2000). *Tutorials for Introduction to Materials Engineering*. Merrion Media.

Mehta, S., & Kalra, M. (2006). Information and Communication Technologies: A bridge for social equity and sustainable development in India. *The International Information & Library Review, 38*(3), 147–160. doi:10.1016/j.iilr.2006.06.008

Plomp, T., Pelgrum, W. J., & Law, N. (2007). SITES2006 - International comparative survey of pedagogical practices and ICT in education. *Education and Information Technologies, 12*(2), 83–92. doi:10.1007/s10639-007-9029-5

Qualters, M. D., Isaacs, J., Cullinane, T., Laird, J., Mcdonald, A., & Corriere, J. (2007). A Game Approach to Teach Environmentally Benign Manufacturing in the Supply Chain. *International Journal for the Scholarship of Teaching and Learning, 2*(2).

Sanyal, B. C. (2001, September 10-12). *New functions of higher education and ICT to achieve education for all*. Paper presented at the Expert Roundtable on University and Technology for Literacy and Education Partnership in Developing Countries, International Institute for Educational Planning, Paris.

Schmidt, J. T. (2007). *Preparing Students for Success in Blended Learning Environments: Future Oriented Motivation & Self-Regulation.* Unpublished PhD thesis.

Scott, N. W. (1996). *A study of the introduction of educational technology into a course in engineering dynamics: classroom environment and learning outcomes.* Unpublished PhD thesis.

Sharma, R. (2003). Barriers in Using Technology for Education in Developing Countries. In *Proceedings of the Information Technology: Research and Education 2003 Conference* (pp. 521-522).

Sidhu, M. (2007). *Development and Applications of Interactive Multimedia TAPS (Technology Assisted Problem Solving) Packages for Engineering.* Unpublished PhD thesis, Universiti Malaya.

Sidhu, M., Cheng, L. K., Der, S. C., & Omar, R. (2009). *Augmented Reality Applications in Education*. Paper presented at the Second Teaching and Learning Conference at UNITEN.

Sidhu, M., & Ramesh, S. (2008). Virtual Worlds: The Next Generation for Solving Engineering Problems. In *Proceedings of the IEEE 8ᵗʰ International Conference on Computer and IT CIT2008*, Sydney, Australia (pp. 303-307).

Sidhu, M., Ramesh, S., & Selvanathan, N. (2005). A Coach-Based Interactive Multimedia Tool For Solving Engineering Problem. *International Multimedia Cyberscape Journal*, 3(2), 28–36.

Smart, K. L., & Cappel, J. L. (2005). An exploratory look at students' perceptions of blended learning. *Issues in Information Systems*, 6(1), 149–155.

Vaughan, R. (1998). The Use of Multimedia in Developing Undergraduate Engineering Courses. *Journal of Materials*, 5(5). Retrieved from http://www.tms.org/pubs/journals/ JOM/9805/Voller/Voller-9805.html.

White, M. (2001). A virtual Interactive Teaching Environment (VITE) Using XML and Augmented Reality. *The International Journal of Electrical Engineering Education*, 38(4), 316–329.

This work was previously published in International Journal of Information Communication Technologies and Human Development, Volume 2, Issue 4, edited by Susheel Chhabra and Hakikur Rahman, pp. 68-79, copyright 2010 by IGI Publishing (an imprint of IGI Global).

Compilation of References

About WifiPDX - Free wireless internet in Portland on WifiPDX. (n.d.). *In Free Portland WiFi - Free wireless internet in Portland on WifiPDX.* Retrieved June 05, 2009 from http://www.WiFipdx.com/about/

Agarwal, R., & Karahanna, E. (2000). Time flies when you're having fun: Cognitive absorption and beliefs about information technology usage. *Management Information Systems Quarterly, 24*(4), 665–694. doi:10.2307/3250951

Agrawal, A. J., & Chandak, M. B. (2007, April 2-4). Mobile Interface for Domain Specific Machine Translation Using Short Messaging Service. In *Proceedings of the 4th International Conference on Information Technology* (pp. 957-958).

ALA (American Library Association). (2006). *Information literacy competency standards for higher education.* Retrieved April 23, 2009, from http://www.ala.org/ala/acrl/acrlstandards/ informationliteracycompetency.cfm

Alexopoulos, G., Koutsouris, A., & Tzouramani, I. (2008, November). *Characteristics of the demand for advisory and educational services in rural areas: Results of field research among young rural inhabitants.* Paper presented at the 10th Panhellenic Conference of Rural Economy, Thessaloniki, Greece.

Alkire, S. (2005). Why the capability approach? *Journal of Human Development and Capabilities, 6*(1), 115–135. doi:10.1080/146498805200034275

Alvesson, M. (2002). *Postmodernism and Social Research.* Buckingham, UK: Open University Press.

Amable, B., & Lung, Y. (2005). The European Socio-Economic Models in a Knowledge- based society: The objectives of the ESEMK project. *Actes du GERPISA.*

Amichai-Hamburger, Y., & Furnham, A. (2007). The positive net. *Computers in Human Behavior, 23*(2), 1033–1045. doi:10.1016/j.chb.2005.08.008

Anau, N., Iwan, R., van Heist, M., Limberg, G., Sudana, M., & Wollenberg, E. (2004). Negotiating more than boundaries: conflict, power and agreement building in the demarcation of village borders in Malinau. In Colfer, C. J. P. (Ed.), *The equitable forest: diversity, community and natural resources.* Washington, DC: Resources for the Future/CIFOR.

Anderson, G. (1993). *Fundamentals of educational research.* London: Falmer Press.

Anderson, S., Bohman, P., Burmeister, O., & Sampson-Wild, G. (2004). User needs and e-Government accessibility: The future impact of WCAG 2.0. In Stary, C., & Stephanidis, C. (Eds.), *User Interface for All* (pp. 289–304). Berlin: Springer Verlag.

Angrist, J., & Krueger, A. (1991). Does compulsory school attendance affect schooling and earnings? *The Quarterly Journal of Economics, 106*(4), 979–1014. doi:10.2307/2937954

Argyris, C., & Schon, D. (1974). *Theory in practice.* San Francisco: Jossey-Bass.

Armitage, D. (2008). Governance and the commons in a multi-level world. *International Journal of the Commons, 2*(1), 7–32.

Asai, K. (2005). Augmented Instructions – A Fusion of Augmented Reality and Printed Learning Materials. In *Proceedings of the 5th IEEE International Conference of Advanced Learning Technologies* (pp. 1-3).

Asgarkhani, M. (2005). Digital government and its effectiveness in public management reform: A local government perspective. *Public Management Review, 7*(3), 465–487. doi:10.1080/14719030500181227

Askar, P., & Usley, Y. (2001). Concerns of administrators and teachers in the diffusion of IT in schools: A case study from Turkey. In McAlister, K., & Reagan, C. (Eds.), *Research: SITE 2001 Section* (pp. 8–9).

Assembly of First Nations (AFN). (2005, March). Recognition and Implementation of First Nation Governments. *Resolve Newsletter*.

Atkins, E., & Vasu, E. S. (1998). Teaching with technology instrument. *Learning and Leading with Technology, 25*(8), 35–39.

Atkins, M. J. (1984). Practitioner as researcher: Some techniques for analyzing semi-structured data in small-scale research. *British Journal of Educational Studies, 32*(3), 251–261. doi:10.1080/00071005.1984.9973691

Atkins, N. E., & Vasu, E. S. (2000). Measuring knowledge of technology usage and stages of concern about computing: A study of middle school teachers. *Journal of Technology and Teacher Education, 8*(4), 279–302.

Baggaley, J. (2007). Distance education technologies: An Asian perspective. *Distance Education, 28*(2), 125–131. doi:10.1080/01587910701439191

Baird, I. G., & Shoemaker, B. (2005). *Aiding or Abetting? Internal Resettlement and International Aid Agencies in the Lao PDR*. Toronto, Canada: Probe International.

Baker, P. M. A., & Bellordre, C. (2003). Factors Influencing Adoption of Wireless Technologies – Key Policy Issues, Barriers, and Opportunities for People with Disabilities. *Information Technology and Disabilities, 9*(2).

Baker, P. M. A., Hanson, J., & Myhill, W. (2009). The Promise of Municipal WiFi and Failed Policies of Inclusion: the Disability Divide. *Information Polity, 14*(1-2).

Baker, J. R., & Moore, S. M. (2008). Blogging as a social tool: A psychosocial examination of the effects of blogging. *Cyberpsychology & Behavior, 11*(6), 747–749. doi:10.1089/cpb.2008.0053

Baker, P. M. A., Bell, A., & Moon, N. W. (2009). Accessibility in municipal wireless networks: System implementation and policy considerations. In Reddick, C. (Ed.), *Strategies for local e-government adoption and implementation: Comparative studies, advances in e-government research book Series*. Hershey, PA: IGI Global.

Baker, P. M. A., & Moon, N. W. (2008). Access Barriers to Wireless Technologies for People with Disabilities: Issues, Opportunities and Policy Options. In Langdon, P., Clarkson, J., & Robinson, P. (Eds.), *Designing inclusive futures*. London: Springer Verlag. doi:10.1007/978-1-84800-211-1_14

Baker, P. M. A., & Ward, A. C. (2002). Bridging temporal and spatial "gaps": The role of information and communication technologies in defining communities. *Information Communication and Society, 5*(2), 207–224. doi:10.1080/13691180210130789

Balit, S. (2003). Forward. In White, S. (Ed.), *Participatory Video: Images that Transform and Empower* (pp. 8–12). New Delhi, India: Sage Publications.

Ballon, P., Audenhove, L., Poel, M., & Staelens, T. (2007). Business models for wireless city networks in the EU and the US: public inputs, and returns. In *Proceedings of the 18th European Regional ITS Conference*, Istanbul, Turkey.

Ballon, P. (2007). Changing business models for Europe's mobile telecommunications industry: The impact of alternative wireless technologies. *Telematics and Informatics, 24*, 192–205. doi:10.1016/j.tele.2007.01.007

Baltuch, J. (2006). St Cloud, Florida citywide Wi-Fi update: Launch plus 30 days. *MuniWireless*. Retrieved June 6, 2009 from http://www.muniwireless.com/municipal/

Baltuch, J. (2005). *Free Municipal Wireless, Pays Big Dividends*. St. Cloud, FL: MRI.

Bangou, F. (2006). Intégration des TICE et apprentissage de l'enseignement: Une approche Systémique. *ALSIC, 9*, 145–159.

Bangou, F., & Wong, S. (2009). Race, and Technology: Where is the Access? In Kuboka, R., & Lin, A. (Eds.), *Race, Culture, and Identities in Second Language Education: Exploring Critically Engaged Practices* (pp. 158–176). London: Routledge.

Baraldi, C. (2003). Children's social participation in the town of adults. In Christensen, P., & O'Brian, M. (Eds.), *Children in the city: Home neighbourhood and community* (pp. 184–205). London: RoutledgeFalmer.

Bardon, R., Hazel, D., & Miller, K. (2007). Preferred information delivery methods of North Carolina forest landowners. *Journal of Extension, 45*(5). Retrieved January 20, 2009, from http://www.joe.org/joe/ 2007october/a3.shtml

Bar, F., & Park, N. (2006). Municipal Wi-Fi Networks: The Goals, Practices, and Policy Implications of the U.S. Case. *Communications and Strategies, 61*(1), 107–126.

Barnes, M. (2002). Bringing difference into deliberation? Disabled people, survivors and local governance. *Policy and Politics, 3*(3), 319–331. doi:10.1332/030557302760094694

Barton, L. (1993). The struggle for citizenship: The case of disabled people. *Disability, Handicap & Society, 8*(3), 235–248. doi:10.1080/02674649366780251

Basu, S., Fernald, J. G., Oulton, N., & Srinivasan, S. (2003). The case of the missing productivity growth, or does information technology explain why productivity accelerated in the united states but not in the united kingdom? *NBER Macroeconomics Annual, 18*, 9–63.

Batinic, B., & Goritz, A. S. (2009). How does social psychology deal with new media? *Social Psychology, 40*(1), 3–5. doi:10.1027/1864-9335.40.1.3

Becker, H. J. (1994). How exemplary computer-using teachers differ from other teachers: Implications for realizing the potential of computers in schools. *Journal of Research on Computing in Education, 26*(3), 291–321.

Bell, D. (2003). Mythscapes: memory, mythology, and national identity. *The British Journal of Sociology, 54*(1), 63–81. doi:10.1080/0007131032000045905

Bell, M. (1998). 1999). The Looking After Children materials. A critical analysis of their use in practice. *Adoption & Fostering, 22*(4), 15–22.

Bell, W., & Freeman, W. (Eds.). (1974). *Ethnicity and Nation-Building*. Beverly Hills, CA: Sage Publications.

Bentler, P. M. (1990). Comparative fit indexes in structural models. *Psychological Bulletin, 107*(2), 238–246. doi:10.1037/0033-2909.107.2.238

Ben-Ze'ev, A. (2004). *Love Online: Emotions on the Internet*. Cambridge, UK: Cambridge University Press. doi:10.1017/CBO9780511489785

Berglund, U., Nordin, K., & Eriksson, M. (2009). *Barnkartor i GIS och trafiksäkerhet* (Children's maps in GIS and traffic safety) (Tech. Rep.). Uppsala, Sweden: Rapporter Institutionen för stad och land.

Berglund, U. (2008). Using children's GIS maps to influence town Planning. *Children. Youth and Environments, 18*(2), 110–132.

Berglund, U., & Nordin, K. (2007). Using GIS to make young people's voices heard in urban planning. *Built Environment, 33*(4), 469–481. doi:10.2148/benv.33.4.469

Bery, R. (2003). Participatory Video that Empowers. In White, S. (Ed.), *Participatory Video: Images that Transform and Empower* (pp. 271–285). New Delhi, India: Sage Publications.

Bestari, N. G., Mongcopa, C., Samson, J., & Ward, K. (2006). *Lao PDR: Governance Issues in agriculture and natural resources: A Case Study from the 2005 Sector Assistance Program Evaluation for the Agriculture and Natural Resources Sector in the Lao People's Democratic Republic. ADB - Governance Issues in Lao PDR*. Manila, Philippines: Asian Development Bank.

Best, S. J., & Kreuger, B. S. (2006). Online interactions and social capital: Distinguishing between new and existing ties. *Social Science Computer Review, 24*(4), 395–410. doi:10.1177/0894439306286855

Beynon-Davies, P. (2007). Models for e-government. *Transforming Government: People. Process and Policy, 1*(1), 7–28.

Bhattacharya, I., & Sharma, K. (2007). India in the knowledge economy – an electronic paradigm. *International Journal of Educational Management, 21*(6), 543–568. doi:10.1108/09513540710780055

Bimber, B. (1998). The Internet and Political Transformation: Populism, Community, and Accelerated Pluralism. *Polity, 31*(1), 133–160. doi:10.2307/3235370

Birraux-Ziegler, P. (2003, December 8-11). *NGO Narrative Report on the Global Forum of Indigenous Peoples and the Information Society*. Geneva, Switzerland: Indigenous Peoples' Centre for Documentation, Research and Information (DoCip). Retrieved September 2009, from http://www.docip.org/anglais/ news_en/reportGFIPIS_eng.rtf

Black, P., & Wiliam, D. (1998). Assessment and classroom learning. *Assessment in Education*, *5*(1), 7–74. doi:10.1080/0969595980050102

Blanchard, M., Metcalf, A., Degney, J., Herman, H., & Burns, J. (2008). Rethinking the digital divide: Findings from a study of marginalised young people's information communication technology (ICT) use. *Youth Studies Australia*, *27*(4), 35–41.

Blanck, P., Hill, E., Siegal, C., Waterstone, M., & Myhill, W. (2006). *Disability civil rights law and policy: Cases and materials* (1st ed.). St. Paul, MN: Thomson/West Publishers.

Block, J. H., & Kollinger, P. (2007). Peer influence in network markets: An empirical investigation. *Schmalenbach Business Review*, *59*, 364–385.

Bollen, K. A. (1989). *Structural Equations with Latent Variables*. New York: Wiley.

Borrini-Feyerabend, G., Pimbert, M., Farvar, M. T., Kothari, A., & Renard, Y. (2004). *Sharing Power: Learning by doing in co-management of natural resources throughout the world*. Tehran, Iran: IIED and IUCN/CEESP/CMWG.

Bottino, R. M. (2003). ICT, national policies, and impact on schools and teachers' development. In *CRPIT 03: Proceedings of the 3.1 and 3.3 Working Groups Conference on International Federation for Information Processing* (pp. 3-6). Darlinghurst, Australia: Australian Computer Society.

Brashear, G., Hollis, G., & Wheeler, M. (2000). Information transfer in the Illinois swine industry: How producers are informed of new technologies. *Journal of Extension*, *38*(1). Retrieved January 20, 2009, from http://joe.org/joe/ 2000february/rb4.html

Breaugh, J. A. (1985). The measurement of work autonomy. *Human Relations*, *38*(6), 551–570. doi:10.1177/001872678503800604

Bricout, J. C., Baker, P. M. A., Ward, A., & Moon, N. (2010). Teleworking and the digital divide. In Ferro, E., Dwivedi, Y., Gil-Garcia, R., & Williams, M. (Eds.), *Overcoming digital divides: constructing an equitable and competitive information society* (pp. 155–178). Hershey, PA: IGI Global.

Bricout, J. C., & Gray, D. B. (2006). Community receptivity: The ecology of disabled persons' participation in the physical, political and social environments. *Scandinavian Journal of Disability Research*, *8*(1), 1–21. doi:10.1080/15017410500335229

British Columbia Treaty Commission (BCTC). (2002, May). Improving the Treaty Process: Report of the Tripartite Working Group. In *First Nations Summit*, BC, Canada. Retrieved December 2007, from http://www.gov.bc.ca/tno/down/ tripartite_working_05_15.pdf

Browne, D. L., & Ritchie, D. C. (1991). Cognitive apprenticeship: A model of staff development for implementing technology in schools. *Contemporary Education*, *64*(1), 28–34.

Brown, J., Collins, A., & Duguid, P. (1989). Situated cognition and the culture of learning. *Educational Researcher*, *18*(1), 32–42.

Brown, J., Shipman, B., & Vetter, R. (2007). SMS: The Short Message Service. *Computer*, *40*(12), 106–110. doi:10.1109/MC.2007.440

Brynjolfsson, E., & Hitt, L. M. (2000). Beyond computation: Information technology, organizational transformation and business performance. *The Journal of Economic Perspectives*, *14*(4), 23–48.

Brynjolfsson, E., Hitt, L. M., Yang, S., Baily, M. N., & Hall, R. E. (2002). Intangible assets: Computers and organizational capital /comments and discussion. *Brookings Papers on Economic Activity*, *1*, 137–198. doi:10.1353/eca.2002.0003

Buddle, K. (2005). Aboriginal Cultural Capital Creation and Radio Production in Urban Ontario. *Canadian Journal of Communication*, *30*, 7–39.

Buente, W., & Robbin, A. (2008). Trends in Internet Information Behavior, 2000-2004. *Journal of the American Society for Information Science and Technology*, *59*(11), 1743–1760. doi:10.1002/asi.20883

Bullen, P. R., & Russell, M. B. (2007). *A Blended Learning Approach to Teaching First Year Engineering.* Paper presented at the International Conference on Engineering Education, Coimbra, Portugal.

Burke, K., & Sewake, K. (2008). Adoption of computer and internet technologies in small firm agriculture: A study of flower growers in Hawaii. *Journal of Extension, 46*(3). Retrieved January 20, 2009, from http://www.joe.org/joe/ 2008june/rb5.shtml

Burnard, P. (1994). Searching for meaning: a method of analysing interview transcripts with a personal computer. *Nurse Education Today, 14*(2), 111–117. doi:10.1016/0260-6917(94)90113-9

Caffarella, R. (2001). *Planning programs for adult learners* (2nd ed.). San Francisco: Jossey-Bass.

Cairncross, S. (2002). *Interactive Multimedia and Learning: Realizing the Benefits.* Unpublished PhD thesis, Napier University, Scotland.

Callister, W. D. (2003). *Student Learning Resources. Materials Science and Engineering an Introduction.* New York: John Wiley & Sons.

Cambridge University. (2010). *Search results of open courseware.* Retrieved March 16, 2010, from http://web-search.cam.ac.uk/ query.html?qt=Open+Courseware

Campanovo, G., & Pigneur, Y. (2003, April 23-26). *Business model analysis applied to mobile business.* Paper presented at the 5th International Conference on Enterprise Information Systems, Angers, France.

Canadian Association of University Teachers. (2009, April). MIT faculty to make articles freely available to public. *CAUT Bulletin,* A4.

Caplan, S. E., & Turner, J. S. (2007). Bringing theory to research on computer-mediated comforting communication. *Computers in Human Behavior, 23*(2), 985–998. doi:10.1016/j.chb.2005.08.003

Carlson, S., & Gadio, C. T. (2005). Teacher professional development in the use of technology. In Haddad, W., & Draxler, A. (Eds.), *Technologies for education: potentials, parameters, and prospects* (pp. 119–132). Paris: UNESCO.

Carlsson, L., & Sandström, A. (2008). Network governance of the commons. *International Journal of the Commons, 2*(1), 33–54.

Cartelli, A., Stanfield, M., Connolly, T., Jimoyiannis, A., Magalhaes, H., & Maillet, K. (2008). Towards the development of a new model for best practice and knowledge construction in virtual campuses. *Journal of Information Technology Education, 7,* 121–134.

Cashmore, J., & Paxman, M. (2006). Wards Leaving Care: Follow up five years on. *Children Australia, 31*(3), 18–25.

CellBazzar. (2009). *SMS Buy – CellBazaar: Mobile phone market.* Retrieved from http://corp.cellbazaar.com/sms.html

Census, U. S. (2002). *Federal, State, and Local Governments: 2002 Census of Governments.* Retrieved July 1, 2009 from http://www.census.gov/ govs/www/cog2002.html

Chadwick, A. (2003). Bringing e-democracy back in: Why it matters for future research on e-governance. *Social Science Computer Review, 21*(4), 443–455. doi:10.1177/0894439303256372

Chai, W. (2009, March 4). Beijing University social studies center announcing the report of an investigation on life in Beijing, Shanghai and Guangzhou: Education attainment's influence on career development is obvious. *China Education Daily,* 2.

Chambers, R. (2004). *Ideas for Development: reflecting forwards* (IDS Working Paper 238). Brighton, UK: University of Sussex, Institute of Development Studies.

Chava, V., Smith, M. R., & Dudley, W. H. (2007). *System and method for in-transit SMS language translation* (U.S. Patent No. 7272406).

Chawla, L. (2002a). Toward better cities for children and youth. In Chawla, L. (Ed.), *Growing up in an Urbanizing World* (pp. 15–34). London: Earthscan.

Chawla, L. (Ed.). (2002b). *Growing up in an urbanising world.* London: Earthscan.

Cheers, D., Kufeldt, K., Klein, R., & Rideout, S. (2007). Comparing Care: The Looking After Children system in Australia and Canada. *Children Australia, 32*(2), 21–28.

Cheers, D., & Morwitzer, J. (2006). Promoting resilient outcomes in Australia with the Looking After Children Electronic System (LACES). In Flynn, R. J., Dudding, P. M., & Barber, J. G. (Eds.), *Promoting Resilience in Child Welfare*. Ottawa, Canada: University of Ottawa Press.

Chen, W., & Wellman, B. (2003). Charting and Bridging Digital Divides. *I-Ways, Digest of electronic commerce policy and regulation, 26*, 155-161.

Chen, Z. (2008). *Fully utilizing the important contribution contemporary distance education makes in building a country with rich human capital.* Retrieved September 7, 2008, from http://www.moe.edu.cn/edoas/website18/98/info1201846559236298.htm

Chen, W., & Wellman, B. (2004). The global digital divide – within and between countries. *IT & Society, 1*(7), 39–45.

Chesley, K. A. (2009). The Future of Municipal Wireless in the United States and Europe. Retrieved May 22, 2009 from http://ssrn.com/abstract=1408808

China Internet Network Information Center. (2009). *CNNIC announces the 23rd Chinese Internet development report.* Retrieved August 31, 2009, from http://research.cnnic.cn/html/1245053573d634.html

Chinn, M. D., & Fairlie, R. W. (2007). The determinants of the global digital divide: A cross-country analysis of computer and internet penetration. *Oxford Economic Papers, 59*, 16–44. doi:10.1093/oep/gpl024

Cho, J., de Zuniga, H., Rojas, H., & Shah, D. (2003). Beyond access: The digital divide and Internet uses and gratifications. *IT & Society, 1*(4), 46–72.

Cholin, V. S. (2005). Study of the application of information technology for effective access to resources in Indian university libraries. *The International Information & Library Review, 37*(3), 189–197. doi:10.1016/j.iilr.2005.07.002

Christensen, H., Griffiths, K., & Jorm, A. F. (2004). Delivering interventions for depression by using the Internet: Randomised controlled trials. *British Medical Journal, 328*(7434), 265–268. doi:10.1136/bmj.37945.566632.EE

Christensen, P. (2003). Place, space and knowledge: Children in the village and the city. In Christensen, P., & O'Brian, M. (Eds.), *Children in the City: Home neighbourhood and community* (pp. 13–28). London: RoutledgeFalmer. doi:10.4324/9780203167236

Christensen, P., & O'Brian, M. (2003). Children in the city: Introducing new perspectives. In Christensen, P., & O'Brian, M. (Eds.), *Children in the city: Home neighbourhood and community* (pp. 1–12). London: RoutledgeFalmer. doi:10.4324/9780203167236

Christensen, P., & Prout, A. (2002). Working with ethical symmetry in social research with children. *Childhood, 9*(4), 447–497. doi:10.1177/0907568202009004007

Cibbora, C. (2005). Interpreting e-government and development. *Information Technology & People, 18*(3), 260–279. doi:10.1108/09593840510615879

City of Decatur. Administrative Services. (2009, January). *Wireless Network Complete* (Press release). Retrieved June 7, 2009 from http://www.decaturga.com/cgs_citysvcs_atr_technology_wireless.aspx

City of Minneapolis. Communications. (2008, December 18). *Wireless Minneapolis results in new funding to help bridge the digital divide* (Press release). Retrieved June 5, 2009 from http://www.ci.minneapolis.mn.us/news/20081218DigitalInclusionAwards.asp

Cleaver, H., & Walker, S. (2004). From Policy to Practice: The implementation of a new framework for social work assessments of children and families. *Child & Family Social Work, 9*, 81–90. doi:10.1111/j.1365-2206.2004.00314.x

Clement, A., & Shade, L. R. (2000). The Access Rainbow: Conceptualising universal Access to the Information/Communication Infrastructure. In Gurstein, M. (Ed.), *Informatics: enabling communities with information and communications technologies* (pp. 32–51). Hershey, PA: IGI Global.

Clement, T., & Bigby, C. (2009). Breaking out a distinct social space: Reflections on supporting community participation for persons with severe and profound intellectual disability. *Journal of Applied Research in Intellectual Disabilities, 22*, 264–275. doi:10.1111/j.1468-3148.2008.00458.x

Coffey, A., & Atkinson, P. (1996). *Making sense of qualitative data: Complementary Research Strategies.* Thousand Oaks, CA: Sage.

Colecchia, A., & Schreyer, P. (2001). *The impact of information communications technology on output growth* (STI Working Paper 2001/7). Paris: OECD.

Colfer, C. J. P. (1983). Communication among "unequals". *International Journal of Intercultural Relations, 7,* 263–283. doi:10.1016/0147-1767(83)90033-0

Coombs, P. H. (1989). Formal and nonformal education: Future strategies. In Titmus, C. (Ed.), *Lifelong learning education for adults* (pp. 57–60). Oxford, UK: Pergamon.

Corbett, J. M., Muir, K., & Singleton, G. (2009). Web 2.0 for Aboriginal Cultural Survival: A new Australian Outback Movement. *Participatory Learning and Action, 59,* 71–78.

Cousins, B., & Earl, L. (1992). The case for participatory evaluation. *Educational Evaluation and Policy Analysis, 14*(4), 397–418.

Crampton, J. W., & Krygier, J. (2006). An introduction to critical cartography. *ACME An International E-Journal for Critical Geographies, 4*(1), 11-33. Retrieved Mach 29, 2009 from http://www.acme-journal.org

Create Foundation. (2001). *Participation in Case Planning Processes. A Consultation with Children and Young People in Care about their Experiences of Decision Making.* Sydney, Australia: Create Foundation.

Creswell, J. (2003). *Research design* (2nd ed.). Thousand Oaks, CA: Sage.

Creswell, J. W. (2003). *Research design: Qualitative, quantitative, and mixed methods approaches.* Thousand Oaks, CA: Sage.

Creswell, J. W. (2008). *Qualitative inquiry and research design.* Thousand Oaks, CA: Sage.

Creswell, J. W., Plano Clark, V. L., Gutmann, M. L., & Hanson, W. E. (2003). Advanced mixed methods research designs. In Tashakkori, A., & Teddlie, C. (Eds.), *Handbook of mixed methods in the social and behavioral sciences* (pp. 209–241). Thousand Oaks, CA: Sage.

Crocker, S. (2003). The Fogo Process: Participatory Communication in a Globalizing World. In White, S. (Ed.), *Participatory Video: Images that Transform and Empower* (pp. 122–144). New Delhi, India: Sage Publications.

Crossing Boundaries National Council (CBNC). (2005). *Aboriginal Voice National Recommendations: From Digital Divide to Digital Opportunity (Crossing Boundaries Papers).* Ottawa, Canada: KTA Centre for Collaborative Government.

Cross, M., & Adam, F. (2007). ICT Policies and Strategies in Higher Education in South Africa: National and Institutional Pathways. *Higher Education Policy, 20*(1), 73–95. doi:10.1057/palgrave.hep.8300144

Crystal, D. (2008). *Txtng: the Gr8 Db8. Oxford University Press.*

Cuban, L. (2001). *Oversold and underused: Computers in the classroom.* Cambridge, MA: Harvard University Press.

Curtis, K., Robert, H., Copperman, J., & Liabo, K. (2004). "How come I don't get asked no questions?" Researching "hard to reach" children and teenagers. *Child & Family Social Work, 9,* 167–175. doi:10.1111/j.1365-2206.2004.00304.x

Cuthell, J. P. (2002). *How do interactive whiteboards enhance learning?* Retrieved February 24, 2004, from http://www.virtuallearning.org.uk/ iwb/Learning_theories.pdf

Cuthell, J. P. (2004). *Interactive whiteboards survey.* Retrieved May 22, 2005, from http://www.virtuallearning.org.uk/ 2003/whiteboards/survey.doc

Cuthell, J. P. (2005). *Seeing the meaning. The impact of interactive whiteboards on teaching and learning.* Paper presented at WCCE 05, Stellenbosch, South Africa.

Dada, D. (2006). The failure of E-Government in developing countries: A literature review. *The Electronic Journal of Information Systems in Developing Countries, 26.* Retrieved May 11, 2009, from http://www.ejisdc.org/ojs2/ index.php/ejisdc/article/ viewFile/277/176

Dahal, G. R., & Adhikari, K. P. (2008). *Bridging, linking, and bonding social capital in collective action: The case of Kalahan Forest Reserve in the Philippines* (CAPRi working paper 79). Washington, DC: International Food Policy Research Institute (IFPRI).

Dahlman, C. J. (2003). Using knowledge for development: a general framework and preliminary assessment of China. In B. Grewal, L. Xue, P. Sheehan, & F. Sun (Eds.), *China's future in the knowledge economy: Engaging the new world* (pp. 35-66). Melbourne, Australia: Centre for Strategic Economic Studies, Victoria University and Tsinghua University Press.

Dahlman, C. J., Routti, J., & Ylä-Anttila, P. (2005). *Finland as a knowledge economy: Elements of success and lessons learned*. Washington, DC: International Bank for Reconstruction and Development European Forecasting Network. (2004). *The Euro area and the Lisbon strategy*. Milan, Italy: Author.

Dahlman, C., Zeng, D., & Wang, S. (2007). *Enhancing China's competitiveness through lifelong learning*. Retrieved September 10, 2008, from http://web.worldbank.org/WBSITE/ EXTERNAL/WBI/WBI-PROGRAMS/KFDLP/ 0,contentMDK:21387573~menuPK:1727232~ pagePK:64156158~piPK:64152884~theSitePK:461198,00.html

Darling, J. (2007). *Investigating the effectiveness and efficiency of games and game based learning communities to support students learning*. Retrieved May, 2009, from http://www.bath.ac.uk/learningandteaching/ recognition/tdf/case_studies

Davis, R. A., Flett, G. L., & Besser, A. (2002). Validation of a new scale for measuring problematic Internet use: Implications for pre-employment screening. *CyberPsychology and Behaviors*, *5*(4), 331–345. doi:10.1089/109493102760275581

Delanty, G., & O'Mahony, P. (2002). *Nationalism and Social Theory: Modernity and Recalcitrance of the Nation*. London: Sage Publications.

Delors, J., Al Mufti, I., Amagi, I., Carneiro, R., Chung, F., & Geremek, B. (1996). *Learning: The treasure within*. Paris: UNESCO Publishing.

Demoussis, M., & Giannakopoulos, N. (2006). Facets of the digital divide in Europe: Determination and extend of Internet use. *Economics of Innovation and New Technology*, *15*(3), 235–246. doi:10.1080/10438590500216016

Denzin, N., & Lincoln, Y. (2008). *Collecting and interpreting qualitative materials*. Thousand Oaks, CA: Sage.

Devaney, L. (2008). Schools lagging in use of digital assessments. *eSchool News*, *11*(8), 22.

Dewan, S., & Riggins, F. (2005). The digital divide: Current and future research directions. *Journal of the Association for Information Systems*, *6*(12), 298–337.

Dewey, J. (1938). *Experience and education*. New York: Collier Books.

DFID (Department for International Development). (1999). *Sustainable guidance sheets: framework*. London: Department for International Development.

Diekmann, F. D. (2009). The new rock stars (economists) & 1 song being sung. *Credit Union Journal*, *13*(16), 6.

Digital Impact Group - Make a Digital Difference. (n.d.). Retrieved June 07, 2009 from http://www.wirelessphiladelphia.org/ digital_partners.cfm

DiMaggio, P., & Hargittai, E. (2001) *From the 'Digital Divide' to 'Digital Inequality': Studying Internet Use as Penetration Increases* (Working Paper 15). Princeton, NJ: Princeton University, Center for Arts and Cultural Policy Studies.

Dimireva, I. (2009, September). Geographical eInclusion. *EU Business News - EUbusiness.com*. Retrieved November 13, 2009 from http://www.eubusiness.com/Internet/Internet/eInclusion/

Dingwall, C. (2007). Municipal Broadband: Challenges and Perspectives. *Federal Communications Law Journal*, *59*(2), 69–106. Retrieved from http://www.law.indiana.edu/ fclj/pubs/v59no2.html.

DLPOD. (2008). *District Leaders Podcast*. Retrieved March 28, 2008, from http://blog.districtleaderspodcast.org

Donnermeyer, J., & Hollifield, A. (2003). Digital divide evidence in four rural towns. *IT & Society*, *1*(4), 107–117.

Dooley, L. M., Metcalf, T., & Martinez, A. (1999). A study of adoption of computer technology by teachers. *Educational Technology & Society*, *2*(4). Retrieved March 10, 2006, from http://ifets.massey.ac.nz/ periodical/vol_4_99/Idooley.html

Dowse, L. (2009). Some people are never going to be able to do that. Challenges for people with intellectual disability in the 21st Century. *Disability & Society, 24*(5), 571–584. doi:10.1080/09687590903010933

Drever, E. (1995). *Using semi-structured interviews in small-scale research: A teacher's guide*. Glasgow, UK: The Scottish Council for Research in Education.

Driskell, D. (2002). *Creating better cities with children and youth*. London: Earthscan.

Drolet, M., & Sauve-Kobylecki, M. (2006). The needs of children in care and the Looking After Children approach: Steps towards promoting children's best interests. In Flynn, R. J., Dudding, P. M., & Barber, J. G. (Eds.), *Promoting Resilience in Child Welfare*. Ottawa, Canada: University of Ottawa Press.

Dudely, M. (2003). The Transformative Power of Video: Ideas, Images, Processes and Outcomes. In White, S. (Ed.), *Participatory Video: Images that Transform and Empower* (pp. 145–156). New Delhi, India: Sage Publications.

Dutta-Bergman, M. (2005). Access to the internet in the context of community participation and community satisfaction. *New Media & Society, 7*(1), 89–109. doi:10.1177/1461444805049146

Dutton, W. (2005, February). *The social dynamics of the Internet*. Paper presented at the International Knowledge and Society Conference, Berkeley, CA.

Ebersold, S. (2007). Affiliating participation for active citizenship. *Scandinavian Journal of Disability Research, 9*(3-4), 237–253. doi:10.1080/15017410701685893

Economist Intelligence Unit. (2004). *Reaping the benefits of ICT Europe's productivity challenge*. Retrieved July 7, 2009, from http://74.125.47.132/search?q= cache:ZI6UMSLbHXYJ:graphics.eiu.com/ files/ad_pdfs/ MICROSOFT_FINAL.pdf +ict+relationship+producti vity&cd =1&hl=en&ct=clnk&gl= us&client=firefox-a

Educause. (2009). *Student Guide to Evaluating Information Technology on Campus*. Retrieved December 18, 2009, from http://www.educause.edu/ studentguide

Edwards, C. (2008). Participative urban renewal? Disability, community and partnership in New Labour's urban policy. *Environment and Planning, 40*(7), 1664–1680. doi:10.1068/a39199

Egbert, J., & Yang, Y. F. (2004). Mediating the digital divide in CALL classrooms: Promoting effective language tasks in limited technology contexts. *ReCALL, 16*(2), 280–291. doi:10.1017/S0958344004000321

Elwood, S. (2002). GIS use in community planning: A multidimensional analysis of empowerment. *Environment & Planning A, 34*, 905–922. doi:10.1068/a34117

Elwood, S. (2006). Critical issues in participatory GIS: Deconstructions, reconstructions, and new research directions. *Transactions in GIS, 10*(5), 693–708. doi:10.1111/j.1467-9671.2006.01023.x

Ertl, H., & Plante, J. (2004). *Connectivity and learning in Canada's schools* (Research Paper No. 56F0004MIE–No. 011). Ottawa, ON: Science, Innovation and Electronic Information Division, Statistics Canada.

eSchool News. (2008). Schools try to reach students via podcast. *eSchool News, 11*(28), 4.

Eteokleous, N. (2008). Evaluating computer technology integration in a centralized school system. *Computers & Education, 51*, 669–686. doi:10.1016/j.compedu.2007.07.004

Evans, K., Velarde, S. J., Prieto, R., Rao, S. N., Sertzen, S., Dávila, K., et al. (2006). In E. Bennett & M. Zurek (Eds.), *Field guide to the Future: Four Ways for Communities to Think Ahead*. Nairobi: Center for International Forestry Research (CIFOR). Retrieved from http://www.asb.cgiar.org/ma/scenarios

Evans, M., Hole, R., Berg, L., Hutchinson, P., & Sookraj, D. Okanagan Urban Aboriginal Research Health Collective. (in press). Common Insights, Differing Methodologies: Towards a Fusion of Indigenous Methodologies, Participatory Action Research, and White Studies in an Urban Aboriginal Research Agenda. *Qualitative Inquiry*.

Fairclough, N. (1992). *Discourse and Social Change*. Cambridge, UK: Polity Press.

Falchikov, N. (2003). Involving students in assessment. *Psychology Learning & Teaching, 3*(2), 102–108.

Fang, G., Zhao, C., & Duan, W. (2008). Building and utilizing post-secondary network education resources. *China Education Info, 19*, 28–32.

Fang, Z. (2009). Understanding new trends in distance education and building high quality distance higher education. *Distance Education in China, 9*, 10–14.

Fernandez, E. (2007). Supporting children and responding to families: Capturing the evidence on family support. *Children and Youth Services Review*. .doi:10.1016/j.childyouth.2007.05.012

Ferreira, G. (2006). Participatory Video for Policy Development. *Canadian Journal of Communication*. Retrieved September 2009, from http://www.cjconline.ca/ index.php/journal/thesis/view/68

Ferreira, G., Ramirez, R., & Walmark, B. (2004, September 18). *Connectivity in Canada's Far North: Participatory Evaluation in Ontario's Aboriginal Communities.* Paper presented at the Measuring the Information Society: What, How, for Who and What? Workshop, Brighton, UK.

Fink, C., & Kenny, C. (2003). W(h)ither the digital divide? *Info, 5*(6), 15–24. doi:10.1108/14636690310507180

Fitchen, C., Ferraro, V., Asuncion, J., Chowjka, C., Barile, M., Nguyen, M., Klomp, R., & Wolforth, J. (2009). Disabilities and e-learning problems and solutions: An exploratory study. *Educational technology & Society, 12*(4), 241-256.

Fitriana, Y. R. (2008). *Landscape and Farming System in Transition: Case Study in Viengkham District, Luang Prabang Province, Lao PDR.* Montpelier, France: Agronomy and Agro-Food Program, Institut des Regions Chaudes-Supagro.

Fleishman, G. (2008, November 17). Second wind for muni WiFi? Mesh-networking startup hopes so. *Ars Technica*. Retrieved May, 2009 from http://arstechnica.com

Flynn, N. (2004). *Instant Messaging Rules: A Business Guide to Managing Policies, Security, and Legal Issues for Safe IM-Communication.* New York: AMACOM/American Management Association.

Flynn, N., & Kahn, R. (2003). *E-Mail Rules: A Business Guide to Managing Policies, Security, and Legal Issues for E-Mail and Digital Communication.* New York: AMACOM/American Management Association.

Flyvbjerg, B. (2001). *Making social science matter: Why social inquiry fails and how it can succeed again.* Cambridge, UK: Cambridge University Press.

Folke, C., Hahn, T., Olsson, P., & Norberg, J. (2005). Adaptive Governance of Social-ecological Systems. *Annual Review of Environment and Resources, 30*, 441–473. doi:10.1146/annurev.energy.30.050504.144511

Forestier, E., Grace, J., & Kenny, C. (2002). Can information and communication technologies be pro-poor? *Telecommunications Policy, 26*, 623–646. doi:10.1016/S0308-5961(02)00061-7

Fostaty-Young, S., & Wilson, R. J. (2000). *Assessment and learning: The ICE approach.* Winnipeg, MB, Canada: Portage and Main Press.

Foster, S. P. (2000). The Digital Divide: Some Reflections. *The International Information & Library Review, 32*(3/4), 437–451. doi:10.1006/iilr.2000.0136

Francis, J. (2002). Implementing the Looking After Children in Scotland materials: Panacea or steppingstone? *Social Work Education, 21*(4), 457–463. doi:10.1080/02615470220150401

Freeman, C., & Aitken-Rose, E. (2005). Future shapers: Children, young people, and planning in New Zealand local government. *Environment and Planning. C, Government & Policy, 23*, 227–256. doi:10.1068/c0433

Freeman, D., & Johnson, K. (1998). Reconceptualizing the knowledge-base of language teacher education. *TESOL Quarterly, 32*(3), 397–416. doi:10.2307/3588114

Freire, P. (1970). *Pedagogy of the oppressed.* New York: Continuum.

Frontline. (2008). *Growing up online.* Retrieved March 15, 2009, from http://www.pbs.org/wgbh/ pages/frontline/kidsonline/

Fruend, P. (2001). Bodies, disability and spaces: The social model and disabling spatial organizations. *Disability & Society, 16*(5), 689–706. doi:10.1080/09687590120070079

Fuchs, C. (2009). The Role of Income Inequality in a Multivariate Cross-National Analysis of the Digital Divide. *Social Science Computer Review, 27*(1), 41–58. doi:10.1177/0894439308321628

Fujita, Y. (2006). Understanding the History of Change in Laos. *Mountain Research and Development, 26*(3), 197–199. doi:10.1659/0276-4741(2006)26[197:UTHOCI]2.0.CO;2

Fujita, Y., & Phengsopha, K. (2008). The Gap between Policy and Practice in Lao PDR. In Colfer, C. J. P., Dahal, G. R., & Capistrano, D. (Eds.), *Lessons from Forest Decentralization: Money, Justice and the Quest for Good Governance in Asia-Pacific*. London: Earthscan/CIFOR.

Fuller, F. F. (1969). Concerns of teachers: A developmental conceptualization. *American Educational Research Journal, 6*(2), 207–226.

Gall, M. D., Gall, J. P., & Borg, W. R. (2003). *Education research: An introduction* (7th ed.). Toronto, ON, Canada: Pearson Education Incorporation.

Galois, R. (1994). *Kwakwaka'wakw Settlement Sites, 1775-1920: A Geographical Analysis and Gazetteer*. Vancouver, Canada: UBC Press.

Garner, C. W. (2004). *Education finance for school leaders*. Upper Saddle River, NJ: Pearson-Merrill Prentice Hall.

Garrett, P. M. (2003). *Remaking Social Work with Children and Families. A Critical Discussion of the "Modernisation" of Social Care*. London: Routledge. doi:10.4324/9780203380765

Garrett, P. M. (2004). The electronic eye: Emerging surveillant practices in social work with children and families. *European Journal of Social Work, 7*(1), 57–71. doi:10.1080/1369145042000217401

Garrett, P. M. (2005). Social work's 'electronic turn': Notes on the deployment of information and communication technologies in social work with children and families. *Critical Social Policy, 25*(4), 529–553. doi:10.1177/0261018305057044

Garrett, R. K., & Danziger, J. N. (2008). IM=interruption management? instant messaging and disruption in the workplace. *Journal of Computer-Mediated Communication, 13*(1), 23–42. doi:10.1111/j.1083-6101.2007.00384.x

Garver, M. S., & Mentzer, J. T. (1999). Logistics research methods: employing structural equation modeling to test for construct validity. *Journal of Business Logistics, 20*(1), 33–57.

George, A. A., Hall, G. E., & Stiegelbauer, S. M. (2006). *Measuring implementation in schools: The Stages of Concern questionnaire*. Austin, TX: Southwest Educational Development Laboratory.

Georgia Centers for Advanced Telecommunications Technology (GCATT). (2004). U.S. Wireless Policy and People with Disabilities: A Status Report. In H. Mitchell, P. M. A. Baker, & A. Bakowsi (Eds.). Atlanta, GA: GCATT and Wireless RERC. Retrieved April 24, 2007 from Gillett, L., & Osorio. (2003, September). *Local Government Broadband Initiatives*. Paper presented at the MIT Program on Internet and Telecoms Convergence.

Gilbertson, R., & Barber, J. C. (2004). The systemic abrogation of standards in foster care. *Australian Journal of Social Work, 57*(1), 31–45. doi:10.1111/j.0312-407X.2003.00112.x

Gilbertson, R., & Barber, J. G. (2002). Obstacles to involving children and young people in foster care research. *Child & Family Social Work, 7*(4), 253–258. doi:10.1046/j.1365-2206.2002.00251.x

Gil-Garcia, R., Helbig, N., & Ferro, E. (2006). Is It Only About Internet Access? An Empirical Test of a Multi-dimensional Digital Divide. In *Proceedings of EGOV 2006* (pp. 139-149). New York: Springer. DOI: 10.1007/11823100

Gille, L. (1986). Growth and telecommunications. *Information, Telecommunications and Development*, 25-61.

Glaser, B. G., & Strauss, A. L. (1967). *The discovery of grounded theory*. Chicago: Aldine.

Gleckman, H. (2009). *Global Governance and Policy Coherence: Before and After the G20 Summit, Global Policy Coherence 2009 Project*. Institute for Environmental Security.

Glotzbach, R., Mordkovich, D., & Radwan, J. (2008). Syndicated RSS feeds for course information distribution. *Journal of Information Technology Education, 7*, 163–183.

Godin, B. (2004). The New Economy: What the concept owes to the OECD. *Research Policy, 33*(5), 679–690. doi:10.1016/j.respol.2003.10.006

Gong, Z. (2007). Open distance education in China and India: A comparison. *Distance Education Journal, 5*, 38–41.

Gordon, C. F., Juang, L. P., & Syed, M. (2007). Internet use and well-being among college students: beyond frequency of use. *Journal of College Student Development, 48*(6), 674–688. doi:10.1353/csd.2007.0065

Görg, C. (2007). Landscape governance: The "politics of scale" and the "natural" conditions of places. *Geoforum*, *38*(5), 954–966. doi:10.1016/j.geoforum.2007.01.004

Gramoll, K. (2001). An Internet Portal for Statics and Dynamics Engineering Courses. In *Proceedings of the International Conference of Engineering* (pp. 1-6).

Graneheim, U. H., & Lundman, B. (2004). Content analysis in nursing research: concepts, procedures and measures to achieve trustworthiness. *Nurse Education Today*, *24*(2), 105–112. doi:10.1016/j.nedt.2003.10.001

Granger, C. A., Morbey, M. L., Lotherington, H., Owston, R. D., & Wideman, H. H. (2002). Factors contributing to teachers' successful implementation of IT. *Journal of Computer Assisted Learning*, *18*(4), 480–488. doi:10.1046/j.0266-4909.2002.00259.doc.x

Greene, M. (1993). The passions of pluralism. *Educational Researcher*, *22*(1), 13–18.

Greene, W. H. (2000). *Econometric Analysis* (4th ed.). Upper Saddle River, NJ: Prentice Hall.

Gubrium, J. F., & Holstein, J. A. (Eds.). (2003). *Postmodern Interviewing*. Thousand Oaks, CA: Sage.

Gunasekaran, V., & Harmantzis, F. C. (2008). Towards a Wi-Fi ecosystem: Technology integration and emerging service models. *Telecommunications Policy*, *32*, 163–181. http://www.cacp.gatech.edu/Policy/ Briefings/EU_Policy_Report_9-21_(B).pdf. doi:10.1016/j.telpol.2008.01.002

Gunkel, D. J. (2003). Second thoughts: toward a critique of the digital divide. *New Media & Society*, *5*(4), 499–522. doi:10.1177/146144480354003

Guzdial, M., & Weingarten, F. W. (Eds.). (1995). *Setting a computer science research agenda for educational technology*. Washington, DC: Computer Research Association.

Habermas, J. (1984). *The theory of communicative action* (*Vol. 1*). Boston, MA: Beacon Press.

Haddad, W. D., & Draxler, A. (Eds.). (2005). *Technologies for education: potentials, parameters, and prospects*. Paris: UNESCO. Retrieved May 1, 2005, from http://unesdoc.unesco.org/ images/0011/001191/119129e.pdf

Hagemann, H. (2008). Consequences of the new information and communication technologies for growth, productivity and employment. *Competitiveness Review: An International Business Journal*, *18*(1/2), 57–69. doi:10.1108/10595420810874600

Hair, J. F., Anderson, R. E., Tatham, R. L., & Black, W. C. (1998). *Multivariate Data Analysis*. Upper Saddle River, NJ: Prentice-Hall.

Hall, G. E., George, A. A., & Rutherford, W. L. (1979). *Measuring Stages of Concern about the innovation: a manual for use of the SoC questionnaire* (Tech. Rep. No. 3032). Austin, TX: Research and Development Center for Teacher Education, University of Texas.

Hall, G. E., Wallace, R. D., Jr., & Dossett, W. A. (1973). *A developmental conceptualization of the adoption process within educational institutions*. Austin, TX: Research and Development Center for Teacher education, University of Texas.

Hall, L., Dunkelberger, J., Ferreira, W., Prevatt, J. W., & Martin, N. (2003). Diffusion-adoption of personal computers and the internet in farm business decisions: Southeastern beef and peanut farmers. *Journal of Extension*, *41*(3). Retrieved January 20, 2009, from http://www.joe.org/joe/ 2003june/a6.shtml

Hall, G. E., & Hord, S. M. (1987). *Change in schools: Facilitating the process*. Ithaca, NY: State University of New York Press.

Hao, L., Wang, Y., & Wang, Y. (2008). A comparison of quality safeguard systems in Chinese and British network higher education. *China Education Info*, *1*, 6–11.

Hargittai, E., & Hinnant, A. (2008). Digital inequality: Differences in young adults' use of the Internet. *Communication Research*, *35*(5), 602–621. doi:10.1177/0093650208321782

Hargreaves, E. (2005). Assessment for learning? Thinking outside the (black) box. *Cambridge Journal of Education*, *35*(2), 213–224. doi:10.1080/03057640500146880

Hargreaves, E. (2007). The validity of collaborative assessment for learning. *Assessment in Education*, *14*(2), 185–199. doi:10.1080/09695940701478594

Harlan, T. (2001). Editors introduction. *Wizaco Sa Revue*, *16*(2), 55–73.

Harris, U. (2009). Transforming images: reimagining women's work through participatory video. *Development in Practice, 19*(4), 538–549. doi:10.1080/09614520902866405

Hart, R. A. (1997). *Children's participation: The theory and practice of involving young citizens in community development and environmental care.* London: Earthscan.

Hassani, S. N. (2006). Locating digital divides at home, work and everywhere else. *Poetics, 34,* 250–272. doi:10.1016/j.poetic.2006.05.007

Hattangdi, H., & Ghosh, A. (2009). Enhancing the quality and accessibility of higher education through the use of Information Communication Technology. *International Journal of Educational Management, 21*(6), 1–12.

Hawkins, B. L., & Oblinger, D. G. (2006). The myth about the digital divide. *EDUCAUSE Review, 41*(4), 12–13.

Healey, P. (1997). *Collaborative planning: Shaping places in fragmented societies.* Basingstoke, UK: Palgrave Macmillan.

Healey, P. (1999). Institutionalist analysis, communicative planning, and shaping places. *Journal of Planning Education and Research, 19*(2), 111–121. doi:10.1177/0739456X9901900201

Helbig, N., Gil-Garcia, R., & Ferro, E. (2009). Understanding the complexity of electronic government: Implications from the digital divide literature. *Government Information Quarterly, 26*(1), 89–97. doi:10.1016/j.giq.2008.05.004

Henman, P., & Adler, M. (2003). Information technology and the governance of social security. *Critical Social Policy, 23*(2), 139–163. doi:10.1177/0261018303023002002

Heptinstall, E. (2000). Gaining access to looked after children for research purposes: Lessons learned. *British Journal of Social Work, 30,* 867–872. doi:10.1093/bjsw/30.6.867

Heritage Foundation. (2009). *Index of economic freedom: Link between economic opportunity and prosperity.* Retrieved October 25, 2009, from http://www.heritage.org/Index/Default.aspx

He, Z. (2008). SMS in China: A Major Carrier of the Nonofficial Discourse Universe. *The Information Society, 24*(3), 182–190. doi:10.1080/01972240802020101

Higa, K., Sheng, R. L., Shin, B., & Figueredo, A. J. (2000). Understanding relationships among teleworkers' e-mail usage, e-mail richness perceptions, and e-mail productivity perceptions under a software engineering environment. *IEEE Transactions on Engineering Management, 47*(2), 163–173. doi:10.1109/17.846784

Hinchey, P. (2008). *Action research.* Thousand Oaks, CA: Sage.

Hoffman, D. L., Novak, T. P., & Schlosser, A. E. (2000). The Evolution of the Digital Divide: How Gaps in Internet Access May Impact Electronic Commerce. *Journal of Computer Mediated Communication, 5*(3). Retrieved October 6, 2009, from http://jcmc.indiana.edu/ vol5/issue3/hoffman.html

Hohlfeld, T. N., Ritzhaupt, A. D., Barron, A. E., & Kember, K. (2008). Examining the digital divide in K-12 public schools: Four-year trends for supporting ICT literacy in Florida. *Computers & Education, 51,* 1648–1663. doi:10.1016/j.compedu.2008.04.002

Holloway, S. L., & Valentine, G. (2003). *Cyberkids: Children in the information age.* London: Routledge Flamer.

Holloway, S., & Valentine, G. (2003). *Cyberkids: Children in the information age.* London: RoutledgeFalmer.

Hong, S., Katterattanakul, P., & Joo, S. (2008). Evaluating government accessibility: A comparative study. *International Journal of Information Technology & Decision Making, 7*(3), 419–515. doi:10.1142/S0219622008003058

Hord, S. M., Rutherford, W. L., Huling, L., & Hall, G. E. (1987). *Taking charge of change.* Alexandria, VA: Association for Supervision and Curriculum Development.

Horelli, L. (1998). Creating child-friendly environments: Case studies on children's participation in three European countries. *Childhood, 5*(2), 225–239. doi:10.1177/0907568298005002008

Horelli, L., & Kaaja, M. (2002). Opportunities and constraints of internet-assisted urban planning with young people. *Journal of Environmental Psychology, 22,* 191–200. doi:10.1006/jevp.2001.0246

Hough, G. (1996). *Information Technology in the Human Services: Whose Dreams, Whose Realities?* Paper presented at the HUSITA 4 Dreams and Realities: Information Technology and the Human Services, Finland.

Howard, L., & Remenyi, Z. (2006). Adaptive Blended Learning Environments. In *Proceedings of the 9ᵗʰ International Conference of Engineering Education* (pp. 1-6).

Howell, J., & Harbon, J. (2004). Agricultural landowners' lack of preference for internet extension. *Journal of Extension, 42*(6). Retrieved January 20, 2009, from http://www.joe.org/joe/ 2004december/a7.shtml

Hoyles, B., & Tregeagle, S. (2007, 1-3 May). *Harnessing Information and Communication Technology in work with young people.* Paper presented at the Are we there yet? Conference, Melbourne, Australia.

Hu, Z. (2009). A study on the diagnosis of student learning in distance education. *Distance Education in China.* Retrieved September 2, 2009, from http://www1.open.edu.cn/ ycjy/jiaoxue.php?id=295

Huang, F. (2009). Quality assurance in cross-border distance education: An international perspective. *Distance Education in China, 3.* Retrieved December 19, 2009, from http://caod.oriprobe.com/articles/ 15993542/Quality_Assurance_in_Cross_border_Distance_Educati.htm

Huang, W. (2007). Introduction of the market mechanism into distance higher education and legal safeguard of the public interest. *Distance Education in China,* 18-21.

Huber, B. (1999). *Communicative aspects of participatory video projects: an exploratory study.* Unpublished master's thesis, Sveriges Lantbruks Universitet, Sweden. Retrieved September 2007, from http://www.maneno.net/pdfs/bernhardsthesis.pdf

Hughes, B. (2009). Disability activisms: social model stalwarts and biological citizens. *Disability & Society, 24*(6), 677–688. doi:10.1080/09687590903160118

Hutchby, I. (2001). Technologies, texts and affordances. *Sociology, 35*(2), 441–456.

Hutchby, I. (2003). Affordances and the analysis of technologically mediated interaction. *Sociology, 37*(3), 581–589. doi:10.1177/00380385030373011

Igoa, C. (1995). *The Inner World of the Immigrant Child.* Mahwah, NJ: Lawrence Erlbaum.

Ikeda, K., & Richey, S. E. (2005). Japanese network capital: The impact of social networks on Japanese political participation. *Political Behavior, 27*(3), 239–252. doi:10.1007/s11109-005-5512-0

ITU. (2009). *Measuring the Information Society - The ICT Development Index, 2009 Edition.* Retrieved from http://www.itu.int/ITU-D/ict/publications/idi/2009/index.html

Jackson, S., & Kilroe, S. (1996). *Looking After Children: Good Parenting, Good Outcomes Reader.* London: The Stationery Office.

Jaeger, P. (2006). Telecommunications policy and individuals with disabilities: Issues of accessibility and social inclusion in the policy and research agenda. *Telecommunications Policy, 30,* 112–124. doi:10.1016/j.telpol.2005.10.001

Jalava, J., & Pohjola, M. (2002). Economic growth in the New Economy: Evidence from advanced economies. *Information Economics and Policy, 14*(2), 189–210. doi:10.1016/S0167-6245(01)00066-X

James, M., & Pedder, D. (2006). Beyond method: assessment and learning practices and values. *Curriculum Journal, 17*(2), 109–138. doi:10.1080/09585170600792712

Jiang, B., Huang, B., & Vasek, V. (2003). Geovisualisation for planning support systems. In Geertman, S., & Stillwell, J. (Eds.), *Planning support system in practice* (pp. 177–191). Berlin: Springer.

Johansson, L., Knippel, V., Waal, D., & Nyamachumbe, F. (2000). Questions and answers about participatory video. *Forest. Trees and People Newsletter, 40/41,* 35–40.

John, P. (2009). Can citizen governance redress the representative bias of political participation? *Public Administration Review, 69*(3-4), 494–502. doi:10.1111/j.1540-6210.2009.01995.x

Johnson, T. (2007). *Some research and examples of white space in web design.* Retrieved September 15, 2007, from http://www.corporatewebsite.com/ articles/some_research_

Johnson, D. R. (2005). *Addressing the growing problem of survey nonresponse.* University Park, PA: Survey Research Center, Penn State University.

Johnson, K. E. (1994). The emerging beliefs and instructional practices of preservice English as a second language teachers. *Teaching and Teacher Education, 10*, 439–452. doi:10.1016/0742-051X(94)90024-8

Joinson, A. N. (2001). Self-disclosure in computer-mediated communication: the role of and visual anonymity. *European Journal of Social Psychology, 31*, 177–192. doi:10.1002/ejsp.36

Joinson, A. N. (2005). Internet Behaviour and the Design of Virtual Methods. In Hine, C. (Ed.), *Virtual Methods: Issues in Social Research on the Internet*. New York: Berg.

Jonassen, D. H., Howland, J., Moore, J., & Marra, R. M. (2003). *Learning to solve problems with technology* (2nd ed.). Upper Saddle River, NJ: Prentice Hall.

Jones, H. (2006). The Integrated Children's System: A resilient system to promote the development in children in care. In Flynn, R. J., Dudding, P. M., & Barber, J. G. (Eds.), *Promoting Resilience in Child Welfare*. Ottowa, Canada: University of Ottowa Press.

Jorgensen, D. W. (2005). *Information Technology and the G7 Economies*. Retrieved July 7, 2009, from http://ws1.ad.economics.harvard.edu/ faculty/jorgenson/files/IT%20and% 20the%20G7%20economies_with%20graphx_05-0301.pdf

Jussi, L. (2006). *Municipal WLAN: Case Examples in Finland (Tech. Rep.)*. Helsinki, Finland: Helsinki University of Technology.

Kalim, R., & Lodhi, S. (2004). *The Knowledge-Based Economy: trends and implications for Pakistan*. Retrieved May 15, 2009, from http://www.pide.org.pk/.../The%20Knowledge%20Based%20Economy.pdf

Katarzyna, M. (2002). *Knowledge Representation, Content Indexing and Effective Teaching of Fluid Mechanics Using Web-Based Content*. Unpublished master's thesis, Massachusetts Institute of Technology.

Kazemikaitiene, E., & Bileviciene, T. (2008). Problems of involvement of disabled persons in eGovernment. *Technology and Economic Development, 14*(2), 184–196. doi:10.3846/1392-8619.2008.14.184-196

Kennedy, D., & Bouchard, R. (2008, May 6). *Tlowitsis rights and title: a discussion paper*. Paper presented at the Tlowitsis Nation, Victoria, Canada.

Khalilov, M., Fonollosa, J. A. R., Zamora-Martinez, F., Castro-Bleda, M. J., & Espaa-Boquera, S. (2008, November 3-5). Neural Network Language Models for Translation with Limited Data. In *Proceedings of the 20th IEEE International Conference on Tools with Artificial Intelligence*, Dayton. *OH. Osteopathic Hospitals, 2*, 445–451.

Kilvington, M., Allen, W., & Kravchenko, C. (1999). *Improving Farmer Motivation Within Tb Vector Control* (Landcare Research Contract Report No. LC9899/110).

Kim, E., Lee, B., & Menon, N. (2009). Social welfare implications of the digital divide. *Government Information Quarterly, 26*, 377–386. doi:10.1016/j.giq.2008.11.004

Kim, G. S., Park, S.-B., & Oh, J. (2008). An examination of factors influencing consumer adoption of short message service (SMS). *Psychology and Marketing, 25*(8), 769–786. doi:10.1002/mar.20238

King, K. P. (2008). Introducing new media into teacher preparation. *ISTE SIGHC, 3*(4), 4–7.

King, K. P., & Gura, M. (2007). *Podcasting for teachers: Using a new technology to revolutionize teaching and learning*. Charlotte, NC: Information Age Publishing.

Kirby, N. F., & Downs, C. T. (2007). Self-assessment and the disadvantaged student: Potential for encouraging self-regulated learning? *Assessment & Evaluation in Higher Education, 32*(4), 475–494. doi:10.1080/02602930600896464

Klease, C. (2008). Silenced stakeholders: Responding to mothers' experiences of the child protection system. *Children Australia, 33*(3), 21–28.

Klein, D., Myhill, W., Hansen, L., Asby, G., Michaelson, S., & Blanck, P. (2003). Electronic Doors to Education: Study of High School Website Accessibility in Iowa. *Behavioral Sciences & the Law, 21*(1), 27–49. doi:10.1002/bsl.521

Ko, H. C., & Kou, F. Y. (2008). Can blogging enhance subjective well-being through self-disclosure. *Cyberpsychology & Behavior, 12*(1), 75–79. doi:10.1089/cpb.2008.016

Kolb, D. A. (1984). *Experiential learning*. Englewood Cliffs, NJ: Prentice-Hall.

Ko, M., Guynes Clark, J., & Ko, D. (2008). Revisiting the impact of information technology investments on productivity: An empirical investigation using Multivariate Adaptive Regression Splines (MARS). *Information Resources Management Journal, 21*(3), 1–23.

Komarudin, H., Siagian, Y., & Colfer, C. J. P. (2008). *Collective action for the poor: A case study in Jambi Province, Indonesia* (CAPRi Working Paper No. 90).

Kong, J., & Luo, J. (2006, October 25-27). The Innovative Business Model behind the Rapid Growth of SMS in China. In *Proceedings of the International Conference on Service Systems and Service Management* (pp. 1472-1477).

Koohang, A., Britz, J., & Seymour, T. (2006, June 25-28). *Hybrid/Blended Learning: Advantages, Challenges, Design, and Future Directions*. Paper presented at the Informing Science and IT Education Joint Conference, Manchester, UK.

Korte, W. B., & Hüsing, T. (2006). *Benchmarking Access and Use of ICT in European Schools 2006*. Retrieved from http://empirica.com/publikationen/ documents/ No08-2006_learnInd.pdf

Korupp, S., & Szydlick, M. (2005). Causes and trends of the digital divide. *European Sociological Review, 21*(4), 409–422. doi:10.1093/esr/jci030

Koufteros, X. A. (1999). Testing a model of pull production: a paradigm for manufacturing research using structural equation modeling. *Journal of Operations Management, 17*(4), 467–488. doi:10.1016/S0272-6963(99)00002-9

Koutsouris, A. (2006). ICTs and rural development: Beyond the hype. *Journal of Extension Systems, 22*(1), 46–62.

Koutsouris, A. (2008). The battlefield of (sustainable) rural development: The case of the Lake Plastiras, Central Greece. *Sociologia Ruralis, 48*(3), 240–256. doi:10.1111/j.1467-9523.2008.00465.x

Kozma, R. (2005). National Policies That Connect ICT-Based Education Reform To Economic And Social Development. *Human Technology, 1*(2), 117–156.

Kramer, R., Lopez, A., & Koonen, A. (2006). Municipal broadband access networks in the Netherlands - three successful cases, and how New Europe may benefit. In *Proceedings of the ACM International Conference on Access networks* (p. 267).

Kraut, R., Kiesler, S., Boneva, B., Cummings, J., Helgeson, V., & Crawford, A. (2002). Internet paradox revisited. *The Journal of Social Issues, 58*(1), 49–74. doi:10.1111/1540-4560.00248

Kriščiūnas, K., & Daugėlienė, R. (2006). The assessment models of Knowledge-Based Economy penetration. *Engineering Economics, 5*(50). ISSN 1392-2785.

Kruger, J., & Dunning, D. (1999). Unskilled and unaware of it: How difficulties in recognizing one's own incompetence lead to inflated self-assessment. *Journal of Personality and Social Psychology, 77*(6), 1121–1134. doi:10.1037/0022-3514.77.6.1121

Kudyba, S., & Diwan, R. K. (2002). *Information technology, corporate productivity, and the new economy*. New York: Quorum Books.

Kufeldt, K., Simard, M., Vachon, J., Baker, J., & Andrews, T. L. (2000). *Looking After Children in Canada: Final Report*. Report to Social Development Partnerships of Human Resources Development Canada: University of New Brunswick University Laval.

Kufeldt, K., McGilligan, L., Klein, R., & Rideout, S. (2006). The Looking After Children assessment process: Promoting resilient children and resilient workers. *Families in Society, 87*(4), 565–574.

Kuznetsov, Y., & Dahlman, C. J. (2008). *Mexico's Transition to a Knowledge-Based Economy Challenges and Opportunities*. Washington, DC: International Bank for Reconstruction and Development.

Kvale, S. (1983). The qualitative research interview; a phenomenological and a hermeneutic mode of understanding. *Journal of Phenomenological Psychology, 14*, 171–196. doi:10.1163/156916283X00090

Kvale, S. (1996). *InterViews: An introduction to qualitative research interviewing*. Thousand Oaks, CA: Sage.

Kyttä, M., Kaaja, M., & Horelli, L. (2004). An internet-based design game as a mediator of children's environmental visions. *Environment and Behavior, 36*(1), 127–151. doi:10.1177/0013916503254839

Lally, E. (2006). Compputing in domestic pattern of life. In Bell, D. (Ed.), *Cybercultures: Critical concepts in media and cultural studies* (pp. 219–241). Abingdon, UK: Routledge.

Lancaster, S., Yen, D. C., Huang, A. H., & Hung, S. Y. (2007). The selection of instant messaging or e-mail: College students' perspective for computer communication. *Information Management & Computer Security, 15*(1), 5–22. doi:10.1108/09685220710738750

Land Management Component. (2006). *Agro-ecosystems analysis and agro-ecological zoning, a handbook. Lao-Swedish Upland Agriculture and Forestry Research Program*. Vientiane, Laos: National Agriculture and Forestry Research Institute.

Lang, U. (2004). Virtual and Augmented Reality Developments for Engineering Applications. In *Proceedings of the European Congress on Computational Methods in Applied Sciences and Engineering* (pp. 1-16).

Lao People's Democratic Republic. (2004, June 8). *Advising Order on Establishing Village and Developing Villages Groups* (No. 09/PB.CP). Lao People Revolutionary Party Political Bureau of Central Party.

Lasley, P., & Bultena, G. (1986). Farmers' opinions about third-wave technologies. *American Journal of Alternative Technology, 1*, 99–110.

Lasley, P., Padgitt, S., & Hanson, M. (2001). Telecommunication technology and its implications for farmers and Extension Services. *Technology in Society, 23*, 109–120. doi:10.1016/S0160-791X(00)00039-7

Lave, J., & Wenger, E. (1991). *Situated learning*. Cambridge, UK: University of Cambridge Press.

Lawrence-Lightfoot, S., & Hoffmann, D. J. (1997). *The art and science of portraiture*. San Francisco: Jossey-Bass.

Lehner, F., & Watson, R. (2001) *From e-commerce to m-commerce: research directions* (working paper). Regensburg, Germany: University of Regensburg, Chair of Business Informatics.

Lekorwe, M., Molomo, M., Molefe, W., & Moseki, K. (2001). *Public attitudes toward democracy, governance and economic development in Botswana* (Afrobarometer Paper No.14). Afrobarometer.

Leonard, M. (2005). *With a capital "G": Gatekeepers and gate-keeping in research with children*.Unpublished manuscript, Queens University Belfast, Ireland.

Leonard, L. N. K., & Riemenschneider, C. K. (2008). What factors influence the individual impact of the Web? An initial model. *Electronic Markets, 18*(1), 75–90. doi:10.1080/10196780701797698

Leung, K. C. (2004). Statistics to measure the knowledge-based economy: The case of Hong Kong, China. In *Proceedings of the 2004 Asia Pacific Technical Meeting of Information and Communication Technology (ICT) Statistic*. Retrieved July 16, 2009, from http://www.unescap.org/.../18.Statistics_to_measure_the_Knowledge-Based_Economy- Hong_Kong.pdf

Leung, L. (2007). Unwillingness-to-communicate and college students' motives in SMS mobile messaging. *Telematics and Informatics, 24*(2), 115–129. doi:10.1016/j.tele.2006.01.002

Leuthold, S. (2001). Rhetorical Dimensions of Native American Documentary. *Wizaco Sa Review, 16*(2), 55–73. doi:10.1353/wic.2001.0022

Leuthold, S., Bargas-Avila, A., & Opwis, K. (2008). Beyond Web content accessibility guidelines: Design of enhanced text user interfaces for blind Internet users. *International Journal of Human-Computer Studies, 66*, 257–270. doi:10.1016/j.ijhcs.2007.10.006

Levin, H., Belfield, C., Muennig, P., & Rouse, C. (2007). *The costs and benefits of an excellent education for all of America's children*. Retrieved April 27, 2009, from http://www.cbcse.org/media/ download_gallery/ Leeds_Report_Final_Jan2007.pdf

Li, D., Yan, J., & Yao, W. (2008). Network education development in regular universities and in TV universities: A comparison. *Distance Education in China*. Retrieved January 8, 2009, from http://www1.open.edu.cn/ ycjy/indexzonghe.php

Li, J. (2007). An evaluation of the regulations in Chinese distance education. *Distance Education in China,* 25-29.

Li, J., & Yu, Q. (2009, April 18). Chinese university presidents reflect on higher education. *People's Daily Overseas Edition*, 4.

Liarokapis, F. (2002). Multimedia Augmented Reality Interface for E-Learning (MARIE). *World Transactions on Engineering and Technology Education, 1*(2), 173–176.

Liarokapis, F. (2004). Web3D Augmented Reality to Support Engineering Education. *World Transactions on Engineering and Technology Education, 3*(1), 11–14.

Li, D., Chau, P. Y. K., & Lou, H. (2005). Understanding Individual Adoption of Instant Messaging: An Empirical Investigation. *Journal of the Association for Information Systems, 6*(4), 102–129.

Lim, C. P., & Chai, C. S. (2004). An activity-theoretical approach to research of ICT integration 13 in Singapore schools: Orienting activities and learner autonomy. *Computers & Education, 43*(3), 215–236. doi:10.1016/j.compedu.2003.10.005

Lim, C. P., & Hang, D. (2003). An activity theory approach to research of ICT integration in Singapore schools. *Computers & Education, 41*(1), 49–63. doi:10.1016/S0360-1315(03)00015-0

Lim, K. G. (2002). The IT way of loafing on the job: Cyberloafing, neutralizing, and organizational justice. *Journal of Organizational Behavior, 23*(5), 675–694. doi:10.1002/job.161

Lin, K. (2008). Building on Components into Traditional Instruction in Pre-Service Teacher Education: The Good, the Bad and the Ugly. *International Journal for Scholarship of Teacher and Learning, 2*(1).

Linquist, B., Keoboualpha, B., Sodarak, H., Horne, P., & Lai, C. (2005). Upland Research in Lao PDR: Experiences with Participatory Research Approaches. In J. Gonsalves, T. Becker, A. Braunet, A. Laguna, A. Braun, D. Campilan, H. de Chavez, E. Fajber, M. Kapiriri, J. Rivaca-Caminade, & J. Vernooy (Eds.), *Participatory Research and Development for sustainable Agriculture and Natural Resource Management: A Sourcebook. Volume 3: Doing Participatory Research and Development* (pp. 58-65). Ottawa, Canada: International Potato Center-Users' Perspectives with Agricultural Research and Development (CIP-UPWARD) and International Development Research Centre (IDRC).

Liu, Y. (2009). *Distance Education and Life Long Learning Forum and Contemporary Distance Education Achievements in the Past 10 Years Exhibition held in Beijing.* Retrieved December 18, 2009, from http://www.moe.gov.cn/edoas/website18/57/info1257844793253457.htm

Liu, Y. (2007). Presentation given at 2007 Innovation and Development in ICT in Chinese Education Forum. *China Education Info, 7*, 5.

Liu, Y., & Huang, C. (2005). Concerns of teachers about technology integration in the USA. *European Journal of Teacher Education, 28*(1), 35–48. doi:10.1080/02619760500039928

Livingstone, D. (1999). Exploring the icebergs of adult learning. *Canadian Journal of Studies in Adult Education, 13*(2), 49–72.

Livingstone, S., & Helsper, E. (2007). Gradation in digital inclusion: Children, young people and the digital divide. *New Media & Society, 9*(4), 671–696. doi:10.1177/1461444807080335

Li, Z. (2008). Current situation of Chinese network coursework and resource development, its difficulties and strategies. *China Education Info, 19*, 12–14.

Lofland, L. H., Snow, D., Anderson, L., & Lofland, J. (2006). *Analyzing social settings* (4th ed.). Wadsworth Publishing Company.

Lopez-Nicolas, C., Molina-Castillo, F. J., & Bouwman, H. (2008). An assessment of advanced mobile services acceptance: Contributions from TAM and diffusion theory models. *Information & Management, 45*(6), 359–364. doi:10.1016/j.im.2008.05.001

Lucas, W. (1998). Effects of e-mail on the organization. *European Management Journal, 16*(1), 18–30. doi:10.1016/S0263-2373(97)00070-4

Lunch, C. (2007). The Most Significant Change: using participatory video for monitoring and evaluation. *Participatory Learning and Action, 56*, 28–32.

Lunch, N., & Lunch, C. (2006). *Insight's into Participatory Video: a handbook for the field.* Oxford, UK: Insight.

Lu, X. (2009). Promoting comprehensive education informationization, building and perfecting a national education information management and public service system. *China Education Info, 15*, 5–7.

Lynch, P., & Horton, S. (2001). *Web style guide* (2nd ed.). Retrieved September 15, 2007, from http://www.webstyleguide.com/ index.html?/sites/site_design.html

Lynch, K. (Ed.). (1977). *Growing up in cities: Studies of the spatial environment of adolescence in Cracow, Melbourne, Mexico City, Salta, Toluca, and Warszawa.* Cambridge, MA: MIT Press.

Ma, L. (2007). TV university distance education from the perspective of internationalization in higher education: Issues and strategies. *Distance Education in China,* 31-34.

MacEachren, A. (2004). *1995). How maps work: Representation, visualization, and design* (pp. iii–iv). New York: Guilford.

Macintosh, A. (2006). eParticipation in Policy-making: the research and the challenges. In P. Cunningham & M. Cunningham (Eds.), *Exploiting the Knowledge Economy: Issues, Applications and Case Studies* (pp. 364-369). Amsterdam: IOS press.

Madon, S. (2005) Evaluating the developmental impact of E-Governance initiatives: An exploratory framework. *The Electronic Journal of Information Systems in Developing Countries, 20.* Retrieved May 11, 2009, from http://www.ejisdc.org/ojs2/ index.php/ejisdc/article/view/123

Maguire, C., Kazlauskas, C., & Weir, A. D. (1994). *Information systems for innovative organizations.* London: Academic Press

Mahatanankoon, P. (2006). Predicting cyber-production deviance in the workplace. *International Journal of Internet and Enterprise Management, 4*(4), 314–330. doi:10.1504/IJIEM.2006.011043

Mahatanankoon, P., & O'Sullivan, P. (2008). Attitude toward mobile text messaging: An expectancy-based perspective. *Journal of Computer-Mediated Communication, 13*(4), 973–992. doi:10.1111/j.1083-6101.2008.00427.x

Maher, D. (2008). Cyberbullying: An ethnographic case study of one Australian upper primary school class. *Youth Studies Australia, 27*(4), 50–57.

Mahrer, H., & Krimmer, R. (2005). Towards the Enhancement of E-democracy: Identifying the Notion of the 'Middleman Paradox'. *Information Systems Journal, 15*(1), 27–42. doi:10.1111/j.1365-2575.2005.00184.x

Makinen, O., & Naarmala, J. (2008). The changing concept of the digital divide. In M. Iskander (Ed.), *Innovative Techniques in Instruction Technology, E-learning, E-assessment, and Education* (pp. 406-409). New York: Springer. DOI: 10.1007/978-1-4020-8739-4_71

Mansel, R. (2002). From Digital Divides to Digital Entitlements in Knowledge Societies. *Current Sociology, 50*(3), 407–426. doi:10.1177/0011392102050003007

March, H. W., & Hocevar, D. (1985). Application of confirmatory factor analysis to the study of self-concept: First- and higher-order factor models and their invariance across groups. *Psychological Bulletin, 97*, 562–582. doi:10.1037/0033-2909.97.3.562

Mariger, H. (2006). *Cognitive Disabilities and the Web: Where Accessibility and Usability Meet?* Retrieved October 11, 2007, from http://ncdae.org/tools/cognitive/

Marshall, C., & Rossman, G. B. (1995). *Designing Qualitative Research* (2nd ed.). Thousand Oaks, CA: Sage.

Marsick, V. J., & Watkins, K. (1990). *Informal and incidental learning in the workplace.* New York: Routledge.

Martinez-Moyano, I., & Gil-Garcia, J. R. (2004). Rules, norms, and individual preferences for action: An institutional framework to understand the dynamics of e-government evolution. In Traunmueller, R. (Ed.), *E-Government 2004* (pp. 194–199). Berlin: Springer-Verlag.

Mason, R. (2000). From distance education to online education. *The Internet and Higher Education, 3*(1-2), 63–74. doi:10.1016/S1096-7516(00)00033-6

Massachusetts Institute of Technology. (2009). *MIT Open Courseware.* Retrieved April 23, 2009, from http://ocw.mit.edu/OcwWeb/ web/home/home/index.htm

Matthews, H., Limb, M., & Taylor, M. (1999). Young people's participation and representation in society. *Geoforum, 30*, 135–144. doi:10.1016/S0016-7185(98)00025-6

Ma, W. (2009). The prospects and dilemmas of Americanizing Chinese higher education. *Asia Pacific Education Review, 10*, 117–124. doi:10.1007/s12564-009-9006-3

Mbarika, V. W., Kah, M. M., Musa, P. F., Meso, P., & Warren, J. (2003). Predictors of growth of teledensity in developing countries: A focus on low and middle income countries. *The Electronic Journal on Information Systems in Developing Countries, 12*, 1–16.

McClimens, A., & Gordon, F. (2009). Presentation of self in E-veryday life: How people labeled with intellectual disability manage identity as they engage the blogosphere. *Sociological Research Online, 13*(4).

McMahon, C. J. (2000). *Tutorials for Introduction to Materials Engineering*. Merrion Media. [CD-ROM]

Mehta, S., & Kalra, M. (2006). Information and Communication Technologies: A bridge for social equity and sustainable development in India. *The International Information & Library Review, 38*(3), 147–160. doi:10.1016/j.iilr.2006.06.008

Merinrath, S., Richard, M., & Middleton, C. (2006, October 19). *Public Forum: Municipal broadband networks: an idea whose time has come?* Lecture presented at the Alternative Telecommunications Policy Forum, Ottawa, Canada. Retrieved June 7, 2009 from www.cwirp.ca

Merriam, S. (1997). *Qualitative research and case study applications in education*. San Francisco: Jossey-Bass.

Ministry of Education. (2009). *2008 Chinese Education Development Statistics*. Retrieved August 31, 2009, from http://www.moe.gov.cn/edoas/ website18/34/info1247820433389334.htm

Ministry of Education. (2009). *Chinese universities receive more international students in the new academic year after overcoming the negative impact of the financial crisis*. Retrieved December 18, 2009, from http://www.moe.gov.cn/edoas/website18/21/info1257818426102421.htm

Ministry of Education. (2010). *2009 over 230,000 international students studied in China*. Retrieved April 2, 2010, from http://www.moe.gov.cn/edoas/ website18/39/info1269244278510339.htm

Ministry of Eduction. (n.d.). *British Columbia District Data Summary*. Retrieved October 17, 2009, from http://www.bced.gov.bc.ca/ reporting/enrol/teach.php

Miniwatts Marketing Group. (2010). *Internet World Stats*. Retrieved March 16, 2010, from http://www.internetworldstats.com/stats.htm

Moahi, K. G. (2007). Globalization, Knowledge Economy and the implication for Indigenous Knowledge. *International Review of Information Ethics (IRIE), 7*. ISSN 1614-1687

Moka, L. L. C. (2009). *Moka Partners with China Mobile for Mobile Chinese to English Language Translation and Language Learning*. Retrieved from http://www.moka.com/ en/news/news-1.htm

Moorman, C., & Matulich, E. (1993). A model for consumers' preventive health motivation and health ability. *The Journal of Consumer Research, 20*(2), 208–228. doi:10.1086/209344

Mueller, J., Wood, E., Willoughby, T., Ross, C., & Specht, J. (2008). Identifying discriminating variables between teachers who fully integrate computers and teachers with limited integration. *Computers & Education, 51*, 1523–1537. doi:10.1016/j.compedu.2008.02.003

Muhlberger, P. (2004). Access, skill and motivation in online political discussion: Testing cyberrealism. In Shane, P. M. (Ed.), *Democracy online: The prospects for political renewal through the Internet* (pp. 225–238). New York: Routledge.

Munro, E. (2001). Empowering looked after children. *Child & Family Social Work, 6*, 129–137. doi:10.1046/j.1365-2206.2001.00192.x

Munro, E. (2005). What tools do we need to improve identification of child abuse. *Child Abuse Review, 14*, 374–388. doi:10.1002/car.921

Nam, C. S., & Smith-Jackson, T. L. (2007). Web-based learning environment: A theory-based design process for development and evaluation. *Journal of Information Technology Education, 6*, 23–43.

National Bureau of Statistics of China. (2002). *89.5% respondents interested in foreign higher education*. Retrieved September 11, 2008, from http://www.stats.gov.cn/tjfx/ rddc/t20020531_21041.htm

National Federation of the Blind et al v. Target Corporation. (2007, March 8). *United States District Court, Northern District of California - San Francisco Division* (Justia, 4,154,104, Dist. file).

Naveh, Z. (1998). Ecological and cultural landscape restoration and the cultural evolution towards a post-industrial symbiosis between human society and nature. *Restoration Ecology*, *6*, 135–143. doi:10.1111/j.1526-100X.1998.00624.x

Neo, R. L., & Skoric, M. M. (2009). Problematic instant messaging use. *Journal of Computer-Mediated Communication*, *14*(3), 627–657. doi:10.1111/j.1083-6101.2009.01456.x

Nicol, D. J., & Macfarlane-Dick, D. (2006). Formative assessment and self-regulated learning: A model and seven principles of good feedback practice. *Studies in Higher Education*, *31*(2), 199–218. doi:10.1080/03075070600572090

Noce, A. A. (2008). A new benchmark for Internet use: A logistic modeling of factors influencing Internet use in Canada, 2005. *Government Information Quarterly*, *25*, 462–476. doi:10.1016/j.giq.2007.04.006

Norrish, P. (1998). Radio and Video for Development. In Richardson, D., & Paisley, L. (Eds.), *The First Mile of Connectivity*. Rome, Italy: Food and Agriculture Organization of the United Nations.

Norris, P. (2001). *Digital divide: Civic engagement, information poverty, and the Internet worldwide*. Cambridge, UK: Cambridge University Press.

Norsk Form. (2005). *Barnetråkk: Barns tilgjengelige uteareal* (Children's tracks: Children's accessible outdoor environments). Retrived June 20, 2009 from http://www.norskform.no/?V_ITEM_ID=1282

Obama, B. (2007, February 10). Illinois Sen. Barack Obama's announcement speech. *The Washington Post*. Retrieved July 7, 2009, from http://www.washingtonpost.com/ wp-dyn/content/article/2007/ 02/10/ AR2007021000879.html

Odendaal, N. (2003). Information and communication technology and local governance: Understanding the difference between cities in developed and emerging economies. *Computers, Environment and Urban Systems*, *27*, 585–607. doi:10.1016/S0198-9715(03)00016-4

OECD. (1997). *The OECD Report on regulatory reform: Synthesis*. Retrieved July 10, 2009, from http://www.oecd.org/dataoecd/ 17/25/2391768.pdf

OECD. (2005a). *Guide to measuring the information society 2005: Directorate for science, technology and industry*. Retrieved July 7, 2009, from http://www.oecd.org/dataoecd/ 41/12/36177203.pdf

OECD. (2005b). *OECD compendium of productivity indicators - 2005*. Retrieved July 7, 2009, from http://www.oecd.org/ dataoecd/6/15/37727582.pdf

OECD. (2006). *Are students ready for a technology rich world*? Retrieved July 20, 2006 from www.pisa.oecd.org

OECD. (2008). *Measuring the impacts of ICT using official statistics 2008: Directorate for science, technology and industry*. Retrieved July 7, 2009, from http://www.oecd.org/dataoecd/ 43/25/39869939.pdf

OECD. (2009a). *OECD member countries*. Retrieved July 7, 2009, from http://www.oecd.org/document/ 58 /0,3343,en_2649_201185_1889402 _1_1_1_1,00.html

OECD. (2009b). *Factbook 2009: Economic, environmental and social statistics; science and technology*. Retrieved July 7, 2009, from http://titania.sourceoecd.org/ vl=10066470/cl=24/nw= 1/rpsv/factbook/index.htm

OGIS - The Observatory for the Greek Information Society. (2009). *The digital Greece indicators: 4th annual report*. Athens, Greece: OGIS.

Oliner, S. D., & Sichel, D. (2000). The resurgence of growth in the late 1990s: Where are we now and where are we going? *The Journal of Economic Perspectives*, *14*(4), 15–44.

Ontario College of Teachers. (2006). *Foundations of professional practice*. Retrieved April 10, 2009, from http://www.oct.ca/ standards/foundations.aspx

Onwuegbuzie, A. J., & Teddlie, C. (2003). A framework for analyzing data in mixed methods research. In Tashakkori, A., & Teddlie, C. (Eds.), *Handbook of mixed methods in social and behavioral research* (pp. 351–383). Thousand Oaks, CA: Sage.

Orgad, S. (2005). From online to offline and back: Moving from online to offline relationships with research informants. In Hine, C. (Ed.), *Virtual Methods: Issues in Social Research on the Internet*. New York: Berg.

Organization for Economic Cooperation and Development. (2007). *Education at a glance 2007*. Retrieved September 10, 2008, from http://www.oecd.org/document/30/ 0,3343,en_2649_39263238_39251550_1_1_1_1,00.html

PĂCEŞILĂ M. (2006). The impact of moving to Knowledge Based Economy in the public sector. *Management & Marketing Craiova, 1*, 113-118. Retrieved June 12, 2009, from http://www.ceeol.com/aspx/ getdocument.aspx?logid=5&id

Paisley, L., & Richardson, D. (1999). *The first mile of connectivity: Why the first mile and not the last?* Rome, Italy: FAO.

Pakula, K. (2006, July 1-2). OMG! Your such a chatterbox. *Sydney Morning Herald,* p. 21.

Palfrey, J., & Gasser, U. (2008). *Born digital: Understanding the first generation of digital natives*. New York: Basic Books.

Papacharissi, Z., & Zaks, A. (2006). Is broadband the future? An analysis of broadband technology potential and diffusion. *Telecommunications Policy, 30*, 64–75. doi:10.1016/j.telpol.2005.08.001

Parker, R., Ward, H., Jackson, S., Aldgate, J., & Wedge, P. (1991). *Looking After Children: Assessing outcomes in child care*. London: HMSO.

Partnership for 21st Century Skills. (2004). *Learning for the 21st century*. Retrieved April 23, 2009, from http://www.21stcenturyskills.org/images/ stories/otherdocs/P21_Report.pdf

Partnership for 21st Century Skills. (2007). *21st century skills standards*. Retrieved May 9, 2009, from http://www.21stcenturyskills.org/documents/ 21st_century_skills_standards.pdf

Parton, N. (2009). Challenge to practice and knowledge in child welfare social work: From the "social" to the "informational"? *Children and Youth Servcies Review,* (doi:10.1016/j.childyouth.2009.01.008).

Parton, N. (2008). Changes in the form of knowledge in social work: From the "social" to the "informational". *British Journal of Social Work, 38*, 253–269. doi:10.1093/bjsw/bcl337

Patton, M. Q. (1997). *Utilization-focused evaluation: The new century text* (3rd ed.). Thousand Oaks, CA: Sage.

Patton, M. Q. (2002). *Qualitative research and evaluation methods* (3rd ed.). Thousand Oaks, CA: Sage.

Pelgrum, W. J. (2001). Obstacles to the integration of ICT in education: results from a worldwide educational assessment. *Computers & Education, 37*, 163–178. doi:10.1016/S0360-1315(01)00045-8

Percy-Smith, B., & Malone, K. (2001). Making children's participation in neighbourhood settings relevant to the everyday lives of young People. *PLA Notes, 42*, 18–22.

Personal Telco Project. (n.d.). Retrieved June 4, 2009 from http://www.personaltelco.net/

Pew Internet & American Life Project. (2008). *Degrees of Access* (May 2008 data). Washington, DC: Pew Research Center's Internet & American Life Project. Retrieved July 1, 2009 from http://www.pewinternet.org/ Presentations/2008/Degrees-of-Access-% 28May-2008-data%29.aspx

Pfund, J., Watts, J. D., Boffa, J., Colfer, C. J. P., Dewi, S., & Guizol, P. (2008). *Integrating Livelihoods and Multiple Biodiversity Values in Landscape Mosaics: Research Guidelines*. Bogor Barat, Indonesia: CIFOR.

Philadelphia Family TIES. (n.d.). Retrieved June 4, 2009 from http://www.phillyhealthinfo.org/ vision_for_equality/index.php/

Philadelphia, W. Communications. (2009, February 27). *Expanded Horizons and Empowerment for Families with Sons and Daughters with Disabilities* (Press release). Retrieved June 4, 2009 from http://www.wirelessphiladelphia.org/ wp_release_vfe_event_022709.pd

Phillips, J. G., & Reddie, L. (2007). Decisional style and self-reported email use in the workplace. *Computers in Human Behavior, 23*(5), 2414–2428. doi:10.1016/j.chb.2006.03.016

Pickles, J. (Ed.). (1995). *Ground truth: The social implications of geographic information systems*. New York: Guilford.

Piggot, L., Sapey, B., & Wilenius, F. (2005). Out of touch: Local government and disabled people's employment needs. *Disability & Society, 20*(6), 599–611. doi:10.1080/09687590500248365

Plante, J., & Beattie, D. (2004). *Connectivity and ICT integration in Canadian elementary and secondary schools: First results from the Information and Communications Technologies in schools survey, 2003-2004.* Retrieved January 3, 2008, from http://www.statcan.ca/english/research/ 81-595-MIE/81-595-MIE2004017.pdf

Plester, B., Blades, M., & Spencer, C. (2006). Children's understanding of environmental representations: Aerial photographs and model towns. In Spencer, C., & Blades, M. (Eds.), *Children and their environments: Learning, using and designing spaces* (pp. 42–56). New York: Cambridge University Press. doi:10.1017/CBO9780511521232.004

Plomp, T., Pelgrum, W. J., & Law, N. (2007). SITES2006 - International comparative survey of pedagogical practices and ICT in education. *Education and Information Technologies, 12*(2), 83–92. doi:10.1007/s10639-007-9029-5

Poelzer, G. (2002). *The Self-Government Landscape.* British Columbia, Canada: BC Treaty Commission. Retrieved October 2007, from http://www.bctreaty.net/files_3/ pdf_documents/self_government_landscape.pdf

Polanyi, M. (1967). *The tacit dimension.* New York: Doubleday.

Polat, R. K. (2005). The Internet and political participation. *European Journal of Communication, 20*(4), 435–459. doi:10.1177/0267323105058251

Powell, A. (2008). WiFi Publics: Producing Community and Technology. *Information Communication and Society, 11*(8), 1068–1088. doi:10.1080/13691180802258746

Powell, A., & Shade, L. R. (2006). Going Wi-Fi in Canada: Municipal and community initiatives. *Government Information Quarterly, 23*(3-4), 381–403. doi:10.1016/j.giq.2006.09.001

Premkumar, G., Ramamurthy, K., & Liu, H. (2008). Internet messaging: an examination of the impact of attitudinal, normative, and control belief systems. *Information & Management, 45*(7), 451–457. doi:10.1016/j.im.2008.06.008

Prensky, M. (2001). Digital natives, digital immigrants. [from http://www.marcprensky.com/writing/]. *Horizon, 9*(5), 1–6. Retrieved April 30, 2009. doi:10.1108/10748120110424816

Primeaux, R. O., & Flint, D. (2004). Instant Messaging: Does it belong in the Workplace? *Intellectual Property & Technology Law Journal, 16*(11), 5–7.

Putman, R. T., & Borko, H. (2000). What do new views of knowledge and thinking have to say about research on teacher learning? *Educational Researcher, 29*(1), 4–15.

Qian, X. (2009). A study of factors affecting the quality of network education services. *Journal of Distance Education, 4*, 54–56.

Qualters, M. D., Isaacs, J., Cullinane, T., Laird, J., Mcdonald, A., & Corriere, J. (2007). A Game Approach to Teach Environmentally Benign Manufacturing in the Supply Chain. *International Journal for the Scholarship of Teaching and Learning, 2*(2).

Quintelier, E., & Vissers, S. (2008). The Effect of Internet Use on Political Participation: An Analysis of Survey Results for 16-Year-Olds in Belgium. *Social Science Computer Review, 26*(4), 411–427. doi:10.1177/0894439307312631

Rajendran, B., & Venkataraman, N. (2009). FOSS solutions for community development. *International Journal of Information Communication Technologies and Human Development, 1*(1), 22–32.

Rakes, G. C., & Casey, H. B. (2002). An analysis of teacher concerns toward instructional technology. *International Journal of Educational Technology, 3*(1). Retrieved June 1, 2006, from http://www.ao.uiuc.edu/ijet/ v3n1/rakes/index.html

Raman, V. (2008). Examining the 'e' in government and governance: A case study in alternatives from Bangalore City, India. *The Journal of Community Informatics, 4*(2). Retrieved May 24, 2009, from http://www.ci-journal.net/index.php/ciej/article/view/437/405

Ramirez, R. (2001). A model for rural and remote information and communication technologies: a Canadian exploration. *Telecommunications Policy, 25*, 315–330. doi:10.1016/S0308-5961(01)00007-6

Ray, A. K. (2008). Measurement of social development: an international comparison. *Social Indicators Research, 86*(1), 1–46. doi:10.1007/s11205-007-9097-3

Raymond, H. (1999). *Learning to Teach Foreign Languages: Case Studies of Six Preservice Teachers in an Education Program*. Unpublished doctoral dissertation, The Ohio State University.

Reddick, A. (2000). *The dual digital divide: The information highway in Canada*. Ottawa, Canada: The Public Interest Advocacy Centre.

Redley, M. (2008). Citizens with learning disabilities and the right to vote. *Disability & Society, 23*(4), 375–384. doi:10.1080/09687590802038894

Reicken, T., Conibear, F., Corrine, M., Lyall, J., Scott, T., & Tanaka, M. (2006). Resistance through Re-representing Culture: Aboriginal Student Filmmakers and a Participatory Action Research Project on Health and Wellness. *Canadian Journal of Education, 29*(1), 265–286. doi:10.2307/20054156

Richardson, V. (1996). The role of attitudes and beliefs in learning to teach. In Sikula, J. (Ed.), *Handbook of Research on Teacher Education* (2nd ed.). New York: Association of Teacher Educators.

Richardson, W. (2006). *Blogs, wikis and podcasts*. Thousand Oaks, CA: Corwin.

Riddington, C., Mansell, J., & Beadle-Brown, J. (2008). Are partnership boards really valuing people? *Disability & Society, 23*(6), 649–665. doi:10.1080/09687590802328550

Ritchie, H., & Blanck, P. (2003). The promise of the internet for disability: A study of on-line services and website accessibility at Centers for Independent Living. *Behavioral Sciences & the Law, 21*, 5–26. doi:10.1002/bsl.520

Roberts, S. (2005, November 8). Working party on indicators for the information society guide to measuring the information society. In *Directorate for Science Technology and Industry*. Retrieved from http://www.oecd.org/dataoecd/41/12/36177203.pdf

Robinson, S. L., & Bennett, R. J. (1995). A topology of workplace deviant behaviors: A multidimensional scaling study. *Academy of Management Journal, 38*(2), 555–572. doi:10.2307/256693

Roca, J. C., Chiu, C. M., & Martinez, F. J. (2006). Understanding e-learning continuance intention: an extension of the Technology Acceptance Model. *International Journal of Human-Computer Studies, 64*(8), 683–696. doi:10.1016/j.ijhcs.2006.01.003

Roe, K., & Broos, A. (2005). Marginality in the information age: The socio-demographics of computer disquietude. *European Journal of Communication, 30*(1), 91–96.

Rogers, E. M. (1995). *Diffusion of Innovations* (4th ed.). New York: The Free Press.

Rogers, E. M. (2003). *Diffusion of innovation*. New York: Free Press.

Rogers, P. (2006). Young people's participation in the renaissance of public space: A case study of Newcastle upon Tyne, UK. *Children. Youth and Environments, 16*(2), 105–130.

Ross, H. (Director) (2006, September 26). The Philadelphia Municipal Wireless Project (Podcast series episode). In *NTEN: Nonprofit Technology News. Portland, Oregon: ODEO*. Retrieved June 5, 2009 from http://odeo.com/episodes/1988269-Part-1- The-Philadelphia-Municipal-Wireless-Project

Rotunda, R. J., Kass, S. J., Sutton, M. A., & Leon, D. T. (2003). Internet use and misuse: preliminary findings from a new assessment. *Behavior Modification, 27*(4), 484–504. doi:10.1177/0145445503255600

Rouibah, K. (2008). Social usage of instant messaging by individuals outside the workplace in Kuwait: A structural equation model. *Information Technology & People, 21*(1), 34–68. doi:10.1108/09593840810860324

Roulstone, A. (2003). Disability, new technology and the redefinition of space-opportunities and challenges. *Cognitive Processing, 4*, 1–12.

Roulstone, A. (2007). Citizenship and vulnerability: Disability and issues of social and political engagement. *Disability & Society, 22*(3), 329–337. doi:10.1080/09687590601141741

Rownok, T., Islam, M. Z., & Khan, M. (2006, December). *Bangla Text Input and Rendering Support for Short Message Service on Mobile Devices*. Paper presented at the 9th International Conference on Computer and Information Technology, Dhaka, Bangladesh.

Rummery, K. (2006). Disabled citizens and social exclusion: The role of direct payments. *Policy and Politics*, *34*(4), 633–650. doi:10.1332/030557306778553132

Rust, C., Price, M., & O'Donovan, B. (2003). Improving students' learning by developing their understanding of assessment criteria and processes. *Assessment & Evaluation in Higher Education*, *28*(2), 147–164. doi:10.1080/02602930301671

Ruth, A. (2008). Don't talk to me about e-mail! Technology's potential contribution to bullying. *International Journal of Organisational Behaviour*, *13*(2), 122–131.

Rutkowski, A. F., Saunders, C., Vogel, D., & van Genuchten, M. (2007). "Is it already 4 a.m. in your time zone?": Focus immersion and temporal dissociation in virtual team. *Small Group Research*, *38*(1), 98–129. doi:10.1177/1046496406297042

Rychen, D. S., & Salganik, L. H. (2003). *Key competencies for a successful life and a well functioning society*. Gottingen, Germany: Hogrefe & Huber.

Saade, R., & Bahli, B. (2005). The impact of cognitive absorption on perceived usefulness and perceived ease of use in on-line learning: An extension of the technology acceptance model. *Information & Management*, *42*(2), 317–327. doi:10.1016/j.im.2003.12.013

Sachs, J. (2005). *The end of poverty: Economic possibilities for our time*. New York: Penguin Group.

Sager, T. (1994). *Communicative Planning Theory. Avebury*. UK: Avebury Press.

Sager, T. (2006). The logic of critical communicative planning: Transaction cost alteration. *Planning Theory*, *5*(3), 223–254. doi:10.1177/1473095206068629

Sanyal, B. C. (2001, September 10-12). *New functions of higher education and ICT to achieve education for all*. Paper presented at the Expert Roundtable on University and Technology for Literacy and Education Partnership in Developing Countries, International Institute for Educational Planning, Paris.

Sapey, B. (1997). Social work tomorrow: Towards a critical understanding of technology in social work. *British Journal of Social Work*, *27*(6), 803–814.

Saran, M., Cagiltay, K., & Seferoglu, G. (2008, March 23-26). Use of Mobile Phones in Language Learning: Developing Effective Instructional Materials. In *Proceedings of the Fifth IEEE International Conference on Wireless, Mobile, and Ubiquitous Technology in Education*, Beijing, China (pp. 39-43).

Saunders, R. J. (1982). Telecommunications in developing countries: Constraints on development. *Communication Economics and Development*, *1982*(b), 190-210.

Saunders, R. J., Warford, J. J., & Wellenius, B. (1983). *Telecommunications and economic development*. Baltimore: John Hopkins.

Saunders, R. J., Warford, J. J., & Wellenius, B. (1994). *Telecommunications and economic development* (2nd ed.). Baltimore: John Hopkins.

Sayer, J., Campbell, B., Petheram, L., Aldrich, M., Ruiz Perez, M., & Endamana, D. (2007). Assessing environment and development outcomes in conservation landscapes. *Biodiversity and Conservation*, *16*, 2677–2694. doi:10.1007/s10531-006-9079-9

Schensul, S., Schensul, J., & LeCompte, M. (1999). *Essential ethnographic methods: Observations, interviews and questionnaires*. Walnut Creek, CA: Altamira Press.

Schmidt, J. T. (2007). *Preparing Students for Success in Blended Learning Environments: Future Oriented Motivation & Self-Regulation*. Unpublished PhD thesis.

Schön, D. A. (1987). *Educating the reflective practitioner*. San Francisco: Jossey-Bass.

Schugurensky, D. (2000). *The forms of informal learning* (Working Paper #19-2000). Toronto, ON, Canada: Centre for the Study of Education and Work, Department of Sociology and Equity Studies in Education & Ontario Institute for Studies in Education of the University of Toronto.

Schur, L., Shields, T., & Schriner, K. (2003). Can I make a difference? Efficacy, employment, and disability. *Political Psychology*, *21*(1), 119–149. doi:10.1111/0162-895X.00319

Scott, N. W. (1996). *A study of the introduction of educational technology into a course in engineering dynamics: classroom environment and learning outcomes*. Unpublished PhD thesis.

Searing, H. (2003). The continuing relevance of case-work ideas to longterm child protection work. *Child & Family Social Work, 8*, 311–320. doi:10.1046/j.1365-2206.2003.00279.x

Seidl, B. (2003). Candid Thoughts on the Not-so-candid Camera: How Video Documentation Radically Alters Development Projects. In White, S. (Ed.), *Participatory Video: Images that Transform and Empower* (pp. 157–194). New Delhi, India: Sage Publications.

Selwyn, N. (2002). *Defining the 'Digital Divide': Developing a Theoretical Understanding of Inequalities in the Information Age* (Occasional Paper 36). Cardiff, UK: Cardiff University, School of Social Sciences.

Selwyn, N. (2004). Reconsidering Political and Popular Understandings of the Digital Divide. *New Media & Society, 6*(3), 381–361. doi:10.1177/1461444804042519

Selwyn, N. (2006). Digital division or digital decision? A study of non-users and low-users of computers. *Poetics, 34*, 273–292. doi:10.1016/j.poetic.2006.05.003

Selwyn, N. (2007). New technologies, young people and social inclusion. In Kutscher, N., & Otto, H. (Eds.), *Grenzenlose cyberwelt? Um verhaltnis von digitaler ungleichheit und neuen bildungszugangen fur jugendliche* (pp. 31–45). Aachen, Germany: Shaker.

Selwyn, N., Gorard, S., & Furlong, J. (2005). Whose internet is it anyway? Exploring adults' (non)use of the internet in everyday life. *European Journal of Communication, 20*(1), 5–26. doi:10.1177/0267323105049631

Shang, R. A., Chen, Y. C., & Shen, L. (2005). Extrinsic versus intrinsic motivations for consumers to shop on-line. *Information & Management, 42*(3), 401–413. doi:10.1016/j.im.2004.01.009

Sharma, R. (2003). Barriers in Using Technology for Education in Developing Countries. In *Proceedings of the Information Technology: Research and Education 2003 Conference* (pp. 521-522).

Shein, D. M. (2005). *Municipal Wireless: A Primer for Public Discussion (Tech. Rep.)*. Rochester, New York: Rochester Institute of Technology, Center for Advancing the Study of Cyber Infrastructure.

Sheng, L. (2008). Exploring the establishment of a legal system to regulate contemporary distance education. *Modern Distance Education Research, 6*, 5–8.

Shen, Y., & Ding, G. (2007). Application of mobile learning in contemporary distance education. *Distance Education Journal, 4*, 37–39.

Shepard, L. A. (2000). The role of assessment in a learning culture. *Educational Researcher, 29*(7), 4–14.

Shepherd, A. W. (2001). *Farm Radio as a Medium for Market Information Dissemination*. Rome, Italy: FAO-Marketing and Rural Finance Service.

Shiers, H. (2001). Pathways to participation: Openings, opportunities and obligations. *Children & Society, 15*, 107–117. doi:10.1002/chi.617

Shin, J., & Harman, G. (2009). New challenges for higher education: global and Asia-Pacific perspectives. *Asia Pacific Education Review, 10*, 1-13. Retrieved September 2, 2009, from http://www.springerlink.com/content/v1153p72h3117723/fulltext.pdf

Shor, I. (1992). *Empowering education*. Chicago: University of Chicago.

Sidhu, M. (2007). *Development and Applications of Interactive Multimedia TAPS (Technology Assisted Problem Solving) Packages for Engineering*. Unpublished PhD thesis, Universiti Malaya.

Sidhu, M., & Ramesh, S. (2008). Virtual Worlds: The Next Generation for Solving Engineering Problems. In *Proceedings of the IEEE 8th International Conference on Computer and IT CIT2008,* Sydney, Australia (pp. 303-307).

Sidhu, M., Cheng, L. K., Der, S. C., & Omar, R. (2009). *Augmented Reality Applications in Education*. Paper presented at the Second Teaching and Learning Conference at UNITEN.

Sidhu, M., Ramesh, S., & Selvanathan, N. (2005). A Coach-Based Interactive Multimedia Tool For Solving Engineering Problem. *International Multimedia Cyberscape Journal, 3*(2), 28–36.

Sina Corporation. (2009). *2008-2009 Chinese network education market research report*. Retrieved September 4, 2009, from http://blog.sina.com.cn/s/blog_5b9aa6e30100e62w.html

Sirbu, M., Lehr, W., & Gillett, S. (2006). Evolving Wireless Access Technologies for Municipal Broadband. *Government Information Quarterly, 23*, 480–502. doi:10.1016/j.giq.2006.09.003

Skolverket. (2009). *IT-användning och IT-kompetens i förskola, skola och vuxenutbildning* (IT usage and IT skills in preschool, school and adult education) (Dnr 75-2007:3775). Retrieved from http://www.skolverket.se/ publikationer?id=2192

Small, T. (2006). Review: Electronic Democracy: Mobilisation, Organisation, and Participation via New ICTs. *Canadian Journal of Communication, 31*(2), 475–476.

Smart, K. L., & Cappel, J. L. (2005). An exploratory look at students' perceptions of blended learning. *Issues in Information Systems, 6*(1), 149–155.

Smith, A. (1999). *Myths and Memories of the Nation*. New York: Oxford University Press.

Snowden, D. (1987). Eyes See; Ears Hear. In Richardson, D., & Paisley, L. (Eds.), *The First Mile of Connectivity*. Rome, Italy: Food and Agriculture Organization of the United Nations.

Soderstrom, S. (2009). Offline social ties and online use of computers: A study of disabled youth and their use of ICT advances. *New Media & Society, 11*(5), 709–727. doi:10.1177/1461444809105347

Song, X. (2007). *2007 International Distance Education Forum opened*. Retrieved September 11, 2008, from http://www.yhedu.syn.cn/ycjy/ ShowArticle.asp?ArticleID=67

Spector, J. M., & Merrill, M. D. (2008). Editorial. *Distance Education, 29*(2), 123–126. doi:10.1080/01587910802154921

Spring, J. (1997). *Deculturalization and the struggle for equality*. New York: McGraw-Hill.

Sridhar, K. S., & Sridhar, V. (2007). Telecommunications Infrastructure and Economic Growth: Evidence from Developing Countries. *Applied Econometrics and International Development, 7*(2), 37–56.

St. Cloud Florida. *CyberSpot General Information*. (n.d.). Retrieved June 5, 2009 from http://www.stcloud.org/index.aspx?NID=402

Stevenson, O. (2008). Ubiquitous presence, partial use: The everyday interaction of children and their families with ICT. *Pedagogy and Education, 17*(2), 115–130. doi:10.1080/14759390802098615

Stienstra, D., & Troschuk, L. (2005). Emerging citizens with disabilities in eDemocracy. *Disability Studies Quarterly, 25*(2), e13.

Stiroh, K. (2002). Are ICT spillovers driving the New Economy? Federal Reserve Bank of New York. *Review of Income and Wealth, 48*, 33–57. doi:10.1111/1475-4991.00039

Stiroh, K. (2008). Information technology and productivity: Old answers and new questions. *CESifo Economic Studies, 54*(3), 356–385. doi:10.1093/cesifo/ifn023

Stucki, G., Reinharrdt, J. D., Grimby, G., & Melvin, J. (2008). Developing research capacity in human functioning and rehabilitation research from the comprehensive perspective based in the ICF-model. *European Journal of Physical Rehabilitation Medicine, 44*, 343–351.

Stuhlmann, J. M., & Taylor, H. G. (1999). Preparing technically competent student- teachers: A three year study of interventions and experiences. *Journal of Technology and Teacher Education, 7*(4), 333–350.

Sun, Y., & Chen, X. (2007). Exploring the establishment of an open university's "mobile campus". *China Education Info, 10*, 7–9.

Sun, Z. (2009). Paying attention to education equity from a technical point of view. *Modern Distance Education, 4*, 6–8.

Su, W. (2009). A study of the development of Chinese distance higher education in transformation. *Modern Distance Education, 3*, 21–23.

Swartz, N. (2005). Workplace e-mail, IM survey reveals risks. *Information Management Journal, 39*(1), 6.

Swiderska, K., Roe, D., Siegele, L., & Grieg-Gran, M. (2009). *The Governance of Nature and the Nature of Governance: Policy that works for biodiversity and livelihoods*. London: IIED.

Täby kommun. (2009a). *Det nya Täby: Översiktsplan 2010-2030, utställningshandling maj 2009, allmänna intressen* (The new Täby: Comprehensive plan 2010-2030, consultation May 2009, public interests). Retrieved June 20, 2009 from http://www.taby.se

Täby kommun. (2009b). *Plats att växa* (Place to grow). Retrieved June 13, 2009 from http://www.taby.se/Miljo-natur-halsa/ Planeringsdokument/Plats-att-vaxa/

Tait, A. (2008). What are open universities for? *Open Learning: The Journal of Open and Distance Learning, 23*(2), 85–93. doi:10.1080/02680510802051871

Tapia, A., & Stone, M. (2005, September 23-25). *Public–private partnership and the role of state and federal legislation in wireless municipal networks.* Paper presented at telecommunications policy research conference (TPRC), Arlington, VA.

Tapia, A., Maitland, C., & Stone, M. (2006). Making It Work for Municipalities: Building Municipal Wireless Networks. *Government Information Quarterly, 23*(3-4), 359–380. doi:10.1016/j.giq.2006.08.004

Taras, M. (2002). Using assessment for learning and learning from assessment. *Assessment & Evaluation in Higher Education, 27*(6), 501–510. doi:10.1080/0260293022000020273

Tashakkori, A., & Teddlie, C. (1998). *Mixed methodology.* Thousand Oaks, CA: Sage.

Tashakkori, A., & Teddlie, C. (Eds.). (2003). *Handbook of mixed methods in the social and behavioral sciences.* Thousand Oaks, CA: Sage.

Television series episode. (2009, May 18). In *Wireless in the City.* New York: Fox News. Retrieved June 5, 2009 from http://www.myfoxny.com

Thatcher, A., Wretschko, G., & Fridjhon, P. (2008). Online flow experiences, problematic internet use and internet procrastination. *Computers in Human Behavior, 24*(5), 2236–2254. doi:10.1016/j.chb.2007.10.008

The FreeChild Project. (2008). Retrieved November 15, 2009 from http://www.freechild.org

The Republic of Korea. (2008, March 28). *R&D spending to reach 5% of GDP: Government.* Retrieved July 7, 2009, from http://www.korea.net/News/ News/newsView.asp?serial_no= 20080320005&part=107&SearchDay

Thomas, N. (2005). Has anything really changed? Managers' views of looked after children's participation in 1997 and 2004. *Adoption & Fostering, 29*(1), 67–77.

Tian, F., Wang, Y., & Wang, Y. (2007). What we have learnt from a comparison of Chinese and British net higher education policies. *Distance Education Journal, 4,* 28–34.

Tidwell, L. C., & Walther, J. B. (2002). Computer-mediated communication effects on disclosure, impressions and interpersonal evaluations. Getting to know one another a bit at a time. *Human Communication Research, 28*(3), 317–348. doi:10.1111/j.1468-2958.2002.tb00811.x

Tilbury, C. (2004). The influence of performance measurement in child welfare policy and practice. *British Journal of Social Work, 34,* 225–241. doi:10.1093/bjsw/bch023

Timmer, M. P., & Van Ark, B. (2005). Does information & communication technology drive EU-US productivity growth differentials? *Oxford Economic Papers, 57,* 693–716. doi:10.1093/oep/gpi032

TKS- Towards a Knowledge Society. (2006). *A proposal for a tertiary education policy for Botswana. Technical report.* Retrieved July 27, 2009, from http://www.tec.org.bw/ tec_doc/tec_rep_10_2006.pdf

Tognozzi, E. (2001). Italian language instruction: The need for teacher development in technology. *Italica, 78*(4), 487–498. doi:10.2307/3656077

Tolley, S. (2005). SCARF: Supporting Children and Responding to Families. *National Child Protection Council Newsletter, 13*(2), 16–19.

Tonucci, F., Prisco, A., & Horelli, L. (2004). A comparison of the models for children's participation in decision-making, in Rome and Helsinki. In L. Horelli & M. Prezza (Eds.), *Child-Friendly Environments: Approaches and lessons* (pp. 83-93). Espoo, Finland: Helsinki University of Technology.

Torres, L., Pina, V., & Basilio, A. (2006). E-governance developments in European Union cities: Reshaping government's relationship with citizens. *Governance: An International Journal of Policy. Administration and Institutions, 19*(2), 277–302.

Tough, A. (1971). *The adult's learning projects learning.* Toronto, ON, Canada: OISE.

Tregeagle, S. (2008). *Service Users' Experiences of Case Managed Interventions.* Paper presented at the Australian National Foster Care Conference.

Tregeagle, S., & Darcy, M. (2007). Child Welfare and Information and Communication Technology: Today's challenge. *British Journal of Social Work.* .doi:10.1093/bjsw/bcm048

Tregeagle, S., & Mason, J. (2008). Service user experience of participation in child welfare case management. *Child & Family Social Work.* .doi:10.1111/j.1365-2206.2008.00564.x

Tress, B., & Tress, G. (2000). Second draft for Recommendations for interdisciplinary landscape research. Workshop no.1. The landscape – from vision to definition. In J. Brandt, B. Tress, & G. Tress (Eds.), *Multifunctional landscapes. Interdisciplinary approaches to landscape research and management. Conference material for the international conference on multifunctional landscapes.* Denmark: University of Roskilde, Centre for landscape research.

Trewin, D. (2002). *Measuring a knowledge-based economy and society.* Canberra, Australia: Australian Bureau of Statistics. Retrieved March 1, 2006, from http://www.abs.gov.au/ausstats/abs@.NSF/66f306f503e529a-5ca25697e0017661f/fe633d1d2b900671ca256c220025e8a3!OpenDocument

Trickett, E. J. (2009). Community psychology: Individuals and interventions in community context. *Annual Review of Psychology, 60,* 395–419. doi:10.1146/annurev.psych.60.110707.163517

Triplett, J. E., & Bosworth, B. P. (2003). Productivity measurement issues in service industries: "Baumol's Disease" has been cured. *Economic Policy Review - Federal Reserve Bank of New York, 9*(3), 23-33.

Trow, M. (1973). *Problems in the Transition from Elite to Mass Higher Education.* Berkeley, CA: Carnegie Commission on Higher Education.

TTPOD. (2005). *TTPOD.* Retrieved April 28, 2009, from http://www.teacherspodcast.org

Turel, O., Serenko, A., & Bontis, N. (2007). User acceptance of wireless short messaging services: Deconstructing perceived value. *Information & Management, 44*(1), 63–73. doi:10.1016/j.im.2006.10.005

Tyler, T. R. (2002). Is the Internet changing social life? It seems the more things change, the more they stay the same. *The Journal of Social Issues, 58*(1), 195–205. doi:10.1111/1540-4560.00256

U.S. Department of Education. (1999). *Preparing tomorrow's teachers to use technology.* Retrieved March 1, 2006, from http://www.ed.gov.teachtech

U.S. NTIA. (2000). *Falling Through the Net: Toward Digital Inclusion.* Washington, DC: Department of Commerce, Economics and Statistics Administration.

U.S. NTIA. (2002). *A Nation Online: Entering the Broadband Age.* Washington, DC: Department of Commerce, Economics and Statistics Administration.

UEGE. (2008). *UEGE 5102 Foundations in American Education.* Retrieved April 28, 2009, from http://uege5102.blogspot.com

ULI. (2008). *Lägesbild GI Sverige: en lägesbild av användandet av geografiska informationssytem i Sverige, resultat från delundersökningen offentliga sektorn* (Situational awareness GI Sweden: Study on use of geographic information and geographic information technology in Sweden, public sector). Retrieved from http://www.geoforum.se/page/158/332

UN. (2003a). *World Public Sector Report 2003: E-Government at the Crossroads.* New York: UN.

UN. (2003b). *UN Global E-government Survey 2003.* Retrieved June 1, 2009, from http://unpan1.un.org/intradoc/groups/public/documents/UN/UNPAN016066.pdf

UN. (2006). *UN Millenium Development Goals Report 2006.* New York: UN.

UN. (2008). *UN E-Government Survey 2008. From E-Government to Connected Governance*. New York: UN.

UNDP. (1996). *Human Development – at the heart of today's policy agenda*. New York: Author.

UNECE. (2002). *Towards a Knowledge-Based Economy: ARMENIA – country readiness assessment report*. Retrieved May 30, 2009, from http://www.unece.org/operact/enterp/ documents/coverpagarmenia.pdf

Unger, L. S., & Kernan, J. B. (1983). On meaning of leisure: An investigation of some determinants of the subjective experience. *The Journal of Consumer Research*, *9*(4), 381–392. doi:10.1086/208932

UNICEF. (1990). Convention on the rights of the child. In *First Call for Children* (pp. 43–79). New York: UNICEF.

UNICEF. (2001, March). *The children as community researchers*. Retrieved November 15, 2009 from http://www.unicef.org/ teachers/researchers/

United Nations Development Program. (2009). *Overcoming barriers: Human mobility and development*. Retrieved December 7, 2009, from http://hdr.undp.org/en/media/HDR_2009_EN_Complete.pdf

United Nations Development Programme. (2001). *The human development report: Making new technologies work for human development*. New York: Author.

United Nations Economic and Social Council (UN). (2008). *Mainstreaming Disability in the Development Agenda, Note by the Secretariat*. Retrieved November 30, 2009 from http://www.un.org/disabilities/

United Nations Educational, Scientific and Cultural Organization. (2009). *Overcoming inequality: Why governance matters*. Retrieved September 5, 2009, from http://unesdoc.unesco.org/ images/0017/001776/177683e.pdf

United Nations. (1993). [*Earth summit - the United Nations programme of action from Rio*. New York: United Nations Dept. of Public Information.]. *Agenda (Durban, South Africa)*, 21.

United States of America, Department of Justice. (n.d.). *Project Civic Access*. Retrieved May, 2009 from http://www.ada.gov/civicac.htm

United States of America, Federal Trade Commission (FTC). (2006). *Municipal Provision of Wireless Internet*. Washington, DC: Federal Trade Commission.

Urban Green Spaces Taskforce. (2002). *Green spaces, better place: Final report*. London: Department for transport, local government, and the regions.

USI Wireless - Wireless Minneapolis History. (n.d.). In *USI Wireless high-speed broadband wireless internet services*. Retrieved June 05, 2009 from http://www.usiwireless.com/ service/minneapolis/history.htm

Using the public airwaves to connect and strengthen communities in New York City. (n.d.). *NYCwireless*. Retrieved June 05, 2009 from http://www.nycwireless.net/about/

Valcour, P. M., & Hunter, L. W. (2004). Technology, organization, and work-life integration. In E. E. Kossek & S. J. Lamber (Eds.), *Work and Life Integration* (pp. 61-84). Mahwah, NJ: Lawrence Erlbaum.

Valentine, G., Butler, R., & Skelton, T. (2001). The ethical and methodological complexities of doing research with "vulnerable" young people. *Ethics Place and Environment*, *4*(2), 119–124. doi:10.1080/13668790120061497

Valkenburg, P. M., & Peter, J. (2007). Online communication and adolescent well-being: testing the stimulation versus the displacement hypothesis. *Journal of Computer-Mediated Communication*, *12*(4), 1169–1182. doi:10.1111/j.1083-6101.2007.00368.x

Van Ark, B., Inklaar, R., & McGuckin, R. (2002). Changing gear? Productivity, ICT and service industries: Europe and the United States. *Economics Program Working Papers, 2*, 1-92.

Van Audenhove, L. V., Ballon, P., Poel, M., & Staelens, T. (2007). Government Policy and Wireless City Networks: A Comparative Analysis of Motivations, Goals, Services and Their Relation to Network Structure. *The Southern African Journal of Information and Communication*, *8*, 108–135.

van Dijk, J. (2005). *The deepening divide: Inequalities in the information society*. Thousand Oaks, CA: Sage.

van Dijk, J. (2006). Digital divide research, achievements and shortcomings. *Poetics*, *34*, 221–235. doi:10.1016/j.poetic.2006.05.004

Van Dijk, J., & Hacker, K. (2003). The digital divide as a complex and dynamic phenomenon. *The Information Society, 19*, 315–326. doi:10.1080/01972240309487

van Noordwijk, M., Tomich, T. P., & Verbist, T. P. (2001). Negotiation support models for integrated natural resource management in tropical forest margins. *Conservation Ecology, 5*(2), 21. Retrieved from http://www.consecol. org/vol5/iss2/art21/

Vanatta, R. A., & Fordham, N. (2004). Teachers disposition as predictors of classroom technology use. *Journal of Research on Technology in Education, 36*, 253–271.

Vaughan, R. (1998). The Use of Multimedia in Developing Undergraduate Engineering Courses. *Journal of Materials, 5*(5). Retrieved from http://www.tms.org/pubs/journals/ JOM/9805/Voller/Voller-9805.html.

Vergot, P., Israel, G., & Mayo, D. (2005). Sources and channels of information used by beef cattle producers in 12 Counties of the Northwest Florida extension eistrict. *Journal of Extension, 43*(2). Retrieved January 20, 2009, from http://www.joe.org/joe/ 2005april/rb6.shtml

Vermunt, J. V. (2005). Relations between student learning patterns and personal and contextual factors and academic performance. *Higher Education, 49*, 205–234. doi:10.1007/s10734-004-6664-2

Victorian Government. (2003). *Public parenting: A review of home-based care in Victoria*. Melbourne, Australia: Victorian Government.

Vonk, G., Geertman, S., & Shot, P. (2005). Bottlenecks blocking widespread usage of planning support systems. *Environment & Planning A, 37*, 909–924. doi:10.1068/ a3712

VPRC. (2007). *Comparative report on the 'National research on new technologies and the information society*. Athens, Greece: VPRC & National Network for Research and Technology.

W3C. (2008). Web content accessibility guidelines (WCAG) 2.0. *W3C Recommendation 11 December 2008*. Retrieved November 7, 2009 from www.w3.org/TR/ WCAG/#guidelines

Wagner, H. (1933). *Spanish Explorations in the Strait of Juan de Fuca*. Santa Ana, CA: Fine Arts Press.

Wakelin, O., & Shadrach, B. (2001). *Impact Assessment of Appropriate and Innovative Technologies in Enterprise Development*. London: Department for International Development. Retrieved August 2009, from http://www. alle.de/transfer/ downloads/MD380.pdf

Walch, R., & Lafferty, M. (2006). *Tricks of the podcasting masters*. Indianapolis, IN: Que.

Wallsten, S. (2005). Broadband Penetration: An Empirical Analysis of State and Federal Policies. *AEI-Brookings Joint Center for Regulatory Studies*. Retrieved April 25, 2007 from http://downloads.heartland.org/17468.pdf

Walther, J. B. (1996). Computer-mediated communication: Impersonal, interpersonal and hyperpersonal interaction. *Human Communication Research, 23*, 3–43.

Wang, C. (2008). Exploring the establishment of a distance education quality assurance system. *Distance Education Journal, 1*, 40–42.

Wang, Y. (2008). Current situation of Chinese digital education resources and its development strategies. *China Education Info, 1*, 9–11.

Wang, Y., Zhao, Y., & Chen, M. (2009). A retrospect of Chinese education informationization in the past 20 years and a look into the future. *China Education Info, 17*, 14–16.

Ward, A., Baker, P. M. A., & Moon, N. (2009). Ensuring the enfranchisement of people with disabilities. *Journal of Disability Policy Studies, 20*, 79–92. doi:10.1177/1044207308325996

Warren, M. F. (2002). Digital divides and the adoption of information and communication technologies in the UK farm sector. *International Journal of Information Technology and Management, 1*(4), 385–405. doi:10.1504/ IJITM.2002.001207

Warschauer, M. (2003). *Technology and Social Inclusion: Rethinking the Digital Divide*. Cambridge, MA: MIT Press.

Warschauer, M. (2004). *Technology and Social Inclusion: Rethinking the Digital Divide*. Cambridge, MA: MIT Press.

Watkins, C. (2008). *SMS text translation and live interpreters arrives on your cell phone with mobile.lingtastic. com*. Retrieved from http://www.lingtastic.com/ Latest-News.htm

Weber, L. E. (1999). Survey of the main challenges facing higher education at the millennium. In Hirsch, W. Z., & Weber, L. E. (Eds.), *Challenges Facing Higher Education at the Millennium* (pp. 3–17). Phoenix, AZ: American Council on Education and the Oryx Press.

Weber, R. P. (1985). *Basic content analysis*. Beverly Hills, CA: Sage.

Weber, S., & Mitchell, C. (1996). Betwixt and between: The culture of student teaching. In Moore, Z. (Ed.), *Foreign language Teacher Education: Multiple Perspectives* (pp. 301–316). Lanham, MD: University Press of America.

Wei, R. (2008). Motivations for using the mobile phone for mass communications and entertainment. *Telematics and Informatics, 25*(1), 36–46. doi:10.1016/j.tele.2006.03.001

Wells, J..G. (2007). Key Design factors in durable instructional technology professional development. *Journal of Technology and Teacher Education, 15*(1), 101–122.

Wen, J. (2009, March 16). The report on the work of the government. *People's Daily Overseas Edition*, 1.

Wheelaghan, S., & Hill, M. (2000). The Looking After Children records system: An evaluation of the Scottish pilot. In Iwaniec, D., & Hill, M. (Eds.), *Child Welfare Policy and Practice* (pp. 143–164). London: Jessica Kingsley Publishers Ltd.

White, M. (2001). A virtual Interactive Teaching Environment (VITE) Using XML and Augmented Reality. *The International Journal of Electrical Engineering Education, 38*(4), 316–329.

White, S. (Ed.). (2003). *Participatory Video: Images that Transform and Empower*. New Delhi, India: Sage Publications.

Whitty, M. T., & Carr, A. N. (2004). New rules in the workplace: Applying object-relations theory to explain problem Internet and e-mail behavior in the workplace. *Computers in Human Behavior, 22*(2), 235–250. doi:10.1016/j.chb.2004.06.005

Wilhjelm, H. (1999). *Hvor har du vært? - ingen steder: Miljøtilknyttende infrastruktur og barns hverdagsliv - en kunnskapsoversikt* (Where have you been? nowhere: Environmental infrastructure and children's everyday life- a review). Trondheim, Norway: Norsk senter for barneforskning.

Wilkinson, M. (2006). Designing an "adaptive" enterprising architecture. *BT Technology Journal, 24*(4), 81–92. doi:10.1007/s10550-006-0099-5

Williams, B. (2008). *Educators' guide to podcasting*. Eugene, OR: ISTE.

Williams, D. (2006). On and off the 'Net: Scales for social capital in an online era. *Journal of Computer-Mediated Communication, 11*, 593–628. doi:10.1111/j.1083-6101.2006.00029.x

Willis, S., & Tranter, B. (2006). Beyond the 'digital divide': Internet diffusion and inequality in Australia. *Journal of Sociology (Melbourne, Vic.), 42*(1), 43–59. doi:10.1177/1440783306061352

Wilmoth, D. (2008). *Innovation in private higher education: the Botswana International University of Science and Technology*. Washington, DC: IFC International Investment Forum on Private Education.

Wims, P. (2007). Analysis of adoption and the use of ICTs among Irish farm families. *Journal of Extension Systems, 23*(1), 14–28.

Wireless Communities Georgia. (2007, June 29). *Civitium. Wireless Philadelphia - Digital Impact Partners*. (n.d.). Retrieved June 4, 2009 from http://wirelessphiladelphia.org/ digital_partners.cfm

Wise, S. (1999). *The UK Looking After Children Approach in Australia*. Paper presented at the 11th Biennial Foster Care Organisation Conference, Melbourne, Australia.

Wise, S. (2003a). An evaluation of a trial of Looking After Children in the State of Victoria, Australia. *Children Australia, 17*, 3–17.

Wise, S. (2003b). Using Looking After Children to create an Australian out-of-home care database. *Children Australia, 28*(2), 38–44.

Wlodkowski, R., & Ginsberg, M. (1995). *Diversity and motivation*. San Francisco: Jossey Bass.

Wollenberg, E., Edmunds, D., & Buck, L. (2000). *Anticipating Change: Scenarios as a tool for adaptive forest management - a guide*. Bogor Barat, Indonesia: Center for International Forestry Research.

Wong, A., Chan, C., Li-Tsang, C., & Lam, C. (2009). Competence of people with intellectual disabilities on using human-computer interface. *Research in Developmental Disabilities, 30*, 107–123. doi:10.1016/j.ridd.2008.01.002

Wong, W., & Welch, E. (2004). Does e-government promote accountability? A comparative analysis of Website openness and government accountability. *Governance: An International Journal of Policy, Administration, and Institutions, 17*(2), 275–297.

Woolcock, M., & Sweetser, A. T. (2002). Bright Ideas: Social Capital—The Bonds That Connect. *ADB Review, 34*(2).

Woolley, H., Spencer, C., Dunn, J., & Rowley, G. (1999). The child as citizen. *Journal of Urban Design, 4*(3), 255–282. doi:10.1080/13574809908724451

World Bank. (n.d.). *Information & Communications Technologies - 2006 Information & Communications for Development (IC4D) - Global Trends and Policies*. Retrieved April 28, 2009, from http://web.worldbank.org/ WBSITE/EXTERNAL/TOPICS/ EXTINFORMATIONANDCOMMUNICATIONANDTECHNOLOGIES/ 0,contentMDK:20831214~pagePK:210058~piPK:210062~theSitePK:282823,00.html

Wozney, L., Venkatesh, V., & Abrami, P. C. (2006). Implementing computer technologies: Teachers' perceptions and practices. *Journal of Technology and Teacher Education, 14*, 120–173.

Wu, L., Lin, C. Y., Aral, S., & Brynjolfsson, E. (2009, February). Financial Revenue of Information Technology Consultant. In *Proceedings of the Winter Information Systems Conference*, Salt Lake City, UT. Retrieved August 10, 2009, from http://smallblue.research.ibm.com/

WWF. (2007). *Landscape Outcomes Assessment Methodology in Practice*. Gland, Switzerland: WWF Forest for Life Programme. Retrieved from http://assets.panda.org/downloads/ loaminpracticemay07.pdf

Xue, W. (2007). From e-learning to u-learning. *China Education Info, 12*, 7–9.

Yan, B. (2007). Establishing a contemporary public distance education service structure. *Distance Education in China*, 12-16.

Yan, B. (2008). Cost and sustainable development of distance education. *Distance Education in China*. Retrieved September 28, 2008, from http://www1.open.edu.cn/ ycjy/indexzonghe.php

Yang, Q., Deng, K., & Cao, F. (2008). Destructive competition in Chinese network education economy. *Distance Education in China, 9*(1). Retrieved September 29, 2008, from http://www1.open.edu.cn/ ycjy/indexzonghe.php

Yan, X., Gong, M., & Thong, J. Y. L. (2006). Two tales of one service: User acceptance of short message service (SMS) in Hong Kong and China. *INFO: The Journal of Policy. Regulation and Strategy, 8*(1), 16–28.

Yin, R. K. (2009). *Case Study Research: Design and Method* (4th ed.). Thousand Oaks, CA: Sage.

Yu, L. (2006). Understanding information inequality: Making sense of the literature of the information and digital divides. *Journal of Librarianship and Information Science, 38*(4), 229–252. doi:10.1177/0961000606070600

Yu, X., Zhang, Y., & Zhu, Z. (2009). A model for measuring competitiveness of education informationalization and a comparison of international indexes. *China Education Info, 17*, 4–10.

Zainudeen, A., Samarajiva, R., & Abeysuria, A. (2006). *Telecom Use on a Shoestring: Strategic Use of Telecom Services by the Financially Constrained in South Asia*. LIRNEasia. Retrieved from http://www.regulateonline.org/ content/view/624/71/

Zeman, K. (2005). *Transformation towards Knowledge-Based Economy. Conference on Medium-Term Economic Assessment*. Retrieved May 10, 2009, from www.aeaf.minfin.bg/.../ Karel_Zeman_paper_CMTEA2005.pdf

Zha, Q. (2009). Diversification or homogenization: how governments and markets have combined to (re)shape Chinese higher education in its recent massification process. *Higher Education, 58*(1), 41-58. Retrieved August 28, 2009, from http://www.springerlink.com.proxy.library.brocku.ca/ content/44217643h4322r17/fulltext.pdf

Zhang, X. (2008). *Deputy Minister of Education Zhang Xinsheng: Opening up and international cooperation of Chinese education*. Retrieved September 16, 2008, from http://www.moe.gov.cn/edoas/website18/ 83/info1218778117003283.htm

Zhang, J., & Lee, S. (2007). A Time Series analysis of international ICT spillover. *Journal of Global Information Management, 15*(4), 65–78.

Zhang, K. (2007). An analysis of Chinese open distance higher education models. *China Education Info, 9*, 15–17.

Zhang, P., & Zhao, H. (2009). Monitoring and supporting network learning. *China Education Info, 15*, 55–58.

Zhang, Z., & Wang, Y. (2007). Social responsibilities of contemporary distance education institutions. *Distance Education Journal, 4*, 8–13.

Zheng, Y., & Walsham, G. (2008). Inequality of what? Social exclusion in the e-society as capability deprivation. *Information Technology & People, 21*(3), 222–243. doi:10.1108/09593840810896000

Zhong, W. (2009, February 13). Distance education provides important support to promote lifelong learning. *China Education Daily*, 7.

Zhou, J. (2007a, October 17). *Continuing to develop education as a priority and striving to provide education that satisfies the people: A retrospect at the education reform and development since the Party's sixteenth congress.* Retrieved September 24, 2008, from http://www.moe.edu.cn/edoas/website18/ level3.jsp?tablename=2038&infoid=33909

Zhou, J. (2007b). Contemporary distance education, a means to realize equity in Chinese higher education. *Contemporary Distance Education, 113*, 9–13.

Zhou, Y., & Chen, Z. (2009). The problems and solutions of higher education institutions' network education. *China Education Info, 5*, 7–9.

Zimmerman, B. J. (2008). Investigating self-regulation and motivation: Historical background, methodological developments, and future prospects. *American Educational Research Journal, 45*(1), 166–183. doi:10.3102/0002831207312909

About the Contributors

Susheel Chhabra is the Associate Professor of Information Technology at Lal Bahadur Shastri Institute of Management (Delhi, India) and is also acting as a programme coordinator, PGDM (MBA). His areas of research and consultancy include e-government, e-business, computer networks, and software engineering. He has published several research papers on international and national level journals. He has co-authored a textbook on human resource information systems, edited a special issue of *International Journal of E-Government Research* on strategic e-business model for government, and also co-authored the edited book *Integrating E-Business Models for Government Solutions: Citizen-Centric Service Oriented Methodologies and Processes* (IGI Global, USA). He is currently engaged in several consultancy and training assignments on social change for human development, e-governance, e-business, and ERP for ISID, NTPC, LBSRC, etc.

* * *

Achilleas Achilleos is currently working as a special scientist in the Department of Computer Science at the University of Cyprus and awaits his PhD defence from the School of Computer Science and Electronic Engineering at the University of Essex. He received his MSc with distinction from University of Essex and a BSc with excellence from the Budapest University of Technology and Economics in Hungary. His research interests include model-driven development, pervasive service creation, context-modelling and mobile computing. His PhD was sponsored by BT and the Engineering and Physical Sciences Research Council (EPSRC) of the UK. Currently he is also engaged in a research project with BT. He research has been published in two international journals and in several international conferences. He has authored a chapter of a book. He served as a referee and a TPC member in several conferences and is a member of the Institute of Electrical and Electronic Engineers (IEEE).

George Alexopoulos is an Agricultural Economist and has obtained an MSc in Regional Development and a Ph.D. in Social Science. He is currently working in the Department of Agricultural Economics and Rural Development, Agricultural University of Athens, Greece. His research interests focus on agricultural policy and rural development with emphasis on the evaluation of agricultural policy measures, rural development projects' design and evaluation and the role of institutions, social economy and civil society in community development. He has published and presented papers in journals and conferences and participated in international meetings and workshops on the aforementioned topics. He is a co-editor in scientific journals, member of international think tanks on co-operatives and member of the boards of relevant scientific societies.

Paul M.A. Baker, Ph.D., is the Director of Research at the Center for Advanced Communications Policy (CACP), and holds the rank of Senior Research Scientist with the Georgia Institute of Technology. He is also the Project Director of Policy Initiatives for both the Rehabilitation Engineering Research Center (RERC) on Mobile Wireless Technologies, and the Workplace Accommodations RERC, and an Adjunct Professor with the School of Public Policy at Georgia Institute of Technology. He is currently researching the role of policy in advancing technology and universal accessibility goals for persons with disabilities; the operation of communities of practice and online communities in virtual environments, and institutional issues involved in public sector information policy development and state and local government use of information and communication technologies. Baker holds a Ph.D. in Public Policy from George Mason University, and is a member of the American Institute of Certified Planners.

Ulla Berglund holds a PhD in urban planning and is an associate professor in landscape planning at the Dept. of Urban and Rural Development at the Swedish University of Agricultural Sciences. She has a long experience within research on people's use of the outdoor environment of different urban contexts in Sweden and in Latvia. In most cases children and young people have been in focus of her studies. Since some years she with Kerstin Nordin is active in the development and application of a methodology for bringing children and young people's knowledge into the spatial planning context with the help of GIS technique.

John C. Bricout, Ph.D. is an associate professor and associate director for research at the University of Central Florida (UCF) School of Social Work since 2007. He also coordinates the social work track in the interdisciplinary public affairs Ph.D. program. Previously, he held a joint faculty appointment in social work and occupational therapy at Washington University in St. Louis. His Ph.D. is in social work from Virginia Commonwealth University, where he was also a pre- and post-doctoral research fellow, funded by the National Institute on Disability and Rehabilitation Research. His research focuses on workplace learning, information and communication technology, and community participation for persons with a disability. He has a strong interest in international and interdisciplinary research. He teaches graduate students on research methods, ethics and community science.

Jon Corbett is an Assistant Professor in the department of Community, Culture and Global Studies at UBC Okanagan. Jon's community-based research explores how digital multimedia technologies can be effectively combined with maps to be used by remote and marginal communities to document, store, manage and communicate their culture, language, history and traditional ecological knowledge. Jon's research also examines how geographic representation of community information using these technologies can strengthen the community internally through the revitalization of culture and traditional environmental management practices, as well as externally through increasing their influence over regional decision-making processes.

Alea Fairchild, Ph.D. teaches at Vesalius College and the Vrije Universiteit Brussel, as well as being a Research Fellow at The Constantia Institute. Her interest is the development and use of intelligence and technology in product planning and business strategy. Dr. Fairchild received her Doctorate in Applied Economics from University of Hasselt in Belgium.

Mohammed Ghanbari (M'78-SM'97-F01) is best known for the pioneering work on two-layer video coding for ATM networks, now known as SNR scalability in the standard video codecs, which earned him a Fellowship of IEEE in 2001. He has published more than 450 technical papers and four books on various aspects of video networking. His book on Video coding: an introduction to standard codecs, received the Rayleigh prize as the best book of year 2000 by the IET. He is a Fellow of IEEE, Fellow of IET and Charted Engineer (CEng).

Jeffrey Hsu is an associate professor of Information Systems at the Silberman College of Business, Fairleigh Dickinson University. He is the author of numerous papers, chapters, and books, and has previous business experience in the software, telecommunications, and financial industries. His research interests include human-computer interaction, e-commerce, IS education, and mobile/ubiquitous computing. He is managing editor of the *International Journal of Data Analysis and Information Systems* (IJDAIS), associate editor of the *International Journal of Information and Communication Technology Education* (IJICTE), and is on the editorial board of several other journals. Dr. Hsu received his PhD in Information Systems from Rutgers University, a MS in computer science from the New Jersey Institute of Technology, and an MBA from the Rutgers Graduate School of Management.

Bwalya Kelvin Joseph is currently a lecturer and researcher at the University of Botswana. He holds a Bachelors of Science and Technology in electrical engineering (Moscow Power Engineering Tech. University) and a Masters in Computer Science (Korea Advanced Institute of Science and Technology) and currently pursuing PhD in information systems (Univ. of Johannesburg). He is also currently, team leader, accreditation committee, Tertiary Education Council (TEC). He previously worked as a director of research at Zambia Research and Development Center. He has published over 10 book chapters, 12 refereed journal articles, 3 modules, 3 working papers and numerous conference proceedings. He sits on editorial bodies of 3 renowned journals.

Vilaphong Kanyasone works for the Northern Agriculture and Forestry Research Centre (NAFReC) in Luang Prabang, Lao PDR. He acts as the facilitator for the intervention component of the Landscape Mosaics Project in the Lao PDR.

Alex Koutsouris has a Ph.D. in Agricultural Extension and Education and is currently an Assistant Professor in the Department of Agricultural Economics and Rural Development, Agricultural University of Athens, Greece. His research interests revolve around sustainable rural development focusing on topics such as extension and communication (including ICT), training and education, and rural tourism with emphasis on systemic and participatory approaches. He has published and presented papers on the abovementioned topics, been a co-editor in scientific journals and publications and served as a member of the boards of relevant scientific societies and international conferences and meetings.

Pruthikrai Mahatanankoon is an associate professor of information systems at the School of Information Technology at Illinois State University. He holds a bachelor's degree in computer engineering, master degrees in management information systems and computer science, and a PhD in management information systems. His current research interests focus upon mobile computing and commerce, Internet usage in the workplace, and career management of IT professionals.

Raquel Mann is a graduate student in the department of Community, Culture and Global Studies at UBC Okanagan. She has been working with digital video for the past six years. Most of her work is dedicated to participatory video.

Sandro Moiron was born in Leiria, Portugal in 1982. He graduated in Electrical Engineering in 2005 from the Polytechnic Institute of Leiria and received the MSc degree in 2007 from University of Coimbra, Portugal. He is currently pursuing the PhD degree at University of Essex, U.K. He is also a research engineer at Instituto de Telecomunicacoes in Portugal. His research interests include video coding and transcoding, compressed-domain signal processing.

Kerstin Nordin is a Landscape Architect (LAR/MSA) and a lecturer at the Department of Urban and Rural Development at the Swedish University of Agricultural Sciences. She is responsible for teaching GIS in connection to Landscape Planning at the department. With a background as professional working with spatial planning at regional levels, she has a special interest in the use of, and access to, information and techniques used in urban planning. Since some years she with Ulla Berglund is active in the development and application of a methodology for bringing children and young people's knowledge into the spatial planning context with the help of GIS technique.

Jessica Pater is a Research Associate at the Georgia Tech Research Institute. Ms. Pater's research focuses on Web 2.0 and social media technologies and their impacts on education and governance with specific interest in identity formation within immersive 3-D environments.

Hakikur Rahman (PhD) is the Project Coordinator of the Sustainable Development Networking Programme (SDNP) in Bangladesh, a global initiative of UNDP since December 1999. He also acts as the Secretary of South Asia Foundation Bangladesh Chapter. Before joining SDNP, he worked as the Director, Computer Division at Bangladesh Open University. He has written several books and many articles/papers on computer education for the informal sector and distance education. He is the Founder-Chairperson of Internet Society Bangladesh Chapter, Editor of the Monthly Computer Bichitra, Founder-Principal and Member Secretary of ICMS Computer College, Head Examiner (Computer) of the Bangladesh Technical Education Board, and Executive Director of BAERIN (Bangladesh Advanced Education Research and Information Network) Foundation. He is also involved in activities related to establishment of a IT based distance education university in Bangladesh.

Swadesh Kumar Samanta is currently director in the Department of Telecommunication, Government of India. He worked for Nuclear Power Corporation, Department of Telecommunication and BSNL in India for more than 14 years and is on study leave since January 2007. He passed BE from University of Calcutta India in 1991 and ranked first in order of merit. He studied MSc in 2003-04 and PhD in 2007-2009 from School of Computer Science and Electronic Engineering, University of Essex, UK. His research is based on an interdisciplinary approach and is investigating the issues related to information delivery in next generation communication networks, cost modelling and cost optimisation for service provisioning and congestion based service charging. His research has been published in number of international journals and conferences. He is regularly invited to give talks at international business conferences.

Manjit Singh Sidhu is currently the Head of Graphics and Multimedia in the College of Information Technology, University Tenaga Nasional, Malaysia. He received his BSc. (Hons) degree in Computer Science from the University of Wolverhampton, UK in 1997 and Masters in Information Technology from University Putra Malaysia in 2000. He completed his Ph.D. in Computer Science from University of Malaya in 2007. He is a Chartered IT Professional and a member of the British Computer Society, a member of the Institute of Electrical and Electronics Engineers (IEEE), a member of the Malaysian Nasional Computer Confederation and Associate Fellow of the Malaysian Scientific Association. His research interests include user interface design approaches in multimedia and virtual reality applications. email:manjit@uniten.edu.my

Irene Tzouramani is an Agricultural Economist (Ph.D.) and currently a Researcher at the Agricultural Economics and Policy Research Institute, National Agricultural Research Foundation, Greece. Her main research interests include agricultural policy, micro-economic analysis, economic evaluation, agricultural financial economics, production economics, risk management and risk analysis in agriculture. She has published and presented papers on the above fields and participated in EU-funded and national research projects.

Susan Tregeagle is the Senior Manager of Program Services for Barnardos Australia which is a large provider of child welfare services. She has many years experience of social work, policy and advocacy in the area of child protection, out of home care, case management, permanency planning, child welfare decision making. She sits on a number of Government committees concerned with data management in child welfare. Susan holds a Bachelor of Social Studies (University of Sydney), Graduate Diploma of Social Administration (University of Technology, Sydney) and PhD from the Social Justice Social Change Research Centre, University of Western Sydney. She has published extensively in Australia and overseas.

Vongvilay Vongkhamsao works in the Cooperation and Planning Division, National Agriculture and Forestry Research Institute (NAFRI) of the Lao PDR. He is a national project coordinator for Landscape Mosaics and focal point on Non-Timber Forest Product (NTFP) Marketing Component in The Agrobiodiversity Initiative (TABI) Project. Since 1993, he has been working on projects relating to NTFPs in Laos.

John Wang is a professor in the Department of Management and Information Systems at Montclair State University, USA. Having received a scholarship award, he came to the USA and completed his PhD in operations research from Temple University. He has published over 100 refereed papers and seven books. He has also developed several computer software programs based on his research findings.

John Daniel Watts works for the Center for International Forestry Research (CIFOR) as a Biodiversity and Governance Officer, based in Luang Prabang, Lao PDR. He supports the implementation of the Landscape Mosaics Project in the Lao project site, focusing on the intervention component of the project. Prior to working in the Lao PDR, he worked as a Research and Communications Officer for the Joint Biodiversity Platform between the Center for International Forestry Research (CIFOR) and World Agroforestry Centre (ICRAF), based in Bogor, Indonesia.

John Woods is a senior lecturer and his interests include image processing, autonomous robotics, intelligent power control, networks and network pricing. During his brief career he has accumulated over 60 journal and conference publications accompanied by grants in these areas. He is a member of the IEE and regularly attends and presents at national and international conferences.

Bin Zhou is an assistant professor in the College of Business and Public Administration, Kean University, USA. He obtained his PhD and MBA degrees in management science and supply chain management from Rutgers Business School, Rutgers University. His research interests include theory and application of supply chain management, logistics and transportation, production and inventory systems, and information technology. His research work has appeared in *International Journal of Production Economics, European Journal of Operational Research, International Journal of Systems Science,* among others. Professor Zhou also serves in the editorial board of *International Journal of Information Systems and Social Change.*

Index

A

Accessibility 24, 61, 91-107, 109-112, 115-116, 118-120, 122, 124, 162, 183, 193, 195, 197, 202-204, 210, 231-232, 236, 260

Accessibility Level (AL) 4, 34-37, 39, 41, 48-50, 58-62, 67, 69, 75, 77-78, 84, 93-96, 113-116, 118-119, 122, 126-128, 137, 142, 144-145, 148, 151-153, 156, 162, 164-165, 167, 171, 179, 194-196, 198-199, 201, 205-206, 209-210, 225, 235, 239, 243

Adaptive Management 143, 152, 154-155

AFL Technologies - See Assessment for Learning.

Africa West Coast Cable 53

Americans with Disabilities Act (ADA) 111, 123-124

Applications Provision 114

Assembly of First Nations 163, 177

Assessment and Evaluation 224-226, 228-230

Assessment and Evaluation Group (AEG) 225, 234-235

Assessment and Evaluation Module (AEM) 225, 227-231, 234-235

Assessment for Learning (AFL) 224-226, 228-231, 233-236

assessment of learning (AOL) 1, 226, 233

Augmented reality (AR) 31, 253, 257-259, 261-262

Automatic SMS Language Translator (ASLT) 39-41

AWCC - See Africa West Coast Cable.

B

Botswana Innovation Hub (BIH) 46

Botswana Research Science and Technology Investment Agency 52

Botswana Telecommunication Company (BTC) 52

Botswana Training Authority (BOTA) 47

British Columbia Treaty Process 158

Broadband Technologies Opportunities Program 110

Bronfenbrenner's social ecology model 97

BRSTIA - See Botswana Research Science and Technology Investment Agency.

Business Model 43, 109, 112, 114-115, 118, 121

Business to Consumer (B2C) 33, 41

C

CellBazzar 42-43

Center for International Forestry Research (CIFOR) 143-144, 155-157

Children's Maps 57-58, 60-61, 63, 66-70

Child Welfare 73-74, 76-78, 84-90

China Internet Network Information Centre 182-183

citizen governance 93, 107

Cognitive Absorption (CA) 1-2, 4-10, 12, 14, 88, 122, 141, 177-179, 191, 205-207, 221-223, 236, 249-250

College Level - See Higher Education.

community building 96

Comparative Fit Index (CFI) 7

computer aided learning (CAL) 254-255, 259

Concerns-Based Adoption Model (CBAM) 195-197, 200

Confirmatory factor analysis (CFA) 6-7, 11

content creators 237

D

Degree of Autonomy 3

democratic governance 93

Demographic Information Questionnaire (DIQ) 196-198, 200

Diffusion of Innovations 195, 197, 207, 250

Digital Cities Survey 98-99

Digital Divide 17, 30, 57, 60, 67, 69, 73, 87, 94-95, 106, 109-111, 113, 121, 123, 125, 127-129, 134, 136-141, 178, 188, 208-211, 221-223

digital persona 105

Distance Education 180, 182-184, 188-189, 191-192

Distance Higher Education - See Distance Education.
District Agriculture and Forestry Office (DAFO) 144, 148, 152-153

E

e-accessibility 109, 111, 115, 117-120
eAdministration 126
East Africa Submarine System (EASSY) 53
Educational Technologies 180, 193, 208, 237
e-governance - See e-government.
e-government 91-106, 108, 126, 140
e-learning 12, 96, 106, 140, 191, 258, 261
Engineering Education 251-254, 256-257, 259-262
eServices 126
European Economic Recovery Plan 110
extended markup language 239, 257, 262

F

Facebook 97-100, 105, 247
First Nations communities 173
Flesch-Kinkaid reading ease 99
Foreign Language Learning 33, 41
Foster Care 73, 82, 88-90
Free Open Source Software (FOSS) 237, 245, 250

G

General Interview Guide 197
Geographical Information System (GIS) 57, 59-61, 63, 68-70, 152-153
Geovisualization 59
GIS-application 57, 60-61, 69
GIScience 58
Government receptivity 105
Gross Domestic Products (GDPs) 16, 20, 22-26, 30, 32, 34, 46, 49-50, 181

H

head mounted device (HMD) 257
Higher Education 17, 56, 131, 142, 180-185, 187-192, 224-225, 228, 235-237, 240, 248, 251, 258, 260-261
Human Development 14, 18, 25, 32, 44, 46-47, 56, 72, 90, 108, 124-125, 129, 137-138, 142, 157, 179-180, 192, 207, 223, 236, 250, 262
Human Development Index (HDI) 25
HyperResearch 199

I

ICRAF - See World Agroforestry Centre.
ICT Diffusion 125
ICT Integration in Teaching 193, 203
Inclusivity 109, 119
Indigenous Communities 158
informal learning 237-239, 241, 245-246, 248, 250
Information and Communications Technologies in Schools Survey (ICTSS) 195, 207
Infrastructure 17-18, 23, 29, 44, 49-50, 52-53, 72, 110, 113, 115, 119, 122, 129, 139, 144, 148, 153, 155, 193, 203
Infrastructure Manufacturing Vending 113
instant messaging (IM) 1-6, 8, 10-12, 14, 43-44, 82-83, 85
interactive whiteboard (IWB) 255-256, 260
International Association for the Evaluation of Educational Achievement (IEA) 195
International Classification of Functioning Disability and Health (ICF) 95
International Comparison 15, 20-21, 26-28, 32
International Distance Education Forum 183, 191
Interventions Knowledge Economy 45
Intra-Rural Digital Divide 125, 137
IT Diffusion - See ICT Diffusion.

J

Java Micro Edition (J2ME) 34, 40

K

Knowledge-Based-Economy (KBE) 46-55
kumban 144, 147-148, 150-152, 154-155

L

Landscape Governance 143-146, 149-151, 154-156
Landscape Management 143, 145-146, 149, 153-155
Landscape Outcomes Assessment Methodology (LOAM) 148, 157
Language Translation 33-35, 37-39, 42-44
Large-Group Format 224, 227-228
Less Favoured Areas (LFAs) 131, 136, 142
Linear Programming 15, 26, 28-29
Local Governance 91, 93, 97, 104, 106-107
Local Knowledge 138, 145, 151-152, 158
Looking After Children (LAC) 74-77, 80, 84, 87-90

M

Ministry of Communications, Science and Technology (MCST) 52
Model chi-Square Statistic 132, 134
multivariate adaptive regression splines (MARS) 18, 31
Municipal Wi-Fi 109-121

N

NAFReC - See Northern Agriculture and Forestry Research Centre.
National Agriculture and Forestry Extension Service (NAFES) 152
National Agriculture and Forestry Research Institute (NAFRI) 143-144, 156
national character 161
National Commission for Science and Technology (NCST) 51
Nationalism 162, 171-172, 177-178
National Organization on Disability (NOD) 99-100
National Statistics Service of Greece (NSSG) 129
National Technical Information Administration 109, 123, 127
Nation Building 158-159, 161-163, 166, 170-177
Natural Resource Governance 143
Network Building 113
Network Operation 113
New Oriental Education Group 184
Normative Fit Index (NFI) 7
Northern Agriculture and Forestry Research Centre 144
NTIA - National Technical Information Administration.
NVIVO 80

O

online-offline boundary 97
Online Social Networks 91, 96-97
Organization of Economic Cooperation and Development (OECD) 16, 18-20, 22, 24, 30-32, 48, 56, 79, 89, 181, 190

P

Pareto Optimization 26, 29
Participatory Video 159, 161, 164-165, 167, 171-172, 174-177, 179
people with disabilities 115-118

personal e-mail (PE) 1-2, 4-8, 14
Place to Grow 61-64, 66-68, 72
Podcasts 122, 124, 237-250
portable document files (PDFs) 31-32, 55-56, 71, 122-123, 141, 157, 177-179, 189-191, 206-207, 232-233, 249, 260
Private/Public Partnership (PPP) 112, 181
Probit model 129, 132, 134
Productivity 1-5, 11, 15-18, 20, 22-25, 29-32, 47-49, 53, 94
Professional Development (PD) 122, 193, 198, 203-205, 210, 223, 237-238, 240-241, 243-244, 248
Professional Learning 237-238, 240, 243, 245, 248
Purchasing Power Parities 24
PV - See Participatory Video.
PWD - See people with disabilities.

R

Really Simply Syndication–feeds (RSS-feeds) 239
Residential Care 73, 75

S

Science and Technology (S&T) 31, 47, 51-52, 56, 138, 183, 259
SDC - See Swiss Agency for Development Cooperation.
Second Language Education (SLE) 208-209, 211-212, 214, 220-221
Sequential Mixed Methods Analysis (SMMA) 241
Service Provision 114, 119
Short Message Entity (SME) 36, 40
Short Messaging Service (SMS) 2, 4, 10, 33-34, 36-44
SLE M.Ed. - See Second Language Education.
Social Networking Site - See Facebook.
Social workers 73-77, 80-86
Southern African Development Community (SADC) 46
square multiple correlations (SMC) 7
Stages of Concern 195-196, 198-206
Stages of Concern Questionnaire (SoCQ) 196, 198, 200, 202, 204, 206
Stakeholder 109, 113, 115, 118-120, 227
Supporting Children and Responding to Families (SCARF) 75, 77, 80, 84, 87, 89
Swiss Agency for Development Cooperation 143-144, 155

T

Teacher candidates (TCs) 211, 225-231, 233-235
Teaching Technologies 193, 237
Teaching with Technology Instrument 204-205
Technological Literacy 127
technology-assisted problem solving (TAPS) 254,
    261
Technology Diffusion - See ICT Diffusion.
Tertiary Education Council (TEC) 52, 56
Tlowitsis 158-161, 164-178
Tucker-Lewis Index (TLI) 7
Twitter 97-100, 105, 247

U

UN Convention of The Rights of the Child 57
UNECE Report 48, 53
UNESCO project 59
UNICEF 57, 59, 72
University Level - See Higher Education.
Urban Planning 57, 60-62, 64, 68-71
Usage Balance 3

V

virtual reality (VR) 253, 256
voice over IP (VOIP) 104, 246

W

Web 2.0 70, 96-98, 178, 237
Web Content Accessibility Guidelines (WCAG) 96,
    99-101, 105, 107
weekly automated assessment scheme (WATS) 258
Wildlife Conservation Society (WCS) 148
Work-Life Balance (WB) 1-2, 4-10, 14
Work-Life Integration 3, 12
World Agroforestry Centre 143-144
World Wide Web Consortium's (W3C) 96, 101, 105

X

XML - See extended markup language.